CAMBRIDGE LIBRARY COLLECTION

Books of enduring scholarly value

Religion

For centuries, scripture and theology were the focus of prodigious amounts
of scholarship and publishing, dominated in the English-speaking world
by the work of Protestant Christians. Enlightenment philosophy and
science, anthropology, ethnology and the colonial experience all brought
new perspectives, lively debates and heated controversies to the study of
religion and its role in the world, many of which continue to this day. This
series explores the editing and interpretation of religious texts, the history of
religious ideas and institutions, and not least the encounter between religion
and science.

The Life of Jesus, Critically Examined

The German theologian David Friedrich Strauss (1808–1874) first published
his highly controversial *The Life of Jesus* in three volumes between 1835
and 1836. This translation, by George Eliot, is based on the fourth German
edition (1840). In this work Strauss applied strict historical methods to the
New Testament gospel narratives and caused scandal across the Protestant
world by concluding that all miraculous elements in the life of Jesus were
mythical and ahistorical. In volume 2 Strauss applies modern historical
criticism to 'de-mythologize' the idea of Jesus as Messiah; the narratives
about the disciples; the discourses in the Synoptic gospels and the Fourth
Gospel; the non-miraculous events; and the miracles narratives. This is a
key text of nineteenth-century theology that pioneered the application of
historical and scientific methods to the study of religions and religious texts.
It is essential reading for any student of the New Testament.

Cambridge University Press has long been a pioneer in the reissuing of out-of-print titles from its own backlist, producing digital reprints of books that are still sought after by scholars and students but could not be reprinted economically using traditional technology. The Cambridge Library Collection extends this activity to a wider range of books which are still of importance to researchers and professionals, either for the source material they contain, or as landmarks in the history of their academic discipline.

Drawing from the world-renowned collections in the Cambridge University Library, and guided by the advice of experts in each subject area, Cambridge University Press is using state-of-the-art scanning machines in its own Printing House to capture the content of each book selected for inclusion. The files are processed to give a consistently clear, crisp image, and the books finished to the high quality standard for which the Press is recognised around the world. The latest print-on-demand technology ensures that the books will remain available indefinitely, and that orders for single or multiple copies can quickly be supplied.

The Cambridge Library Collection will bring back to life books of enduring scholarly value (including out-of-copyright works originally issued by other publishers) across a wide range of disciplines in the humanities and social sciences and in science and technology.

The Life of Jesus, Critically Examined

VOLUME 2

DAVID FRIEDRICH STRAUSS

CAMBRIDGE UNIVERSITY PRESS

Cambridge, New York, Melbourne, Madrid, Cape Town, Singapore,
São Paolo, Delhi, Dubai, Tokyo

Published in the United States of America by Cambridge University Press, New York

www.cambridge.org
Information on this title: www.cambridge.org/9781108019576

© in this compilation Cambridge University Press 2010

This edition first published 1846
This digitally printed version 2010

ISBN 978-1-108-01957-6 Paperback

THE LIFE OF JESUS.

LONDON:

GEORGE WOODFALL AND SON,

ANGEL COURT, SKINNER STREET.

THE

LIFE OF JESUS,

CRITICALLY EXAMINED

BY

DR. DAVID FRIEDRICH STRAUSS.

Translated from the Fourth German Edition.

IN THREE VOLUMES.

VOL. II.

LONDON:

CHAPMAN, BROTHERS, 121, NEWGATE STREET.

MDCCCXLVI.

CONTENTS

THE SECOND VOLUME.

SECOND PART CONTINUED.

HISTORY OF THE PUBLIC LIFE OF JESUS.

CHAPTER IV.

JESUS AS THE MESSIAH.

CHAPTER V.

THE DISCIPLES OF JESUS.

CHAPTER VI.

THE DISCOURSES OF JESUS IN THE THREE FIRST GOSPELS.

CHAPTER VII.

DISCOURSES OF JESUS IN THE FOURTH GOSPEL.

CHAPTER VIII.

EVENTS IN THE PUBLIC LIFE OF JESUS, EXCLUSIVE OF THE MIRACLES.

CHAPTER IX.

MIRACLES OF JESUS.

THE LIFE OF JESUS.

CHAPTER IV

JESUS AS THE MESSIAH *.

§ 61.

JESUS, THE SON OF MAN.

IN treating of the relation in which Jesus conceived himself
to stand to the messianic idea, we can distinguish his dicta
concerning his own person from those concerning the work he
had undertaken.

The appellation which Jesus commonly gives himself in the
gospels is, *the Son of man*, ὁ υἱὸς τοῦ ἀνθρώπου. The exactly corresponding Hebrew expression בֶּן־אָדָם is in the Old Testament
a frequent designation of man in general, and thus we might be
induced to understand it in the mouth of Jesus. This interpretation would suit some passages; for example, Matt. xii. 8.
where Jesus says: *The Son of man is lord also of the Sabbath
day*, κύριος γάρ ἐστι τοῦ σαββάτου ὁ υἱὸς τοῦ ἀνθρώπου,—words
which will fitly enough take a general meaning, such as Grotius

---

* All that relates to the idea of the Messiah as suffering, dying, and rising again, is
here omitted, and reserved for the history of the Passion.

affixes to them, namely, that man is lord of the Sabbath, especially if we compare Mark (ii. 27), who introduces them by the proposition, *The Sabbath was made for man, and not man for the Sabbath,* τὸ σάββατον διὰ τὸν ἄνθρωπον ἐγένετο, οὐχ ὁ ἄνθρωπος διὰ τὸ σάββατον. But in the majority of cases, the phrase in question is evidently used as a special designation. Thus, Matt. viii. 20, a scribe volunteers to become a disciple of Jesus, and is admonished to count the cost in the words, *The Son of man hath not where to lay his head,* ὁ υἱὸς τοῦ ἀνθρώπου οὐκ ἔχει, ποῦ τὴν κεφαλὴν κλίνῃ : here some particular man must be intended, nay, the particular man into whose companionship the scribe wished to enter, that is, Jesus himself. As a reason for the self-application of this term by Jesus, it has been suggested that he used the third person after the oriental manner, to avoid the *I* [1]. But for a speaker to use the third person in reference to himself, is only admissible, if he would be understood, when the designation he employs is precise, and inapplicable to any other person present, as when a father or a king uses his appropriate title of himself ; or when, if the designation be not precise, its relation is made clear by a demonstrative pronoun, which limitation is eminently indispensable if an individual speak of himself under the universal designation *man.* We grant that occasionally a gesture might supply the place of the demonstrative pronoun ; but that Jesus in every instance of his using this habitual expression had recourse to some visible explanatory sign, or that the evangelists would not, in that case, have supplied its necessary absence from a written document by some demonstrative addition, is inconceivable. If both Jesus and the evangelists held such an elucidation superfluous, they must have seen in the expression itself the key to its precise application. Some are of opinion that Jesus intended by it to point himself out as the ideal man—man in the noblest sense of the word [2]; but this is a modern theory, not an historical inference, for there is no trace of such an interpreta-

---

[1] Paulus, exeget. Handb. 1, 6. s. 465 ; Fritzsche, in Matth. p. 320.
[2] Thus after Herder, Köster e. g. in Immanuel. s. 265.

tion of the expression in the time of Jesus [3], and it would be more easy to show, as others have attempted, that the appellation, *Son of man*, so frequently used by Jesus, had reference to his lowly and despised condition [4]. Apart however from the objection that this acceptation also would require the addition of the demonstrative pronoun, though it might be adapted to many passages, as Matt. viii. 20, John i. 51, there are others, (such as Matt. xvii. 22, where Jesus, foretelling his violent death, designates himself ὁ υἱὸς τοῦ ἀνθρώπου,) which demand the contrast of high dignity with an ignominious fate. So in Matt. x. 23. the assurance given to the commissioned disciples that before they had gone over the cities of Israel the Son of Man would come, could have no weight unless this expression denoted a person of importance ; and that such was its significance is proved by a comparison·of Matt. xvi. 28, where there is also a mention of an ἔρχεσθαι, *a coming* of the Son of man, but with the addition ἐν τῇ βασιλείᾳ αὐτοῦ. As this addition can only refer to the messianic kingdom, the υἱὸς τοῦ ἀνθρώπου must be the Messiah.

How so apparently vague an appellation came to be appropriated to the Messiah, we gather from Matt. xxvi. 64 parall., where the Son of Man is depicted as coming *in the clouds of heaven*. This is evidently an allusion to Dan. vii. 13 f. where after having treated of the fall of the four beasts, the writer says : *I saw in the night visions, and behold, one like the Son of Man* (כְּבַר אֱנָשׁ, ὡς υἱὸς ἀνθρώπου, LXX.) *came with the clouds of heaven, and came to the Ancient of days. And there was given him dominion, and glory, and a kingdom, that all people, nations and languages should serve him : his dominion is an everlasting dominion.* The four beasts (v. 17 ff.) were symbolical of the four great empires, the last of which was the Macedonian, with its offshoot, Syria. After their fall, the kingdom was to be given in perpetuity to the People of

---

[3] Lücke, Comm. zum Joh. 1, s. 397 f.
[4] e. g. Grotius.

God, *the saints of the Most High:* hence, he who was to come
with *clouds of heaven* could only be, either a personification of
the holy people [5], or a leader of heavenly origin under whom
they were to achieve their destined triumph,—in a word, the
Messiah ; and this was the customary interpretation among the
Jews [6]. Two things are predicated of this personage,—that he
was like the Son of Man, and that he came with the clouds of
heaven ; but the *former* particular is his distinctive characteristic, and imports either that he had not a superhuman form,
that of an angel for instance, though descending from heaven,
or else that the kingdom about to be established presented in
its humanity a contrast to the inhumanity of its predecessors,
of which ferocious beasts were the fitting emblems [7]. At a later
period, it is true, the Jews regarded the coming with the clouds
of heaven עָנָנֵי עָטֵ־שְׁמַיָּא as the more essential attribute of the
Messiah, and hence gave him the name Anani, after the Jewish
taste of making a merely accessory circumstance the permanent
epithet of a person or thing [8]. If, then, the expression ὁ υἱὸς
τοῦ ἀνθρώπου necessarily recalled the above passage in Daniel,
generally believed to relate to the Messiah, it is impossible that
Jesus could so often use it, and in connexion with declarations
evidently referring to the Messiah, without intending it as the
designation of that personage.

That by the expression in question Jesus meant himself,
without relation to the messianic dignity, is less probable than
the contrary supposition, that he might often mean the Messiah
when he spoke of the *Son of Man*, without relation to his own
person.   When, Matt. x. 23, on the first mission of the twelve
apostles to announce the kingdom of heaven, he comforts them

---

[5] Abenesra, see Hävernick, ut sup. Comm. zum Daniel, s. 244.

[6] Schöttgen, horæ, ii. s. 63, 73 ; Hävernick, ut sup. s. 243 f.

[7] See for the most important opinions, Hävernick, ut sup. s. 242 f.

[8] Let the reader bear in mind the designation of David's elegy, 2 Sam. i. 17 ff. as
קֶשֶׁת, and the denomination of the Messiah as צֶמַח. Had Schleiermacher considered the nature of Jewish appellatives, he would not have called the reference of
υἱὸς τοῦ ἀ. to the passage in Daniel, a strange idea. (Glaubensl. § 99. s. 99. Anm.).

under the prospect of their future persecutions by the assurance that they would not *have gone over all the cities of Israel before the coming of the Son of Man*, we should rather, taking this declaration alone, think of a third person, whose speedy messianic appearance Jesus was promising, than of the speaker himself, seeing that he was already come, and it would not be antecedently clear how he could represent his own coming as one still in anticipation. So also when Jesus (Matt. xiii. 37 ff.) interprets the Sower of the parable to be the Son of Man, who at the end of the world will have a harvest and a tribunal, he might be supposed to refer to the Messiah as a third person distinct from himself. This is equally the case, xvi. 27 f., where, to prove the proposition that the loss of the soul is not to be compensated by the gain of the whole world, he urges the speedy coming of the Son of Man, to administer retribution. Lastly, in the connected discourses, Matt. xxiv. xxv. parall., many particulars would be more easily conceived, if the υἱὸς τοῦ ἀνθρώπου whose παρουσία Jesus describes, were understood to mean another than himself.

But this explanation is far from being applicable to the majority of instances in which Jesus uses this expression. When he represents the Son of Man, not as one still to be expected, but as one already come and actually present, for example, in Matt. xviii. 11, where he says: *The Son of Man is come to save that which was lost ;* when he justifies his own acts by the authority with which the Son of Man was invested, as in Matt. ix. 6 ; when, Mark viii. 31 ff. comp. Matt. xvi. 22, he speaks of the approaching sufferings and death of the Son of Man, so as to elicit from Peter the exclamation, οὐ μὴ ἔσται σοι τοῦτο, *this shall not be unto thee ;* in these and similar cases he can only, by the υἱὸς τοῦ ανθρωπου, have intended himself. And even those passages, which, taken singly, we might have found capable of application to a messianic person, distinct from Jesus, lose this capability when considered in their entire connexion. It is possible, however, either that the writer may

have misplaced certain expressions, or that the ultimately prevalent conviction that Jesus was *the Son of Man* caused what
was originally said merely of the latter, to be viewed in immediate relation to the former.

Thus besides the fact that Jesus on many occasions called
himself the Son of Man, there remains the possibility that
on many others, he may have designed another person; and
if so, the latter would in the order of time naturally precede the
former. Whether this possibility can be heightened to a reality,
must depend on the answer to the following question : Is there,
in the period of the life of Jesus, from which all his recorded
declarations are taken, any fragment which indicates that he
had not yet conceived himself to be the Messiah ?

§ 62.

HOW SOON DID JESUS CONCEIVE HIMSELF TO BE THE MESSIAH, AND FIND RECOGNITION AS SUCH FROM OTHERS?

Jesus held and expressed the conviction that he was the
Messiah ; this is an indisputable fact. Not only did he, according to the evangelists, receive with satisfaction the confession of
the disciples that he was the Χριστός (Matt. xvi. 16 f.) and the
salutation of the people, *Hosanna to the Son of David* (xxi.
15 f.) ; not only did he before a public tribunal (Matt. xxvi.
64, comp. John xviii. 37,) as well as to private individuals
(John iv. 26, ix. 37, x. 25,) repeatedly declare himself to be the
Messiah : but the fact that his disciples after his death believed
and proclaimed that he was the Messiah, is not to be comprehended, unless, when living, he had implanted the conviction in their minds.

To the more searching question, how soon Jesus began to
declare himself the Messiah and to be regarded as such by others,
the evangelists almost unanimously reply, that he assumed that
character from the time of his baptism. All of them attach to
his baptism circumstances which must have convinced himself,
if yet uncertain, and all others who witnessed or credited them
that he was no less than the Messiah ; John makes his earliest

disciples recognise his right to that dignity on their first interview (i. 42 ff.), and Matthew attributes to him at the very beginning of his ministry, in the sermon on the mount, a representation of himself as the Judge of the world (vii. 21 ff,) and therefore the Messiah.

Nevertheless, on a closer examination, there appears a remarkable divergency on this subject between the synoptical statement and that of John. While, namely, in John, Jesus remains throughout true to his assertion, and the disciples and his followers among the populace to their conviction, that he is the Messiah; in the synoptical gospels there is a vacillation discernible—the previously expressed persuasion on the part of the disciples and people that Jesus was the Messiah, sometimes vanishes and gives place to a much lower view of him, and even Jesus himself becomes more reserved in his declarations. This is particularly striking when the synoptical statement is compared with that of John; but even when they are separately considered, the result is the same.

According to John (vi. 15), after the miracle of the loaves the people were inclined to constitute Jesus their (messianic) King; on the contrary, according to the other three evangelists, either about the same time (Luke ix. 18 f.) or still later (Matt. xvi. 13 f. Mark viii. 27 f.) the disciples could only report, on the opinions of the people respecting their master, that some said he was the resuscitated Baptist, some Elias, and others Jeremiah or one of the old prophets : in reference to that passage of John, however, as also to the synoptical one, Matt. xiv. 33, according to which, some time before Jesus elicited the above report of the popular opinion, the people who were with him in the ship[1] when he had allayed the storm, fell at his feet and worshipped him as the Son of God, it may be observed that when Jesus had spoken or acted with peculiar impressiveness, individuals, in the exaltation of the moment, might be penetrated with a conviction that he was the Messiah, while the general

---

[1] That the expression οἱ ἐν τῷ πλοίῳ includes more than the disciples, vid. Fritzsche, in loc.

and calm voice of the people yet pronounced him to be merely
a prophet.

But there is a more troublesome divergency relative to the
disciples. In John, Andrew, after his first interview with Jesus,
says to his brother, *we have found the Messiah,* εὑρήκαμεν τὸν
Μεσσίαν (i. 42) ; and Philip describes him to Nathanael as the
person foretold by Moses and the prophets (v. 46) ; Nathanael
salutes him as the Son of God and King of Israel (v. 50) ; and the
subsequent confession of Peter appears merely a renewed avowal
of what had been long a familiar truth. In the synoptical
evangelists it is only after prolonged intercourse with Jesus, and
shortly before his sufferings, that the ardent Peter arrives at the
conclusion that Jesus is the Χριστος, ὁ υἱὸς τοῦ θεοῦ τοῦ ζῶντος
(Matt. xvi. 16, parall.). It is impossible that this confession
should make so strong an impression on Jesus that, in consequence of it, he should pronounce Peter blessed, and his confession the fruit of immediate divine revelation, as Matthew
narrates ; or that, as all the three evangelists inform us, (xvi.
20, viii. 30, ix. 21,) he should, as if alarmed, forbid the dis·
ciples to promulgate their conviction, unless it represented not
an opinion long cherished in the circle of his disciples, but a
new light, which had just flashed on the mind of Peter, and
through him was communicated to his associates.

There is a third equally serious discrepancy, relative to the
declarations of Jesus concerning his Messiahship. According to
John, he sanctions the homage which Nathanael renders to him
as the Son of God and King of Israel, in the very commencement of his public career, and immediately proceeds to speak of
himself under the messianic title, Son of Man (i. 51 f.) : to the
Samaritans also after his first visit to the passover (iv. 26, 39 ff.),
and to the Jews on the second (v. 46), he makes himself known
as the Messiah predicted by Moses. According to the synoptical writers, on the contrary, he prohibits, in the instance above
cited and in many others, the dissemination of the doctrine of
his Messiahship, beyond the circle of his adherents. Farther,
when he asks his disciples, *Whom do men say that I am?*

(Matt. xvi. 15) he seems to wish[2] that they should derive their conviction of his Messiahship from his discourses and actions, and when he ascribes the avowed faith of Peter to a revelation from his heavenly Father, he excludes the possibility of his having himself previously made this disclosure to his disciples, either in the manner described by John, or in the more indirect one attributed to him by Matthew in the Sermon on the Mount; unless we suppose that the disciples had not hitherto believed his assurance, and that hence Jesus referred the new-born faith of Peter to divine influence.

Thus, on the point under discussion the synoptical statement is contradictory, not only to that of John, but to itself; it appears therefore that it ought to be unconditionally surrendered before that of John, which is consistent with itself, and one of our critics has justly reproached it with deranging the messianic economy in the life of Jesus[3]. But here again we must not lose sight of our approved canon, that in glorifying narratives, such as our gospels, where various statements are confronted, that is the least probable which best subserves the object of glorification. Now this is the case with John's statement; according to which, from the commencement to the

---

[2] There is a difficulty involved in the form of the question, put by Jesus to his disciples: τίνα με λίγουσιν οἱ ἄνθρωποι εἶναι, τὸν υἱὸν τοῦ ἀνθρώπου; i. e. what opinion have the people of me, the Messiah? This, when compared with the sequel, seems a premature disclosure; hence expositors have variously endeavoured to explain away its primâ facie meaning. Some (e. g. Beza) understand the subordinate clause, not as a declaration of Jesus concerning his own person, but as a closer limitation of the question: For whom do the people take me? for the Messiah? But this would be a leading question, which, as Fritzsche well observes, would indicate an eagerness for the messianic title, not elsewhere discernible in Jesus. Others, therefore, (as Paulus and Fritzsche,) give the expression υἱὸς τ. ἀ. a general signification, and interpret the question thus: Whom do men say that I, the individual addressing you, am? But this explanation has been already refuted in the foregoing section. If, then, we reject the opinion that the υἱὸς τ. ἀ. is an addition which the exuberant faith of the writer was apt to suggest even in an infelicitous connexion, we are restricted to De Wette's view, (exeg. Handb. 1, 1, s. 86 f), namely, that the expression, ὁ υιος τ. α. was indeed an appellation of the Messiah, but an indirect one, so that it might convey that meaning, as an allusion to Daniel, to Jesus and those already aware of his messiahship, while to others it was merely the equivalent of, this man.

[3] Schneckenburger, über den Ursprung u. s. f. s. 28 f.

close of the public life of Jesus, his Messiahship shines forth in
unchanging splendour, while, according to the synoptical
writers, it is liable to a variation in its light. But though this
criterion of probability is in favour of the first three evangelists,
it is impossible that the order in which they make ignorance
and concealment follow on plain declarations and recognitions of
the Messiahship of Jesus can be correct ; and we must suppose
that they have mingled and confounded two separate periods
of the life of Jesus, in the latter of which alone he presented
himself as the Messiah. We find, in fact, that the watchword
of Jesus on his first appearance differed not, even verbally, from
that of John, who professed merely to be a forerunner ; it is the
same *Repent, for the kingdom of heaven is at hand* (Matt.
iv. 17) with which John had roused the Jews (iii. 2); and indicates in neither the one nor the other an assumption of the character of Messiah, with whose coming the kingdom of heaven was
actually to commence, but merely that of a teacher who points
to it as yet future [4]. Hence the latest critic of the first gospel
justly explains all those discourses and actions therein narrated,
by which Jesus explicitly claims to be the Messiah, or, in consequence of which this dignity is attributed to him and accepted,
if they occur before the manifestation of himself recorded in
John v., or before the account of the apostolic confession (Matt.
xvi.), as offences of the writer against chronology or literal
truth [5]. We have only to premise, that as chronological confusion prevails throughout, the position of this confession
shortly before the history of the Passion, in nowise obliges us
to suppose that it was so late before Jesus was recognised as
the Messiah among his disciples, since Peter's avowal may have
occurred in a much earlier period of their intercourse. This,
however, is incomprehensible—that the same reproach should
not attach even more strongly to the fourth gospel than to the
first, or to the synoptical writers in general. For it is surely

---

[4] This distinction of two periods in the public life of Jesus is also made by
Fritzsche, Comm. in Matth. s. 213. 536. and Schneckenburger ut sup.

[5] Schneckenburger, ut sup. s. 29.

more pardonable that the first three evangelists should give us
the pre-messianic memoirs in the wrong place, than that the
fourth should not give them at all ; more endurable in the
former, to mingle the two periods, than in the latter, quite to
obliterate the earlier one.

If then Jesus did not lay claim to the Messiahship from the
beginning of his public career, was this omission the result of
uncertainty in his own mind ; or had he from the first a conviction that he was the Messiah, but concealed it for certain
reasons ? In order to decide this question, a point already
mentioned must be more carefully weighed. In the first three
evangelists, but not so exclusively that the fourth has nothing
similar, when Jesus effects a miracle of healing he almost invariably forbids the person cured to promulgate the event, in these
or similar words, ὅρα μηδενὶ εἴπης ; e. g. the leper, Matt. viii. 4 ;
parall. ; the blind men, Matt. ix. 30 ; a multitude of the healed,
Matt. xii. 16 ; the parents of the resuscitated damsel, Mark
v. 43 ; above all he enjoins silence on the demoniacs, Mark
i. 34. iii. 12. ; and John v. 13, it is said, after the cure of the
man at the pool of Bethesda, *Jesus had conveyed himself
away, a multitude being in that place.* Thus also he forbade
the three who were with him on the mount of the Transfiguration, to publish the scene they had witnessed, (Matt. xvii. 9);
and after the confession of Peter, he charges the disciples to tell
no man the conviction it expressed (Luke ix. 21). This prohibition of Jesus could hardly, as most commentators suppose[6], be
determined by various circumstantial motives, at one time having
relation to the disposition of the person healed, at another to the
humour of the people, at another to the situation of Jesus :
rather, as there is an essential similarity in the conditions under
which he lays this injunction on the people, if we discern
a probable motive for it on any occasion, we are warranted
in applying the same motive to the remaining cases. This
motive is scarcely any other than the desire that the belief that

[6] Fritzsche, in Matth. p. 309. comp. 352. Olshausen, s. 265.

he was the Messiah should not be too widely spread. When (Mark i. 34) Jesus would not allow the ejected demons to speak *because they knew him,* when he charged the multitudes *that they should not make him known* (Matt. xii. 16), he evidently intended that the former should not proclaim him in the character in which their more penetrative, demoniacal glance had viewed him, nor the latter in that revealed by the miraculous cure he had wrought on them—in short, they were not to betray their knowledge that he was the Messiah. As a reason for this wish on the part of Jesus, it has been alleged, on the strength of John vi. 15., that he sought to avoid awakening the political idea of the Messiah's kingdom in the popular mind, with the disturbance which would be its inevitable result[7]. This would be a valid reason; but the synoptical writers represent the wish, partly as the effect of humility[8]; Matthew, in connexion with a prohibition of the kind alluded to, applying to Jesus a passage in Isaiah (xlii. 1 f.) where the servant of God is said to be distinguished by his stillness and unobtrusiveness: partly, and in a greater degree, as the effect of an apprehension that the Messiah, at least such an one as Jesus, would be at once proscribed by the Jewish hierarchy.

From all this it might appear that Jesus was restrained merely by external motives, from the open declaration of his messiahship, and that his own conviction of it existed from the first in equal strength; but this conclusion cannot be maintained in the face of the consideration above mentioned, that Jesus began his career with the same announcement as the Baptist, an announcement which can scarcely have more than one import— an exhortation to prepare for a coming Messiah. The most natural supposition is that Jesus, first the disciple of the Baptist, and afterwards his successor, in preaching repentance and the approach of the kingdom of heaven, took originally the same position as his former master in relation to the messianic

[7] Fritzsche, p. 352. Olshausen, ut sup.

[8] The opposite view is held by the Fragmentist, who thinks the prohibition was intended to stimulate the popular eagerness.

kingdom, notwithstanding the greater reach and liberality of his mind, and only gradually attained the elevation of thinking himself the Messiah. This supposition explains in the simplest manner the prohibition we have been considering, especially that annexed to the confession of Peter. For as often as the thought that he might be the Messiah suggested itself to others, and was presented to him from without, Jesus must have shrunk, as if appalled, to hear confidently uttered that which he scarcely ventured to surmise, or which had but recently become clear to himself. As, however, the evangelist often put such prohibitions into the mouth of Jesus unseasonably, (witness the occasion mentioned, Matt. viii. 4, when after a cure effected before a crowd of spectators, it was of little avail to enjoin secrecy on the cured, [9]) it is probable that evangelical tradition. enamoured of the mysteriousness that lay in this incognito of Jesus [10], unhistorically multiplied the instances of its adoption.

§ 63.

JESUS, THE SON OF GOD.

In Luke i. 35, we find the narrowest and most literal interpretation of the expression, ὁ υἱὸς τοῦ θεου; namely, as derived from his conception by means of the Holy Ghost. On the contrary, the widest moral and metaphorical sense is given to the expression in Matt. v. 45, where those who imitate the love of God towards his enemies are called the sons of the Father in heaven. There is an intermediate sense which we may term the metaphysical, because while it includes more than mere conformity of will, it is distinct from the notion of actual paternity, and implies a spiritual community of being. In this sense it is profusely employed and referred to in the fourth gospel; as when Jesus says that he speaks and does nothing of himself, but only what as a son he has learned from the Father (v. 19; xii. 49, and elsewhere), who, moreover, is in him (xvii. 21),

---

[9] Fritzsche, s. 309.
[10] Comp. Schleiermacher, über den Lukas. s. 74.

and notwithstanding his exaltation over him (xiv. 28), is yet
one with him (x. 30). There is yet a fourth sense in which
the expression is presented. When (Matt. iv. 3) the devil
challenges Jesus to change the stones into bread, making the
supposition, *If thou be the Son of God;* when Nathanael says
to Jesus, *Thou art the Son of God, the King of Israel* (John
i. 49) ; when Peter confesses, *Thou art the Christ, the Son of
the living God* (Matt. xvi. 16; comp. John vi. 69); when
Martha thus expresses her faith in Jesus, *I believe that thou
art the Christ, the Son of God* (John xi. 27) ; when the high
priest adjures Jesus to tell him if he be *the Christ, the Son of
God* (Matt. xxvi. 63) : it is obvious that the devil means nothing more than, If thou be the Messiah ; and that in the other
passages the υἱὸς τοῦ θεοῦ, united as it is with Χριστὸς and βασιλεὺς, is but an appellation of the Messiah.

    In Hos. xi. 1, Exod. iv. 22, the people of Israel, and in
2 Sam. vii. 14, Ps. ii. 7, (comp. lxxxix. 28) the king of that
people, are called the son and the first-born of God.   The
kings (as also the people) of Israel had this appellation, in
virtue of the love which Jehovah bore them, and the tutelary
care which he exercised over them (2 Sam. vii. 14) ; and from
the second psalm we gather the farther reason, that as earthly
kings choose their sons to reign with or under them, so the
Israelitish kings were invested by Jehovah, the supreme ruler,
with the government of his favourite province.   Thus the
designation was originally applicable to every Israelitish king
who adhered to the principle of the theocracy ; but when the
messianic idea was developed, it was pre-eminently assigned to
the Messiah, as the best-beloved Son, and the most powerful
vicegerent of God on earth [1].

    If, then, such was the original historical signification of the
epithet, *Son of God,* as applied to the Messiah, we have to
ask : is it possible that Jesus used it of himself in this signification only, or did he use it also in either of the three senses

----

[1] Comp. the excellent treatise of Paulus on the following question in the Einl.
zum Leben Jesu, 1, a. s. 28 ff.

previously adduced ? The narrowest, the merely physical import
of the term is not put into the mouth of Jesus, but into that
of the annunciating angel, Luke i. 35 ; and for this the evangelist alone is responsible. In the intermediate, metaphysical
sense, implying unity of essence and community of existence
with God, it might possibly have been understood by Jesus,
supposing him to have remodelled in his own conceptions the
theocratic interpretation current among his compatriots. It is
true that the abundant expressions having this tendency in the
gospel of John, appear to contradict those of Jesus on an occasion recorded by the synoptical writers (Mark x. 17 f; Luke
xviii. 18 f), when to a disciple who accosts him as *Good
Master*, he replies ; *Why callest thou me good ? there is none
good but one, that is God.* Here Jesus so tenaciously maintains the distinction between himself and God, that he renounces the predicate of (perfect) goodness, and insists on its
appropriation to God alone [2]. Olshausen supposes that this
rejection related solely to the particular circumstances of the
disciple addressed, who regarding Jesus as a merely human
teacher, ought not from his point of view to have given him
a divine epithet, and that it was not intended by Jesus as a
denial that he was, according to a just estimate of his character, actually the ἀγαθὸς in whom the one good Being was reflected as in a mirror ; but this is to take for granted what is first
to be proved, namely, that the declarations of Jesus concerning
himself in the fourth gospel are on a level as to credibility
with those recorded by the synoptical writers. Two of these
writers cite some words of Jesus which have an important bearing on our present subject : *All things are delivered to me of
my Father : and no man knoweth the Son but the Father :
neither knoweth any man the Father, but the Son, and he to
whomsoever the Son will reveal him,* Matt. xi. 27. Taking
this passage in connexion with the one before quoted, we must

---

[2] Even if a different reading be adopted for the parallel passage in Matthew
(xix. 16 f), it must remain questionable whether his statement deserve the preference
to that of the two other evangelists.

infer that Jesus had indeed an intimate communion of thought and will with God, but under such limitations, that the attribute of perfect goodness, as well as of absolute knowledge (e. g. of the day and hour of the last day, Mark xiii. 32 parall.) belonged exclusively to God, and hence the boundary line between divine and human was strictly preserved. Even in the fourth gospel Jesus declares, *My Father is greater than I*, ὁ πατήρ μου μείζων μου ἐστὶ, (xiv. 28), but this slight echo of the synoptical statement does not remove the difficulty of conciliating the numerous discourses of a totally different tenor in the former, with the rejection of the epithet ἀγαθός in the latter. It is surprising, too, that Jesus in the fourth gospel appears altogether ignorant of the theocratic sense of the expression υἱὸς τοῦ θεοῦ, and can only vindicate his use of it in the metaphysical sense, by retreating to its vague and metaphorical application. When, namely, (John x. 34 ff,) to justify his assumption of this title, he adduces the scriptural application of the term θεοὶ to other men, such as princes and magistrates, we are at a loss to understand why Jesus should resort to this remote and precarious argument, when close at hand lay the far more cogent one, that in the Old Testament, a theocratic king of Israel, or according to the customary interpretation of the most striking passages, the Messiah, is called the Son of Jehovah, and that therefore he, having declared himself to be the Messiah (v. 25), might consistently claim this appellation.

With respect to the light in which Jesus was viewed as the Son of God by others, we may remark that in the addresses of well-affected persons the title is often so associated as to be obviously a mere synonym of Χριστὸς, and this even in the fourth gospel; while on the other hand the contentious Ἰουδαῖοι of this gospel seem in their objections as ignorant as Jesus in his defence, of the theocratic, and only notice the metaphysical meaning of the expression. It is true that, even in the synoptical gospels, when Jesus answers affirmatively the question whether he be the Christ, the Son of the living God (Matt. xxvi. 65 parall.), the high priest taxes him with blasphemy;

but he refers merely to what he considers the unwarranted arrogation of the theocratic dignity of the Messiah, whereas in the fourth gospel, when Jesus represents himself as the Son of God (v. 17 f. x. 30 ff.) the Jews seek to kill him for the express reason that he thereby makes himself ἴσον τῷ θεῷ, nay even ἑαυτὸν θεόν. According to the synoptical writers, the high priest so unhesitatingly considers the idea of the Son of God to pertain to that of the Messiah, that he associates the two titles as if they were interchangeable, in the question he addresses to Jesus: on the contrary the Jews in the Gospel of John regard the one idea as so far transcending the other, that they listen patiently to the declaration of Jesus that he is the Messiah (x. 25), but as soon as he begins to claim to be the Son of God, *they take up stones to stone him.* In the synoptical gospels the reproach cast on Jesus is, that being a *common* man, he gives himself out for the Messiah; in the fourth gospel, that being a mere *man*, he gives himself out for a *divine* being. Hence Olshausen and others have justly insisted that in those passages of the latter gospel to which our remarks have reference, the υἱὸς τοῦ θεοῦ is not synonymous with Messiah, but is a name far transcending the ordinary idea of the Messiah [3]; they are not, however, warranted in concluding that therefore in the first three evangelists also [4] the same expression imports more than the Messiah. For the only legitimate interpretation of the high priest's question in Matthew makes ὁ υἱὸς τοῦ θεοῦ a synonym of ὁ Χριστὸς, and though in the parallel passage of Luke, the judges first ask Jesus if he be the Christ (xxii. 67.) ? and when he declines a direct answer,—predicting that they will behold the Son of Man seated at the right hand of God,—hastily interrupt him with the question, *Art thou the Son of God?* (v. 70) ; yet, after receiving what they consider an affirmative answer, they accuse him before Pilate as one who pretends to be Christ, a king (xxiii. 2), thus clearly

---

[3] Bibl. Comm. 2, s. 130. 253.
[4] Olshausen, ut sup. 1, s. 108 ff.

showing that Son of Man, Son of God, and Messiah, must have been regarded as interchangeable terms. It must therefore be conceded that there is a discrepancy on this point between the synoptical writers and John, and perhaps also an inconsistency of the latter with himself; for in several addresses to Jesus he retains the customary form, which associated *Son of God* with *Christ* or *King of Israel,* without being conscious of the distinction between the signification which υιος τ. θ. must have in such a connexion, and that in which he used it elsewhere—a want of perception which habitual forms of expression are calculated to induce. We have before cited examples of this oversight in the fourth evangelist (John i. 49. vi. 69. xi. 27).

The author of the Probabilia reasonably considers it suspicious that, in the fourth gospel, Jesus and his opponents should appear entirely ignorant of the theocratic sense which is elsewhere attached to the expression ὁ υἱὸς τοῦ θεοῦ, and which must have been more familiar to the Jews than any other, unless we suppose some of them to have partaken of Alexandrian culture. To such, we grant, as well as to the fourth evangelist, judging from his prologue, the metaphysical relation of the λόγος μονογενὴς to God would be the most cherished association.

§ 64.

THE DIVINE MISSION AND AUTHORITY OF JESUS. HIS PRE-EXISTENCE.

The four evangelists are in unison as to the declaration of Jesus concerning his divine mission and authority. Like every prophet, he is sent by God (Matt. x. 40. John v. 23 f. 56 f.), acts and speaks by the authority, and under the immediate guidance of God (John v. 19 ff.), and exclusively possesses an adequate knowledge of God, which it is his office to impart to men (Matt. xi. 27. John iii. 13). To him, as the Messiah, all power is given (Matt. xi. 27); first, over the kingdom which he is appointed to found and to rule with all its members (John x. 29. xvii. 6); next, over mankind in general (John xvii. 2), and even external nature (Matt. xxviii. 18); consequently, should the interests of the messianic kingdom demand it, power to effect a thorough revolution in the whole world. At the future commencement of his reign, Jesus, as Messiah, is authorized to awake the dead (John v. 28.), and to sit as a judge, separating those worthy to partake of the heavenly kingdom from the unworthy (Matt. xxv. 31 ff. John v. 22. 29.); offices which Jewish opinion attributed to the Messiah [1], and which Jesus, once convinced of his messiahship, would necessarily transfer to himself.

The evangelists are not equally unanimous on another point. According to the synoptical writers, Jesus claims, it is true, the highest human dignity, and the most exalted relation with God, for the present and future, but he never refers to an existence anterior to his earthly career : in the fourth gospel, on the contrary, we find several discourses of Jesus which contain the repeated assertion of such a pre-existence. We grant that when Jesus describes himself as coming down from heaven (John iii. 13. xvi. 28.), the expression, taken alone, may be understood as a merely figurative intimation of his superhuman origin. It is more difficult, but perhaps admissible, to interpret, with the Socinian Crell, the declaration of Jesus *Before Abraham was, I am,* πρὶν Αβραὰμ γενέσθαι, ἐγώ εἰμι (John viii. 58.), as referring to a purely ideal existence in the pre-determination of God; but scarcely possible to consider the prayer to the Father (John xvii. 5.) to confirm the δόξα (*glory*) which Jesus had with Him *before the world was,* πρὸ τοῦ τὸν κόσμον εἶναι, as an entreaty for the communication of a glory predestined for Jesus from eternity. But the language of Jesus John vi. 62., where he speaks of the Son of Man *reascending* ἀναβαίνειν *where he was before* ὅπου ἦν τὸ πρότερον, is, in its intrinsic meaning, as well as in that which is reflected on it from other passages, unequivocally significative of actual, not merely ideal, pre-existence.

It has been already conjectured [2] that these expressions, or

---

[1] Bertholdt, Christol. Judæor. §§ 8. 35. 42.
[2] Bretschneider, Probab. p. 59.

at least the adaptation of them to a real pre-existence, are
derived, not from Jesus, but from the author of the fourth
gospel, with whose opinions, as propounded in his introduction,
they specifically agree ; for if *the Word was in the beginning
with God* (ἐν ἀρχῇ πρὸς τὸν θεόν), Jesus, in whom it was *made
flesh*, might attribute to himself an existence before Abraham,
and a participation of glory with the Father before the foundation of the world.   Nevertheless, we are not warranted in
adopting this view, unless it can be shown, that neither was the
idea of the pre-existence of the Messiah extant among the Jews
of Palestine before the time of Jesus, nor is it probable that
Jesus attained such a notion, independently of the ideas peculiar
to his age and nation.

The latter supposition, that Jesus spoke from his own
memory of his pre-human and pre-mundane existence, is liable
to comparison with dangerous parallels in the history of
Pythagoras, Ennius, and Apollonius of Tyana, whose alleged
reminiscences of individual states which they had experienced
prior to their birth [3], are now generally regarded either as subsequent fables, or as enthusiastic self-delusions of those celebrated men.   For the other alternative, that the idea in question
was common to the Jewish nation, a presumption may be found
in the description, already quoted from Daniel, of the Son of
Man coming in the clouds of heaven, since the author, possibly, and, at all events, many readers, imagined that personage
to be a superhuman being, dwelling beforehand with God, like
the angels.   But that every one who referred this passage to the
Messiah, or that Jesus in particular, associated with it the
notion of a pre-existence, is not to be proved ; for, if we exclude
the representation of John, Jesus depicts his coming in the
clouds of heaven, not as if he had come as a visitant to earth
from his home in heaven, but, according to Matt. xxvi. 65.
(comp. xxiv. 25), as if he, the earth-born, after the completion

---

[3] Porphyr. Vita Pythag. 26 f.   Jamblich. 14. 63.   Diog. Laert. viii. 4 f. 14.
Baur, Apollonius von Tyana, p. 64 f. 98 f. 185 f.

of his earthly course, would be received into heaven, and from thence would return to establish his kingdom : thus making the coming from heaven not necessarily include the idea of pre-existence. We find in the Proverbs, in Sirach, and the Book of Wisdom, the idea of a personified and even hypostasized Wisdom of God, and in the Psalms and Prophets, strongly marked personifications of the Divine word[4]; and it is espe-cially worthy of note, that the later Jews, in their horror of anthropomorphism in the idea of the Divine being, attributed his speech, appearance, and immediate agency, to the *Word* (מימרא) or the *dwelling place* (שכינתא) of Jehovah, as may be seen in the venerable[5] Targum of Onkelos[6]. These ex-pressions, at first mere paraphrases of the name of God, soon received the mystical signification of a veritable hypostasis, of a being, at once distinct from, and one with God. As most of the revelations and interpositions of God, whose organ this personified Word was considered to be, were designed in favour of the Israelitish people, it was natural for them to assign to the manifestation which was still awaited from Him, and which was to be the crowning benefit of Israel,—the manifestation, namely, of the Messiah,—a peculiar relation with the Word or Shechina[7]. From this germ sprang the opinion that with the Messiah the Shechina would appear, and that what was ascribed to the Shechina pertained equally to the Messiah : an opinion not confined to the Rabbins, but sanctioned by the Apostle Paul. According to it, the Messiah was, even in the wilderness, the invisible guide and benefactor of God's people (1 Cor. x. 4, 9.)[8]; he was with our first parents in Paradise[9]; he was the agent in creation (Col. i. 16.); he even existed before the crea-

---

[4] See a notification and exposition of the passages in Lücke, Comm. zum Ev. Joh. 1, s. 211 ff.

[5] Winer, de Onkeloso, p. 10. Comp. De Wette, Einleit. in das A. T. § 58.

[6] Bertholdt, Christol. Judæor. §§ 23—25. Comp. Lücke ut sup. s. 244. note.

[7] Schöttgen, ii. s. 6 f.

[8] Targ. Jes. xvi. 1 : *Iste (Messias) in deserto fuit rupes ecclesiæ Zionis.* In Bertholdt, ut sup. p. 145.

[9] Sohar chadasch f. lxxxii. 4, ap. Schöttgen, ii, s. 440.

tion [10], and prior to his incarnation in Jesus, was in a glorious fellowship with God (Phil. ii. 6.).

As it is thus evident that, immediately after the time of Jesus, the idea of a pre-existence of the Messiah was incorporated in the higher Jewish theology, it is no far-fetched conjecture, that the same idea was afloat when the mind of Jesus was maturing, and that in his conception of himself as the Messiah, this attribute was included. But whether Jesus were as deeply initiated in the speculations of the Jewish schools as Paul, is yet a question, and as the author of the fourth gospel, versed in the Alexandrian doctrine of the λογὸς, stands alone in ascribing to Jesus the assertion of a pre-existence, we are unable to decide whether we are to put the dogma to the account of Jesus, or of his biographer.

§ 65.

THE MESSIANIC PLAN OF JESUS.   INDICATIONS OF A POLITICAL ELEMENT.

The Baptist pointed to a future individual, and Jesus to himself, as the founder of the kingdom of heaven. The idea of that messianic kingdom belonged to the Israelitish nation; did Jesus hold it in the form in which it existed among his cotemporaries, or under modifications of his own?

The idea of the Messiah grew up amongst the Jews in soil half religious, half political: it was nurtured by national adversity, and in the time of Jesus, according to the testimony of the gospels, it was embodied in the expectation that the Messiah would ascend the throne of his ancestor David, free the Jewish people from the Roman yoke, and found a kingdom which would last for ever (Luke i. 32 f. 68 ff. Acts i. 6.). Hence our first question must be this. Did Jesus include this political element in his messianic plan?

---

[10] Nezach Israël c. xxxv. f. xlviii. 1. Schmidt, Bibl. für Kritik u. Exegese, 1, s. 38: מְשִׁיחַ מִפְּנֵי תּוֹרוֹ. Sohar Levit. f. xiv. 56. Schöttgen, ii. s. 436: *Septem (lumina condita sunt, antequam mundus conderetur), nimirum . . . . . . et lumen Messiæ.* Here we have the pre-existence of the Messiah represented as a real one: for a more ideal conception of it, see Bereschith Rabba, sect. 1, f. iii. 3 (Schöttgen).

That Jesus aspired to be a temporal ruler, has at all times been an allegation of the adversaries of Christianity, but has been maintained by none with so much exegetical acumen as by the author of the Wolfenbüttel Fragments[1], who, be it observed, by no means denies to Jesus the praise of aiming at the moral reformation of his nation. According to this writer, the first indication of a political plan on the part of Jesus is, that he unambiguously announced the approaching messianic kingdom, and laid down the conditions on which it was to be entered, without explaining what this kingdom was, and wherein it consisted[2], as if he supposed the current idea of its nature to be correct. Now the fact is, that the prevalent conception of the messianic reign had a strong political bias; hence, when Jesus spoke of the Messiah's kingdom without a definition, the Jews could only think of an earthly dominion, and as Jesus could not have presupposed any other interpretation of his words, he must have wished to be so understood. But in opposition to this it may be remarked, that in the Parables by which Jesus shadowed forth the kingdom of heaven; in the Sermon on the Mount, in which he illustrates the duties of its citizens; and lastly, in his whole demeanour and course of action, we have sufficient evidence, that his idea of the messianic kingdom was peculiar to himself. There is not so ready a counterpoise for the difficulty, that Jesus sent the apostles, with whose conceptions he could not be unacquainted, to announce the Messiah's kingdom throughout the land (Matt. x.). These, who disputed which of them should be greatest in the kingdom of their master (Matt. xviii. 1. Luke xxii. 24); of whom two petitioned for the seats at the right and left of the messianic king (Mark x. 35 ff.); who, even after the death and resurrection of Jesus, expected a restoration of the kingdom to Israel (Acts i. 6);—these had clearly from the beginning to the end of their intercourse with Jesus, no other than the popular notion of the Messiah; when, therefore, Jesus despatched them as

---

[1] Von dem Zweck Jesu und seiner Jünger, s. 108—157.
[2] Comp. Fritzsche, in Matth. s. 114.

heralds of his kingdom, it seems necessarily a part of his design, that they should disseminate in all places their political
messianic idea.

Among the discourses of Jesus there is one especially worthy
of note in Matt. xix. 28. (comp. Luke xxii. 30.). In reply to
the question of Peter, *We have left all and followed thee;
what shall we have therefore?* Jesus promises to his disciples
that in the παλιγγενεσία, *when the Son of Man shall sit on his
throne, they also shall sit on twelve thrones, judging the
twelve tribes of Israel.* That the literal import of this promise
formed part of the tissue of the messianic hopes cherished by
the Jews of that period, is not to be controverted. It is argued,
however, that Jesus spoke figuratively on this occasion, and
only employed familiar Jewish images to convey to the apostles
an assurance, that the sacrifices they had made here would be
richly compensated in their future life by a participation in his
glory[3]. But the disciples must have understood the promise
literally, when, even after the resurrection of Jesus, they har-
boured anticipations of worldly greatness; and as Jesus had
had many proofs of this propensity, he would hardly have
adopted such language, had he not intended to nourish their
temporal hopes. The supposition that he did so merely to animate the courage of his disciples, without himself sharing their
views, imputes duplicity to Jesus;—a duplicity in this case
quite gratuitous, since, as Olshausen justly observes, Peter's
question would have been satisfactorily answered by any other
laudatory acknowledgment of the devotion of the disciples.
Hence it appears a fair inference, that Jesus himself shared the
Jewish expectations which he here sanctions: but expositors
have made the most desperate efforts to escape from this unwelcome conclusion. Some have resorted to an arbitrary alteration
of the reading[4]; others to the detection of irony, directed
against the disproportion between the pretensions of the dis-

[3] Kuinöl, Comm. in Matt. p. 518.   Olshausen also, p. 744, understands the discourse symbolically, though he attaches to it a different meaning.

[4] Paulus, exeget. Handb. 2, s. 613. f.

ciples, and their trivial services [5] ; others to different expedients, but all more unnatural than the admission, that Jesus, in accordance with Jewish ideas, here promises his disciples the dignity of being his assessors in his visible messianic judgment, and that he thus indicates the existence of a national element in his notion of the Messiah's kingdom. It is observable, too, that in the Acts (i. 7.), Jesus, even after his resurrection, does not deny that he will restore the kingdom to Israel, but merely discourages curiosity as to the times and seasons of its restoration.

Among the actions of Jesus, his last entry into Jerusalem (Matt. xxi. 1 ff.) is especially appealed to as a proof that his plan was partly political. According to the Fragmentist, all the circumstances point to a political design : the time which Jesus chose,—after a sufficiently long preparation of the people in the provinces; the passover, which they visited in great numbers; the animal on which he rode, and by which, from a popular interpretation of a passage in Zachariah, he announced himself as the destined King of Jerusalem; the approval which he pronounces when the people receive him with a royal greeting ; the violent procedure which he hazards in the temple; and finally, his severe philippic on the higher class of the Jews (Matt. xxiii.), at the close of which he seeks to awe them into a reception of him as their messianic king, by the threat that he will show himself to them no more in any other guise.

§ 66.

DATA FOR THE PURE SPIRITUALITY OF THE MESSIANIC PLAN OF JESUS. BALANCE.

Nowhere in our evangelical narratives is there a trace of Jesus having sought to form a political party. On the contrary, he withdraws from the eagerness of the people to make him a king (John vi. 15.) ; he declares that the messianic kingdom comes not with observation, but is to be sought for in the

---

[5] Liebe, in Winer's exeg. Studien, 1, 59. ff.

recesses of the soul (Luke xvii. 20 f.) ; it is his principle to
unite obedience to God with obedience to temporal authority,
even when heathen (Matt. xxii. 21.) ; on his solemn entry into
the capital, he chooses to ride the animal of peace, and afterwards escapes from the multitude, instead of using their excitement for the purposes of his ambition ; lastly, he maintains
before his judge, that his kingdom is not *from hence* οὐκ
ἐντεῦθεν, *is not of this world* οὐκ ἐκ τοῦ κόσμου τούτου (John xvi.
36.), and we have no reason in this instance to question either
his or the evangelist's veracity.

Thus we have a series of indications to counterbalance those
detailed in the preceding section.   The adversaries of Christianity have held exclusively to the arguments for a political, or
rather a revolutionary, project, on the part of Jesus, while the
orthodox theologians adhere to those only which tell for the pure
spirituality of his plan [1] ; and each party has laboured to invalidate by hermeneutical skill the passages unfavourable to its
theory.   It has of late been acknowledged that both are equally
partial, and that there is need of arbitration between them.

This has been attempted chiefly by supposing an earlier and
a later form of the plan of Jesus [2].   Although, it has been said,
the moral improvement and religious elevation of his people
were from the first the primary object of Jesus, he nevertheless,
in the beginning of his public life, cherished the hope of reviving,
by means of this internal regeneration, the external glories of the
theocracy, when he should be acknowledged by his nation as the
Messiah, and thereby be constituted the supreme authority in
the state.   But in the disappointment of this hope, he recognized the Divine rejection of every political element in his plan,
and thenceforth refined it into pure spirituality.   It is held to

---

[1] So Reinhard, über den Plan, welchen der Stifter der christlichen Religion zum
Besten der Menschheit entwarf. s. 57 ff. (4te Aufl.)

[2] Paulus, Leben Jesu 1, b. s. 85. 94. 106 ff. ; Venturini, 2, s. 310 f. Hase, Leben
Jesu, 1 ed. §§ 68. 84.   Hase has modified this opinion in his 2d edition, §§ 49, 50.
(comp. theol. Streitschrift, 1. s. 61. ff.), though with apparent reluctance, and he now
maintains that Jesus had risen above the political notion of the messianic kingdom
before his public appearance.

be a presumption in favour of such a change in the plan of
Jesus, that there is a gladness diffused over his first appearance,
which gives place to melancholy in the latter period of his
ministry; that instead of the acceptable year of the Lord, announced in his initiative address at Nazareth, sorrow is the
burthen of his later discourses, and he explicitly says of
Jerusalem, that he had attempted to save it, but that now its
fall, both religious and political, was inevitable. As, however,
the evangelists do not keep the events and discourses proper to
these distinct periods within their respective limits, but happen
to give the two most important data for the imputation of a
political design to Jesus, (namely the promise of the twelve
thrones and the public entrance into the capital,) near the close
of his life; we must attribute to these writers a chronological
confusion, as in the case of the relation which the views of Jesus
bore to the messianic idea in general : unless as an alternative
it be conceivable, that Jesus uttered during the same period, the
declarations which seem to indicate, and those which disclaim,
a political design.

This, in our apprehension, is not inconceivable; for Jesus
might anticipate a καθίζεσθαι ἐπὶ θρόνους for himself and his disciples, not regarding the means of its attainment as a political
revolution, but as a revolution to be effected by the immediate
interposition of God. That such was his view may be inferred
from his placing that judiciary appearance of his disciples in
the παλιγγενεσία; for this was not a political revolution, any
more than a spiritual regeneration,—it was a resurrection of the
dead, which God was to effect through the agency of the
Messiah, and which was to usher in the messianic times [3]. Jesus
certainly expected to restore the throne of David, and with his
disciples to govern a liberated people; in no degree, however,
did he rest his hopes on the sword of human adherents (Luke
xxii. 38. Matt. xxvi. 52.), but on the legions of angels,
which his heavenly Father could send him (Matt. xxvi. 53.).
Wherever he speaks of coming in his messianic glory, he

---

[3] Fritzsche, in Matt. p. 606 f.

depicts himself surrounded by angels and heavenly powers
(Matt. xvi. 27, xxiv. 30 f. xxv. 31 ; John i. 52.) ; before the
majesty of the Son of Man, coming in the clouds of heaven,
all nations are to bow without the coercion of the sword, and
at the sound of the angel's trumpet, are to present themselves,
with the awakened dead, before the judgment-seat of the
Messiah and his twelve apostles. All this Jesus would not
bring to pass of his own will, but he waited for a signal from
his heavenly Father, who alone knew the appropriate time for
this catastrophe (Mark xiii. 32.), and he apparently was not
disconcerted when his end approached without his having
received the expected intimation. They who shrink from this
view, merely because they conceive that it makes Jesus an en-
thusiast [4], will do well to reflect how closely such hopes corresponded with the long cherished messianic idea of the Jews [5], and
how easily, in that day of supernaturalism, and in a nation
segregated by the peculiarities of its faith, an idea, in itself extravagant, if only it were consistent, and had, in some of its
aspects, truth and dignity, might allure even a reasonable man
beneath its influence.

With respect to that which awaits the righteous after judgment,—everlasting life in the kingdom of the Father,—it is true
that Jesus, in accordance with Jewish notions [6], compares it to a
feast (Matt. viii. 11 ; xxii. 2 ff.), at which he hopes himself to
taste the fruit of the vine (Matt. xxvi. 29.), and to celebrate the
passover (Luke xxii. 16.) : but his declaration that in the αἰὼν
μέλλων the organic relation between the sexes will cease, and
men will be *like the angels* (ἰσάγγελοι, Luke xx. 35 ff.), seems
more or less to reduce the above discourses to a merely symbolical significance.

Thus we conclude that the messianic hope of Jesus was not
political, nor even merely earthly, for he referred its fulfilment
to supernatural means, and to a supermundane theatre (the regenerated earth) : as little was it a purely spiritual hope, in the

---

[4] De Wette, Bibl. Dogm. § 216.
[5] Bertholdt, Christol. Judæor. §§ 30 ff.
[6] Ibid, § 39.

modern sense of the term, for it included important and unprecedented changes in the external condition of things: but it was the national, theocratic hope, spiritualized and ennobled by his own peculiar moral and religious views.

§ 67.

THE RELATION OF JESUS TO THE MOSAIC LAW.

The Mosaic institutions were actually extinguished in the church of which Jesus was the founder; hence it is natural to suppose that their abolition formed a part of his design:—a reach of vision, beyond the horizon of the ceremonial worship of his age and country, of which apologists have been ever anxious to prove that he was possessed [1]. Neither are there wanting speeches and actions of Jesus which seem to favour their effort. Whenever he details the conditions of participation in the kingdom of heaven, as in the sermon on the mount, he insists, not on the observance of the Mosaic ritual, but on the spirit of religion and morality; he attaches no value to fasting, praying, and almsgiving, unless accompanied by a corresponding bent of mind (Matt. vi. 1—18); the two main elements of the Mosaic worship, sacrifice and the keeping of sabbaths and feasts, he not only nowhere enjoins, but puts a marked slight on the former, by commending the scribe who declared that the love of God and one's neighbour was *more than whole burnt-offerings and sacrifices,* as one *not far from the kingdom of God* (Mark xii. 23 f.) [2], and he ran counter in action as well as in speech to the customary mode of celebrating the Sabbath (Matt. xii. 1—13; Mark ii. 23—28; iii. 1—5; Luke vi. 1—10; xiii. 10. ff. ; xiv. 1. ff.; John v. 5. ff. ; vii. 22 ; ix. 1. ff.), of which in his character of Son of Man he claimed to be Lord. The Jews, too, appear to have expected a revision of the Mosaic law by their Messiah [3]. A somewhat analogous

[1] E. g. Reinhard, Plan Jesu, s. 14 ff.
[2] For an exaggeration in the Ebionite Gospel, vid. Epiphanius, hæres. xxx. 16.
[3] Bertholdt, ut sup. § 31.

sense is couched in the declarations attributed by the fourth
evangelist to Jesus (ii. 19.) ; Matthew (xxvi. 61.) and Mark
(xiv. 58.) represent him as being accused by false witnesses of
saying, *I am able to destroy* (John, *destroy*) *the temple of
God* (Mark, *that is made with hands*), *and to build it in three
days* (Mark, *I will build another made without hands*). The
author of the Acts has something similar as an article of accusation against Stephen, but instead of the latter half of the sentence it is thus added, *and* (he, i. e. Jesus) *shall change the
customs which Moses delivered us ;* and perhaps this may be
regarded as an authentic comment on the less explicit text.
In general it may be said that to one who, like Jesus, is so
far alive to the absolute value of the internal compared with
the external, of the bent of the entire disposition compared
with isolated acts, that he pronounces the love of God and our
neighbour to be the essence of the law (Matt. xxii. 36 ff.),—
to him it cannot be a secret, that all precepts of the law which
do not bear on these two points are unessential.   But the argument apparently most decisive of a design on the part of Jesus
to abolish the Mosaic worship, is furnished by his prediction
that the temple, the centre of Jewish worship (Matt. xxiv. 2.
parall.), would be destroyed, and that the adoration of God
would be freed from local fetters, and become purely spiritual
(John iv. 21 ff.).

The above, however, presents only one aspect of the position
assumed by Jesus towards the Mosaic law; there are also data
for the belief that he did not meditate the overthrow of the ancient constitution of his country.   This side of the question has
been, at a former period, and from easily-conceived reasons, the
one which the enemies of Christianity in its ecclesiastical form,
have chosen to exhibit[4]; but it is only in recent times that, the
theological horizon being extended, the unprejudiced expositors
of the church[5] have acknowledged its existence.   In the first

---

[4] This is done the most concisely in the Wolfenbüttel Fragments, von dem Zweck
u. s. f. s. 66 ff.

[5] Especially Fritzsche, in Matt. s. 214 ff.

place, during his life Jesus remains faithful to the paternal law; he attends the synagogue on the sabbath, journeys to Jerusalem at the time of the feast, and eats of the paschal lamb with his disciples. It is true that he heals on the sabbath, allows his disciples to pluck ears of corn (Matt. xii. 1. ff.), and requires no fasting or washing before meat in his society (Matt. iv. 14 ; xv. 2). But the Mosaic law concerning the sabbath simply prescribed cessation from common labour, מְלָאכָה, (Exod. xx. 8. ff.; xxxi. 12. ff. ; Deut. v. 12. ff.), including ploughing, reaping, (Ex. xxxiv. 21), gathering of sticks (Numb. xv. 32. ff.) and similar work, and it was only the spirit of petty observance, the growth of a later age, that made it an offence to perform cures, or pluck a few ears of corn [6]. The washing of hands before eating was but a rabbinical custom [7] ; in the law one general yearly fast was alone prescribed (Lev. xvi. 29 ff. ; xxiii. 27 ff.) and no private fasting required ; hence Jesus cannot be convicted of infringing the precepts of Moses [8]. In that very sermon on the mount in which Jesus exalts spiritual religion so far above all ritual, he clearly presupposes the continuation of sacrifices (Matt. v. 23 f.), and declares that he is not come to destroy the law and the prophets, but to fulfil (Matt. v. 17.). Even if πληρῶσαι, in all probability, refers chiefly to the accomplishment of the Old Testament prophecies, οὐκ ἦλθον καταλῦσαι must at the same time be understood of the conservation of the Mosaic law, since in the context, perpetuity is promised to its smallest letter, and he who represents its lightest precept as not obligatory, is threatened with the lowest rank in the kingdom of heaven [9]. In accordance with this, the apostles adhered strictly to the Mosaic law, even after the Feast of Pentecost; they went at the hour of prayer into the temple (Acts iii. 1.), clung to the synagogues and to the Mosaic injunctions

---

[6] Winer, bibl. Realwörterb. 2, s. 406 ff.

[7] Comp. Paulus, exeg. Handb. 2, s. 273.

[8] Winer, b. Realw. 1 Bd. s. 426.

[9] Fritzsche, s. 214 ff.

respecting food (x. 14), and were unable to appeal to any express declaration of Jesus as a sanction for the procedure of Barnabas and Paul, when the judaizing party complained of their baptizing Gentiles without laying on them the burthen of the Mosaic law.

This apparent contradiction in the conduct and language of Jesus, has been apologetically explained by the supposition, that not only the personal obedience of Jesus to the law, but also his declarations in its favour, were a necessary concession to the views of his cotemporaries, who would at once have withdrawn their confidence from him, had he announced himself as the destroyer of their holy and venerated law[10].   We allow that the obedience of Jesus to the law in his own person, might be explained in the same way as that of Paul, which, on his own showing, was a measure of mere expediency (1 Cor. ix. 20. comp. Acts xvi. 3.).   But the strong declarations of Jesus concerning the perpetuity of the law, and the guilt of him who dares to violate its lightest precept, cannot possibly be derived from the principle of concession; for to pronounce that indispensable, which one secretly holds superfluous, and which one even seeks to bring gradually into disuse, would, leaving honesty out of the question, be in the last degree injudicious.

Hence others have made a distinction between the moral and the ritual law, and referred the declaration of Jesus that he wished not to abrogate the law, to the former alone, which he extricated from a web of trivial ceremonies, and embodied in his own example[11].   But such a distinction is not found in those striking passages from the Sermon on the Mount; rather, in the νόμος and προφῆται, *the law and the prophets*, we have the most comprehensive designation of the whole religious constitution of the Old Testament[12], and under the most trivial

---

[10] Reinhard, s. 15 ff. Planck, Geschichte des Christenthums in der Periode seiner Einführung, 1, s. 175 ff.

[11] De Wette, Bibl. Dogm. § 210.

[12] Fritzsche, s. 214.

commandment, and the smallest letter of the law, alike pronounced imperishable, we cannot well understand any thing
else than the ceremonial precepts [13].

A happier distinction is that between really Mosaic institutes,
and their traditional amplifications [14]. It is certain that the
Sabbath cures of Jesus, his neglect of the pedantic ablutions
before eating, and the like, ran counter, not to Moses, but to
later rabbinical requirements, and several discourses of Jesus
turn upon this distinction. Matt. xv. 3 ff., Jesus places the
commandment of God in opposition to the tradition of the
elders, and Matt. xxiii. 23, he declares that where they are
compatible, the former may be observed without rejecting the
latter, in which case he admonishes the people to do all that the
Scribes and Pharisees enjoin ; where, on the contrary, either the
one or the other only can be respected, he decides that it is
better to transgress the tradition of the Elders, than the commandment of God as given by Moses (Matt. xv. 3 ff.). He
describes the mass of traditional precepts, as a burthen grievous
to be borne, which he would remove from the oppressed people,
substituting his own light burthen and easy yoke; whence it
may be seen, that with all his forbearance towards existing institutions, so far as they were not positively pernicious, it was
his intention that all these *commandments of men*, as plants
which his heavenly Father had not planted, should be rooted up
(xv. 9. 13.). The majority of the Pharisaical precepts referred to
externals, and had the effect of burying the noble morality of
the Mosaic law under a heap of ceremonial observances ; a gift
to the temple sufficed to absolve the giver from his filial duties
(xv. 5.), and the payment of tithe of anise and cummin,
superseded justice, mercy, and faith (xxiii. 23.). Hence this
distinction is in some degree identical with the former, since in
the rabbinical institutes it was their merely ceremonial tendency
that Jesus censured, while, in the Mosaic law, it was the kernel
of religion and morality that he chiefly valued. It must only

[13] Vid. the Fragmentist, s. 69.
[14] Paulus, exeg. Handb. 1, b, s. 600 f. Leben Jesu, 1, a, s. 296. 312.

not be contended that he regarded the Mosaic law as permanent solely in its spiritual part, for the passages quoted, especially from the Sermon on the Mount, clearly show that he did not contemplate the abolition of the merely ritual precepts.

Jesus, supposing that he had discerned morality and the spiritual worship of God to be the sole essentials in religion, must have rejected all which, being merely ritual and formal, had usurped the importance of a religious obligation, and under this description must fall a large proportion of the Mosaic precepts ; but it is well known how slowly such consequences are deduced, when they come into collision with usages consecrated by antiquity.   Even Samuel, apparently, was aware that obedience is better than sacrifice (1 Sam. xv. 22), and Asaph, that an offering of thanksgiving is more acceptable to God than one of slain animals (Ps. l.) ; yet how long after were sacrifices retained together with true obedience, or in its stead!   Jesus was more thoroughly penetrated with this conviction than those ancients; with him, the true commandments of God in the Mosaic law were simply, *Honour thy father and thy mother, Thou shalt not kill,* &c., and above all, *Thou shalt love the Lord thy God with all thy heart, and thy neighbour as thyself.*   But his deep-rooted respect for the sacred book of the law, caused him, for the sake of these essential contents, to honour the unessential ; which was the more natural, as in comparison with the absurdly exaggerated pedantry of the traditional observances, the ritual of the Pentateuch must have appeared highly simple.   To honour this latter part of the law as of Divine origin, but to declare it abrogated on the principle, that in the education of the human race, God finds necessary for an earlier period an arrangement which is superfluous for a later one, implies that idea of *the law* as *a schoolmaster,* νόμος παιδαγωγὸς (Gal. iii. 24.), which seems first to have been developed by the apostle Paul ; nevertheless, its germ lies in the declaration of Jesus, that God had permitted to the early Hebrews, *on account of the hardness of their hearts,* (Matt. xix. 8 f.,) many things which, in a more advanced stage of culture, were inadmissible.

A similar limitation of the duration of the law is involved in the predictions of Jesus, (if indeed they were uttered by Jesus, a point which we have to discuss,) that the temple would be destroyed at his approaching advent (Matt. xxiv. parall.), and that devotion would be freed from all local restrictions (John iv.); for with these must fall the entire Mosaic system of external worship. This is not contradicted by the declaration that the law would endure until heaven and earth should pass away (Matt. v. 18.), for the Hebrew associated the fall of his state and sanctuary with the end of the old world or dispensation, so that the expressions, so long as the temple stands, and so long as the world stands, were equivalent [15]. It is true that the words of Jesus, Luke xvi. 16., ὁ νόμος καὶ οἱ προφῆται ἕως 'Ιωάννου' seem to imply, that the appearance of the Baptist put an end to the validity of the law; but this passage loses its depreciatory sense when compared with its parallel, Matt. xi. 13. On the other hand, Luke xvi. 17. controls Matt. v. 18., and reduces it to a mere comparison between the stability of the law, and that of heaven and earth. The only question then is, in which of the gospels are the two passages more correctly stated? As given in the first, they intimate that the law would retain its supremacy until, and not after, the close of the old dispensation. With this agrees the prediction, that the temple would be destroyed; for the spiritualization of religion, and, according to Stephen's interpretation, the abolition of the Mosaic law, which were to be the results of that event, were undoubtedly identified by Jesus with the commencement of the αἰὼν μέλλων of the Messiah. Hence it appears, that the only difference between the view of Paul and that of Jesus is this: that the latter anticipated the extinction of the Mosaic system as a concomitant of his glorious advent or return to the regenerated earth, while the former believed its abolition permissible on the old, unregenerated earth, in virtue of the Messiah's first advent [16].

---

[15] Comp. Paulus, exeg. Handb. 1, b. s. 598 f.

[16] Comp. Hase, L. J. s. 84. Rabbinical notions of the abrogation of the Law in Schöttgen, ii. s. 611 ff.

§ 68.

Although the church founded by Jesus did, in fact, early extend itself beyond the limits of the Jewish people, there are yet indications which might induce a belief that he did not contemplate such an extension[1]. When he sends the twelve on their first mission, his command is, *Go not into the way of the Gentiles—Go rather to the lost sheep of the house of Israel* (Matt. x. 5 f.). That Matthew alone has this injunction, and not the two other synoptists, is less probably explained by the supposition that the Hebrew author of the first gospel interpolated it, than by the opposite one, namely, that it was wilfully omitted by the Hellenistic authors of the second and third gospels. For, as the judaizing tendency of Matthew is not so marked that he assigns to Jesus the intention of limiting the messianic kingdom to the Jews; as, on the contrary, he makes Jesus unequivocally foretel the calling of the Gentiles (viii. 11 f. xxi. 33 ff. xxii. 1 ff. xxviii. 19 f.): he had no motive for fabricating this particularizing addition; but the two other evangelists had a strong one for its omission, in the offence which it would cause to the Gentiles already within the fold. Its presence in Matthew, however, demands an explanation, and expositors have thought to furnish one by supposing the injunction of Jesus to be a measure of prudence[2]. It is unquestionable that, even if the plan of Jesus comprehended the Gentiles as well as the Jews, he must at first, if he would not for ever ruin his cause with his fellow-countrymen, adopt, and prescribe to the disciples, a rule of national exclusiveness. This necessity on his part might account for his answer to the Canaanitish woman, whose daughter he refuses to heal, because he was only sent to the lost sheep of the house of Israel (Matt.

---

[1] Thus the Wolfenbüttel Fragmentist, ut sup. s. 72 ff.

[2] Reinhard : Planck, Geschichte des Christenthums in der Per. seiner Einführung, 1, s. 179 ff.

xv. 24), were it not that the boon which he here denies is not
a reception into the messianic kingdom, but a temporal benefit,
such as even Elijah and Elisha had conferred on those who
were not Israelites (1 Kings xvii. 9 ff. 2 Kings v. 1 ff.)—examples to which Jesus elsewhere appeals (Luke iv. 25 ff.).
Hence the disciples thought it natural and unobjectionable to
grant the woman's petition, and it could not be prudential considerations that withheld Jesus, for a time, from compliance.
That an aversion to the Gentiles may not appear to be his
motive, it has been conjectured[3] that Jesus, wishing to preserve
an incognito in that country, avoided the performance of any
messianic work. But such a design of concealment is only
mentioned by Mark (vii. 25.), who represents it as being de-
feated by the entreaties of the woman, contrary to the inclina-
tions of Jesus; and as this evangelist omits the declaration of
Jesus, that he was not sent but to the lost sheep of the house
of Israel, we must suspect that he was guided by the wish to
supply a less offensive motive for the conduct of Jesus, rather
than by historical accuracy. Had Jesus really been influenced
by the motive which Mark assigns, he must at once have alleged
it to his disciples instead of a merely ostensible one, calculated
to strengthen their already rigid exclusiveness. We should
therefore rather listen to the opinion that Jesus sought, by his
repeated refusal, to prove the faith of the woman, and furnish
an occasion for its exhibition[4], if we could find in the text the
slightest trace of mere dissimulation; and none of a real change
of mind[5]. Even Mark, bent as he was on softening the features
of the incident, cannot have thought of a dissimulation of this
kind; otherwise, instead of omitting the harsh words and making
the inadequate addition, *and would have no man know it*, he
would have removed the offence in the most satisfactory manner,
by an observation such as, *he said this to prove her* (comp.
John vi. 6.). Thus it must be allowed that Jesus in this case

---

[3] Paulus, Leben Jesu, 1, a, s. 380 f. Hase, L. J. § 102.

[4] Olshausen, 1, s. 507.

[5] Hase, ut sup.

seems to share the antipathy of his countrymen towards the
Gentiles, nay, his antipathy seems to be of a deeper stamp than
that of his disciples; unless their advocacy of the woman be a
touch from the pencil of tradition, for the sake of contrast and
grouping.

This narrative, however, is neutralized by another, in which
Jesus is said to act in a directly opposite manner.   The centurion of Capernaum, also a Gentile, (as we gather from the
remarks of Jesus,) has scarcely complained of a distress similar
to that of the Canaanitish woman, when Jesus himself volunteers
to go and heal his servant (Matt. viii. 5.).   If, then, Jesus
has no hesitation, in this instance, to exercise his power of healing in favour of a heathen, how comes it that he refuses to do so
in another quite analogous case ?   Truly if the relative position
of the two narratives in the gospels have any weight, he must
have shown himself more harsh and narrow at the later period
than at the earlier one.   Meanwhile, this single act of benevolence
to a Gentile, standing as it does in inexplicable contradiction to
the narrative above examined, cannot prove, in opposition to the
command expressly given to the disciples, not to go to the Gentiles, that Jesus contemplated their admission as such into the
messianic kingdom.

Even the prediction of Jesus that the kingdom of heaven
would be taken from the Jews and given to the Gentiles, does not
prove this.   In the above interview with the centurion of Capernaum, Jesus declares that *many shall come from the east and
the west*, and sit down with the patriarchs in *the kingdom of
heaven*, while the *children of the kingdom*, (obviously the
Jews,) for whom it was originally designed, will be cast out
(Matt. viii. 11 f.).   Yet more decidedly, when applying the
parable of the husbandmen in the vineyard, he warns his
countrymen that *the kingdom of God shall be taken from them,
and given to a nation bringing forth the fruits thereof* (Matt.
xxi. 43.).   All this may be understood in the sense intended
by the prophets, in their promises that the messianic kingdom
would extend to all nations ; namely, that the Gentiles would

turn to the worship of Jehovah, embrace the Mosaic religion in its entire form, and afterwards be received into the Messiah's kingdom. It would accord very well with this expectation, that, prior to such a conversion, Jesus should forbid his disciples to direct their announcement of his kingdom to the Gentiles. But in the discourses concerning his re-appearance, Jesus regards the publication of the Gospel to all nations as one of the circumstances that must precede that event; (Matt. xxiv. 14. Mark xiii. 10.), and after his resurrection, according to the synoptists, he gave his disciples the command, *Go ye, and teach all nations, baptizing them,* &c. (Matt. xxviii. 19; Mark xvi. 15; Luke xxiv. 47.); i. e. go to them with the offer of the Messiah's kingdom, even though they may not beforehand have become Jews. Not only, however, do the disciples, after the first Pentecost, neglect to execute this command, but when a case is thrust on them which offers them an opportunity for compliance with it, they act as if they were altogether ignorant that such a direction had been given by Jesus (Acts x. xi.). The heathen centurion Cornelius, worthy, from his devout life, of a reception into the messianic community, is pointed out by an angel to the apostle Peter. But because it was not hidden from God, with what difficulty the apostle would be induced to receive a heathen, without further preliminary, into the Messiah's kingdom, he saw it needful to prepare him for such a step by a symbolical vision. In consequence of such an admonition Peter goes to Cornelius; but to impel him to baptize him and his family, he needs a second sign, the pouring out of the Holy Ghost on these uncircumcised. When, subsequently, the Jewish Christians in Jerusalem call him to account for this reception of Gentiles, Peter appeals in his justification solely to the recent vision, and to the Holy Ghost given to the centurion's family. Whatever judgment we may form of the credibility of this history, it is a memorial of the many deliberations and contentions which it cost the apostles after the departure of Jesus, to convince themselves of the eligibility of Gentiles for a participation in the kingdom of their

Christ, and the reasons which at last brought them to a decision. Now if Jesus had given so explicit a command as that above quoted, what need was there of a vision to encourage Peter to its fulfilment? or, supposing the vision to be a legendary investiture of the natural deliberations of the disciples, why did they go about in search of the reflection, that all men ought to be baptized, because before God all men and all animals, as his creatures, are clean, if they could have appealed to an express injunction of Jesus? Here, then, is the alternative: if Jesus himself gave this command, the disciples cannot have been led to the admission of the Gentiles by the means narrated in Acts x. xi.; if, on the other hand, that narrative is authentic, the alleged command of Jesus cannot be historical. Our canon decides for the latter proposition. For that the subsequent practice and pre-eminent distinction of the Christian Church, its accessibility to all nations, and its indifference to circumcision or uncircumcision, should have lain in the mind of its founder, is the view best adapted to exalt and adorn Jesus; while, that, first after his death, and through the gradual development of relations, the church, which its Founder had designed for the Gentiles only in so far as they became Jews, should break through these limits, is in the simple, natural, and therefore the probable course of things.

§ 69.

RELATION OF THE MESSIANIC PLAN OF JESUS TO THE SAMARITANS.   HIS INTERVIEW
WITH THE WOMAN OF SAMARIA.

There is the same apparent contradiction in the position which Jesus took, and prescribed to his disciples, towards the inhabitants of Samaria. While in his instructions to his disciples, (Matt. x. 5,) he forbids them to visit any city of the Samaritans, we read in John (iv.) that Jesus himself in his journey through Samaria laboured as the Messiah with great effect, and ultimately stayed two days in a Samaritan town; and in the Acts (i. 8), that before his ascension he charged the disciples to be his witnesses, not only in Jerusalem and in all Judea, but also in Samaria. That Jesus did not entirely shun Samaria, as that prohibition might appear to intimate, is evident from Luke ix. 52. (comp. xvii. 11.), where his disciples bespeak lodgings for him in a Samaritan village, when he has determined to go to Jerusalem ; a circumstance which accords with the information of Josephus, that those Galileans who journeyed to the feasts usually went through Samaria [1]. That Jesus was not unfavourable to the Samaritans, nay, that in many respects he acknowledged their superiority to the Jews, is evident from his parable of the Good Samaritan (Luke x. 30 ff.) ; he also bestows a marked notice on the case of a Samaritan, who, among ten cleansed, was the only one that testified his gratitude (Luke xvii. 16.) ; and, if we may venture on such a conclusion from John iv. 25, and subsequent records [2], the inhabitants of Samaria themselves had some tincture of the messianic idea.

However natural it may appear that Jesus should avail himself of this susceptible side of the Samaritans, by opportunely announcing to them the messianic kingdom; the aspect which the four evangelists bear to each other on this subject must excite surprise. Matthew has no occasion on which Jesus comes in contact with the Samaritans, or even mentions them, except in the prohibition above quoted ; Mark is more neutral than Matthew, and has not even that prohibition ; Luke has two instances of contact, one of them unfavourable, the other favourable, together with the parable in which Jesus presents a Samaritan as a model, and his approving notice of the gratitude of one whom he had healed ; John, finally, has a narrative in which Jesus appears in a very intimate and highly favourable relation to the Samaritans. Are all these various accounts well-founded ? If so, how could Jesus at one time prohibit his disciples from including the Samaritans in the messianic plan, and at another time, himself receive them without hesitation ? Moreover, if the chronological order of the evangelists deserve regard, the

---

[1] Antiq. xx. vi. 1. For some rabbinical rules not quite in accordance with this, see Lightfoot, p. 991.

[2] Bertholdt, Christol. Judæor. § 7.

ministry of Jesus in Samaria must have preceded the prohibition contained in his instructions to his disciples on their first mission. For the scene of that mission being Galilee, and there being no space for its occurrence during the short stay which, according to the fourth evangelist, Jesus made in that province before the first passover (ii. 1—13.), it must be placed after that passover; and, as the visit to Samaria was made on his journey, after that visit also. How, then, could Jesus, after having with the most desirable issue, personally taught in Samaria, and presented himself as the Messiah, forbid his disciples to carry thither their messianic tidings? On the other hand, if the scenes narrated by John occurred after the command recorded by Matthew, the disciples, instead of wondering that Jesus talked so earnestly with a *woman* (John iv. 27.), ought rather to have wondered that he held any converse with a *Samaritan* [3].

Since then of the two extreme narratives at least, in Matthew and John, neither presupposes the other, we must either doubt the authenticity of the exclusive command of Jesus, or of his connexion with the inhabitants of Samaria.

In this conflict between the gospels, we have again the advantage of appealing to the Book of Acts as an umpire. Before Peter, at the divine instigation, had received the first fruits of the Gentiles into the Messiah's kingdom, Philip the deacon, being driven from Jerusalem by the persecution of which Stephen's death was the commencement, journeyed to the city of Samaria, where he preached Christ, and by miracles of all kinds won the Samaritans to the faith, and to the reception of baptism (Acts viii. 5 ff.). This narrative is a complete contrast to that of the first admission of the Gentiles: while in the one there was need of a vision, and a special intimation from the Spirit, to bring Peter into communication with the heathens; in the other, Philip, without any precedent, unhesitatingly baptizes the Samaritans. And lest it should be said that the deacon was perhaps of a more liberal spirit than the apostle, we

[3] Some erroneously attribute this meaning to their question: see in Lücke 1, s. 533.

have Peter himself coming forthwith to Samaria in company
with John,—an incident which forms another point of opposition between the two narratives; for, while the first admission
of the Gentiles makes a highly unfavourable impression on the
mother church at Jerusalem, the report that *Samaria had
received the word of God* meets with so warm an approval
there, that the two most distinguished apostles are commissioned
to confirm and consummate the work begun by Philip. The
tenor of this proceeding makes it not improbable that there
was a precedent for it in the conduct of Jesus, or at least a
sanction in his expressions.

The narrative in the fourth Gospel (iv.) would form a perfect precedent in the conduct of Jesus, but we have yet to
examine whether it bear the stamp of historical credibility. We
do not, with the author of the Probabilia, stumble at the designation of the locality, and the opening of the conversation
between Jesus and the woman[4]; but from v. 16 inclusively,
there are, as impartial expositors confess[5], many grave difficulties. The woman had entreated Jesus to give her of the water
which was for ever to extinguish thirst, and Jesus immediately
says, *Go, call thy husband.* Why so? It has been said that Jesus,
well knowing that the woman had no lawful husband, sought to
shame her, and bring her to repentance[6]. Lücke, disapproving the
imputation of dissimulation to Jesus, conjectures that, perceiving
the woman's dulness, he hoped by summoning her husband,
possibly her superior in intelligence, to create an opportunity
for a more beneficial conversation. But if Jesus, as it presently
appears, knew that the woman had not at the time any proper
husband, he could not in earnest desire her to summon him;
and if, as Lücke allows, he had that knowledge in a supernatural
manner, it could not be hidden from him, who knew what was
in man, that she would be little inclined to comply with his injunction. If however, he had a prescience that what he required

[4] Bretschneider, ut sup. s. 47 ff. 97 f.
[5] Lücke, 1, s. 520 ff.
[6] Tholück, in loc.

would not be done, the injunction was a feint, and had some latent object. But that this object was the penitence of the woman there is no indication in the text, for the ultimate effect on her is not shame and penitence, but faith in the prophetic insight of Jesus (v. 19). And this was doubtless what Jesus wished, for the narrative proceeds as if he had attained his purpose with the woman, and the issue corresponded to the design. The difficulty here lies, not so much in what Lücke terms dissimulation,—since this comes under the category of blameless temptation ($\pi \epsilon \iota \rho \acute{a} \zeta \epsilon \iota \nu$), elsewhere occurring,—as in the violence with which Jesus wrests an opportunity for the display of his prophetic gifts.

By a transition equally abrupt, the woman urges the conversation to a point at which the Messiahship of Jesus may become fully evident. As soon as she has recognized Jesus to be a prophet, she hastens to consult him on the controversy pending between the Jews and Samaritans, as to the place appropriated to the true worship of God (v. 20.). That so vivid an interest in this national and religious question is not consistent with the limited mental and circumstantial condition of the woman, the majority of modern commentators virtually confess, by their adoption of the opinion, that her drift in this remark was to turn away the conversation from her own affairs [7]. If then the implied query concerning the place for the true worship of God, had no serious interest for the woman, but was prompted by a false shame calculated to hinder confession and repentance, those expositors should remember what they elsewhere repeat to satiety [8], that in the gospel of John the answers of Jesus refer not so much to the ostensible meaning of questions, as to the under current of feeling of which they are the indications. In accordance with this method, Jesus should not have answered the artificial question of the woman as if it had been one of deep seriousness; he ought rather to have evaded it, and recurred to the already detected stain on her conscience, which

---

[7] Lücke and Tholück, in loc. Hase, L. J. 67.
[8] E. g. Tholück, in many passages.

she was now seeking to hide, in order if possible to bring her to
a full conviction and open avowal of her guilt. But the fact is
that the object of the evangelist was to show that Jesus had been
recognized, not merely as a prophet, but as the Messiah, and he
believed that to turn the conversation to the question of the legitimate place for the worship of God, the solution of which was
expected from the Messiah [9], would best conduce to that end.

Jesus evinces (v. 17.) an acquaintance with the past history
and present position of the woman. The rationalists have
endeavoured to explain this by the supposition, that while Jesus
sat at the well, and the woman was advancing from the city,
some passer-by hinted to him that he had better not engage in
conversation with her, as she was on the watch to obtain a
sixth husband [10]. But not to insist on the improbability that a
passer-by should hold a colloquy with Jesus on the character
of an obscure woman, the friends as well as the enemies of the
fourth gospel now agree, that every natural explanation of that
knowledge on the part of Jesus, directly counteracts the design
of the evangelist [11]. For according to him, the disclosure which
Jesus makes of his privity to the woman's intimate concerns, is
the immediate cause, not only of her own faith in him, but of
that of many inhabitants of the city (v. 39.), and he obviously
intends to imply that they were not too precipitate in receiving
him as a prophet, on that ground alone. Thus in the view of
the evangelist, the knowledge in question was an effluence of
the higher nature of Jesus, and modern supranaturalists adhere to
this explanation, adducing in its support the power which John
attributes to him (ii. 24 f.), of discerning what is in man without the aid of external testimony [12]. But this does not meet
the case; for Jesus here not only knows what is in the woman,
—her present equivocal state of mind towards him who is not
her husband,—he has cognizance also of the extrinsic fact that

[9] Comp. Schöttgen, horæ, i. s. 970 f. Wetstein, s. 863.
[10] Paulus, Leben Jesu, 1, a, 187; Comment. 4, in loc.
[11] Comp. Olshausen in loc. and Bretschneider, Probab. s. 50.
[12] Olshausen, Lücke, in loc.

she has had five hushands, of whom we cannot suppose that each had left a distinct image in her mind traceable by the observation of Jesus. That by means of the penetrative acumen with which he scrutinized the hearts of those with whom he had to do, Jesus should also have a prophetic insight into his own messianic destiny, and the fortunes of his kingdom, may under a certain view of his person appear probable, and in any case must be deemed in the highest degree dignified; but that he should be acquainted, even to the most trivial details, with the adventitious history of obscure individuals, is an idea that degrades him in proportion to the exaltation of his prophetic dignity. Such empirical *knowingness* (not omniscience) would moreover annihilate the human consciousness which the orthodox view supposes to co-exist in Jesus [13]. But the possession of this knowledge, however it may clash with our conception of dignity and wisdom, closely corresponds to the Jewish notion of a prophet, more especially of the Messiah; in the Old Testament, Daniel recites a dream of Nebuchadnezzar, which that monarch himself had forgotten (Dan. ii.); in the Clementine Homilies, the true prophet is ὁ πάντοτε πάντα εἰδώς· τὰ μὲν γεγονότα ὡς ἐγένετο, τὰ δὲ γινόμενα ὡς γίνεται, τὰ δὲ ἐσόμενα ὡς ἔσται [14]; and the rabbins number such a knowledge of personal secrets among the signs of the Messiah, and observe that from the want of it, Bar-Cocheba was detected to be a pseudo-Messiah [15].

Farther on (v. 23.) Jesus reveals to the woman what Hase terms the sublimest principle of his religion, namely, that the service of God consists in a life of piety; tells her that all ceremonial worship is about to be abolished; and that he is the personage who will effect this momentous change, that is, the Messiah. We have already shown it to be improbable that Jesus, who did not give his disciples to understand that he was the Messiah until a comparatively late period, should make an

---

[13] Comp. Bretschneider, ut sup. s. 49 f.
[14] Homil. ii. 6. comp. iii. 12.
[15] Schöttgen, horæ, ii. p. 371 f.

early and distinct disclosure on the subject to a Samaritan
woman. In what respect was she worthy of a communication
more explicit than ever fell to the lot of the disciples? What
could induce Jesus to send roaming into the futurity of religious
history, the contemplation of a woman, whom he should rather
have induced to examine herself, and to ponder on the corrup-
tions of her own heart? Nothing but the wish to elicit from her,
at any cost, and without regard to her moral benefit, an acknowledgment, not only of his prophetic gifts, but of his Messiahship ; to which end it was necessary to give the conversation
the above direction. But so contracted a design can never
be imputed to Jesus, who on other occasions, exemplifies a
more suitable mode of dealing with mankind : it is the design
of the glorifying legend, or of an idealizing biographer.

Meanwhile, continues the narrative (v. 27.), the disciples of
Jesus returned from the city with provisions, and marvelled that
he talked with a woman, contrary to rabbinical rule [16]. While
the woman, excited by the last disclosure of Jesus, hastens homeward to invite her fellow-citizens to come and behold the
Messiah-like stranger, the disciples entreat him to partake of the
food they have procured ; he answers, *I have meat to eat that
ye know not of* (v. 32). They, misunderstanding his words,
imagine that some person has supplied him with food in their
absence : one of those carnal interpretations of expressions
intended spiritually by Jesus, which are of perpetual recurrence in the fourth gospel, and are therefore suspicious.
Then follows a discourse on sowing and reaping (v. 35 ff.),
which, compared with v. 37., can only mean that what Jesus
has sown, the disciples will reap [17]. We admit that this is susceptible of the general interpretation, that the germ of the kingdom of God, which blossomed and bore fruit under the cultivation of the apostles, was first deposited in the world by Jesus :
but it cannot be denied that a special application is also intended. Jesus foresees that the woman, who is hastening

---

[16] Lightfoot, p. 1002.
[17] Lücke, 1, s. 542.

towards the city, will procure him an opportunity of sowing the seed of the gospel in Samaria, and he promises the disciples that they at a future time shall reap the fruits of his labours. Who is not here reminded of the propagation of Christianity in Samaria by Philip and the apostles, as narrated in the Acts[18]?   That, even abstracting all supernaturalism from our idea of the person of Jesus, he might have foreseen this progress of his cause in Samaria from his knowledge of its inhabitants, is not to be denied ; but as the above figurative prediction forms part of a whole more than improbable in an historical point of view, it is equally liable to suspicion, especially as it is easy to show how it might originate without any foundation in fact.   According to the prevalent tradition of the early church, as recorded in the synoptical gospels, Jesus laboured personally in Galilee, Judea, and Perea only,—not in Samaria, which, however, as we learn from the Acts, embraced the gospel at no remote period from his death.   How natural the tendency to perfect the agency of Jesus, by representing him to have sown the heavenly seed in Samaria, thus extending his ministry through all parts of Palestine ; to limit the glory of the apostles and other teachers to that of being the mere reapers of the harvest in Samaria ; and to put this distinction, on a suitable occasion, into the mouth of Jesus !

The result, then, of our examination of John's Samarian narrative is, that we cannot receive it as a real history : and the impression which it leaves as a whole tends to the same conclusion.   Since Heracleon and Origen[19], the more ancient commentators have seldom refrained from giving the interview of Jesus with the woman of Samaria an allegorical interpretation, on the ground that the entire scene has a legendary and poetic colouring.   Jesus is seated at a well,—that idyllic locality with which the old Hebrew legend associates so many critical incidents; at the identical well, moreover, which a tradition, founded on Gen. xxxiii. 19 ; xlviii. 22 ; Josh. xxiv. 32, reported to have

---

[18] Lücke, s. 540, note. Bretschneider, s. 52.
[19] Comm. in Joan, tom. 13.

been given by Jacob to his son Joseph ; hence the spot, in addition to its idyllic interest, has the more decided consecration of national and patriarchal recollections, and is all the more worthy of being trodden by the Messiah. At the well Jesus meets with a woman who has come out to draw water, just as, in the Old Testament, the expectant Eliezer encounters Rebekah with her pitcher, and as Jacob meets with Rachel, the destined ancestress of Israel, or Moses with his future wife. Jesus begs of the woman to let him drink ; so does Eliezer of Rebekah ; after Jesus has made himself known to the woman as the Messiah, she runs back to the city, and fetches her neighbours : so Rebekah, after Eliezer has announced himself as Abraham's steward, and Rachel, after she has discovered that Jacob is her kinsman, hasten homeward to call their friends to welcome the honoured guest. It is, certainly, not one blameless as those early mothers in Israel, whom Jesus here encounters ; for this woman came forth as the representative of an impure people, who had been faithless to their marriage bond with Jehovah, and were then living in the practice of a false worship ; while her good-will, her deficient moral strength, and her obtuseness in spiritual things, perfectly typify the actual state of the Samaritans. Thus, the interview of Jesus with the woman of Samaria, is only a poetical representation of his ministry among the Samaritans narrated in the sequel; and this is itself a legendary prelude to the propagation of the gospel in Samaria after the death of Jesus.

Renouncing the event in question as unhistorical, we know nothing of any connexion formed by Jesus with the Samaritans, and there remain as indications of his views regarding them, only his favourable notice of an individual from among them (Luke xvii. 16.) ; his unpropitious reception in one of their villages (Luke ix. 53.) ; the prohibition with respect to them, addressed to his disciples (Matt. x. 5.) ; the eulogistic parable, (Luke x. 30. ff.) ; and his valedictory command, that the gospel should be preached in Samaria (Acts i. 8). This express command being subsequent to the resurrection of Jesus, its reality must remain problematical for us until we have examined the evidence for that capital fact; and it is to be questioned whether without it, and notwithstanding the alleged prohibition, the unhesitating conduct of the apostles, Acts viii., can be explained.   Are we then to suppose on the part of the apostolic history, a cancelling of hesitations and deliberations that really occurred; or on the part of Matthew, an unwarranted ascription of national bigotry to Jesus; or, finally, on the part of Jesus, a progressive enlargement of view?

CHAPTER V.

THE DISCIPLES OF JESUS.

§ 70.

THE first two evangelists agree in stating that Jesus, when walking by the sea of Galilee, called, first, the two brothers Andrew and Peter, and immediately after, James and John, to forsake their fishing nets, and to follow him (Matt. iv. 18—22 ; Mark i. 16—20). The fourth evangelist also narrates (i. 35—51,) how the first disciples came to attach themselves to Jesus, and among them we find Peter and Andrew, and, in all probability, John, for it is generally agreed that the nameless companion of Andrew was that ultimately favourite apostle. James is absent from this account, and instead of his vocation, we have that of Philip and Nathanael. But even when the persons are the same, all the particulars of their meeting with Jesus are variously detailed. In the two synoptical gospels, the scene is the coast of the Galilean sea : in the fourth, Andrew, Peter, and their anonymous friend, unite themselves to Jesus in the vicinity of the Jordan ; Philip and Nathanael, on the way from thence into Galilee. In the former, again, Jesus in two instances calls a pair of brothers; in the latter, it is first Andrew and his companion, then Peter, and anon Philip and Nathanael, who meet with Jesus. But the most important difference is this :

E 2

while, in Matthew and Mark, the brethren are called from their
fishing immediately by Jesus; in John, nothing more is said
of the respective situations of those who were summoned, than
that they *come*, and *are found*, and Jesus himself calls only
Philip; Andrew and his nameless companion being directed to
him by the Baptist, Peter brought by Andrew, and Nathanael
by Philip.

Thus the two narratives appear to refer to separate events;
and if it be asked which of those events was prior to the other,
we must reply that John seems to assign the earlier date to
his incidents, for he represents them as taking place before the
return of Jesus from the scene of his baptism into Galilee; while
the synoptists place theirs after that journey, especially if,
according to a calculation often adopted, we regard the return
into Galilee, which they make so important an epoch, as being
that from the first passover, not from the baptism.   It is evident, too, from the intrinsic nature of the occurrences reported
by the fourth evangelist, that they could not have succeeded
those in Matthew and Mark.   For if, as these writers tell us,
Andrew and John had already followed Jesus, they could not
again be in the train of the Baptist, as we see them in the
fourth gospel, nor would it have been necessary for that teacher
to have directed their attention to Jesus; neither if Peter had
already been called by Jesus himself to become a fisher of men,
was there any need for his brother Andrew to bring him to his
already elected master.   Nevertheless, expositors with one
voice declare that the two narratives are equally adapted to precede, or follow, each other.   The fourth gospel, say they [1], re-
counts merely the first introduction of these men to Jesus; they
did not forthwith become his constant followers, but were first
installed by Jesus in their proper discipleship on the occasion
which the synoptists have preserved.

Let us test the justness of their view.   In the synoptical
narrative Jesus says to his future disciples, *Come after me,*

---

[1] Kuinöl, Comm. in Matth. s. 100; Lücke, Comm. z. Joh. 1, s. 388; Olshausen
bibl. Comm., 1, s. 197; Hase, Leben Jesu, § 56. 61.

δεῦτε ὀπίσω μου, and the result is that they follow him (ἠκολού-
θησαν αὐτῷ). If we understand from this that the disciples
thenceforth constantly followed Jesus, how can we give a different interpretation to the similar expression in the fourth
gospel, *Follow me*, ἀκολούθει μοι? It is therefore a laudable
consistency in Paulus, to see, in both instances, merely an invitation to a temporary companionship during a walk in the immediate neighbourhood[2]. But this interpretation is incompatible with the synoptical history. How could Peter, at a
later period, say so emphatically to Jesus, *We have left all, and
followed thee: what shall we have therefore?*—how could
Jesus promise to him and to every one who had forsaken
houses, &c. a hundredfold recompense (Matt. xix. 27 ff.),
if this forsaking and following had been so transient and interrupted? From these considerations alone it is probable that
the ἀκολούθει μοι in John also denotes the commencement of a
permanent connexion; but there are besides the plainest indications that this is the case in the context to the narrative.
Precisely as in the synoptical gospels, Jesus appears alone
before the scene of the vocation, but after this on every fit occasion the attendance of his disciples is mentioned: so in the
fourth gospel, from the time of the occurrence in question, the
previously solitary Jesus appears in the company of his disciples (ii. 2; xii. 17; iii. 22; iv. 8, 27, &c.). To say that these
disciples, acquired in Peræa, again dispersed themselves after
the return of Jesus into Galilee[3], is to do violence to the gospels out of harmonistic zeal. But even supposing such a dis-
persion, they could not, in the short time which it is possible
to allow for their separation from Jesus, have become so completely strangers to him, that he would have been obliged to
re-open an acquaintance with them after the manner narrated
by the synoptical writers. Still less probable is it that Jesus,
after having distinguished Simon in the most individual manner
by the surname Cephas on their first interview, would on a later

---

[2] Leben Jesu, 1, a, s. 212.
[3] Paulus, Leben Jesu, 1, a, s. 213; Sieffert, über den Ursprung u. s. f., s. 72

occasion address to him the summons to be a *fisher of men*—
a destination which was common to all the disciples.

The rationalistic commentators perceive a special advantage
in their position of the two narratives. It accounts, say they,
for what must otherwise be in the highest degree surprising,
namely, that Jesus merely in passing, and at the first glance,
should choose four fishermen for his disciples, and that among
them he should have alighted on the two most distinguished
apostles ; that, moreover, these four men, actively employed in
their business, should leave it on the instant of their receiving
an enigmatical summons from a man with whom they had no
intimate acquaintance, and devote themselves to him as his
followers. Now on comparing the fourth gospel, we see that
Jesus had learned to know these men long before, and that
they, too, had had demonstration of his excellence, whence it is
easy to understand the felicity of his choice, and their readiness
to follow him. But this apparent advantage is the condemning
circumstance in the above position ; for nothing can more
directly counteract the intention of the first two evangelists,
than to suppose a previous acquaintance between Jesus and the
brethren whom he summons to follow him. In both gospels,
great stress is laid on the fact that they *immediately* εὐθέως
left their nets, resolved to follow Jesus : the writers must therefore have deemed this something extraordinary, which it certainly was not, if these men had previously been in his train.
In relation to Jesus also, the point of the narrative lies in his
having, with a prophetic spirit, and at the first glance, selected
the right individuals, *not needing that any should testify of
man, for he knew what was in man,* according to John ii. 25,
and thus presenting one of the characteristics which the Jews
expected in their Messiah.

If, then, each of these two diverse narratives professes to
describe the first acquaintance of Jesus with his most distinguished disciples, it follows that one only can be correct, while
the other is necessarily erroneous[4]. It is our task to inquire

---

[4] See Fritzsche, in Matt. p. 189.

which has the more intrinsic proofs of veracity. With respect to the synoptical representation, we share the difficulty which is felt by Paulus, in regarding it as a true account of the first interview between the parties. A penetration into the character of men at the first glance, such as is here supposed to have been evinced by Jesus, transcends all that is naturally possible to the most fortunate and practised knowledge of mankind. The nature of man is only revealed by his words and actions; the gift of discerning it without these means, belongs to the visionary, or to that species of intuition for which the rabbinical designation of this messianic attribute, *odorando judicare* [5], is not at all too monstrous. Scarcely less improbable is the unhesitating obedience of the disciples, for Jesus had not yet acquired his Galilean fame; and to account for this promptitude we must suppose that the voice and will of Jesus had a coercive influence over minds, independently of preparation and motives [6], which would be to complete the incredibility of the narrative by adding a magical trait to the visionary one already exposed.

If these negative arguments are deemed strong enough to annul the pretensions of the narrative to an historical character, the alternative is to assign to it a mythical interpretation, if we can show on positive grounds that it might have been constructed in a traditional manner without historical foundation. As adequate inducements to the formation of such a legend, we may point, not only to the above cited Jewish notion of the Messiah as the searcher of hearts, but to a specific type of this vocation of the apostles, contained in the narrative (1 Kings xix. 19—21,) of the mode in which the prophet Elijah summoned Elisha to become his follower. Here Jesus calls the brethren from their nets and their fishing; there the prophet calls his future disciple from the oxen and the plough; in both cases there is a transition from simple, physical labour, to the highest spiritual office—a contrast which, as is exemplified in

---

[5] Schöttgen, horæ, ii. p. 372.

[6] Paulus, ut sup.

the Roman history, tradition is apt either to cherish or to create. Further, the fishermen, at the call of Jesus, forsake their nets and follow him; so Elisha, when Elijah cast his mantle over him, *left the oxen, and ran after Elijah.* This is one apparent divergency, which is a yet more striking proof of the relation between the two narratives, than is their general similarity. The prophet's disciple entreated that before he attached himself entirely to Elijah, he might be permitted to take leave of his father and mother; and the prophet does not hesitate to grant him this request, on the understood condition that Elisha should return to him. Similar petitions are offered to Jesus (Luke ix. 59 ff.; Matt. viii. 21 f.) by some whom he had called, or who had volunteered to follow him; but Jesus does not accede to these requests: on the contrary, he enjoins the one who wished previously to bury his father, to enter on his discipleship without delay; and the other, who had begged permission to bid farewell to his friends, he at once dismisses as unfit for the kingdom of God. In strong contrast with the divided spirit manifested by these feeble proselytes, it is said of the apostles, that they, without asking any delay, immediately forsook their occupation, and, in the case of James and John, their father. Could any thing betray more clearly than this one feature, that the narrative is an embellished imitation of that in the Old Testament, intended to show that Jesus, in his character of Messiah, exacted a more decided adhesion, accompanied with greater sacrifices, than Elijah, in his character of Prophet merely, required or was authorized to require[7]? The historical germ of the narrative may be this: several of the most eminent disciples of Jesus, particularly Peter, dwelling on the shores of the sea of Galilee, had been fishermen, whence Jesus during their subsequent apostolic agency may have sometimes styled them *fishers of men.* But without doubt, their relation with Jesus was formed gradually, like other human relations, and is only elevated into a marvel through the obliviousness of tradition.

[7] Paulus, exeg. Handb. 1. b. s. 464.

By removing the synoptical narrative we make room for that of John; but whether we are to receive it as historical, can only be decided by an examination of its matter. At the very outset, it excites no favourable prejudice, that John the Baptist is the one who directs the first two disciples to Jesus; for if there be any truth in the representation given in a former chapter of the relation between Jesus and the Baptist, some disciples of the latter might, indeed, of their own accord attach themselves to Jesus, formerly their fellow-disciple, but nothing could be farther from the intention of the Baptist than to resign his own adherents to Jesus. This particular seems indebted for its existence to the apologetic interest of the fourth gospel, which seeks to strengthen the cause of Jesus by the testimony of the Baptist. Further, that Andrew, after one evening's intercourse with Jesus, should announce him to his brother with the words, *We have found the Messiah* (i. 42.); that Philip too, immediately after his call, should speak of him in a similar manner to Nathanael (v. 46); is an improbability which I know not how to put strongly enough. We gather from the synoptical statement, which we have above decided to be trustworthy, that some time was necessary for the disciples to recognize Jesus as the Messiah, and openly confess their belief through their spokesman Peter, whose tardy discernment Jesus would have been incorrect in panegyrizing as a divine revelation, if it amounted to no more than what was communicated to him by his brother Andrew at the commencement of his discipleship. Equally unnatural is the manner in which Jesus is said to have received Simon. He accosts him with the words, *Thou art Simon, the son of Jona,*—a mode of salutation which seems, as Bengel has well remarked [8], to imply that Jesus had a supernatural acquaintance with the name and origin of a man previously unknown to him, analogous to his cognizance of the number of the Samaritan woman's husbands, and of Nathanael's presence under the fig-tree. Jesus then proceeds to bestow on Simon

---

[8] Gnomen, in loc.

the significant surname of Cephas or Peter. If we are not inclined to degrade the speech of Jesus into buffoonery, by referring this appellation to the bodily organization of the disciple [9],
we must suppose that Jesus at the first glance, with the eye of
him who knew hearts, penetrated into the inmost nature of
Simon, and discovered not only his general fitness for the
apostleship, but also the special, individual qualities which
rendered him comparable to a rock.   According to Matthew, it
was not until after long intercourse with Jesus, and after he
had given many manifestations of his peculiar character, that
this surname was conferred on Simon, accompanied by an explanation of its meaning (xvi. 18.) : evidently a much more
natural account of the matter than that of the fourth evangelist,
who makes Jesus discern at the first glance the future value of
Simon to his cause, an *odorando judicare* which transcends
the synoptical representation in the same ratio as the declaration, *Thou shalt be called Cephas,* presupposes a more intimate knowledge, than the proposal, *I will make you fishers
of men.*   Even after a more lengthened conversation with
Peter, such as Lücke supposes [10], Jesus could not pronounce so
decidedly on his character, without being a searcher of hearts,
or falling under the imputation of forming too precipitate a
judgment.   It is indeed possible that the Christian legend,
attracted by the significance of the name, may have represented
Jesus as its author, while, in fact, Simon had borne it from his
birth.

The entire narrative concerning Nathanael is a tissue of improbabilities.   When Philip speaks to him of a Messiah from
Nazareth, he makes the celebrated answer, *Can any good thing
come out of Nazareth* (v. 47.) ?   There is no historical datum
for supposing that Nazareth, when Jesus began his ministry,
was the object of particular odium or contempt [11], and there is
every probability that the adversaries of Christianity were the

[9] Paulus, Leben Jesu, 1. a. s. 168.
[10] S. 385.
[11] Vid. Lücke, s. 389 f.

first to cast an aspersion on the native city of the Messiah whom
they rejected. In the time of Jesus, Nazareth was only depre-
ciated by the Jews, as being a Galilean city—a stigma which it
bore in common with many others : but in this sense it could
not be despised by Nathanael, for he was himself a Galilean
(xxi. 2.). The only probable explanation is that a derisive
question, which, at the time of the composition of the fourth
gospel, the Christians had often to hear from their opponents,
was put into the mouth of a cotemporary of Jesus, that by the
manner in which he was divested of his doubt, others might be
induced to comply with the invitation, *to come and see.* As
Nathanael approaches Jesus, the latter pronounces this judgment
on his character, *Behold an Israelite indeed, in whom is no
guile* (v. 48.) ! Paulus is of opinion that Jesus might have previously gathered some intimations concerning Nathanael at
Cana, where he had just been attending a marriage of some relations [12]. But if Jesus had become acquainted with Nathanael's
character in a natural way, he must, in answer to the question
Whence knowest thou me ? either have reminded him of the
occasion on which they had had an earlier interview, or referred
to the favourable report of others. Instead of this he speaks of
his knowledge that Nathanael had been tarrying under a fig-
tree : a knowledge which from its result is evidently intended to
appear supernatural. Now to use information, obtained by
ordinary means, so as to induce a belief that it has been communicated supernaturally, is charlatanism, if anything deserve
the name. As, however, the narrator certainly did not mean to
impute such artifice to Jesus, it is undeniably his intention to
ascribe to him a supernatural knowledge of Nathanael's character. As little are the words, *When thou wast under the fig-
tree, I saw thee,* explained by the exclamation of Paulus, "How
often one sees and observes a man who is unconscious of one's
gaze !" Lücke and Tholück are also of opinion, that Jesus observed Nathanael under the fig-tree in a natural manner ; they

[12] Ut sup.

add, however, the conjecture, that the latter was engaged in
some occupation, such as prayer or the study of the law, which
afforded Jesus a key to his character.   But if Jesus meant to
imply, " How can I fail to be convinced of thy virtue, having
watched thee during thy earnest study of the law, and thy fervent
prayer under the fig-tree?" he would not have omitted the word
προσευχόμενον (*praying*), or ἀναγινώσκοντα (*reading*), for want of
which we can extract no other sense from his declaration than
this : " Thou mayest be assured of my power to penetrate into
thy inmost soul, from the fact that I beheld thee when thou
wast in a situation from which all merely human observers were
excluded." Here the whole stress is thrown not on any peculiarity in the situation of the person seen, but on the fact that
Jesus saw him, whence it is necessarily inferred that he did so
by no ordinary, natural, means.   To imagine that Jesus possessed such a second sight, is, we grant, not a little extravagant;
but for that very reason, it is the more accordant with the then
existing notions of a prophet, and of the Messiah. A like power of
seeing and hearing beyond the limits assigned to human organs,
is attributed to Elisha in the Old Testament.   When (2 Kings
vi. 8, ff.) the king of Syria makes war against Israel, Elisha
indicates to the king of Israel every position of the enemy's
camp ; and when the king of Syria expresses his suspicion that
he is betrayed by deserters, he is told that the Israelitish prophet knows all the words that he, the king of Syria, speaks in
his private chamber.   Thus also (xxi. 32,) Elisha knows that
Joram has sent out messengers to murder him.   How could it
be endured that the Messiah should fall short of the prophet in
his powers of vision ? This particular, too, enables our evangelist to form a climax, in which Jesus ascends from the penetration of one immediately present (v. 42), to that of one approaching for the first time (v. 48), and finally, to the perception of one out of the reach of human eyesight.   That Jesus
goes a step farther in the climax, and says, that this proof
of his messianic second sight is a trifle compared with what
Nathanael has yet to see,—that on him, the Son of man, the

angels of God shall descend from the opened heavens (v. 51), —in nowise shows, as Paulus thinks, that there was nothing miraculous in that first proof, for there is a gradation even in miracles.

Thus in the narrative of John we stumble at every step on difficulties, in some instances greater than those with which the synoptical accounts are encumbered: hence we learn as little from the one as the other, concerning the manner in which the first disciples attached themselves to Jesus. I cannot agree with the author of the Probabilia [13], in deriving the divergency of the fourth evangelist from his predecessors, from the wish to avoid mentioning the derided fishing-trade of the most distinguished apostles; since in chap. xxi., which Bretschneider allows to be by the same hand as the rest of the gospel, he unhesitatingly introduces the obnoxious employment. I rather surmise that the idea of their having received their decisive apostolic call while actually engaged with their fishing-nets, was not afloat in the tradition from which the fourth evangelist drew; and that this writer formed his scenes, partly on the probably historical report that some disciples of Jesus had belonged to the school of the Baptist, and partly from the wish to represent in the most favourable light the relation between Jesus and the Baptist, and the supernatural gifts of the former.

§ 71.

PETER'S DRAUGHT OF FISHES.

We have hitherto examined only two accounts of the vocation of Peter and his companions; there is a third given by Luke (v. 1—11.). I shall not dilate on the minor points of difference [1] between his narrative and that of the first two evangelists; the essential distinction is, that in Luke the disciples do not, as in Matthew and Mark, unite themselves to Jesus on a simple invitation, but in consequence of a plentiful draught of fishes,

[13] P. 141.
[1] Storr, Ueber den Zweck der ev. Gesch. und der Br. Joh., s. 350.

to which Jesus has assisted Simon. If this feature be allowed
to constitute Luke's narrative a separate one from that of his
predecessors, we have next to inquire into its intrinsic credibility, and then to ascertain its relation to that of Matthew and
Mark.

Jesus, oppressed by the throng of people on the shore of the
Galilean sea, enters into a ship, that he may address them with
more ease at a little distance from land. Having brought his
discourse to a close, he desires Simon, the owner of the boat,
to launch out into the deep, and let down his nets for a draught.
Simon, although little encouraged by the poor result of the last
night's fishing, declares himself willing, and is rewarded by so
extraordinary a draught, that Peter and his partners, James
and John (Andrew is not here mentioned), are struck with
astonishment, the former even with awe, before Jesus, as a
superior being. Jesus then says to Simon, *Fear not; from
henceforth thou shalt catch men,* and the issue is that the three
fishermen forsake all, and follow him.

The rationalistic commentators take pains to show that what
is above narrated might occur in a natural way. According to
them, the astonishing consequence of letting down the net was
the result of an accurate observation on the part of Jesus, assisted by a happy fortuity. Paulus[2] supposes that Jesus at first
wished to launch out farther into the deep merely to escape from
the crowd, and that it was not until after sailing to some distance,
that, descrying a place where the fish were abundant, he desired
Peter to let down the net. But he has fallen into a twofold contradiction of the evangelical narrative. In close connexion with
the command to launch out into the deep, Jesus adds, *Let down
your nets for a draught* (ἐπανάγαγε εἰς τὸ βάθος, καὶ χαλάσατε
τὰ δίκτυα, κ. τ. λ.), as if this were one of his objects in changing
the locality; and if he spoke thus when at a little distance only
from the shore, his hope of a successful draught could not be
the effect of his having observed a place abundant in fish on the

[2] Exeg. Handb. 1, b. s. 449.

main sea, which the vessel had not yet reached.   Our rationalists must therefore take refuge in the opinion of the author of
the Natural History of the Great Prophet of Nazareth, who
says, Jesus conjectured on general grounds, that under existing
circumstances (indicative probably of an approaching storm),
fishing in the middle of the sea would succeed better than it
had done in the night.   But, proceeding from the natural point
of view, how could Jesus be a better judge in this matter, than
the men who had spent half their life on the sea in the employment of fishing ?   Certainly if the fishermen observed nothing
which could give them hope of a plentiful draught, neither in a
natural manner could Jesus ; and the agreement between his
words and the result, must, adhering to the natural point of
view, be put down wholly to the account of chance.   But what
senseless audacity, to promise at random a success, which,
judging from the occurrences of the past night, was little likely
to follow !   It is said, however, that Jesus only desires Peter to
make another attempt, without giving any definite promise.
But, we must rejoin, in the emphatic injunction, which Peter's
remark on the inauspicious aspect of circumstances for fishing
does not induce him to revoke, there is a latent promise, and
the words, *Let down your nets,* &c., in the present passage,
can hardly have any other meaning than that plainly expressed
in the similar scene, John xxi. 6., *Cast the net on the right
side of the ship, and ye shall find.*   When, moreover, Peter
retracts his objection in the words, *Nevertheless at thy word I
will let down the net,* ἐπὶ δὲ τῷ ῥήματί σου χαλάσω το δίκτυον,
though ῥῆμα may be translated by *command* rather than by
promise, in either case he implies a hope that what Jesus enjoins will not be without result.   If Jesus had not intended to
excite this hope, he must immediately have put an end to it, if
he would not expose himself to disgrace in the event of failure ;
and on no account ought he to have accepted the attitude and
expressions of Peter as his due, if he had only merited them by
a piece of lucky advice given at a venture.

The drift of the narrative, then, obliges us to admit that the writer intended to signalize a miracle. This miracle may be viewed either as one of power, or of knowledge. If the former, we are to conceive that Jesus, by his supernatural power, caused the fish to congregate in that part of the sea where he commanded Peter to cast in his net. Now that Jesus should be able, by the immediate action of his will, to influence men, in the nature of whose minds his spiritual energy might find a fulcrum, may to a certain extent be conceived, without any wide deviation from psychological laws; but that he could thus influence irrational beings, and those not isolated animals immediately present to him, but shoals of fish in the depths of the sea, it is impossible to imagine out of the domain of magic. Olshausen compares this operation of Jesus to that of the divine omnipotence in the annual migrations of fish and birds[3]; but the comparison is worse than lame,—it lacks all parallelism; for the latter is an effect of the divine agency, linked in the closest manner with all the other operations of God in external nature, with the change of seasons, &c. : while the former, even presupposing Jesus to be actually God, would be an isolated act, interrupting the chain of natural phenomena; a distinction that removes any semblance of parallelism between the two cases. Allowing the possibility of such a miracle, (and from the supranaturalistic point of view, nothing is in itself impossible,) did it subserve any apparent object, adequate to determine Jesus to so extravagant a use of his miraculous powers? Was it so important that Peter should be inspired by this incident with a superstitious fear, not accordant with the spirit of the New Testament? Was this the only preparation for engrafting the true faith? or did Jesus believe that it was only by such signs that he could win disciples? How little faith must he then have had in the force of mind and of truth! how much too meanly must he have estimated Peter, who, at a later period at least (John vi. 68), clung to his society, not on account of the miracles which he beheld Jesus perform, but for the sake of *the words of eternal life,* which came from his lips!

[3] Bibl. Comm. 1, p. 283.

Under the pressure of these difficulties, refuge may be sought in the other supposition as the more facile one; namely, that Jesus, by means of his superhuman knowledge, was merely aware that in a certain place there was then to be found a multitude of fishes, and that he communicated this information to Peter. If by this it be meant that Jesus, through the possession of an omniscience such as is commonly attributed to God, knew at all times, all the fish, in all seas, rivers, and lakes; there is an end to his human consciousness. If, however, it be merely meant that when he crossed any water he became cognizant of its various tribes of fish, with their relative position; even this would be quite enough to encumber the space in his mind that was due to more weighty thoughts. Lastly, if it be meant that he knew this, not constantly and necessarily, but as often as he wished; it is impossible to understand how, in a mind like that of Jesus, a desire for such knowledge should arise,—how he, whose vocation had reference to the depths of the human heart, should be tempted to occupy himself with the fish-frequented depths of the waters.

But before we pronounce on this narrative of Luke, we must consider it in relation to the cognate histories in the first two synoptical gospels. The chronological relation of the respective events is the first point. The supposition that the miraculous draught of fishes in Luke was prior to the vocation narrated by the two other evangelists, is excluded by the consideration, that the firm attachment which that miracle awakened in the disciples, would render a new call superfluous; or by the still stronger objection, that if an invitation, accompanied by a miracle, had not sufficed to ally the men to Jesus, he could hardly flatter himself that a subsequent bare summons, unsupported by any miracle, would have a better issue. The contrary chronological position presents a better climax; but why a second invitation, if the first had succeeded? For to suppose that the brethren who followed him on the first summons, again left him until the second, is to cut the knot, instead of untying it. Still more complicated is the difficulty, when we take in addition the narrative of the fourth evangelist: for what shall we think of the connexion between Jesus and his disciples, if it began in the manner described by John; if, after this, the disciples having from some unknown cause separated from their master, he again called them, as if nothing of the kind had before occurred, on the shore of the Galilean sea; and if, this invitation also producing no permanent adherence, he for the third time summoned them to follow him, fortifying this final experiment by a miracle? The entire drift of Luke's narrative is such as to exclude, rather than to imply, any earlier and more intimate relation between Jesus and his ultimate disciples. For the indifferent mention of two ships on the shore, whose owners were gone out of them to wash their nets, Simon being unnamed until Jesus chooses to avail himself of his boat, seems, as Schleiermacher has convincingly shewn [4], to convey the idea that the two parties were entire strangers to each other, and that these incidents were preparatory to a relation yet to be formed, not indicative of one already existing: so that the healing of Peter's mother-in-law, previously recounted by Luke, either occurred, like many other cures of Jesus, without producing any intimate connexion, or has too early a date assigned to it by that evangelist. The latter conjecture is supported by the fact that Matthew places the miracle later.

Thus, it fares with the narrative of Luke, when viewed in relation to that of Matthew and Mark, as it did with that of John, when placed in the same light; neither will bear the other to precede, or to follow it,—in short, they exclude each other [5]. Which then is the correct narrative? Schleiermacher prefers that of the evangelist on whom he has commented, because it is more particular [6]; and Sieffert [7] has recently asserted with great emphasis, that no one has ever yet doubted the superiority of Luke's narrative, as a faithful picture of the

[4] Ueber den Lukas, s. 70.
[5] This, with the legendary character of both narratives, is acknowledged by De Wette, exeg. Handb. 1, 1, s. 47. 1, 2, s. 38 f.
[6] Neander is of the same opinion, L. J. s. 249 f.
[7] Ueber den Ursprung des ersten kan. Ev. s. 73.

entire occurrence, the number of its special, dramatic, and intrinsically authenticated details, advantageously distinguishing it from the account in the first (and second) gospel, which by its omission of the critical incident, the turning point in the narrative (the draught of fishes), is characterized as the recital of one who was not an eye-witness. I have already presented myself elsewhere [8] to this critic, as one hardy enough to express the doubt of which he denies the existence, and I here repeat the question : supposing one only of the two narratives to have been modified by oral tradition, which alternative is more in accordance with the nature of that means of transmission,—that the tangible fact of a draught of fishes should evaporate into a mere saying respecting fishers of men, or that this figurative expression should be condensed into a literal history ? The answer to this question cannot be dubious ; for when was it in the nature of the legend to spiritualize ? to change the real, such as the story of a miracle, into the ideal, such as a mere verbal image ? The stage of human culture to which the legend belongs, and the mental faculty in which it originates, demand that it should give a stable body to fleeting thought, that it should counteract the ambiguity and changeableness of words, by affixing them to the permanent and universally understood symbol of action.

It is easy to show how, out of the expression preserved by the first evangelist, the miraculous story of the third might be formed. If Jesus, in allusion to the former occupation of some of his apostles, had called them fishers of men ; if he had compared the kingdom of heaven to a net cast into the sea, in which all kinds of fish were taken (Matt. xiii. 47) ; it was but a following out of these ideas to represent the apostles as those who, at the word of Jesus, cast out the net, and gathered in the miraculous multitude of fishes [9]. If we add to this, that the

[8] Berliner Jahrbücher für wissenschaftliche Kritik, 1834, Nov. ; now in the Charakteristiken u. Kritiken, s. 264 f.

[9] According to De Wette, the copious draught of fishes was a symbolical miracle, typifying the rich fruits of the apostolic ministry.

ancient legend was fond of occupying its wonder-workers with
affairs of fishing, as we see in the story related of Pythagoras
by Jamblichus and Porphyry[10]; it will no longer appear improbable, that Peter's miraculous draught of fishes is but the
expression about the fishers of men, transmuted into the history
of a miracle, and this view will at once set us free from all the
difficulties that attend the natural, as well as the supranatural,
interpretation of the narrative.

A similar miraculous draught of fishes is recorded in the appendix to the fourth gospel, as having occurred after the resurrection (ch. xxi.). Here again Peter is fishing on the Galilean
sea, in company with the sons of Zebedee and some other disciples, and again he has been toiling all night, and has taken
nothing[11]. Early in the morning, Jesus comes to the shore,
and asks, without their recognizing him, if they have any meat?
On their answering in the negative, he directs them to cast the
net on the right side of the ship, whereupon they have an extremely rich draught, and are led by this sign to recognize
Jesus. That this history is distinct from the one given by Luke,
is, from its great similarity, scarcely conceivable; the same narrative has doubtless been placed by tradition in different periods
of the life of Jesus[12].

Let us now compare these three fishing histories,—the two
narrated of Jesus, and that narrated of Pythagoras,—and their
mythical character will be obvious. That which, in Luke, is
indubitably intended as a miracle of power, is, in the history of
Jamblichus, a miracle of knowledge; for Pythagoras merely tells
in a supernatural manner the number of fish already caught by
natural means. The narrative of John holds a middle place,
for in it also the number of the fish (153) plays a part; but

[10] Porphyr. vita Pythagoræ, no. 25. ed. Kiessling; Jamblich. v. P. no. 36. ders.
Ausg. It is fair to adduce this history, because, being less marvellous than the
gospel narrative, it can hardly be an imitation, but must have arisen independently,
and hence it evinces a common tendency of the ancient legend.

[11] Luke v. 5: δι' ὅλης τῆς νυκτὸς κοπιάσαντες οὐδὲν ἐλάβομεν.   John xxi. 3:
καὶ ἐν ἐκείνῃ τῇ νυκτὶ ἐπίασαν οὐδέν.

[12] Comp. de Wette, exeg. Handb., 1, 3, s. 213.

instead of being predetermined by the worker of the miracle, it is simply stated by the narrator. One legendary feature common to all the three narratives, is the manner in which the multitude and weight of the fishes are described; especially as this sameness of manner accompanies a diversity in particulars. According to Luke, the multitude is so great that the net is broken, one ship will not hold them, and after they have been divided between the two vessels, both threaten to sink. In the view of the tradition given in the fourth gospel, it was not calculated to magnify the power of the miraculous agent, that the net which he had so marvellously filled should break; but as here also the aim is to exalt the miracle by celebrating the number and weight of the fishes, they are said to be μεγάλοι (*great*), and it is added that the men *were not able to draw the net for the multitude of fishes*: instead, however, of lapsing out of the miraculous into the common by the breaking of the net, a second miracle is ingeniously made,—that *for all there were so many, yet was not the net broken.* Jamblichus presents a further wonder (the only one he has, besides the know ledge of Pythagoras as to the number of the fish): namely, that while the fish were being counted, a process that must have required a considerable time, not one of them died. If there be a mind that, not perceiving in the narratives we have compared the finger-marks of tradition, and hence the legendary character of these evangelical anecdotes, still leans to the historical interpretation, whether natural or supernatural; that mind must be alike ignorant of the true character both of legend and of history, of the natural and the supernatural.

§ 72.

CALLING OF MATTHEW. CONNEXION OF JESUS WITH THE PUBLICANS.

The first gospel (ix. 9 ff.) tells of *a man named Matthew*, to whom, when sitting at the receipt of custom, Jesus said, *Follow me*. Instead of Matthew, the second and third gospels have *Levi*, and Mark adds that he was *the son of Alpheus* (Mark

ii. 14 ff. ; Luke v. 27 ff.).   At the call of Jesus, Luke says that he left all; Matthew merely states, that he followed Jesus and prepared a meal, of which many publicans and sinners partook, to the great scandal of the Pharisees.

From the difference of the names it has been conjectured that the evangelists refer to two different events[1]; but this difference of the name is more than counterbalanced by the similarity of the circumstances.   In all the three cases the call of the publican is preceded and followed by the same occurrences; the subject of the narrative is in the same situation; Jesus addresses him in the same words; and the issue is the same[2].   Hence the opinion is pretty general, that the three synoptists have in this instance detailed only one event.   But did they also understand only one person under different names, and was that person the apostle Matthew?

This is commonly represented as conceivable on the supposition that Levi was the proper name of the individual, and Matthew merely a surname[3]; or that after he had attached himself to Jesus, he exchanged the former for the latter[4].   To substantiate such an opinion, there should be some indication that the evangelists who name the chosen publican Levi, intend under that designation no other than the Matthew mentioned in their catalogues of the apostles (Mark iii. 18; Luke vi. 15; Acts i. 13.).   On the contrary, in these catalogues, where many surnames and double names occur, not only do they omit the name of Levi as the earlier or more proper appellation of Matthew, but they leave him undistinguished by the epithet, ὁ τελώνης (*the publican*), added by the first evangelist in his catalogue (x. 3.); thus proving that they do not consider the apostle Matthew to be identical with the Levi summoned from the receipt of custom[5].

---

[1] Vid. Kuinöl, in Matth. p. 255.
[2] Sieffert, ut sup. p. 55.
[3] Kuinöl, ut sup.   Paulus, exeg. Handb., 1, b, s. 513.   L. J., 1, a, 240.
[4] Bertholdt, Einleitung, 3, s. 1255 f.   Fritzsche, s. 340.
[5] Sieffert, s. 56 ; De Wette, exeg. Handb., 1, 1, s. 91.

If then the evangelists describe the vocation of two different men in a precisely similar way, it is improbable that there is accuracy on both sides, since an event could hardly be repeated in its minute particulars. One of the narratives, therefore, is in error; and the burthen has been thrown on the first evangelist, because he places the calling of Matthew considerably after the sermon on the mount; while according to Luke (vi. 13. ff.), all the twelve had been chosen before that discourse was delivered [6]. But this would only prove, at the most, that the first gospel gives a wrong position to the history; not that it narrates that history incorrectly. It is therefore unjust to impute special difficulties to the narrative of the first evangelist: neither are such to be found in that of Mark and Luke, unless it be thought an inconsistency in the latter to attribute a *forsaking of all, καταλιπὼν ἄπαντα*, to one whom he does not include among the constant followers of Jesus [7]. The only question is, do they not labour under a common difficulty, sufficient to stamp both accounts as unhistorical?

The close analogy between this call and that of the two pairs of brethren, must excite attention. They were summoned from their nets; he from the custom-house; as in their case, so here, nothing further is needed than a simple *Follow me;* and this call of the Messiah has so irresistible a power over the mind of the called, that the publican, like the fishermen, *leaves all, and follows him.* It is not to be denied, that as Jesus had been for a considerable time exercising his ministry in that country, Matthew must have long known him; and this is the argument with which Fritzsche repels the accusation of Julian and Porphyry, who maintain that Matthew here shows himself rash and inconsiderate. But the longer Jesus had observed him, the more easily might he have found opportunity for drawing him gradually and quietly into his train, instead of hurrying him in so tumultuary a manner from the midst of his business.

[6] Sieffert, s. 60.
[7] De Wette, ut sup.

Paulus indeed thinks that no call to discipleship, no sudden forsaking of a previous occupation, is here intended, but that Jesus having brought his teaching to a close, merely signified to the friend who had given him an invitation to dinner, that he was now ready to go home with him, and sit down to table[8]. But the meal appears, especially in Luke, to be the consequence, and not the cause, of the summons; moreover, a modest guest would say to the host who had invited him, *I will follow thee*, ἀκολουθήσω σοι, not *Follow me*, ἀκολούθει μοι; and in fine, this interpretation renders the whole anecdote so trivial, that it would have been better omitted[9]. Hence the abruptness and impetuosity of the scene return upon us, and we are compelled to pronounce that such is not the course of real life, nor the procedure of a man who, like Jesus, respects the laws and formalities of human society; it is the procedure of legend and poetry, which love contrasts and effective scenes, which aim to give a graphic conception of a man's exit from an old sphere of life, and his entrance into a new one, by representing him as at once discarding the implements of his former trade, leaving the scene of his daily business, and straightway commencing a new life. The historical germ of the story may be, that Jesus actually had publicans among his disciples, and possibly that Matthew was one. These men had truly left the custom-house to follow Jesus; but only in the figurative sense of this concise expression, not in the literal one depicted by the legend.

It is not less astonishing that the publican should have a great feast in readiness for Jesus immediately after his call. For that this feast was not prepared until the following day[10], is directly opposed to the narratives, the two first especially. But it is entirely in the tone of the legend to demonstrate the joy of the publican, and the condescension of Jesus, and to create an occasion for the reproaches cast on the latter on ac-

[8] Exeg. Handb. 1, b, s. 510. L. J. 1, a, 240.
[9] Schleiermacher, über den Lukas, s. 76.
[10] Gratz, Comm. z. Matth. 1, s. 470.

count of his intimacy with sinners, by inventing a great feast, given to the publicans at the house of their late associate immediately after his call.

Another circumstance connected with this narrative merits particular attention. According to the common opinion concerning the author of the first gospel, Matthew therein narrates his own call. We may consider it granted that there are no positive indications of this in the narrative ; but it is not so clear that there are no negative indications which render it impossible or improbable. That the evangelist does not here speak in the first person, nor when describing events in which he had a share in the first person plural, like the author of the Acts of the Apostles, proves nothing ; for Josephus and other historians not less classical, write of themselves in the third person, and the *we* of the pseudo-Matthew in the Ebionite gospel has a very suspicious sound. The use of the expression, ἄνθρωπον, Ματθαῖον λεγόμενον, which the Manicheans made an objection [11], as they did the above-mentioned circumstance, is not without a precedent in the writings of Xenophon, who in his Anabasis introduces himself as *Xenophon, a certain Athenian,* Ξενοφῶν τις Ἀθηναῖος [12]. The Greek, however, did not fall into this style from absorption in his subject, nor from unaffected freedom from egotism,—causes which Olshausen supposes in the evangelist ; but either from a wish not to pass for the author, as an old tradition states [13], or from considerations of taste, neither of which motives will be attributed to Matthew. Whether we are therefore to consider that expression as a sign that the author of the first gospel was not Matthew, may be difficult to decide [14] : but it is certain that this history of the publican's call is throughout less clearly narrated in that gospel than in the third. In the former, we are at a loss to understand why it is abruptly said that Jesus sat at meat in the house, if the evangelist were him-

---

[11] Augustin c. Faust. Manich. xvii. 1.
[12] iii. i. 4.
[13] Plutarch. de gloria Atheniens., at the beginning.
[14] Schulz, Ueber das Abendmahl, s. 308.

self the hospitable publican, since it would then seem most natural for him to let his joy on account of his call appear in the
narrative, by telling, as Luke does, that he immediately made a
great feast in his house.   To say that he withheld this from
modesty, is to invest a rude Galilean of that age with the
affectation belonging to the most refined self-consciousness of
modern days.

To this feast at the publican's, of which many of the same
obnoxious class partook, the evangelists annex the reproaches
cast at the disciples by the Pharisees and Scribes, because their
master ate with publicans and sinners.   Jesus, being within
hearing of the censure, repelled it by the well-known text on the
destination of the physician for the sick, and the Son of man
for sinners (Matt. ix. 11 ff. parall.).   That Jesus should be
frequently taunted by his pharisaical enemies with his too great
predilection for the despised class of publicans (comp. Matt.
xi. 19), accords fully with the nature of his position, and is
therefore historical, if anything be so : the answer, too, which
is here put into the mouth of Jesus, is from its pithy and concise
character well adapted for literal transmission.   Further, it is
not improbable that the reproach in question may have been
especially called forth, by the circumstance that Jesus ate with
publicans and sinners, and went under their roofs.   But that
the cavils of his opponents should have been accompaniments
of the publican's dinner, as the evangelical account leads us
to infer, especially that of Mark (v. 16), is not so easily conceivable [15].   For as the feast was *in the house* (εν τῇ οἰκίᾳ), and as
the disciples also partook of it, how could the Pharisees utter
their reproaches to them, while the meal was going forward,
without defiling themselves by becoming the *guests of a man
that was a sinner*,—the very act which they reprehended in
Jesus ? (Luke xix. 7.)   It will hardly be supposed that they
waited outside until the feast was ended.   It is difficult for
Schleiermacher to maintain, even on the representation of Luke

---

[15] Comp. de Wette, exeg. Handb. 1, 2, p. 134.

taken singly, that the evangelical narrative only implies, that the publican's feast was the cause of the Pharisees' censure, and not that they were cotemporary[16]. Their immediate connexion might easily originate in a legendary manner; in fact, one scarcely knows how tradition, in its process of transmuting the abstract into the concrete, could represent the general idea that the Pharisees had taken offence at the friendly intercourse of Jesus with the publicans, otherwise than thus : Jesus once feasted in a publican's house, in company with many publicans ; the Pharisees saw this, went to the disciples and expressed their censure, which Jesus also heard, and parried by a laconic answer.

After the Pharisees, Matthew makes the disciples of John approach Jesus with the question, why his disciples did not fast, as they did (v. 14 f.) ; in Luke (v. 33 ff.) ; it is still the Pharisees who vaunt their own fasts and those of John's disciples, as contrasted with the eating and drinking of the disciples of Jesus ; Mark's account is not clear (v. 18). According to Schleiermacher, every unprejudiced person must perceive in the statement of Matthew compared with that of Luke, the confusing emendations of a second editor, who could not explain to himself how the Pharisees came to appeal to the disciples of John ; whereas, thinks Schleiermacher, the question would have been puerile in the mouth of the latter ; but it is easy to imagine that the Pharisees might avail themselves of an external resemblance to the disciples of John when opposing Jesus, who had himself received baptism of that teacher. It is certainly surprising that after the Pharisees, who were offended because Jesus ate with publicans, some disciples of John should step forth as if they had been cited for the purpose, to censure generally the unrestricted eating and drinking of Jesus and his disciples. The probable explanation is, that evangelical tradition associated the two circumstances from their intrinsic similarity, and that the first evangelist erroneously gave them the

additional connexion of time and place. But the manner in
which the third evangelist fuses the two particulars, appears a
yet more artificial combination, and is certainly not historical,
because the reply of Jesus could only be directed to John's disciples, or to friendly inquirers: to Pharisees, he would have
given another and a more severe answer [17].

Another narrative, which is peculiar to Luke (xix. 1—10),
treats of the same relation as that concerning Matthew or Levi.
When Jesus, on his last journey to the feast, passes through
Jericho, a *chief among the publicans* ἀρχιτελώνης, named
Zacchæus, that he might, notwithstanding his short stature, get
a sight of Jesus among the crowd, climbed a tree, where Jesus
observed him, and immediately held him worthy to entertain
the Messiah for the night.   Here, again, the favour shown to a
publican excites the discontent of the more rigid spectators ; and
when Zácchæus has made vows of atonement and beneficence,
Jesus again justifies himself, on the ground that his office had
reference to sinners.   The whole scene is very dramatic, and
this might be deemed by some an argument for its historical
character ; but there are certain internal obstacles to its reception.   We are not led to infer that Jesus previously knew
Zacchæus, or that some one pointed him out to Jesus by
name [18] ; but, as Olshausen truly says, the knowledge of
Zacchæus that Jesus here suddenly evinced, is to be referred to
his power of discerning what was in men without the aid of
testimony.   We have before decided that this power is a
legendary attribute ; hence the above particular, at least, cannot
be historical, and the narrative is possibly a variation on the
same theme as that treated of in connexion with the account of
Matthew's call, namely, the friendly relation of Jesus to the
publicans.

---

[17] De Wette, exeg. Handb. 1, 1, p. 93.
[18] Paulus, exeg. Handb., 3, a, s. 48.   Kuinöl, in Luc. p. 632

§ 73.

The men whose vocation we have been considering, namely, the sons of Jonas and of Zebedee, with Philip and Matthew (Nathanael alone being excepted), form the half of that narrow circle of disciples which appears throughout the New Testament under the name of *the twelve*, οἱ δώδεκα, *the twelve disciples* or *apostles*, οἱ δώδεκα μαθήται or ἀπόστολοι. The fundamental idea of the New Testament writers concerning the twelve, is that Jesus himself chose them (Mark iii. 13 f. ; Luke vi. 13 ; John vi. 70 ; xv. 16.). Matthew does not give us the history of the choice of all the twelve, but he tacitly presupposes it by introducing them as a college already instituted (x. 1.). Luke, on the contrary, narrates how, after a night spent on the mountain in vigils and prayer, Jesus selected twelve from the more extensive circle of his adherents, and then descended with them to the plain, to deliver what is called the Sermon on the Mount (vi. 12.). Mark also tells us in the same connexion, that Jesus when on a mountain made a voluntary choice of twelve from the mass of his disciples (iii. 13.). According to Luke, Jesus chose the twelve immediately before he delivered the sermon on the mount, and apparently with reference to it : but there is no discoverable motive which can explain this mode of associating the two events, for the discourse was not specially addressed to the apostles [1], neither had they any office to execute during its delivery. Mark's representation, with the exception of the vague tradition from which he sets out, that Jesus chose the twelve, seems to have been wrought out of his own imagination, and furnishes no distinct notion of the occasion and manner of the choice [2]. Matthew has adopted the best method in merely presupposing, without describing, the particular vocation of the apostles ; and John pursues the same plan, beginning (vi. 67.)

[1] Schleiermacher, über den Lukas, s. 85.
[2] Ib.

to speak of *the twelve*, without any previous notice of their appointment.

Strictly speaking, therefore, it is merely presupposed in the gospels, that Jesus himself fixed the number of the apostles. Is this presupposition correct ?   There certainly is little doubt that this number was fixed during the lifetime of Jesus ; for not only does the author of the Acts represent the twelve as so compact a body immediately after the ascension of their master, that they think it incumbent on them to fill up the breach made by the apostacy of Judas by the election of a new member (i. 15 ff.) ; but the apostle Paul also notices an appearance of the risen Jesus, specially to *the twelve* (1 Cor. xv. 5.).   Schleiermacher, however, doubts whether Jesus himself chose the twelve, and he thinks it more probable that the peculiar relation ultimately borne to him by twelve from amongst his disciples, gradually and spontaneously formed itself [3].   We have, indeed, no warrant for supposing that the appointment of the twelve was a single solemn act; on the contrary, the gospels explicitly narrate, that six of them were called singly, or by pairs, and on separate occasions ; but it is still a question whether the number twelve was not determined by Jesus, and whether he did not willingly abide by it as an expedient for checking the multiplication of his familiar companions.   The number is the less likely to have been fortuitous, the more significant it is, and the more evident the inducements to its choice by Jesus.   He himself, in promising the disciples (Matt. xix. 28.) *that they shall sit on twelve thrones, judging the twelve tribes of Israel,* gives their number a relation to that of the tribes of his people ; and it was the opinion of the highest Christian antiquity that this relation determined his choice [4].   If he and his disciples were primarily sent to the *lost sheep of the house of Israel* (Matt. x. 6; xv. 24), it might seem appropriate that the number of the shepherds should correspond to that of the shepherdless tribes (Matt. ix. 36.).

[3] Ut sup. s. 88.

[4] Ep. Barnab. 8, and the Gospel of the Ebionites ap. Epiphanius, hær. xxx. 13.

The destination of the twelve is only generally intimated in John (xv. 16.) ; in Mark, on the contrary, it is particularly, and without doubt accurately, stated. *He ordained twelve*, it is here said, *that they should be with him*, that is, that he might not be without companionship, aid, and attendance on his journeys ; and accordingly we find them helpful to him in procuring lodgings (Luke ix. 52 ; Matt. xxvi. 17 f.), food (John iv. 8.), and other travelling requisites (Matt. xxi. 1 ff.) ; but above all they were in his society to become *scribes well instructed unto the kingdom of heaven* (Matt. xiii. 52.). To this end they had the opportunity of being present at most of the discourses of Jesus, and even of obtaining private elucidations of their meaning (Matt. xiii. 10 ff. 36 ff.) ; of purifying their minds by his severe but friendly discipline (Matt. viii. 26 ; xvi. 23 ; xviii. 1 ff. 21 ff. ; Luke ix. 50, 55 f. ; John xiii. 12 ff. &c.), and of elevating their souls by the contemplation of his example (John xiv. 19.). Another motive of Jesus in choosing the twelve, was, according to Mark, *that he might send them forth to preach*, that is, to preach the kingdom of heaven during his life, according to the immediate meaning of Mark ; but the promulgation of his cause after his death, must be supposed as an additional object on the part of Jesus. (Mark proceeds to enumerate the powers of healing and of casting out devils ; but on these points we cannot dilate until we reach a future stage of our inquiry.)

It was this latter destination that won for them the distinguished name of *apostles*, ἀπόστολοι (Matt. x. 2 ; Mark vi. 30 ; Luke vii. 13. &c.). It has been doubted whether Jesus himself conferred this name on the twelve, according to Luke vi. 13, and it has been suggested that it was not given them until later, *ex eventu* [5]. But that Jesus should have called them his envoys cannot be improbable, if he really sent them on a journey to announce the approaching kingdom of the Messiah. We grant that it is possible to regard this journey

---

[5] Schleiermacher, ut sup. s. 87.

as an event transposed from the period after the death of Jesus to his lifetime, in order that a sort of rehearsal of the subsequent mission of the apostles might pass under the eye of Jesus; but as it is not improbable that Jesus, perhaps even before he had a full conviction of his own Messiahship, sent out messengers to announce the Messiah's kingdom, we are not warranted to urge such a doubt.

John knows nothing of this mission, recorded by the synoptists. On the other hand, they are ignorant of a circumstance alleged by John, namely, that the disciples baptized during the life of Jesus (iv. 2.). According to the synoptical evangelists, it was not until after the resurrection, that Jesus gave his disciples authority to baptize (Matt xxviii. 19. parall.). As, however, the rite of baptism was introduced by John, and we have reason to believe that Jesus, for a time, made that teacher his model, it is highly probable that he and his disciples also practised baptism, and hence that the positive statement of the fourth gospel is correct. But the negative statement that *Jesus himself baptized not* (iv. 2.), has the appearance of an after-thought, intended to correct the import of the previous passages (iii. 22 ; iv. 1.), and is most probably to be accounted for by the tendency of the fourth gospel to exalt Jesus above the Baptist, and by a corresponding dread of making Jesus exercise the function of the mere forerunner. The question whether Jesus did not baptize at least the apostles, afterwards occasioned much demur in the church.

With the exception of the mission mentioned above, the gospels speak of no important separation between Jesus and his twelve disciples, for there is nothing certain to be gathered from the resumption of their business after his death (John xxi. 2 ff.). No one could detect in our gospels any indications of a repeated interruption to the intercourse of Jesus with his disciples, but theologians, whose harmonistic zeal wished to find room for a second and third vocation ; or expositors, who, in their unwearied application to details, cast about for a means of subsistence for so many indigent men, and thought it necessary to suppose that they were occasionally provided for by a return to their secular labours. As to the subsistence of Jesus and his disciples, we have sufficient sources for it in the hospitality of the East, which, among the Jews, was especially available to the rabbins; in the companionship of rich women *who ministered unto him of their substance* (Luke viii. 2 f.); and finally in the γλωσσόκομον, mentioned, it is true, only by the fourth evangelist (xii. 6; xiii. 29), which was ample enough to furnish assistance to the poor, as well as to supply the wants of the society, and in which, it is probable, presents from wealthy friends of Jesus were deposited. They who do not hold these means adequate without the labour of the disciples, or who think, on more general grounds, that the total renunciation of their secular employment on the part of the twelve, is improbable, must not try to force their opinion on the evangelists, who by the stress which they lay on the expression of the apostles, *we have left all* (Matt. xix. 27 ff.), plainly intimate the opposite view.

We gather, as to the rank of the twelve disciples of Jesus, that they all belonged to the lower class: four, or perhaps more (John xxi. 2), were fishermen, one a publican, and for the others, it is probable from the degree of cultivation they evince, and the preference always expressed by Jesus for the *poor*, πτωχοὺς, and *the little ones*, νηπίους (Matt. v. 3; xi. 5, 25), that they were of a similar grade.

§ 74.

THE TWELVE CONSIDERED INDIVIDUALLY.   THE THREE OR FOUR MOST
CONFIDENTIAL DISCIPLES OF JESUS.

We have in the New Testament four catalogues of the apostles; one in each of the synoptical gospels, and one in the Acts (Matt. x. 2—4; Mark iii. 6—10; Luke vi. 14—16; Acts i. 13). Each of these four lists may be divided into three quaternions; in each corresponding quaternion the first member is the same; and in the last, the concluding member also, if we except Acts i. 13, where he is absent: but the intermediate members are differently arranged, and in the concluding quaternions there is a difference of names or of persons.

At the head of the first quaternion in all the catalogues, and in Matthew with the prefix πρῶτος (*the first*), stands Simon Peter, the son of Jonas (Matt. xvi. 17); according to the fourth gospel, of Bethsaida (i. 45); according to the synoptists, resident in Capernaum [1] (Matt. viii. 14. parall.). We hear an echo of the old polemical dispute, when Protestant expositors ascribe this position to mere chance,—an assumption which is opposed by the fact that all four of the catalogues agree in giving the precedence to Peter, though they differ in other points of arrangement; or when those expositors allege, in explanation, that Peter was first called [2], which, according to the fourth gospel, was not the case. That this invariable priority is indicative of a certain pre-eminence of Peter among the twelve, is evident from the part he plays elsewhere in the evangelical history. Ardent by nature, he is always beforehand with the rest of the apostles, whether in speech (Matt. xv. 15; xvi. 16, 22; xvii. 4; xviii. 21; xxvi. 33; John vi. 68), or in action (Matt. xiv. 28; xxvi. 58; John xviii. 16); and if it is not seldom the case that the speech and action are faulty, and that his prompt courage quickly evaporates, as his denial shows, yet he is, according to the synoptical statement, the first who expresses a decided conviction of the Messiahship of Jesus (Matt. xvi. 16. parall.). It is true that of the eulogies and prerogatives bestowed on him on that occasion, that which is implied in his surname is the only one that remains peculiarly his; for the authority to *bind and to loose*, that is, to forbid and to permit [3], in the newly-founded Messianic kingdom, is soon after extended to all the apostles (xviii. 18). Yet more

---

[1] If ἡ πόλις Ἀνδρέου καὶ Πέτρου, John i. 45, mean the same as ἡ ἰδία πόλις, Matth. ix. 1, that is, the place where they were resident, there exists a contradiction on this point between John and the synoptists.

[2] Comp. Fritzsche, in Matt. p. 358.

[3] Comp. Lightfoot, in loc.

decidedly does this pre-eminence of Peter among the original apostles appear in the Acts, and in the epistles of Paul.

Next to Peter, the catalogue of the first and third gospels places his brother Andrew ; that of the second gospel and the Acts, James, and after him, John. The first and third evange lists are evidently guided by the propriety of uniting the couples of brethren ; Mark, and the author of the Acts, by that of pre- ferring the two apostles next in distinction to Peter to the less conspicuous Andrew, whom they accordingly put last in the quaternion. We have already considered the manner in which these four apostles are signalized in the Christian legend by a special history of their vocation. They appear together in other passages of Mark ; first (i. 29), where Jesus, in company with the sons of Zebedee, enters the house of Simon and Andrew : as, however, the other evangelists only mention Peter on this occasion, Mark may have added the other names inferentially, concluding that the four fishermen, so recently called, would not be apart from Jesus, and that Andrew had a share in his brother's house, a thing in itself probable [4]. Again, Mark xiii. 3, our four apostles concur in asking Jesus *privately* ($\varkappa\alpha\tau'$ $i\delta i\alpha\nu$) concerning the time of the destruction of the temple, and of his second advent. But the parallel passages in the other gospels do not thus particularize any of the disciples. Matthew says, *The disciples came to him privately* (xxiv. 3) ; hence it is pro- bable that Mark's limitation is an erroneous one. Possibly the words $\varkappa\alpha\tau'$ $i\delta i\alpha\nu$, being used in the document to which he re- ferred to denote the separation of the twelve from the multitude, appeared to him, from association, an introductory form, of which there are other examples (Matt. xvii. 1 ; Mark ix. 2), to a private conference of Jesus with Peter, James and John, to whom he might add Andrew on account of the fraternity. Luke, on the other hand, in his account of the miraculous draught of fishes, and the vocation of the fishermen (v. 10), omits Andrew, though he is included in the corresponding nar-

---

[4] Comp. Saunier, über die Quellen des Markus, s. 55 t.

ratives, probably because he does not elsewhere appear as one
of the select apostles; for except on the occasions already noticed, he is only mentioned by John (vi. 9; xii. 22), and that in
no very important connexion.

The two sons of Zebedee are the only disciples whose distinction rivals that of Peter. Like him, they cvince an ardent
and somewhat rash zeal (Luke ix. 54; once John is named alone,
Mark ix. 38; Luke ix. 49); and it was to this disposition, apparently, that they owed the surname *Sons of Thunder*, בְּנֵי רֶגֶשׁ
υἱοὶ βροντῆς (Mark iii. 17)[5], conferred on them by Jesus. So
high did they stand among the twelve, that either they (Mark
xi. 35 ff.), or their mother for them (Matt. xx. 20 ff.), thought
they might claim the first place in the Messiah's kingdom. It
is worthy of notice that not only in the four catalogues, but elsewhere when the two brothers are named, as in Matt. iv. 21;
xvii. 1; Mark i. 19, 29; v. 37; ix. 2; x. 35; xiii. 3; xiv. 33; Luke
v. 10; ix. 54; with the exception of Luke viii. 51; ix. 28; James
is always mentioned first, and John is appended to him as *his
brother* (ὁ ἀδελφὸς αὐτοῦ). This is surprising; because, while
we know nothing remarkable of James, John is memorable as
the favourite disciple of Jesus. Hence it is supposed that this
precedence cannot possibly denote a superiority of James to
John, and an explanation has been sought in his seniority[6].
Nevertheless, it remains a doubt whether so constant a precedence do not intimate a pre-eminence on the part of James; at
least, if, in the apprehension of the synoptists, John had been
as decidedly preferred as he is represented to have been in the
fourth gospel, we are inclined to think that they would have
named him before his brother James, even allowing him to be
the younger. This leads us to a difference between the first
three evangelists and the fourth which requires a closer examination.

In the synoptical gospels, as we have observed, Peter, James,
and John, form the select circle of disciples whom Jesus admits

---

[5] Comp. de Wette, in loc.
[6] Paulus, exeg. Handb. 1, b, s. 556.

to certain scenes, which the rest of the twelve were not
spiritually mature enough to comprehend; as the transfiguration, the conflict in Gethsemane, and, according to Mark (v. 37),
the raising of the daughter of Jairus [7]. After the death of Jesus,
also, a James, Peter and John appear as the *pillars* of the
church (Gal. ii. 9) ; this James, however, is not the son of
Zebedee, who had been early put to death (Acts xii. 2), but
James, the brother of the Lord (Gal. i. 19), who even in the
first apostolic council appears to have possessed a predominant
authority, and whom many hold to be the second James of the
apostolic catalogue given in Acts i. [8]. It is observable from
the beginning of the Acts, that James the son of Zebedee, is
eclipsed by Peter and John. As, then, this James the elder was
not enough distinguished or even known in the primitive church,
for his early martyrdom to have drawn much lustre on his
name, tradition had no inducement from subsequent events, to
reflect an unhistorical splendour on his relation to Jesus ; there
is therefore no reason to doubt the statement as to the prominent
position held by James, in conjunction with Peter and John,
among the twelve apostles.

So much the more must it excite surprise to find, in the
fourth gospel the triumvirate almost converted into a monarchy:
James, like another Lepidus, is wholly cast out, while Peter
and John are in the position of Antony and Octavius, the
latter having nearly stripped his rival of all pretensions to
an equal rank with himself, to say nothing of a higher. James
is not even named in the fourth gospel; only in the appendix
(xxi. 2) is there any mention of the *sons of Zebedee;* while
several narratives of the vocations of different apostles are
given, apparently including that of John himself, no James

---

[7] This is probably a mere inference of Mark. Because Jesus excluded the multitude, and forbade the publication of the event, the evangelist saw in it one of those
secret scenes, to which Jesus was accustomed to admit only the three favoured
apostles.

[8] In the ancient church it was thought that Jesus had communicated to these three
individuals the γνῶσις, to be mysteriously transmitted. Vid. in Gieseler, K. G. 1,
s. 234.

appears in them, neither is there any speech of his, as of many
other apostles, throughout this gospel.

Quite differently does the fourth evangelist treat Peter. He
makes him one of the first who enter the society of Jesus, and
gives him a prominent importance not less often than the
synoptists; he does not conceal that Jesus bestowed on him an
honourable surname (i. 43); he puts in his mouth (vi. 68 f.)
a confession which seems but a new version of the celebrated
one in Matt. xvi. 16; according to him, Peter once throws
himself into the sea that he may more quickly reach Jesus
(xxi. 7); at the last supper, and in the garden of Gethsemane,
he makes Peter more active than even the synoptists represent
him (xiii. 6 ff.; xviii. 10 f.); he accords him the honour of
following Jesus into the high priest's palace (xviii. 15), and of
being one of the first to visit the grave of Jesus after the resurrection (xx. 3 ff.); nay, he even details a special conversation
between the risen Jesus and Peter (xxi. 15 ff.). But these advantages of Peter are in the fourth gospel invalidated in a
peculiar manner, and put into the shade, in favour of John.
The synoptists tell us that Peter and John were called to the
apostleship in the same way, and the former somewhat before
the latter; the fourth evangelist prefers associating Andrew with
the nameless disciple who is taken for John, and makes Peter
come to him through the instrumentality of his brother [9]. He
also admits the honourable interpretation of the surname Peter,
and the panegyric on Peter's confession ; but this he does in
common with Mark and Luke, while the speeches and the action
attributed in the fourth gospel to Peter during the last supper
and in the garden, are to be classed as only so many mistakes.
The more we approach the catastrophe, the more marked is the
subordination of Peter to John. At the last supper indeed,
Peter is particularly anxious for the discovery of the traitor : he
cannot, however, apply immediately to Jesus (xiii. 23 ff.), but is
obliged to make John, *who was leaning on Jesus' bosom,* his

---

[9] Even Paulus, L. J. 1, a, s. 167 f , remarks that the fourth evangelist seems to
have had a design in noticing this circumstance.

medium of communication. While, according to the synoptists, Peter alone followed Jesus into the palace of the high priest; according to the fourth evangelist, John accompanied him, and under such circumstances, that without him Peter could not have entered,—John, as one known to the high priest, having to obtain admission for him (xviii. 15 f.). In the synoptical gospels, not one of the disciples is bold enough to venture to the cross; but in the fourth, John is placed under it, and is there established in a new relation to the mother of his dying master: a relation of which we elsewhere find no trace (xix. 26 f.). On the appearance of the risen Jesus at the Galilean sea (xxi.), Peter, as the θερμότερος, casts himself into the sea; but it is not until after John, as the διορατικώτερος (Euthymius), has recognized the Lord in the person standing on the shore. In the ensuing conversation, Peter is indeed honoured with the commission, *Feed my sheep;* but this honour is overshadowed by the dubitative question, *Lovest thou me?* and while the prospect of martyrdom is held up to him, John is promised the distinction of tarrying till Jesus came again, an advantage which Peter is warned not to envy. Lastly, while, according to Luke (xxiv. 12), Peter, first among the apostles, and alone, comes to the vacant grave of his risen master, the fourth gospel (xx. 3), gives him a companion in John, who outruns Peter and arrives first at the grave. Peter goes into the grave before John, it is true; but it is the latter in whose honour it is recorded, that he *saw and believed,* almost in contradiction to the statement of Luke, that Peter went home *wondering in himself at that which was come to pass.* Thus in the fourth gospel, John, both literally and figuratively, *outruns Peter,* for the entire impression which the attentive reader must receive from the representation there given of the relative position of Peter and John, is that the writer wished a comparison to be drawn in favour of the latter [10].

[10] This has not escaped the acumen of Dr. Paulus. In a review of the first volume of the second ed of Lücke's Comm. zum Johannes, im Lit. Bl. zur allg. Kir-chenzeitung, Febr. 1834, no. 18, s. 137 f., he says: "The gospel of John has only

But John is moreover especially distinguished in the gospel which bears his name, by the constant epithet, *the beloved disciple, the disciple whom Jesus loved*, ὁ μαθητὴς ὃν ἠγάπα, or ἐφίλει ὁ Ἰησοῦς, (xiii. 23 ; xix. 26 ; xx. 2 ; xxi. 7, 20). It is true that we have no absolute proof from the contents of the fourth gospel, whether intrinsically or comparatively considered, that by the above formula, or the more indeterminate one, *the other* ὁ ἄλλος, or *another disciple,* ἄλλος μαθητὴς (x. 15 f. ; xx. 3, 4, 8), which, as it appears from xx. 2 f., is its equivalent, we are to understand the apostle John. For neither is the designation in question anywhere used interchangeably with the name of the apostle, nor is there anything narrated in the fourth gospel of the favourite disciple, which in the three first is ascribed to John. Because in xxi. 2. the sons of Zebedee are named among the assistants, it does not follow that the disciple mentioned v. 7 as the one whom Jesus loved must be John ; James, or one of the *two other disciples* mentioned in v. 2, might be meant. Nevertheless, it is the immemorial tradition of the church that the disciple whom Jesus loved was John, nor are all reasons for such a belief extinct even to us ; for in the Greek circle from which the fourth gospel sprang, there could scarcely be among the apostles whom it leaves unnamed, one so well known as to be recognized under that description unless it were John, whose residence at Ephesus is hardly to be rejected as a mere fable.

It may appear more doubtful whether the author intended by this title to designate himself, and thus to announce himself as the apostle John.   The conclusion of the twenty-first chapter, v. 24, does certainly make the favourite disciple the testifier and writer of the preceding history ; but we may assume it as granted that this passage is an addition by a strange

---

preserved the less advantageous circumstances connected with Peter (excepting vi. 68), *such as place him in marked subordination to John* [here the passages above considered are cited].   An adherent of Peter can hardly have had a hand in the gospel of John." We may add that it seems to have proceeded from an antagonist of Peter, for it is probable that he had such of the scoohl of John, as well as of Paul.

hand[11]. When, however, in the genuine text of the gospel, (xix. 35), the writer says of the effect produced by the piercing of the side of Jesus, *he that saw bare record,* ὁ ἑωρακὼς μεμαρτύρηκε ; no other than the favourite disciple can be intended, because he alone among all the disciples (the only parties eligible as witnesses in the case), is supposed to be present at the cross. The probability that the author here speaks of himself is not at all affected by his use of the third person ; but the preterite annexed to it may well excite a doubt whether an appeal be not here made to the testimony of John, as one distinct from the writer[12]. This mode of expression, however, may be explained also in accordance with the other supposition[13], which is supported by the circumstance that the author in i. 14, 16, seems to announce himself as the eye-witness of the history he narrates.

Was that author, then, really the apostle John, as he apparently wishes us to surmise ? This is another question, on which we can only pronounce when we shall have completed our investigation. We will merely allude to the difficulty of supposing that the apostle John could give so unhistorical a sketch of the Baptist as that in the fourth gospel. But we ask, is it at all probable that the real John would so unbecomingly neglect the well-founded claims of his brother James to a special notice ? and is not such an omission rather indicative of a late Hellenistic author, who scarcely had heard the name of the brother so early martyred ? The designation, *the disciple whom Jesus loved,* which in xxi. 20 has the prolix addition, *who also leaned on his breast at supper, and said, Lord, which is he that betrayeth thee?* is not to be considered as an offence against modesty[14]. It is certainly far too laboured and embellished for one who, without any ulterior view, wishes to

[11] Vid. Lücke, Comm. zum Joh. 2, s. 708.
[12] Paulus, in his review of Bretschneider's Probabilien, in the Heidelberger Jahrbüchern, 1821, no. 9, s. 138.
[13] Lücke, ut sup. s. 664.
[14] Bretschneider, Probabilia, p. 111 f.

indicate himself, for such an one would, at least sometimes, have simply employed his name: but a venerator of John, issuing perhaps from one of his schools, might very naturally be induced to designate the revered apostle under whose name he wished to write, in this half honourable, half mysterious manner[15].

§ 75.

THE REST OF THE TWELVE, AND THE SEVENTY DISCIPLES.

The second quaternion in all the four catalogues begins with Philip. The three first gospels know nothing more of him than his name. The fourth alone gives his birth-place, Bethsaida, and narrates his vocation (i. 44 f.); in this gospel he is more than once an interlocutor, but his observations are founded on mistakes (vi. 7; xiv. 8); and he perhaps appears with most dignity, when the Ἕλληνες, who wish to see Jesus, apply immediately to him (xii. 21).

The next in the three evangelical lists is Bartholomew; a name which is nowhere found out of the catalogues. In the synoptical gospels Bartholomew is coupled with Philip; in the history of the vocations given by the fourth evangelist (i. 46), Nathanael appears in company with the latter, and (xxi. 2) is again presented in the society of the apostles. Nathanael, however, finds no place among the twelve, unless he be indentical with one otherwise named by the synoptists. If so, it is thought that Bartholomew is the most easily adapted to such an alias, as the three first gospels couple him with Philip, just as the fourth, which has no Bartholomew, does Nathanael; to which it may be added that בר תלמי is a mere patronymic, which must have been accompanied by a proper name, such as Nathanael[1]. But we have no adequate ground for such an identification, since the juxtaposition of Bartholomew and Philip is shown to be accidental, by our finding the former (Acts i. 13), as well

---

[15] Comp. Paulus, ut sup. s. 137.

[1] Thus most of the expositors, Fritzsche, Matth., s. 359; Winer Realwörterb. 1, s. 163 f. Comp. De Wette, exeg. Handb. 1, 1, s. 98.

as the latter (John xxi. 2), linked with different names; the absence of Bartholomew from the fourth gospel is not peculiar to him among the twelve; finally, second names as surnames were added to proper as well as to patronymic names, as Simon Peter, Joseph Caiaphas, John Mark, and the like; so that any other apostle not named by John might be equally well identified with Nathanael, and hence the supposed relation between the two appellations is altogether uncertain.

In the catalogue given in the Acts, Philip is followed, not by Bartholomew, but by Thomas, who in the list of the first gospel comes after Bartholomew, in that of the others, after Matthew. Thomas, in Greek Δίδυμος, appears in the fourth gospel, on one occasion, in the guise of mournful fidelity (xi. 16): on another, in the more noted one of incredulity (xx. 24. ff.) ; and once again in the appendix (xxi. 2). Matthew, the next in the series, is found nowhere else except in the history of his vocation.

The third quaternion is uniformly opened by James the son of Alpheus, of whom we have already spoken. After him comes in both Luke's lists, Simon, whom he calls Zelotes, or the zealot, but whom Matthew and Mark (in whose catalogues he is placed one degree lower) distinguish as the Canaanite ὁ κανανίτης (from קַנָּא, to be zealous). This surname seems to mark him as a former adherent of the Jewish sect of zealots for religion [2], a party which, it is true, did not attain consistence until the latest period of the Jewish state, but which was already in the process of formation. In all the lists that retain the name of Judas Iscariot, he occupies the last place, but of him we must not speak until we enter on the history of the passion. Luke, in his filling up of the remaining places of this quaternion, differs from the two other evangelists, and perhaps these also differ from each other ; Luke has a second Judas, whom he styles the brother of James; Matthew, Lebbeus; and Mark, Thaddeus. It is true that we now commonly read in Matthew,

[2] Joseph. bell. jud. iv. iii. 9.

Lebbeus, whose surname was Thaddeus; but the vacillation in the early readings seems to betray these words to be a later addition intended to reconcile the first two evangelists [3]; an attempt which others have made by pointing out a similarity of meaning between the two names, though such a similarity does not exist [4]. But allowing validity to one or other of these harmonizing efforts, there yet remains a discrepancy between Matthew and Mark with their Lebbeus-Thaddeus, and Luke with his Judas, the brother of James. Schleiermacher justly disapproves the expedients, almost all of them constrained and unnatural, which have been resorted to for the sake of proving that here also, we have but one person under two different names. He seeks to explain the divergency, by supposing, that during the lifetime of Jesus, one of the two men died or left the circle of the apostles, and the other took his place; so that one list gives the earlier, the other the later member [5]. But it is scarcely possible to admit that any one of our catalogues was drawn up during the life of Jesus; and after that period, no writer would think of including a member who had previously retired from the college of apostles; those only would be enumerated who were ultimately attached to Jesus. It is the most reasonable to allow that there is a discrepancy between the lists, since it is easy to account for it by the probability that while the number of the apostles, and the names of the most distinguished among them, were well known, varying traditions supplied the place of more positive data concerning the less conspicuous.

Luke makes us acquainted with a circle of disciples, intermediate to the twelve and the mass of the partisans of Jesus. He tells us (x. 1 ff.) that besides the twelve, Jesus chose *other seventy also,* and sent them two and two before him into all the districts which he intended to visit on his last journey, that they might proclaim the approach of the kingdom of heaven. As the other evangelists have no allusion to this event, the most

---

[3] Comp. Credner, Einleitung, 1, s. 64; De Wette, exeg. Handb. 1, 1, s. 98 f.
[4] De Wette, ut sup.
[5] Ueber den Lukas, s. 88 f.

recent critics have not hesitated to make their silence on this head a reproach to them, particularly to the first evangelist, in his supposed character of apostle[6]. But the disfavour towards Matthew on this score ought to be moderated by the consideration, that neither in the other gospels, nor in the Acts, nor in any apostolic epistle, is there any trace of the seventy disciples, who could scarcely have passed thus unnoticed, had their mission been as fruitful in consequences, as it is commonly supposed. It is said, however, that the importance of this appointment lay in its significance, rather than in its effects. As the number of the twelve apostles, by its relation to that of the tribes of Israel, shadowed forth the destination of Jesus for the Jewish people; so the seventy, or as some authorities have it, the seventy-two disciples, were representatives of the seventy or seventy-two peoples, with as many different tongues, which, according to the Jewish and early Christian view, formed the sum of the earth's inhabitants[7], and hence they denoted the universal destination of Jesus and his kingdom[8]. Moreover, seventy was a sacred number with the Jewish nation; Moses deputed seventy elders (Num. xi. 16, 25); the Sanhedrim had seventy members[9]; the Old Testament, seventy translators.

Had Jesus, then, under the pressing circumstances that mark his public career, nothing more important to do than to cast about for significant numbers, and to surround himself with inner and outer circles of disciples, regulated by these mystic measures? or rather, is not this constant preference for sacred numbers, this assiduous development of an idea to which the number of the apostles furnished the suggestion, wholly in the spirit of the primitive Christian legend? This, supposing it imbued with Jewish prepossessions, would infer, that as Jesus

---

[6] Schulz, über das Abendmahl, s. 307.; Schneckenburger, ueber den Ursprung, s. 13 f.

[7] Tuf haarez, f. xix. c. iii.; Clem. hom. xviii. 4; Recognit. Clement. ii. 42. Epiphan. hær. i. 5.

[8] Schneckenburger, ut sup.; Gieseler, über Entstehung der schriftl. Evangelien, s. 127 f.

[9] Lightfoot, p. 786.

had respect to the twelve tribes in fixing the number of his apostles, he would extend the parallel by appointing seventy subordinate disciples, corresponding to the seventy elders; or, supposing the legend animated by the more universal sentiments of Paul, it could not escape the persuasion that to the symbol of the relation of his office to the Israelitish people, Jesus would annex another, significative of its destination for all the kindreds of the earth.   However agreeable this class of seventy disciples may have always been to the church, as a series of niches for the reception of men who, without belonging to the twelve, were yet of importance to her, as Mark, Luke and Matthew; we are compelled to pronounce the decision of our most recent critic precipitate, and to admit that the gospel of Luke, by its acceptance of such a narrative, destitute as it is of all historical confirmation, and of any other apparent source than dogmatical interests, is placed in disadvantageous comparison with that of Matthew.   We gather, indeed, from Acts i. 21 f. that Jesus had more than the twelve as his constant companions; but that these formed a body of exactly seventy, or that that number was selected from them, does not seem adequately warranted [10].

[10] De Wette, exeget. Handb., 1, 1, s. 99 f. 1, 2, s. 61. 1, 3, s. 220.; Theile, zur Biogr. J., § 24.   For the contrary opinion, see Neander, L. J. Chr., s. 498 f.

CHAPTER VI.

THE DISCOURSES OF JESUS IN THE THREE FIRST GOSPELS *.

---

§ 76.

THE SERMON ON THE MOUNT.

In reviewing the public life of Jesus, we may separate from the events those discourses which were not merely incidental, but which stand independent and entire. This distinction, however, is not precise, for many discourses, owing to the occurrences that suggested them, may be classed as events; and many events, from the explanations annexed to them, seem to range themselves with the discourses. The discourses of Jesus given in the synoptical gospels, and those attributed to him in the fourth, differ widely both in form and matter, having only a few isolated sentences in common : they must, therefore, be subjected to a separate examination. Again, there is a dissimilitude between the three first evangelists : Matthew affects long discourses, and collects into one mass a number of sayings, which in Luke are distributed among various places and occasions; each of these two evangelists has also some discourses peculiar to himself. In Mark, the element of discourses exists in a very small proportion. Our purpose will, therefore, be best answered, if we make Matthew's comprehensive discourses our starting point; ascertain all the corresponding ones in the

* All that relates to the sufferings, death, and resurrection of Jesus is here excluded.

other gospels; inquire which amongst them has the best arrangement and representation of these discourses; and, finally, endeavour to form a judgment as to how far they really proceeded from the lips of Jesus. The first long discourse in Matthew is that known as the sermon on the mount (v.—vii.). The evangelist, having recorded the return of Jesus after his baptism into Galilee, and the calling of the fishermen, informs us, that Jesus went through all Galilee, teaching and healing; that great multitudes followed him from all parts of Palestine; and that for their instruction he ascended a mountain, and delivered the sermon in question (iv. 23, ff.). We seek in vain for its parallel in Mark, but Luke (vi. 20—49) gives a discourse which has the same introduction and conclusion, and presents in its whole tenor the most striking similarity with that of Matthew; moreover, in both cases, Jesus, at the termination of his discourse, goes to Capernaum, and heals the centurion's servant. It is true that Luke gives a later insertion to the discourse, for previous to it he narrates many journeyings and cures of Jesus, which Matthew places after it; and while the latter represents Jesus as ascending a mountain, and being seated there during delivery of his discourse, Luke says, almost in contradiction to him, that Jesus *came down and stood in the plain.* Further, the sermon in Luke contains but a fourth part of that in Matthew, while it has some elements peculiarly its own.

To avoid the unpleasant admission that one of two inspired evangelists must be in error,—which is inevitable if in relation to the same discourse one of them makes Jesus deliver it on the mountain, the other in the plain; the one sitting, the other standing; the one earlier, the other later; if either the one has made important omissions, or the other as important additions;—the ancient harmonists pronounced these discourses to be distinct[1], on the plea that Jesus must frequently have treated of

---

[1] Augustin. de consens. ev. ii. 19.; Storr, über den Zweck des Evang. u. d. Br. Joh., s. 347 ff. For further references see Tholück's Auslegung der Bergpredigt, Einl., § 1.

the essential points of his doctrine, and may therefore have repeated word for word certain impressive enunciations. This may be positively denied with respect to long discourses, and even concise maxims will always be reproduced in a new guise and connexion by a gifted and inventive teacher; to say the least, it is impossible that any but a very barren mind should repeat the same formal exordium, and the same concluding illustration, on separate occasions.

The identity of the discourses being established, the first effort was to conciliate or to explain the divergencies between the two accounts so as to leave their credibility unimpeached. In reference to the different designation of the locality, Paulus insists on the ἐπὶ of Luke, which he interprets to imply that Jesus stood *over* the plain and therefore on a hill. Tholück, more happily, distinguishes the *level space*, τόπος πεδινὸς, from the plain properly so called, and regards it as a less abrupt part of the mountain. But as one evangelist makes Jesus ascend the mountain to deliver his discourse, while the other makes him descend for the same purpose, these conciliators ought to admit, with Olshausen, that if Jesus taught in the plain, according to Luke, Matthew has overlooked the descent that preceded the discourse; or if, as Matthew says, Jesus taught seated on the mountain, Luke has forgotten to mention that after he had descended, the pressure of the crowd induced him to reascend before he commenced his harangue. And without doubt each was ignorant of what he omits, but each knew that tradition associated this discourse with a sojourn of Jesus on a mountain. Matthew thought the mountain a convenient elevation for one addressing a multitude; Luke, on the contrary, imagined a descent necessary for the purpose: hence the double discrepancy, for he who teaches from a mountain is sufficiently elevated over his hearers to sit, but he who teaches in a plain will naturally stand. The chronological divergencies, as well as the local, must be admitted, if we would abstain from fruitless efforts at conciliation [2].

[2] Comp. De Wette, exeg. Handb., 1, 1, s. 47 ff. 1. 2. s. 44.

H

The difference as to the length and contents of the discourse is susceptible of three explanations : either the concise record of Luke is a mere extract from the entire discourse which Matthew gives without abridgment; or Matthew has incorpo rated many sayings belonging properly to other occasions; or lastly, both these causes of variety have concurred. He who, with Tholück, wishes to preserve intact the *fides divina*, or with Paulus, the *fides humana* of the evangelists, will prefer the first supposition, because to withhold the true is more innocent than to add the false. The above theologians hold that the train of thought in the sermon on the mount as given by Matthew, is closely consecutive, and that this is a proof of its original unity. But any compiler not totally devoid of ability, can give a tolerable appearance of connectedness to sayings which did not originally belong to each other ; and even these commentators are obliged to admit [3] that the alleged consecutiveness extends over no more than half the sermon, for from vi. 19, it is a string of more or less isolated sentences, some of them very unlikely to have been uttered on the occasion. More recent criticism has therefore decided that the shorter account of Luke presents the discourse of Jesus in its original form, and that Matthew has taken the license of incorporating with this much that was uttered by Jesus at various times, so as to retain the general sketch—the exordium, peroration, and essential train of thought; while between these compartments he inserted many sayings more or less analogous borrowed from elsewhere [4]. This view is especially supported by the fact that many of the sentences, which in Matthew make part of the sermon on the mount, are in Mark and Luke dispersed through a variety of scenes. Compelled to grant this, yet earnestly solicitous to avert from the evangelist an imputation that might invalidate his claim to be considered an eyewitness, other theologians maintain that Matthew did not compile the discourse under the idea that it was actually spoken

---

[3] Tholück, s. 24 ; Paulus, exeg. Handb., 1, b, s. 584.
[4] Schulz, vom Abendmahl, s. 313 f.; Sieffert, s. 74 ff. ; Fritzsche, s. 301.

on a single occasion, but with the clearest knowledge that such was not the case [5]. It is with justice remarked in opposition to this, that when Matthew represents Jesus as ascending the mountain before he begins his discourse, and descending after its close, he obviously makes these two incidents the limits of a single address; and that when he speaks of the impression which the discourse produced on the multitude, whose presence he states as the inducement to its delivery, he could not but intend to convey the idea of a continuous harangue [6]. As to Luke's edition of the sermon, there are parts in which the interrupted connexion betrays deficiencies, and there are additions which do not look genuine [7]; it is also doubtful whether he assigns a more appropriate connexion to the passages in the position of which he differs from Matthew [8]; and hence, as we shall soon see more fully, he has in this instance no advantage over his predecessor.

The assemblage to whom the sermon on the mount was addressed, might from Luke's account be supposed a narrow circle, for he states that the choice of the apostles immediately preceded the discourse, and that at its commencement Jesus *lifted up his eyes on his disciples*, and he does not, like Matthew, note the *multitude*, ὄχλους, as part of the audience. On the other hand, Matthew also mentions that before the sermon the disciples gathered round Jesus and were taught by him; and Luke represents the discourse as being delivered *in the audience of the people* (vii. 1); it is therefore evident that Jesus spoke to the crowd in general, but with a particular view to the edification of his disciples [9]. We have no reason to doubt that a real harangue of Jesus, more than ordinarily

---

[5] Olshausen, Bibl. Comm., 1, s. 197; Kern, in der Tüb. schrift, 1834, 2, s. 33.

[6] Schulz, ut sup. s. 315; Schneckenburger, Beiträge, s. 26; Credner, Einleit. 1, s. 69.

[7] Schleiermacher, über den Lukas, s. 89 f.

[8] Tholück, p. 11, and my Review of the writings of Sieffert and others in the Jahrbuch, f. wiss. Kritik, Nov. 1834; now in my Charakteristiken u. Kritiken, s. 252 ff.

[9] Comp. Tholück, ut sup. s. 25 ff.; De Wette, exeget. Handb., 1, 1, s. 49.

solemn and public, was the foundation of the evangelical accounts before us.

Let us now proceed to an examination of particulars. In both editions, the sermon on the mount is opened by a series of beatitudes; in Luke, however, not only are several wanting which we find in Matthew, but most of those common to both are in the former taken in another sense than in the latter [10]. The *poor*, πτωχοὶ, are not specified as in Matthew by the addition, *in spirit*, τῷ πνεύματι; they are therefore not those who have a deep consciousness of inward poverty and misery, but the literally poor; neither is the hunger of the πεινῶντες (*hungering*) referred to τὴν δικαιοσύνην (*righteousness*); it is therefore not spiritual hunger, but bodily; moreover, the adverb νῦν, *now*, definitively marks out *those who hunger* and *those who weep*, the πεινῶντες and κλαίοντες. Thus in Luke the antithesis is not, as in Matthew, between the present sorrows of pious souls, whose pure desires are yet unsatisfied, and their satisfaction about to come; but between present suffering and future well-being in general [11]. This mode of contrasting the αἰὼν οὗτος and the αἰὼν μέλλων, *the present age* and *the future*, is elsewhere observable in Luke, especially in the parable of the rich man; and without here inquiring which of the two representations is probably the original, I shall merely remark, that this of Luke is conceived entirely in the spirit of the Ebionites,—a spirit which has of late been supposed discernible in Matthew. It is a capital principle with the Ebionites, as they are depicted in the Clementine Homilies, that he who has his portion in the present age, will be destitute in the age to come; while he who renounces earthly possessions, thereby accumulates heavenly treasures [12]. The last beatitude relates to those who are persecuted for the sake of Jesus. Luke in the parallel passage has, *for the Son of man's sake;* hence

---

[10] Storr, Ueber den Zweck u. s. w., s. 348 f. Olshausen.

[11] De Wette, exeg. Handb., 1, 2, s. 44 f.; Neander, L. J. Chr., s. 155 f. Anm.

[12] Homil. xv. 7; comp. Credner in Winer's Zeitschrift f. wiss. Theologie, 1, s. 298 f.; Schneckenburger, über das Evangelium der Aegyptier, § 6.

the words *for my sake* in Matthew, must be understood to refer to Jesus solely in his character of Messiah [13].

The beatitudes are followed in Luke by as many *woes οὐαὶ*, which are wanting in Matthew. In these the opposition established by the Ebionites between this world and the other, is yet more strongly marked ; for woe is denounced on the rich, the full, and the joyous, simply as such, and they are threatened with the evils corresponding to their present advantages, under the new order of things to be introduced by the Messiah ; a view that reminds us of the Epistle of James, v. 1 ff. The last woe is somewhat stiffly formed after the model of the last beatitude, for it is evidently for the sake of the contrast to the true prophets, so much calumniated, that the false prophets are said, without any historical foundation, to have been spoken well of by all men. We may therefore conjecture, with Schleiermacher [14], that we are indebted for these maledictions to the inventive fertility of the author of the third gospel. He added this supplement to the beatitudes, less because, as Schleiermacher supposes, he perceived a chasm, which he knew not how to fill, than because he judged it consistent with the character of the Messiah, that, like Moses of old, he should couple curses with blessings. The sermon on the mount is regarded as the counterpart of the law, delivered on Mount Sinai ; but the introduction, especially in Luke, reminds us more of a passage in Deuteronomy, in which Moses commands that on the entrance of the Israelitish people into the promised land, one half of them shall take their stand on Mount Gerizim, and pronounce a manifold blessing on the observers of the law, the other half on Mount Ebal, whence they were to fulminate as manifold a curse on its transgressors. We read in Josh. viii. 33 ff. that this injunction was fulfilled [15].

---

[13] Schneckenburger, über den Ursprung, s. 29.

[14] Ut sup. s. 90. Neander agrees with him, ut sup.

[15] The Rabbins also attached weight to these Mosaic blessings and curses, vid. Lightfoot, p. 255. As here we have eight blessings, they held that Abraham had been blessed *benedictionibus septem* (Baal Turim, in Gen. xii. Lightfoot, p. 256.) :

With the beatitudes, Matthew suitably connects the representation of the disciples as *the salt of the earth*, and *the light
of the world* (v. 13 ff.). In Luke, the discourse on the salt
is, with a rather different opening, introduced in another place
(xiv. 34 f.), where Jesus admonishes his hearers to ponder the
sacrifices that must be made by those who would follow him,
and rather to abstain from the profession of discipleship than
to maintain it dishonourably; and to this succeeds aptly enough
the comparison of such degenerate disciples to salt that has lost
its savour. Thus the dictum accords with either context, and
from its aphoristical conciseness would be likely to recur, so
that it may have been really spoken in both discourses. On the
contrary, it cannot have been spoken in the sequence in which
it is placed by Mark (ix. 50) : for the idea that every one shall
be salted with fire (in allusion to hell), has no internal connexion with the comparison of the true disciples of Jesus to
salt, denoting their superiority : the connexion is merely external, resulting from the verbal affinity of ἁλίζειν and ἅλας,—it is
the connexion of the dictionary [16]. The altered sequel which
Mark gives to the apothegm (*have salt in yourselves, and be at
peace one with another*), might certainly be united to it without
incongruity, but it would accord equally well with quite a different
train of thought. The apothegm on the light which is not to
be hidden, as the salt is not to be without savour, is also wanting
in the sermon on the mount as given by Luke; who, however, omitting the special application to the disciples, has substantially the same doctrine in two different places. We find
it first (viii. 16.) immediately after the interpretation of the
parable of the sower, where it also occurs in Mark (iv. 21). It
must be admitted that there is no incoherence in associating
the shining of the light with the fructification of the seed;

David, Daniel with his three companions, and the Messiah, *benedictionibus sex.*
(Targ. Ruth. 3. ibid.) They also counted together with the twenty *beatitudines* in
the Psalms, as many *væ* in Isaiah. (Midrasch Tehillim in Ps. i. ib.)

[16] Schneckenburger, Beiträge, s. 58. Neander tries to show, very artificially, a
real connexion of thought, s. 157, Anm.

still, a judicious teacher will pause on the interpretation of a parable, and will not disturb its effect by a hasty transition to new images. At any rate there is no intrinsic connexion between the shining of the inward light, and the declaration appended to it by Luke, that all secrets shall be made manifest. We have here a case which is of frequent recurrence with this evangelist; that, namely, of a variety of isolated sayings being thrown confusedly together between two independent discourses or narratives. Thus between the parable of the sower and the narrative of the visit paid to Jesus by his mother and brethren, the apothegm on the light is inserted on account of its internal analogy with the parable: then, because in this apothegm there occurs the opposition between concealment and manifestation, it suggested to the writer the otherwise heterogeneous discourse on the revelation of all secrets; whereupon is added, quite irrelevantly to the context, but with some relation to the parable, the declaration, *Whosoever hath, to him shall be given.* In the second passage on the manifestation of the light (xi. 33), the subject has absolutely no connexion, unless we interpolate one [17], with that of the context, which turns on the condemnation of the cotemporaries of Jesus by the Ninevites. The fact is, that here again, between the discourses against the demand for signs and those at the Pharisee's dinner, we have a chasm filled up with disjointed fragments of harangues.

At v. 17 ff. follows the transition to the main subject of the sermon; the assurance of Jesus that he came not to destroy the law and the prophets, but to fulfil, &c. Now as Jesus herein plainly presupposes that he is himself the Messiah, to whom was ascribed authority to abolish a part of the law, this declaration cannot properly belong to a period in which, if Matt. xvi. 13 ff. be rightly placed, he had not yet declared himself to be the Messiah. Luke (xvi. 17) inserts this declaration together with the apparently contradictory one, that the law and the prophets were in force until the coming of John. These are

---

[17] Olshausen in loc. The true reading is indicated by Schneckenburger, Beiträge, s. 58; Tholück, ut sup. s. 11.

two propositions that we cannot suppose to have been uttered consecutively; and the secret of their conjunction in Luke's gospel lies in the word νόμος, *law*, which happens to occur in both [18]. It is to be observed that between the parable of the steward and that of the rich man, we have another of those pauses in which Luke is fond of introducing his fragments.

So little, it appears from v. 20, is it the design of Jesus to inculcate a disregard of the Mosaic law, that he requires a far stricter observance of its precepts than the Scribes and Pharisees, and he makes the latter appear in contrast to himself as the underminers of the law.   Then follows a series of Mosaic commandments, on which Jesus comments so as to show that he penetrates into the spirit of the law, instead of cleaving to the mere letter, and especially discerns the worthlessness of the rabbinical glosses (48).   This section, in the order and completeness in which we find it in Matthew, is wanting in Luke's sermon on the mount; a decisive proof that the latter has deficiencies.   For not only does this chapter contain the fundamental thought of the discourse as given by Matthew, but the desultory sayings which Luke gives, concerning the love of enemies, mercifulness and beneficence, only acquire a definite purpose and point of union in the contrast between the spiritual interpretation of the law given by Jesus, and the carnal one given by the doctors of the time.   The words, too, with which Luke makes Jesus proceed after the last woe : *But I say unto you*, and those at v. 39, *And he spake a parable unto them*, have been correctly pointed out as indicative of chasms [19].   As regards the isolated parallel passages, the admonition to a quick reconciliation with an adversary (v. 25 f.), is, to say the least, not so easily brought into connexion with the foregoing matter in Luke (xii. 58.) as in Matthew [20].   It is still worse with the passage in Luke which is parallel with Matt. v. 32 ; this text (relative to divorce), which in Matthew is linked in the general chain

---

[18] This cause is overlooked by Schleiermacher, s. 205 ; comp. De Wette, in loc.

[19] Schleiermacher, ut sup. s. 90.   Tholück, s. 21.

[20] Tholück, s. 12, 187 ; De Wette, in loc.

of ideas, is in Luke (xvi. 18.) thrust into one of the apertures we have noticed, between the assurance of the perpetuity of the law and the parable of the rich man. Olshausen tries to find a thread of connexion between the passage and the one preceding it, by interpreting *adultery,* μοιχεύειν, allegorically, as faithlessness to the divine law; and Schleiermacher [21] attaches it to the succeeding parable by referring it to the adulterous Herod: but such interpretations are altogether visionary [22]. Probably tradition had apprized the evangelist that Jesus, after the foregoing declaration as to the perpetuity of the Mosaic law, had enunciated his severe principle on the subject of divorce, and hence he gave it this position, not knowing more of its original connexion. In Matt. xix. 9, we find a reiteration of this principle on an occasion very likely to call it forth. The exhortations to patience and submissiveness, form, in Matthew, the spiritual interpretation of the old rule, *an eye for an eye,* &c., and are therefore a following out of the previous train of thought. In Luke (vi. 29.), they are introduced with much less precision by the command concerning love to enemies: which command is also decidedly better given in Matthew as the rectification of the precept, *Thou shalt love thy neighbour, and hate thine enemy* (43 ff.). Again: the observation that to love friends is nothing more than bad men can do, is, in Matthew, made, in order to controvert the traditional perversion of the Mosaic injunction to love one's neighbour, into a permission to hate enemies: in Luke, the observation follows the rule, *Whatsoever ye would that men should do to you,* &c., which in Matthew occurs farther on (vii. 12.) without any connexion. On the whole, if the passage in Luke from vi. 2—36, be compared with the corresponding one in Matthew, there will be found in the latter an orderly course of thought; in the former, considerable confusion [23].

The warnings against Pharisaic hypocrisy (vi. 1—6) are

[21] Ut sup. 206 f.
[22] Comp. De Wette exeg. Handb. 1, 2, s. 86.
[23] De Wette, exeg. Handb. 1, 1, s. 48.

without a parallel in Luke; but he has one of the model prayer, which recent criticism has turned not a little to the disadvantage of Matthew. The ancient harmonists, it is true, had no hesitation in supposing that Jesus delivered this prayer twice,—in the connexion in which it is given by Matthew, as well as under the circumstances narrated by Luke (xi. 1 ff.) [24]. But if Jesus had already in the sermon on the mount given a model prayer, his disciples would scarcely have requested one afterwards, as if nothing of the kind had occurred; and it is still more improbable that Jesus would repeat the same formulary, without any recollection that he had delivered it to these disciples long before. Hence our most recent critics have decided that Luke alone has preserved the natural and true occasion on which this prayer was communicated, and that like many other fragments, it was interpolated in Matthew's sermon on the mount by the writer [25]. But the vaunted naturalness of Luke's representation, I, for one, cannot discover. Apart from the improbability, admitted even by the above critics, that the disciples of Jesus should have remained without any direction to pray until the last journey, in which Luke places the scene; it is anything but natural that Jesus should abstain from giving his disciples the exemplar which was in his mind until they sought for it, and that then he should forthwith fall into prayer. He had, doubtless, often prayed in their circle from the commencement of their intercourse; and if so, their request was superfluous, and must, as in John xiv. 9, have produced only an admonition to recollect what they had long seen and heard in his society. The account of Luke seems to have been framed on mere conjecture; it was known that the above prayer proceeded from Jesus, and the further question as to the motive for its communication, received the gratuitous answer: without doubt his disciples had asked him for such an exemplar. Without, therefore, maintaining that Matthew has preserved to us the connexion in which

---

[24] Orig. de. orat. xviii. and Hess, Gesch. Jesu, 2, s. 48 f.

[25] Schleiermacher, ut sup. s. 173; Olshausen, 1, s. 235; Sieffert, s. 78 ff. Neander, s. 235 f. note.

this prayer was originally uttered by Jesus, we are not the less in doubt whether it has a more accurate position in Luke [26]. With regard to the elements of the prayer, it is impossible to deny what Wetstein says : *tota hæc oratio ex formulis Hebræorum concinnata est* [27] ; but Fritzsche's observation is also just, that desires of so general a nature might be uttered in the prayers of various persons, even in similar phraseology, without any other cause than the broad uniformity of human feeling [28]. We may add that the selection and allocation of the petitions in the prayer are entirely original, and bear the impress of that religious consciousness which Jesus possessed and sought to impart to his followers [29]. Matthew inserts after the conclusion of the prayer two propositions, which are properly the corollary of the third petition, but which seem inaptly placed, not only because they are severed by the concluding petition from the passage to which they have reference, but because they have no point of coincidence with the succeeding censures and admonitions which turn on the hypocrisy of the Pharisaic fasts. Mark, however, has still more infelicitously appended these propositions to the discourse of Jesus on the efficacy of believing prayer (xi. 25) [30].

At vi. 19, the thread of strict connexion is broken, according to the admission of Paulus, and so far all expositors are bound to agree with him. But his position, that notwithstanding the admitted lack of coherence in the succeeding collection of sentences, Jesus spoke them consecutively, is not equally tenable ; on the contrary, our more recent critics have all the probabilities on their side when they suppose, that in this latter half of the sermon on the mount Matthew has incorporated a variety of sayings uttered by Jesus on different occasions. First stands the apothegm on earthly and heavenly treasures (19—21),

[26] Comp. De Wette, exeg. Handb. 1, 1, s. 69. 1, 2, s. 65.

[27] N. T. 1, 323. The parallels may be seen in Wetstein and Lightfoot.

[28] Comm. in Matt. p. 265.

[29] Comp. De Wette, 1, 1, s. 69 ff. ; Neander, s. 237 ff.

[30] Comp. De Wette, 1, 2, s. 176.

which Luke, with more apparent correctness, inserts in a discourse of Jesus, the entire drift of which is to warn his adherents against earthly cares (xii. 33 f.).   It is otherwise with the
next sentence, on the eye being the light of the body. Luke an
nexes this to the apothegm already mentioned on the light that
is to be exhibited ; now as the *light*, λύχνος, placed on a candlestick, denotes something quite distinct from what is intended
by the comparison of the eye to a *light*, λύχνος, the only reason
for combining the two apothegms lies in the bare word λύχνος : a
rule of association which belongs properly to the dictionary, and
which, beyond it, is worse than none.   Then follows, also without any apparent connexion, the apothegm on the two masters,
appended by Luke to the parable of the steward, with which it
happens to have the word *Mammon,* μαμωνᾶς, in common. Next
comes, in Matthew v. 25—34, a dissuasion from earthly solicitude, on the ground that natural objects flourish and are sustained without anxiety on their part ; in Luke, this doctrine is
consistently united with the parable (found only in the third
gospel) of the man who, in the midst of amassing earthly treasures, is summoned away by death (xii. 22 ff.) [31]. The warning not to be blind to our own faults while we are sharp-sighted
and severe towards those of others (vii. 1—5), would, if we rejected the passage from v. 19, of chap. vi. to the end, form a suitable continuation to the previous admonition against Pharisaic
sanctimoniousness (vi. 16—18), and might, therefore, have belonged to the original body of the discourse [32]. This is the more
probable because Luke has the same warning in his sermon on
the mount (37 f. 41 f.), where it happens to assort very well with
the preceding exhortation to mercifulness ; but at v. 39 and 40,
and part of 38, it is interrupted by subjects altogether irrelevant.
The text, *With what measure ye mete,* &c., is very inappropriately interposed by Mark (iv. 24), in a passage similar in

[31] From vi. 19 to the end of the chapter, even Neander finds no orderly association, and conjectures that the editor of the Greek Gospel of Matthew was the
compiler of this latter half of the discourse (p. 169, note).

[32] Neander, ut sup. ; De Wette, in loc.

kind to one of Luke's intermediate miscellanies. V. 6, in Matthew, is equally destitute of connexion and parallel; but the succeeding assurances and arguments as to the efficacy of prayer (v. 7—11), are found in Luke xi. 9, very fitly associated with another parable peculiar to that evangelist: that of the friend awaked at midnight. The apothegm, *What ye would that men should do unto you*, &c., is quite isolated in Matthew; in Luke, it has only an imperfect connexion [33]. The following passage (v. 13 f.) on the *strait gate*, στενὴ πύλη, is introduced in Luke (xiii. 23.) by the question, addressed to Jesus: *Are there few that be saved?* εἰ ὀλίγοι οἱ σωζόμενοι; which seems likely enough to have been conceived by one who knew that Jesus had uttered such a saying as the above, but was at a loss for an occasion that might prompt the idea; moreover, the image is far less completely carried out in Luke than in Matthew, and is blended with parabolical elements [34]. The apothegm on the tree being known by its fruits (v. 16—20), appears in Luke (vi. 43 ff.), and even in Matthew, farther on (xii. 33 ff.), to have a general application, but in Matthew's sermon on the mount, it has a special relation to the false prophets; in Luke, it is in the last degree misplaced. The denunciation of those who say to Jesus, *Lord, Lord,* but who, on account of their evil deeds will be rejected by him at the day of judgment (21—23), decidedly presupposes the Messiahship of Jesus, and cannot, therefore, have well belonged to so early a period as that of the sermon on the mount; hence it is more appropriately placed by Luke (xiii. 25 ff.). The peroration of the discourse is, as we have mentioned, common to both evangelists.

The foregoing comparison shows us that the discourses of Jesus, like fragments of granite, could not be dissolved by the flood of oral tradition; but they were not seldom torn from their natural connexion, floated away from their original situation, and deposited in places to which they did not properly belong.

---

[33] De Wette, 1, 2, s. 45.
[34] Ib. in loc. des Lukas.

Relative to this effect, there is this distinction between the three first evangelists; Matthew, like an able compiler, though far from being sufficiently informed to give each relic in its original connexion, has yet for the most part succeeded in judiciously associating analogous materials; while the two other evangelists have left many small fragments just where chance threw them, in the intervals between longer discourses. Luke has laboured in some instances to combine these fragments artificially, but he could not thus compensate for the absence of natural connexion.

§ 77.

INSTRUCTIONS TO THE TWELVE.   LAMENTATIONS OVER THE GALILEAN CITIES.   JOY
OVER THE CALLING OF THE SIMPLE.

The first gospel (x.) reports another long discourse as having been delivered by Jesus, on the occasion of his sending out the twelve to preach the kingdom of heaven. Part of this discourse is peculiar to the first gospel; that portion of it which is common to the two other synoptists is only partially assigned by them to the same occasion, Luke introducing its substance in connexion with the mission of the seventy (x. 2 ff.), and in a subsequent conversation with the disciples (xii. 2 ff.). Some portion of the discourse is also found repeated both in Matthew and the other evangelists, in the prophetic description given by Jesus of his second advent.

In this instance again, while the older harmonists have no hesitation in supposing a repetition of the same discourse [1], our more recent critics are of opinion that Luke only has the true occasions and the original arrangement of the materials, and that Matthew has assembled them according to his own discretion [2]. Those expositors who are apologetically inclined, maintain that Matthew was not only conscious of here associating sayings uttered at various times, but presumed that this

---

[1] E. g. Hess, Gesch. Jesu, 1, s. 545.
[2] Schulz, ut. sup. s. 308, 314 ; Sieffert, s. 80 ff.

would be obvious to his readers[3]. On the other hand, it is justly observed that the manner in which the discourse is introduced by the words: *These twelve Jesus sent forth, and commanded them* (v. 5); and closed by the words: *when Jesus made an end of commanding his twelve disciples,* &c. (xi. 1.); proves clearly enough that it was the intention of the evangelist to give his compilation the character of a continuous harangue[4].

Much that is peculiar to Matthew in this discourse, appears to be merely an amplification on thoughts which are also found in the corresponding passages of the two other synoptists; but there are two particulars in the opening of the instructions as detailed by the former, which differ specifically from anything presented by his fellow evangelists. These are the limitation of the agency of the disciples to the Jews (v. 5, 6), and the commission (associated with that to announce the kingdom of heaven and heal the sick, of which Luke also speaks, ix. 2,) to raise the dead: a surprising commission, since we know of no instances previous to the departure of Jesus, in which the apostles raised the dead; and to suppose such when they are not narrated, after the example of Olshausen, is an expedient to which few will be inclined.

All that the synoptists have strictly in common in the instructions to the twelve, are the rules for their external conduct; how they were to journey, and how to behave under a variety of circumstances (Matt. v. 9—11, 14; Mark vi. 8—11; Luke ix. 3—5). Here, however, we find a discrepancy; according to Matthew and Luke, Jesus forbids the disciples to take with them, not only gold, a scrip, and the like, but even *shoes, ὑποδήματα,* and a *staff, ῥάβδον*; according to Mark, on the contrary, he merely forbids their taking more than a *staff* and *sandals, εἰ μὴ ῥάβδον μόνον* and *σανδάλια.* This discrepancy is most easily accounted for by the admission, that tradition only preserved a reminiscence of Jesus having signified the sim-

---

[3] Olshausen, in loc. The latter bold assertion in Kern, über den Ursprung des Evang. Matth., s. 63.

[4] Schulz, s. 315.

plicity of the apostolic equipment by the mention of the staff and shoes, and that hence one of the evangelists understood that Jesus had interdicted all travelling requisites except these; the other, that these also were included in his prohibition. It was consistent with Mark's love of the picturesque to imagine a wandering apostle furnished with a staff, and therefore to give the preference to the former view.

It is on the occasion of the mission of the seventy, that Luke (x. 2) puts into the mouth of Jesus the words which Matthew gives (ix. 37 f.) as the motive for sending forth the twelve, namely, the apothegm, *The harvest truly is ready, but the labourers are few;* also the declaration that the labourer is worthy of his hire (v. 7. comp. Matt. x. 10); the discourse on the apostolic salutation and its effect (Matt. v. 12 f. Luke v. 5 f.); the denunciation of those who should reject the apostles and their message (Matt. v. 15; Luke v. 12); and finally, the words, *Behold, I send you forth as lambs,* &c.(Matt. v. 16; Luke v. 3.) The sequence of these propositions is about equally natural in both cases. Their completeness is alternately greater in the one than in the other; but Matthew's additions generally turn on essentials, as in v. 16; those of Luke on externals, as in v. 7, 8, and in v. 4, where there is the singular injunction to salute no man by the way, which might appear an unhistorical exaggeration of the urgency of the apostolic errand, did we not know that the Jewish greetings of that period were not a little ceremonious[5]. Sieffert observes that the instructions which Jesus gave—according to Matthew, to the twelve, according to Luke, to the seventy—might, so far as their tenor is concerned, have been imparted with equal fitness on either occasion; but I doubt this, for it seems to me improbable that Jesus should, as Luke states, dismiss his more confidential disciples with scanty rules for their outward conduct, and that to the seventy he should make communications of much greater moment and pathos[6]. The above critic at length decides in favour of Luke,

---

[5] Vid. De Wette, Archäol. § 265, and in loc.
[6] Comp. De Wette, exeg. Handb. 1, 1, s. 99.

whose narrative appears to him more precise, because it distinguishes the seventy from the twelve. We have already discussed this point, and have found that a comparison is rather to the advantage of Matthew. The blessing pronounced on him who should give even a cup of cold water to the disciples of Jesus (v. 42), is at least more judiciously inserted by Matthew as the conclusion of the discourse of instructions, than in the endless confusion of the latter part of Mark ix. (v. 41), where ἐάν, (*if*), and ὃς ἄν, (*whosoever*), seem to form the only tie between the successive propositions.

The case is otherwise when we regard those portions of the discourse which Luke places in his twelfth chapter, and even later, and which in Matthew are distinguishable as a second part of the same discourse. Such are the directions to the apostles as to their conduct before tribunals (Matt. x. 19 f. ; Luke xii. 11) ; the exhortation not to fear those who can only kill the body (Matt. v. 28 ; Luke v. 4 f.) ; the warning against the denial of Jesus (Matt. v. 32 f.; Luke v. 8 f.) ; the discourse on the general disunion of which he would be the cause (Matt. v. 34 ff.; Luke v. 51 ff.) ; a passage to which Matthew, prompted apparently by the enumeration of the members of a family, attaches the declaration of Jesus that these are not to be valued above him, that his cross must be taken, &c., which he partly repeats on a subsequent occasion, and in a more suitable connexion (xvi. 24 f.) ; further, predictions which recur in the discourse on the Mount of Olives, relative to the universal persecution of the disciples of Jesus (v. 17 f. 22. comp. xxiv. 9, 13) ; the saying which Luke inserts in the sermon on the mount (vi. 40), and which also appears in John (xv. 20), that the disciple has no claim to a better lot than his master (v. 24 f.) ; lastly, the direction, which is peculiar to the discourse in Matthew, to flee from one city to another, with the accompanying consolation (v. 23). These commands and exhortations have been justly pronounced by critics[7] to be unsuitable to the first

[7] Schulz, s. 308; Sieffert, s. 82 ff.

mission of the twelve, which, like the alleged mission of the seventy, had no other than happy results (Luke ix. 10; x. 17); they presuppose the troublous circumstances which supervened after the death of Jesus, or perhaps in the latter period of his life. According to this, Luke is more correct than Matthew in assigning these discourses to the last journey of Jesus[8]; unless, indeed, such descriptions of the subsequent fate of the apostles and other adherents of Jesus were produced *ex eventu*, after his death, and put into his mouth in the form of prophecies; a conjecture which is strongly suggested by the words, *He who taketh not up his cross*, &c. (v. 38.)[9].

The next long discourse of Jesus in Matthew (chap. xi.) we have already considered, so far as it relates to the Baptist. From v. 20—24, there follow complaints and threatenings against the Galilean cities, in which *most of his mighty works were done*, and which, nevertheless, *believed not*. Our modern critics are perhaps right in their opinion that these apostrophes are less suitable to the period of his Galilean ministry, in which Matthew places them, than to that in which they are introduced by Luke (x. 13 ff.); namely, when Jesus had left Galilee, and was on his way to Judea and Jerusalem, with a view to his final experiment[10]. But a consideration of the immediate context seems to reverse the probability. In Matthew, the description of the ungracious reception which Jesus and John had alike met with, leads very naturally to the accusations against those places which had been the chief theatres of the ministry of the former; but it is difficult to suppose, according to Luke, that Jesus would speak of his past sad experience to the seventy, whose minds must have been entirely directed to the future, unless we conceive that he chose a subject so little adapted to

---

[8] The satisfactory connexion which modern criticism finds throughout the 12th chap. of Luke, I am as little able to discover as Tholück, Auslegung der Bergpredigt, s. 13 f., who has strikingly exposed the partiality of Schleiermacher for Luke, to the prejudice of Matthew.

[9] Vid. De Wette in loc.

[10] Schleiermacher, über den Lukas, s. 169 f. ; Schneckenburger, über den Ursprung u. s. f., s. 32 f.

the exigencies of those whom he was addressing, in order to unite the threatened judgment on the Galilean cities, with that which he had just denounced against the cities that should reject his messengers. But it is more likely that this association proceeded solely from the writer, who, by the comparison of a city that should prove refractory to the disciples of Jesus, to Sodom, was reminded of the analogous comparison to Tyre and Sidon, of places that had been disobedient to Jesus himself, without perceiving the incongruity of the one with the circumstances which had dictated the other[11].

The *joy*, ἀγαλλίασις, expressed by Jesus (v. 25—27) on account of the insight afforded to *babes*, νηπίοις, is but loosely attached by Matthew to the preceding maledictions. As it supposes a change in the mental frame of Jesus, induced by pleasing circumstances, Luke (x. 17. 21 ff.) would have all the probabilities on his side, in making the return of the seventy with satisfactory tidings the cause of the above expression; were it not that the appointment of the seventy, and consequently their return, are altogether problematical; besides, it is possible to refer the passage in question to the return of the twelve from their mission. Matthew connects with this rejoicing of Jesus his invitation to the *weary and heavy laden* (v. 28—30). This is wanting in Luke, who, instead, makes Jesus turn to his disciples *privately*, and pronounce them blessed in being privileged to see and hear things which many prophets and kings yearned after in vain (23 f.): an observation which does not so specifically agree with the preceding train of thought, as the context assigned to it by Matthew, and which is moreover inserted by the latter evangelist in a connexion (xiii. 16 f.) that may be advantageously confronted with that of Luke.

[11] Comp. De Wette, exeg. Handb., 1, 1, s. 110. 1, 2, s. 62.

§ 78.

According to Matthew (chap. xiii.), Jesus delivered seven parables, all relating to the βασιλεία τῶν οὐρανῶν. Modern criticism, however, has doubted whether Jesus really uttered so many of these symbolical discourses on one occasion [1]. The parable, it has been observed, is a kind of problem, to be solved by the reflection of the hearer; hence after every parable a pause is requisite, if it be the object of the teacher to convey real instruction, and not to distract by a multiplicity of ill-understood images [2]. It will, at least, be admitted, with Neander, that parables on the same or closely-related subjects can only be spoken consecutively, when, under manifold forms, and from various points of view, they lead to the same result [3]. Among the seven parables in question, those of the mustard-seed and the leaven have a common fundamental idea, differently shadowed forth—the gradual growth and ultimate prevalence of the kingdom of God : those of the net and the tares represent the mingling of the good with the bad in the kingdom of God; those of the treasure and the pearl inculcate the inestimable and all-indemnifying value of the kingdom of God; and the parable of the sower depicts the unequal susceptibility of men to the preaching of the kingdom of God. Thus there are no less than four separate fundamental ideas involved in this collection of parables—ideas which are indeed connected by their general relation to the kingdom of God, but which present this object under aspects so widely different, that for their thorough comprehension a pause after each was indispensable. Hence, it has been concluded, Jesus would not merit the praise of being a judicious teacher, if as Matthew represents, he had spoken all the above parables in rapid succession [4].

[1] Schulz, über das Abendmahl, s. 314.
[2] Olshausen, bibl. Comm. 1, s. 437.
[3] L. J. Chr., s. 175.
[4] Schneckenburger, über den Ursprung u. s. f., s. 33.

If we suppose in this instance, again, an assemblage of discourses similar in kind, but delivered on different occasions, we are anew led to the discussion as to whether Matthew was aware of the latter circumstance, or whether he believed that he was recording a continuous harangue. The introductory form, *And he spake many things to them in parables* (v. 3): καὶ ἐλάλησεν αὐτοῖς πολλὰ ἐν παραβολαῖς, and the concluding one, *when Jesus had finished these parables* (v. 53): ὅτε ἐτέλεσεν ὁ Ἰησοῦς τὰς παραβολὰς ταύτας, seem to be a clear proof that he did not present the intermediate matter as a compilation. Mark, indeed, narrates (iv. 10), that at the close of the first parable, the disciples being again, καταμόνας, *in private*, with Jesus, asked him for its interpretation; and hence it has been contended [5] that there was an interruption of the discourse at this point; but this cannot serve to explain the account of Matthew, for he represents the request of the disciples as being preferred on the spot, without any previous retirement from the crowd; thus proving that he did not suppose such an interruption. The concluding form which Matthew inserts after the fourth parable (v. 34 f.), might, with better reason, be adduced as intimating an interruption, for he there comprises all the foregoing parables in one address by the words, *All these things spake Jesus in parables*, &c., ταῦτα πάντα ἐλάλησεν ὁ Ἰησοῦς ἐν παραβολαῖς κ. τ. λ., and makes the pause still more complete by the application of an Old Testament prophecy; moreover, Jesus is here said (36) to change his locality, to dismiss the multitude to whom he had hitherto been speaking on the shore of the Galilean sea, and enter *the house*, εἰς τὴν οἰκίαν, where he gives three new parables, in addition to the interpretation which his disciples had solicited of the second. But that the delivery of the last three parables was separated from that of the preceding ones by a change of place, and consequently by a short interval of time, very little alters the state of the case. For it is highly improbable that Jesus would without intermission tax the memory of the populace.

whose minds it was so easy to overburthen, with four parables,
two of which were highly significant; and that he should forthwith overwhelm his disciples, whose power of comprehension he
had been obliged to aid in the application of the first two parables, with three new ones, instead of ascertaining if they were
capable of independently expounding the third and fourth.
Further, we have only to look more closely at Matthew's narrative, in order to observe that he has fallen quite involuntarily
on the interruption at v. 34 ff. If it were his intention to com-
municate a series of parables, with the explanations that Jesus
privately gave to his disciples of the two which were most important, and were therefore to be placed at the head of the
series, there were only three methods on which he could proceed. First, he might make Jesus, immediately after the enun-
ciation of a parable, give its interpretation to his disciples in
the presence of the multitude, as he actually does in the case of
the first parable (10—23). But the representation is beset
with the difficulty of conceiving how Jesus, surrounded by a
crowd, whose expectation was on the stretch, could find leisure
for a conversation aside with his disciples[6]. This inconvenience Mark perceived, and therefore chose the second resource
that was open to him—that of making Jesus with his disciples
withdraw after the first parable into *the house*, and there deliver
its interpretation. But such a proceeding would be too great a
hindrance to one who proposed publicly to deliver several parables one after the other; for if Jesus returned to the house immediately after the first parable, he had left the scene in which
the succeeding ones could be conveniently imparted to the
people. Consequently, the narrator in the first gospel cannot,
with respect to the interpretation of the second parable, either
repeat his first plan, or resort to the second; he therefore
adopts a third, and proceeding uninterruptedly through two
further parables, it is only at their close that he conducts Jesus
to the house, and there makes him impart the arrear of inter-

[6] Schleiermacher, s. 120.

pretation. Herewith there arose in the mind of the narrator a sort of rivalry between the parables which he had yet in reserve, and the interpretation, the arrear of which embarrassed him ; as soon as the former were absent from his recollection, the latter would be present with its inevitably associated form of conclusion and return homeward ; and when any remaining parables recurred to him, he was obliged to make them the sequel of the interpretation. Thus it befel with the three last parables in Matthew's narration ; so that he was reduced almost against his will to make the disciples their sole participants, though it does not appear to have been the custom of Jesus thus to clothe his private instructions ; and Mark (v. 33 f.) plainly supposes the parables which follow the interpretation of the second, to be also addressed to the people [7].

Mark, who (iv. 1) depicts the same scene by the sea-side, as Matthew, has in connexion with it only three parables, of which the first and third correspond to the first and third of Matthew, but the middle one is commonly deemed peculiar to Mark [8]. Matthew has in its place the parable wherein the kingdom of heaven is likened to a man who sowed good seed in his field ; but while men slept, the enemy came and sowed tares among it, which grew up with the wheat. The servants know not from whence the tares come, and propose to root them up ; but the master commands them to let both grow together until the harvest, when it will be time enough to separate them. In Mark, Jesus compares the kingdom of heaven to a man who casts seed into the ground, and while he sleeps and rises again, the seed passes, he knows not how, from one stage of development to another: *and when it is ripe, he puts in the sickle, because the harvest is come.* In this parable there is wanting what constitutes the dominant idea in that of Matthew, the tares, sown by the enemy ; but as, nevertheless, the other ideas, of sowing, sleeping, growing one knows not how, and

[7] Fritzsche, Comm. in Marc. s. 120, 128, 134 ; De Wette, in loc.

[8] Comp. Saunier, über die Quellen des Markus, s. 74 ; Fritzsche ut sup. ; De Wette in loc.

harvest, wholly correspond, it may be questioned whether Mark does not here merely give the same parable in a different version, which he preferred to that of Matthew, because it seemed more intermediate between the first parable of the sower, and the third of the mustard-seed.

Luke, also, has only three of the seven parables given in Matt. xiii. ; namely, those of the sower, the mustard-seed, and the leaven; so that the parables of the buried treasure, the pearl, and the net, as also that of the tares in the field, are peculiar to Matthew. The parable of the sower is placed by Luke (viii. 4 ff.) somewhat earlier, and in other circumstances, than by Matthew, and apart from the two other parables which he has in common with the first evangelist's series. These he introduces later, xiii. 18—21'; a position which recent critics unanimously acknowledge as the correct one[9]. But this decision is one of the most remarkable to which the criticism of the present age has been led by its partiality to Luke. For if we examine the vaunted connectedness of this evangelist's passages, we find that Jesus, having healed a woman *bowed down by a spirit of infirmity*, silences the punctilious ruler of the synagogue by the argument about the ox and ass, after which it is added (v. 17), *And when he had said these things, all his adversaries were ashamed; and all the people rejoiced for all the glorious things that were done by him.* Surely so complete and marked a form of conclusion is intended to wind up the previous narrative, and one cannot conceive that the sequel went forward in the same scene; on the contrary, the phrases, *then said he,* and *again he said,* by which the parables are connected, indicate that the writer had no longer any knowledge of the occasion on which Jesus uttered them, and hence inserted them at random in this indeterminate manner, far less judiciously than Matthew, who at least was careful to associate them with analogous materials[10].

---

[9] Schleiermacher, ut. sup. s. 192; Olshausen, 1, s. 431 ; Schneckenburger, ut sup. s. 33.

[10] Comp. De Wette, exeg. Handb., 1, 2, s. 73 f.

We proceed to notice the other evangelical parables [11], and first among them, those which are peculiar to one evangelist. We come foremost in Matthew to the parable of the servant (xviii. 23 ff.) who, although his lord had forgiven him a debt of ten thousand talents, had no mercy on his fellow-servant who owed him a hundred; tolerably well introduced by an exhortation to placability (v. 15), and the question of Peter, *How oft shall my brother sin against me, and I forgive him?* Likewise peculiar to Matthew is the parable of the labourers in the vineyard (xx. 1 ff.), which suitably enough forms a counterpoise to the foregoing promise of a rich recompense to the disciples. Of the sentences which Matthew appends to this parable (v. 16), the first, *So the last shall be first, and the first last,* by which he had also prefaced it (xix. 30), is the only one with which it has any internal connexion; the other, *for many are called, but few chosen,* rather gives the moral of the parable of the royal feast and the wedding garment, in connexion with which Matthew actually repeats it (xxii. 14). It was well adapted, however, even torn from this connexion, to circulate as an independent apothegm, and as it appeared fitting to the evangelist to annex one or more short sentences to the end of a parable, he might be induced, by some superficial similarity to the one already given, to place them in companionship. Farther, the parable of the two sons sent into the vineyard, is also peculiar to Matthew (xxi. 28 ff.), and is not ill-placed in connexion with the foregoing questions and retorts between Jesus and the Pharisees; its anti-Pharisaic significance is also well brought out by the sequel (31 f.).

Among the parables which are peculiar to Luke, that of the two debtors (vii. 41 ff.); that of the good Samaritan (x. 30 ff.); that of the man whose accumulation of earthly treasure is interrupted by death (xii. 16 ff. comp. Wis. xi. 17 ff.); and also the two which figure the efficacy of importunate prayer (xi. 5 ff. xviii. 2 ff.); have a definite, clear signification, and with the ex-

[11] Analogies to these parables and apothegms, are given out of the rabbinical literature by Wetstein, Lightfoot, and Schöttgen, in loc.

ception of the last, which is introduced abruptly, a tolerably
consistent connexion.   We may learn from the two last parables, that it is often necessary entirely to abstract particular
features from the parables of Jesus, seeing that in one of them
God is represented by a lukewarm friend, in the other by an
unjust judge.   To the latter is annexed the parable of the
Pharisee and Publican (9—14), of which only Schleiermacher,
on the strength of a connexion, fabricated by himself between
it and the foregoing, can deny the antipharisaic tendency[12].
The parables of the lost sheep, the piece of silver, and the
prodigal son (Luke xv. 3—32), have the same direction.
Matthew also has the first of these (xviii. 12 ff.), but in a different connexion, which determines its import somewhat differently, and without doubt, as will presently be shown, less correctly.   It is easy to imagine that these three parables were
spoken in immediate succession, because the second is merely a
variation of the first, and the third is an amplification and
elucidation of them both.   Whether, according to the opinion
of modern criticism, the two succeeding parables also belong
with the above to one continuous discourse[13], must be determined by a closer examination of their contents, which are in
themselves noteworthy.

The parable of the unjust steward, notoriously the *crux in-
terpretum*, is yet without any intrinsic difficulty.   If we read
to the end of the parable, including the moral (v. 9), we gather
the simple result, that the man who without precisely using
unjust means to obtain riches, is yet in the sight of God an
unprofitable servant, δοῦλος ἀχρεῖος (Luke xvii. 10), and, in
the employment of the gifts intrusted to him by God, a *steward
of injustice*, οἰκονόμος τῆς ἀδικίας, may best atone for this per-
vading unfaithfulness by lenity and beneficence towards his
fellow-men, and may by their intervention procure a place in
heaven.   It is true that the beneficence of the fictitious steward
is a fraud; but we must abstract this particular, as, in the case

---

[12] Ueber den Lukas, s. 220.
[13] Schleiermacher, ut sup. s. 202 ff.   Olshausen in loc.

of two previous parables, we have to abstract the lukewarmness of the friend, and the injustice of the judge: nay, the necessity for such an abstraction is intimated in the narrative itself, for from v. 8 we gather that what the steward did in a worldly spirit is, in the application, to be understood in a more exalted sense of the *children of light.* Certainly, if we suppose the words, *He that is faithful in that which is least,* &c. (10—12) to have been uttered in their present connexion, it appears as if the steward were set forth as a model, deserving in some sense or other the praise of faithfulness; and when (v. 13) it is said that no servant can serve two masters, the intended inference seems to be that this steward had held to the rightful one. Hence we have expositions such as that of Schleiermacher, who under the master understands the Romans; under the debtors, the Jewish people; under the steward, the publicans, who were generous to the latter at the expense of the former; thus, in the most arbitrary manner, transforming the master into a violent man, and justifying the steward [14]. Olshausen carries the perversion of the parable to the extreme, for he degrades the master, who, by his judicial position evidently announces himself as the representative of God, into ἄρχων τοῦ κόσμου τούτου, *the prince of this world,* while he exalts the steward into the image of a man who applies the riches of this world to spiritual objects. But as in the moral (v. 9) the parable has a consistent ending; and as inaccurate association is by no means unexampled in Luke; it is not admissible to concede to the following verses any influence over the interpretation of the parable, unless a close relation of idea can be made manifest. Now the fact is, that the very opposite, namely, the most perplexing diversity, exists. Moreover, it is not difficult to show what might have seduced Luke into a false association. In the parable there was mention of the *mammon of unrighteousness,* μαμωνᾶς τῆς ἀδικίας; this suggested to him the saying of Jesus, that he who proves faithful in the ἀδίκῳ μαμωνᾷ, *the unrighteous*

[14] Ut sup.

mammon, as that which is least, may also have the true riches committed to his trust.   But the word *mammon* having once taken possession of the writer's mind, how could he avoid recollecting the well-known aphorism of Jesus on God and Mammon, as two incompatible masters, and adding it (v. 13), however superfluously, to the preceding texts? [15].   That by this addition the previous parable was placed in a thoroughly false light, gave the writer little concern, perhaps because he had not seized its real meaning, or because, in the endeavour completely to disburthen his evangelical meaning, he lost all solicitude about the sequence of his passages.   It ought, in general, to be more considered, that those of our evangelists who, according to the now prevalent opinion, noted down oral traditions, must, in the composition of their writings, have exerted their memory to an extent that would repress the activity of reflection; consequently the arrangement of the materials in their narratives is governed by the association of ideas, the laws of which are partly dependent on external relations; and we need not be surprised to find many passages, especially from the discourses of Jesus, ranged together for the sole cause that they happen to have in common certain striking consonant words.

If from hence we glance back on the position, that the parable of the unjust steward must have been spoken in connexion with the foregoing one of the prodigal son, we perceive that it rests merely on a false interpretation.   According to Schleiermacher, it is the defence of the publicans against the Pharisees, that

---

[15] Schneckenburger has decided, Beiträge, No. V. where he refutes Olshausen's interpretation of the parable, that this verse does not really belong to its present position, while with respect to the preceding verses from v. 9, he finds it possible to hold the contrary opinion.   De Wette also considers that v. 13 is the only one decidedly out of place.   He thinks it possible, by supplying an intermediate proposition, which he supposes the writer to have omitted, and which led from the *prudent* use of riches to faithfulness in preserving those entrusted to us, to give a sufficient connexion to v. 9 and 10—12, without necessarily referring the idea of faithfulness to the conduct of the steward.   The numerous attempts, both ancient and modern, to explain the parable of the steward without a critical dislocation of the associated passages, are only so many proofs that it is absolutely requisite to a satisfactory interpretation.

forms the bond; but there is no trace of publicans and Pharisees in the latter parable. According to Olshausen, the compassionate love of God, represented in the foregoing parable, is placed in juxtaposition with the compassionate love of man, represented in the succeeding one; but simple beneficence is the sole idea on which the latter turns, and a parallel between this and the manner in which God meets the lost with pardon, is equally remote from the intention of the teacher and the nature of the subject. The remark (v. 14) that the Pharisees heard all these things, and, being covetous, derided Jesus, does not necessarily refer to the individuals mentioned xv. 2, so as to imply that they had listened to the intermediate matter as one continuous discourse; and even if that were the case, it would only show the view of the writer with respect to the connectedness of the parables; a view which, in the face of the foregoing investigation, cannot possibly be binding on us [16].

We have already discussed the passage from v. 15 to 18; it consists of disconnected sayings, and to the last, on adultery, is annexed the parable of the rich man, in a manner which, as we have already noticed, it is attempted in vain to show as a real connexion. It must, however, be conceded to Schleiermacher, that if we separate them, the alternative, namely, the common application of the parable to the penal justice of God, is attended with great difficulties [17]. For there is no indication throughout the parable, of any actions on the part of the rich man and Lazarus, that could, according to our notions, justify the exaltation of the one to a place in Abraham's bosom, and the condemnation of the other to torment; the guilt of the one appears to lie in his wealth, the merit of the other in his poverty. It is indeed generally supposed of the rich man, that he was immoderate in his indulgence, and that he had treated Lazarus unkindly [18]. But the latter is nowhere intimated; for the picture of the beggar lying at the door of the rich man, is not

[16] Comp. De Wette, exeg. Handb. 1, 2, s. 80.
[17] Ut. sup. s. 208.
[18] Vid. Kuinöl, in loc.

intended in the light of a reproach to the latter, because he
might easily have tendered his aid, and yet neglected to do so ;
it is designed to exhibit the contrast, not only between the
earthly condition of the two parties, but between their proximity
in this life, and their wide separation in another. So the other
particular, that the beggar was eager for the crumbs that fell
from the rich man's table, does not imply that the rich man
denied him this pittance, or that he ought to have given him
more than the mere crumbs ; it denotes the deep degradation of
the earthly lot of Lazarus compared with that of the rich man,
in opposition to their reversed position after death, when the
rich man is fain to entreat for a drop of water from the hand of
Lazarus.   On the supposition that the rich man had been
wanting in compassion towards Lazarus, the Abraham of the
parable could only reply in the following manner : " Thou hadst
once easy access to Lazarus, and yet thou didst not relieve him;
how then canst thou expect him to traverse a long distance to
give thee alleviation ?"   The sumptuous life of the rich man,
likewise, is only depicted as a contrast to the misery of the
beggar ; for if he had been supposed guilty of excess, Abraham
must have reminded him that he had taken too much of the
good things of this life, not merely that he had received his
share of them.   Equally groundless is it, on the other hand, to
suppose high moral excellencies in Lazarus, since there is no
intimation of such in the description of him, which merely regards his outward condition,—neither are such ascribed to him
by Abraham : his sole merit is, the having received evil in this
life.   Thus, in this parable the measure of future recompense is
not the amount of good done, or wickedness perpetrated, but
of evil endured, and fortune enjoyed [19], and the aptest motto for
this discourse is to be found in the sermon on the mount, according to Luke's edition : *Blessed be ye poor, for yours is the
kingdom of God! Woe to you that are rich! for ye have
received your consolation;* a passage concerning which we

---

[19] Comp. De Wette, 1, 2, s. 86 f.

have already remarked, that it accords fully with the Ebionite view of the world. A similar estimation of external poverty is ascribed to Jesus by the other synoptists, in the narrative of the rich young man, and in the aphorisms on the camel and the needle's eye (Matt. xix. 16 ff. ; Mark x. 17 ff.; comp. Luke xviii. 18 ff.). Whether this estimation belong to Jesus himself, or only to the synoptical tradition concerning him, it was probably generated by the notions of the Essenes [20]. We have hitherto considered the contents of the parable down to v. 27 ; from whence to the conclusion the subject is, the writings of the Old Testament as the adequate and only means of grace.

In conclusion, we turn to a group of parables, among which some, as relating to the death and return of Christ, ought, according to our plan, to be excepted from the present review ; but so far as they are connected with the rest, it is necessary to include them. They are the three parables of the rebellious husbandmen in the vineyard (Matt. xxi. 33 ff. parall.), of the talents or minæ (Matt. xxv. 14 ff. ; Luke xix. 12 ff.), and the marriage feast (Matt. xxii. 2 ff.; Luke xiv. 16 ff.). Of these the parable of the husbandmen in all the accounts, that of the talents in Matthew, and that of the marriage feast in Luke, are simple parables, unattended with difficulty. Not so the parable of the minæ in Luke, and of the marriage feast in Matthew That the former is fundamentally the same with that of the talents in Matthew, is undeniable, notwithstanding the many divergencies. In both are found the journey of a master ; the assembling of the servants to entrust them with a capital, to be put into circulation ; after the return of the master, a reckoning in which three servants are signalized, two of them as active, the third as inactive, whence the latter is punished, and the former rewarded ; and in the annunciation of this issue the words of the master are nearly identical in the two statements. The principal divergency is, that besides the relation between

---

[20] On the Essenes as *contemners of riches* ($\varkappa\alpha\tau\alpha\varphi\rho\sigma\nu\eta\tau\grave{\alpha}\varsigma$ $\pi\lambda\sigma\acute{\nu}\tau\sigma\nu$), comp. Joseph. b. j. ii. viii. 3 ; Credner, über Essener und Ebioniten, in Winer's Zeitschrift, 1, s. 217 ; Gfrörer, Philo, 2, s. 311.

the master who journeys into a far country and his servants, in
Luke there is a second relation between the former and certain
rebellious citizens; and accordingly, while in Matthew the
master is simply designated ἄνθρωπος, *a man*, in Luke he is
styled ἄνθρωπος εὐγενὴς, a *nobleman*, and a *kingdom* is assigned
to him, the object of his journey being to *receive for himself a
kingdom :* an object of which there is no mention in Matthew.
The subjects of this personage, it is farther said, hated him,
and after his departure renounced their allegiance.   Hence at
the return of the lord, the rebellious citizens, as well as the
slothful servant, are punished ; but in their case the retribution
is that of death : the faithful servants, on the other hand, are
not only rewarded generally by an entrance into the joy of their
Lord, but royally, by the gift of a number of cities.   There
are other divergencies of less moment between Luke and
Matthew ; such as, that the number of servants is undetermined
by the one, and limited to ten by the other ; that in Matthew
they receive talents, in Luke minæ ; in the one unequal sums,
in the other equal ; in the one, they obtain unequal profits
from unequal sums by an equal expenditure of effort, and are
therefore equally rewarded ; in the other, they obtain unequal
profits from equal sums by an unequal expenditure of effort,
and are therefore unequally rewarded.

Supposing this parable to have proceeded from the lips of
Jesus on two separate occasions, and that Matthew and Luke
are right in their respective arrangements, he must have delivered it first in the more complex form given by Luke, and
then in the simple one given by Matthew [21] ; since the former
places it before, the latter after the entrance into Jerusalem.
But this would be contrary to all analogy.   The first presentation of an idea is, according to the laws of thought, the most
simple ; with the second new relations may be perceived, the
subject may be viewed under various aspects, and brought into
manifold combinations.   There is, therefore, a foundation for

[21] Thus Kuinöl, Comm. in Luc. p. 635.

Schleiermacher's opinion, that contrary to the arrangement in the Gospels, Jesus first delivered the parable in the more simple form, and amplified it on a subsequent occasion [22]. But for our particular case this order is not less inconceivable than the other. The author of a composition such as a parable, especially when it exists only in his mind and on his lips, and is not yet fixed in writing, remains the perfect master of his materials even on their second and more elaborate presentation; the form which he had previously given to them is not rigid and inflexible, but pliant, so that he can adapt the original thoughts and images to the additional ones, and thus give unity to his production. Hence, had he who gave the above parable the form which it has in Luke, been its real author, he would, after having transformed the master into a king, and inserted the particulars respecting the rebellious citizens, have intrusted arms to the servants instead of money (comp. Luke xxii. 36.)[23], and would have made them show their fidelity rather by conflict with the rebels, than by increasing their capital; or in general would have introduced some relation between the two classes of persons in the parable, the servants and the citizens; instead of which, they are totally unconnected throughout, and form two ill-cemented divisions [24]. This shows very decisively that the parable was not enriched with these additional particulars by the imagination of its author, but that it was thus amplified by another in the process of transmission. This cannot have been effected in a legendary manner, by the gradual filling up of the original sketch, or the development of the primitive germ; for the idea of rebellious citizens could never be evolved from that of servants and talents, but must have been added from without, and therefore have previously existed as part of an independent whole. This amounts to the position that we have here an

---

[22] Ueber den Lukas, 239 f.   Neander agrees with him, L. J. Chr. p. 188.

[23] This is a reply to Neander's objection, p. 191, note.

[24] How Paulus, exeg. Handb. 3, a. p. 76, can pronounce the more complex form of the parable in Luke as not only the most fully developed but the best wound up, I am at a loss to understand.

example of two originally distinct parables, the one treating of
servants and talents, the other of rebellious citizens, flowing
together in consequence of their mutually possessing the images
of a ruler's departure and return[25]. The proof of our proposition must depend on our being able easily to disentangle the
two parables; and this we can effect in the most satisfactory
manner, for by extracting v. 12, 14, 15, and 27, and slightly
modifying them, we get in a rather curtailed but consistent form,
the parable of the rebellious citizens, and we then recognise the
similarity of its tendency with that of the rebellious husbandmen
in the vineyard[26].

A similar relation subsists between the form in which the
parable of the marriage feast is given by Luke (xiv. 16 ff.), and
that in which it is given by Matthew (xxii. 2 ff.) ; only that in
this case Luke, as in the other, Matthew, has the merit of
having preserved the simple original version. On both sides,
the particulars of the feast, the invitation, its rejection, and the
consequent bidding of other guests, testify the identity of the
two parables; but, on the other hand, the host who in Luke is
merely *a certain man*, ἄνθρωπός τις, is in Matthew *a king*,
βασιλεὺς, whose feast is occasioned by the marriage of his son ;
the invited guests, who in Luke excuse themselves on various
pleas to the messenger only once sent out to them, in Matthew
refuse to come on the first invitation, and on the second more
urgent one, some go to their occupations, while others maltreat
and kill the servants of the king, who immediately sends forth
his armies to destroy those murderers, and burn up their city.
Nothing of this is to be found in Luke; according to him, the
host merely causes the poor and afflicted to be assembled in
place of the guests first invited, a particular which Matthew also

---

[25] Comp. De Wette, 1, 1, s. 208 f.

[26] V. 12. Ἄνθρωπός τις εὐγενὴς ἐπορεύθη εἰς χώραν μακρὰν, λαβεῖν ἑαυτῷ βασιλείαν,
καὶ ὑποστρέψαι. 14. οἱ δὲ πολῖται αὐτοῦ ἐμίσουν αὐτὸν, καὶ ἀπέστειλαν πρεσβείαν
ὀπίσω αὐτοῦ, λέγοντες· οὐ θέλομεν τοῦτον βασιλεῦσαι ἐφ' ἡμᾶς. 15. καὶ ἐγένετο ἐν τῷ
ἐπανελθεῖν αὐτὸν λαβόντα τὴν βασιλείαν, καὶ εἶπε φωνηθῆναι αὐτῷ τοὺς δούλους—(καὶ
εἶπεν αὐτοῖς·) 27. —τοὺς ἐχθρούς μου ἐκείνους, τοὺς μὴ θελήσαντάς με βασιλεῦσαι ἐπ'
αὐτοὺς, ἀγάγετε ὧδε καὶ κατασφάξατε ἔμπροσθέν μου.

appends to his fore-mentioned incidents. Luke closes the parable with the declaration of the host, that none of the first bidden guests shall partake of his supper; but Matthew proceeds to narrate how, when the house was full, and the king had assembled his guests, one was discovered to be without a wedding garment, and was forthwith carried away into outer darkness.

The maltreatment and murder of the king's messengers are features in the narrative of Matthew which at once strike us as inconsistent—as a departure from the original design. Disregard of an invitation is sufficiently demonstrated by the rejection of it on empty pretexts such as Luke mentions; the maltreatment and even the murder of those who deliver the invitation, is an exaggeration which it is less easy to attribute to Jesus than to the Evangelist. The latter had immediately before communicated the parable of the rebellious husbandmen; hence there hovered in his recollection the manner in which they were said to have used the messengers of their lord, beating one, killing and stoning others, (λαβόντες τοὺς δούλους αὐτοῦ ὃν μὲν ἔδειραν, ὃν δὲ ἀπέκτειναν, ὃν δὲ ἐλιθοβόλησαν,) and he was thus led to incorporate similar particulars into the present parable (κρατήσαντες τοὺς δούλους αὐτοῦ ὕβρισαν καὶ ἀπέκτειναν,) overlooking the circumstance that what might have been perpetrated with sufficient motive against servants who appeared with demands and authority to enforce them, had in the latter case no motive whatever. That hereupon, the king, not satisfied with excluding them from this feast, sends out his armies to destroy them and burn up their city, necessarily follows from the preceding incidents, but appears, like them, to be the echo of a parable which presented the relation between the master and the dependents, not in the milder form of a rejected invitation, but in the more severe one of an insurrection; as in the parable of the husbandmen in the vineyard, and that of the rebellious citizens, which we have above separated from the parable of the minæ. Yet more decidedly does the drift of the last particular in Matthew's parable, that of the wedding garment, betray that it was not originally associated with the rest. For if the king

K 2

had commanded that all, *both bad and good*, who were to be found in the highways, should be bidden to the feast, he could not wonder that they had not all wedding attire. To assume that those thus suddenly summoned went home to wash, and adjust their dress, is an arbitrary emendation of the text[27]. Little preferable is the supposition that, according to oriental manners, the king had ordered a caftan to be presented to each guest, and might therefore justly reproach the meanest for not availing himself of the gift[28]; for it is not to be proved that such a custom existed at the period[29], and it is not admissible to presuppose it merely because the anger of the king appears otherwise unfounded. But the addition in question is not only out of harmony with the imagery, but with the tendency of this parable. For while hitherto its aim had been to exhibit the national contrast between the perversity of the Jews, and the willingness of the gentiles : it all at once passes to the moral one, to distinguish between the worthy and the unworthy. That after the Jews had contemned the invitation to partake of the kingdom of God, the heathens would be called into it, is one complete idea, with which Luke very properly concludes his parable ; that he who does not prove himself worthy of the vocation by a corresponding disposition, will be again cast out of the kingdom, is another idea, which appears to demand a separate parable for its exhibition. Here again it may be conjectured that the conclusion of Matthew's parable is the fragment of another, which, from its also referring to a feast, might in tradition, or in the memory of an individual, be easily mingled with the former, preserved in its purity by Luke[30]. This other parable must have simply set forth, that a king had invited various guests to a wedding feast, with the tacit condition that

---

[27] Fritzsche, p. 656. This remark serves to refute De Wette's vindication of the above particular in his exeg. Handb.

[28] Paulus, exeg. Handb. 3, a, s. 210 ; Olshausen, bibl. Comm. 1, s. 811.

[29] Vid. Fritzsche, ut sup.

[30] From the appendix to Schneckenburger's Beiträgen, I see that a reviewer in the Theol. Literaturblatt, 1831, No. 88, has also conjectured that we have here a blending of two originally distinct parables.

they should provide themselves with a suitable dress, and that he delivered an individual who had neglected this observance to his merited punishment. Supposing our conjectures correct, we have here a still more compound parable than in the former case: a parable in which, 1stly, the narrative of the ungrateful invited parties (Luke xiv.) forms the main tissue, but so that, 2ndly, a thread from the parable of the rebellious husbandmen is interwoven; while, 3rdly, a conclusion is stitched on, gathered apparently from an unknown parable on the wedding garment.

This analysis gives us an insight into the procedure of evangelical tradition with its materials, which must be pregnant with results.

§ 79.

MISCELLANEOUS INSTRUCTIONS AND CONTROVERSIES OF JESUS.

As the discourses in Matt. xv. 1—20 have been already considered, we must pass on to xviii. 1 ff., Mark ix. 33 ff., Luke ix. 46 ff., where various discourses are connected with the exhibition of a little child, occasioned by a contention for pre-eminence among the disciples. The admonition to become as a little child, and to humble one's self as a little child, in Matthew forms a perfectly suitable comment on the symbolical reproof (v. 3, 4.); but the connexion between this and the following declaration of Jesus, that whosoever receives one such little child in his name, receives him, is not so obvious. For the child was set up to teach the disciples in what they were to imitate it, not how they were to behave towards it, and how Jesus could all at once lose sight of his original object, it is difficult to conceive. But yet more glaring is the irrelevance of the declaration in Mark and Luke; for they make it follow immediately on the exhibition of the child, so that, according to this, Jesus must, in the very act, have forgotten its object, namely, to present the child to his ambitious disciples as worthy of imitation, not as in want of reception[1]. Jesus was accustomed to say of his disciples, that whosoever received them,

[1] Comp. De Wette, 1, 1, s. 152.

received him, and in him, the Father who had sent him (Matt.
x. 40 ff. ; Luke x. 16 ; John xiii. 20). Of children he elsewhere
says merely, that whosoever does not receive the kingdom of
heaven as a little child cannot enter therein (Mark x. 15. Luke
xviii. 17.) This declaration would be perfectly adapted to the
occasion in question, and we may almost venture to conjecture
that ὃς ἐὰν μὴ δέξηται τὴν βασιλείαν τῶν οὐρανῶν ὡς παιδίον, was the
original passage, and that the actual one is the result of its confusion with Matt. x. 40, ὃς ἐὰν δέξηται παιδίον τοιοῦτον ἓν ἐπὶ τῷ
ὀνόματί μου.

Closely connected by the word ἀποκριθεὶς, *answering*, with
the sentences just considered, Mark (ix. 38 f.) and Luke (ix.
49 f.) introduce the information which John is said to give to
Jesus, that the disciples having seen one casting out devils in
the name of Jesus, without attaching himself to their society,
had forbidden him. Schleiermacher explains the connexion
thus : because Jesus had commanded the reception of children
in his name, John was led to the confession, that he and his
associates had hitherto been so far from regarding the performing of an act in the name of Jesus as the point of chief importance, that they had interdicted the use of his name to one
who followed not with them[2]. Allowing this explanation to be
correct, we must believe that John, arrested by the phrase, *in my
name* (which yet is not prominent in the declaration of Jesus,
and which must have been thrown still farther into the background, by the sight of the child set up in the midst), drew from
it the general inference, that in all actions the essential point is
to perform them *in the name of Jesus ;* and with equal rapidity,
leaped to the remote reflection, that the conduct of the disciples
towards the exorcist was in contradiction with this rule. But
all this supposes the facility of combination which belongs to a
Schleiermacher, not the dulness which still characterized the
disciples. Nevertheless, the above critic has unquestionably
opened on the true vein of connexion between the preceding apo-

---

[2] Ueber den Lukas, s. 153 f.

thegm and this ἀπόκρισις of John; he has only failed to perceive that this connexion is not intrinsic and original, but extrinsic and secondary. It was quite beyond the reach of the
disciples to apply the words *in my name*, by a train of deduc-
tions, to an obliquely connected case in their own experience ;
but, according to our previous observations, nothing could be
more consistent with the habit of association that characterizes
the writer of the evangelical tradition in the third Gospel,
whence the second evangelist seems to have borrowed, than that
he should be reminded by the striking phrase, *in my name*,
in the preceding discourse of Jesus, of an anecdote containing
the same expression, and should unite the two for the sake of
that point of external similarity alone [3]

To the exhortation to receive such little children, Matthew
annexes the warning against *offending one of these little ones*,
σκανδαλίζειν ἕνα τῶν μικρῶν τούτων, an epithet which, in x. 42, is
applied to the disciples of Jesus, but in this passage, apparently,
to children [4]. Mark (v. 42) has the same continuation, notwithstanding the interruption above noticed, probably because he forsook Luke (who here breaks off the discourse, and does not introduce the admonition against offences until later, xvii. 1 f., and
apart from any occasion that might prompt it), and appealed to
Matthew [5]. Then follows in Matthew (v. 8 f.) and Mark (v. 43 f.)
a passage which alone ought to open the eyes of commentators to
the mode in which the synoptists arrange the sayings of Jesus.
To the warning against the *offending*, σκανδαλίζειν, of the little
ones, and the woe pronounced on those by whom *offences come*,
τὸ σκάνδαλον ἔρχεται, they annex the apothegm on the *offending*, σκανδαλίζειν, of the hand, eye, &c. Jesus could not proceed thus,—for the injunctions: Mislead not the little ones !
and, Let not your sensuality mislead you ! have nothing in
common but the word *mislead*. It is easy, however, to account

[3] Comp. De Wette, in loc.
[4] Vid. Fritsche and De Wette, in loc.
[5] Saunier, über die Quellen des Markus, s. 111.

for their association by the writer of the first Gospel[6]. The word σκανδαλίζειν recalled to his mind all the discourses of Jesus containing a similar expression that had come to his knowledge, and although he had previously presented the admonitions concerning seduction by the members, in a better connexion, as part of the sermon on the mount, he could not resist the temptation of reproducing them here, for the sake of this slight verbal affinity with the foregoing text. But at v. 10 he resumes the thread which he had dropped at v. 7, and adds a further discourse on the *little ones*, μικρούς. Matthew makes Jesus confirm the value of the little ones by the declaration, that the Son of Man was come to seek the lost, and by the parable of the lost sheep (v. 11—14). It is not, however, evident why Jesus should class the μικρούς with the ἀπολωλός (*lost*); and both the declaration and the parable seem to be better placed by Luke, who introduces the former in the narrative of the calling of Zaccheus (xix. 10.), and the latter, in a reply to the objections of the Pharisees against the amity of Jesus with the publicans (xv. 3 ff.). Matthew seems to have placed them here, merely because the discourse on the little ones reminded him of that on the lost,—both exemplifying the mildness and humility of Jesus.

Between the moral of the above parable (v. 14) and the following rules for the conduct of Christians under injuries (v. 15 ff.), there is again only a verbal connexion, which may be traced by means of the words, ἀπόληται, should perish, and ἐκέρδησας, *thou hast gained;* for the proposition : God wills not that one of these little ones should perish, might recall the proposition : We should endeavour to win over our brother, by showing a readiness to forgive. The direction to bring the offender before the *church*, ἐκκλησία, is generally adduced as a proof that Jesus intended to found a church. But he here speaks of the ἐκκλησία as an institution already existing : hence we must either refer the expression to the Jewish synagogue,

---

[6] Comp. De Wette, in loc. Matt.

an interpretation which is favoured by the analogy of this direction with Jewish precepts; or if, according to the strict meaning of the word and its connexion, ἐκκλησία must be understood as the designation of the Christian community, which did not then exist, it must be admitted that we have here, at least in the form of expression, an anticipation of a subsequent state of things [7]. The writer certainly had in view the new church, eventually to be founded in the name of Jesus, when, in continuation, he represented the latter as imparting to the body of the disciples the authority to bind and to loose, previously given to Peter, and thus to form a messianic religious constitution. The declarations concerning the success of unanimous prayer, and the presence of Jesus among two or three gathered together in his name, accord with this prospective idea [8].

The next discourse that presents itself (Matt. xix. 3—12, Mark x. 2—12), though belonging, according to the evangelists, to the last journey of Jesus, is of the same stamp with the disputations which they, for the most part, assign to the last residence of Jesus in Jerusalem. Some Pharisees propose to Jesus the question, at that time much discussed in the Jewish schools [9], whether it be lawful for a man to put away his wife for every cause. To avoid a contradiction between modern practice and the dictum of Jesus, it has been alleged that he here censures the species of divorce, which was the only one known at that period, namely, the arbitrary dismissal of a wife; but not the judicial separation resorted to in the present day [10]. But this very argument involves the admission, that Jesus denounced all the forms of divorce known to him; hence the question still remains whether, if he could have had cognizance of the modern procedure in dissolving matrimony, he would

---

[7] Vid. de Wette, exeg. Handb. 1, 1, p. 155.

[8] Analogous passages from Jewish writings are given in Wetstein, Lightfoot, Schöttgen, in loc.

[9] Bemidbar R. ad. Num. v. 30, in Wetstein, p. 303.

[10] E. g. Paulus, L. J. 1, b. s. 46.

have held it right to limit his general censure. Of the succeeding declaration, prompted by a question of the disciples[11], namely, that celibacy may be practised for the kingdom of heaven's sake, Jesus himself says, that it cannot be understood by all, but only by those *to whom it is given* (v. 11). That the doctrine of Jesus may not run counter to modern opinion, it has been eagerly suggested, that his panegyric on celibacy had relation solely to the circumstances of the coming time, or to the nature of the apostolic mission, which would be impeded by family ties[12]. But there is even less intimation of this special bearing in the text, than in the analogous passage 1 Cor. vii. 25 ff.[13], and, adhering to a simple interpretation, it must be granted that we have here one of the instances in which ascetic principles, such as were then prevalent, especially among the Essenes[14], manifest themselves in the teaching of Jesus, as represented in the synoptical gospels.

The controversial discourses which Matthew, almost throughout in agreement with the other synoptists, places after the entrance of Jesus into Jerusalem (xxi. 23—27 ; xxii. 15—46)[15], are certainly pre-eminently genuine fragments, having precisely the spirit and tone of the rabbinical dialectics in the time of Jesus. The third and fifth among them are particularly worthy of note, because they exhibit Jesus as an interpreter of Scripture. With respect to the former, wherein Jesus endeavours to convince the Sadducees that there will be a resurrection of the dead, from the Mosaic designation of God as the God of Abraham, of Isaac, and of Jacob, maintaining that he is not

---

[11] For probable doubts as to the correctness of the position given to this discourse of Jesus, vid. Neander, L. J. Chr. s. 525, Anm.

[12] Paulus, ib. s. 50, exeg. Handb. 2, s. 599.

[13] In this passage, it is true that celibacy is at first recommended as good for *the present distress;* but the Apostle does not rest there ; for at v. 32 ff. he adds, *He that is unmarried careth for the things of the Lord—he that is married for the things of the world :*—a motive to celibacy which must be equally valid under all circumstances, and which affords us a glimpse into the fundamental asceticism of Paul's views. Comp. Rückert's Commentary in loc.

[14] Vid. Gfrörer, Philo. 2, s. 310 f.

[15] A concise elucidation of them may be found in Hase, L. J. § 129.

the God of the dead, but of the living (Matt. xxii. 31—33 parall.) : Paulus admits that Jesus here argues subtilly, while he contends that the conclusion is really involved in the premises. But in the expression אֱלֹהֵי־אַבְרָהָם *the God of Abraham*, &c., which had become a mere formula, nothing more is implied than that Jehovah, as he had been the protecting Deity of these men, would for ever continue such to their posterity. An individual relation subsisting between Jehovah and the patriarchs after their death, is nowhere else alluded to in the Old Testament, and could only be discovered in the above form by rabbinical interpreters, at a time when it was thought desirable, at any cost, to show that the idea of immortality, which had become prevalent, was contained in the law; where, however, it is not to be met with by unprejudiced eyes. We find the relation of God to Abraham, Isaac, and Jacob, adduced as a guarantee of immortality elsewhere in rabbinical argumentations, all of which could hardly have been modelled on this one of Jesus [16]. If we look into the most recent commentaries, we nowhere find a candid confession as to the real character of the argumentation in question. Olshausen has wonders to tell of the deep truth contained in it, and thinks that he can deduce from it, in the shortest way, the authenticity and divinity of the Pentateuch. Paulus sees the validity of the proof between the lines of the text; Fritzsche is silent. Wherefore these evasions? Why is the praise of having seen clearly, and spoken openly, in this matter, abandoned to the Wolfenbüttel Fragmentist [17]? What spectres and double-sighted beings, must Moses and Jesus have been, if they mixed with their cotemporaries without any real participation in their opinions and weaknesses, their joys and griefs; if, mentally dwelling apart from their age and nation, they conformed to these relations only externally and by accommodation, while, internally and according to their nature, they stood among the

[16] Vid. Gemara Hieros. Berac. f. v. 4, in Lightfoot, p. 423, and R. Manasse Ben Isr. in Schöttgen, i. p. 180.
[17] See his 4th Fragment, Lessing's 4tem Beitrag, s. 434 ff.

foremost ranks of the enlightened in modern times! Far more noble were these men, nay, they would then only engage our sympathy and reverence, if, in a genuinely human manner, struggling with the limitations and prejudices of their age, they succumbed to them in a hundred secondary matters, and only attained perfect freedom, in relation to the one point by which each was destined to contribute to the advancement of mankind.

A controversial question concerning the Messiah is proposed (v. 41—46) to the Pharisees by Jesus, namely, How can the same personage be at once the Lord and the son of David? Paulus maintains that this is a model of interpretation in conformity with the text [18]; an assertion which is no good augury that his own possesses that qualification. According to him, Jesus, in asking how David could call the Messiah, *Lord*, when in the general opinion he was his son, intended to apprise the Pharisees, that in this Psalm it is not David who is speaking of the Messiah, but another poet who is speaking of David as his lord, so that to suppose this warlike psalm a messianic one, is a mistake. Why, asks Paulus, should not Jesus have found out this interpretation, since it is the true one? But this is the grand error of his entire scheme of interpretation—to suppose that what is truth in itself, or more correctly, for us, must, even to the minutest details, have been truth for Jesus and the apostles. The majority of ancient Jewish interpreters apply this psalm to the Messiah [19]; the apostles use it as a prophecy concerning Christ (Acts ii. 34 f.; 1 Cor. xv. 25); Jesus himself, according to Matthew and Mark, adds ἐν πνεύματι to Δαβὶδ καλεῖ αὐτὸν Κύριον, thus plainly giving his approval to the notion that it is David who there speaks, and that the Messiah is his subject: how then can it be thought that he held the contrary opinion? It is far more probable, as Olshausen has well shown, that Jesus believed the psalm to be a messianic one: while, on the other hand, Paulus is equally correct in maintaining that it

---

[18] L. J. 1, b. s. 115 ff.

[19] Vid. Wetstein, in loc. Hengstenberg, Christol. 1, a, s. 140 f.; also Paulus himself, exeg. Handb. 3, a, s. 283 f.

originally referred, not to the Messiah, but to some Jewish ruler, whether David or another.   Thus we find that Jesus here gives a model of interpretation, in conformity, not with the text, but with the spirit of his time ; a discovery which, if the above observations be just, ought to excite no surprise.   The solution of the enigma which Jesus here proposes to the Pharisees, lay without doubt, according to his idea, in the doctrine of the higher nature of the Messiah ; whether he held that, in virtue of this, he might be styled the Lord of David, while, in virtue of his human nature, he might also be regarded as his son ; or whether he wished to remove the latter notion as erroneous [20]. The result, however, and perhaps also the intention of Jesus with respect to the Pharisees, was merely to convince them that he was capable of retaliating on them, in their own way, by embarrassing them with captious questions, and that with better success than they had obtained in their attempts to entrap him. Hence the evangelists place this passage at the close of the disputations prompted by the Pharisees, and Matthew adds, *Neither durst any man from that day forth ask him any more questions :*   a concluding form which is more suitable here than after the lesson administered to the Sadducees, where it is placed by Luke (xx. 40), or than after the discussion on the greatest commandment, where it is introduced by Mark (xii. 34.).

Immediately before this question of Jesus, the first two evangelists narrate a conversation with a *lawyer,* νομικὸς, or *scribe,* γραμματεὺς, concerning the greatest commandment. (Matt. xxii. 34 ff. ; Mark xii. 28 ff.)   Matthew annexes this conversation to the dispute with the Sadducees, as if the Pharisees wished, by their question as to the greatest commandment, to avenge the defeat of the Sadducees.   It is well known, however, that these sects were not thus friendly ; on the contrary, we read in the Acts (xxiii. 7), that the Pharisees were inclined to go over to the side of one whom they had previously persecuted, solely

[20] Comp. De Wette, in loc.

because he had had the address to take the position of an oppo-
nent towards the Sadducees.   We may here quote Schneckenburger's observation [21], that Matthew not seldom (iii. 7 ; xvi. 1)
places the Pharisees and Sadducees side by side in a way that
represents, not their real hostility, but their association in the
memory of tradition, in which one opposite suggested another.
In this respect, Mark's mode of annexing this conversation to
the foregoing, is more consistent ; but all the synoptists seem
to labour under a common mistake in supposing that these discussions, grouped together in tradition on account of their
analogy, followed each other so closely in time, that one colloquy
elicited another.   Luke does not give the question concerning
the greatest commandment in connexion with the controversies
on the resurrection and on the Messiah ; but he has a similar
incident earlier, in his narrative of the journey to Jerusalem
(x. 25 ff.).   The general opinion is that the first two evangelists
recount the same occurrence, and the third, a distinct one [22].
It is true that the narrative of Luke differs from that of Matthew and Mark, in several not immaterial points.   The first
difference, which we have already noticed, relates to chronological
position, and this has been the chief inducement to the supposition of two events.   The next difference lies in the nature of
the question, which, in Luke, turns on the rule of life calculated
to insure the inheritance of eternal life, but, in the other evangelists, on the greatest commandment.   The third difference is
in the subject who pronounces this commandment, the first two
synoptists representing it to be Jesus, the third, the lawyer.
Lastly, there is a difference as to the issue, the lawyer in Luke
putting a second, self-vindicatory, question, which calls forth
the parable of the good Samaritan ; while in the two other
evangelists, he retires either satisfied, or silenced by the answer
to the first.   Meanwhile, even between the narrative of Matthew
and that of Mark, there are important divergencies.   The principal relates to the character of the querist, who in Matthew

[21] Ueber den Ursprung u. s. f., s. 45, 47.
[22] Paulus and Olshausen, in loc.

proposes his question with a view to *tempt* Jesus (πειράζων) ; in Mark, with good intentions, because he had perceived that Jesus had answered the Sadducees well. Paulus, indeed, although he elsewhere (Luke x. 25) considers the act of tempting (ἐκπειράζων) as the putting a person to the proof to subserve interested views, pronounces that the word πειράζων in this instance can only be intended in a good sense. But the sole ground for this interpretation lies, not in Matthew, but in Mark, and in the unfounded supposition that the two writers could not have a different idea of the character and intention of the inquiring doctor of the law. Fritzche has correctly pointed out the difficulty of conciliating Matthew and Mark as lying, partly in the meaning of the word πειράζων, and partly in the context, it being inadmissible to suppose one among a series of malevolent questions friendly, without any intimation of the distinction on the part of the writer. With this important diversity is connected the minor one, that while in Matthew, the scribe, after Jesus has recited the two commandments, is silent, apparently from shame, which is no sign of a friendly disposition on his part towards Jesus ; in Mark, he not only bestows on Jesus the approving expression, *Well, Master, thou hast said the truth*, but enlarges on his doctrine so as to draw from Jesus the declaration that he has *answered discreetly*, and is *not far from the kingdom of God*. It may be also noticed that while in Matthew Jesus simply repeats the commandment of love, in Mark he prefaces it by the words, *Hear, O Israel, the Lord thy God is one Lord*. Thus, if it be held that the differences between the narrative of Luke, and that of the two other evangelists, entail a necessity for supposing that they are founded on two separate events ; the no slighter differences between Mark and Matthew, must in all consistency be made a reason for supposing a third. But it is so difficult to credit the reality of three occurrences essentially alike, that the other alternative, of reducing them to one, must, prejudice apart, be always preferred. The narratives of Matthew and Mark are the most easily identified ; but there are not wanting points of contact between Matthew and Luke, for in both the *lawyer* νομικὸς appears as a tempter (πειράζων), and is not impressed in favour of Jesus by his answer; nor even between Luke and Mark, for these agree in appending explanatory remarks to the greatest commandment, as well as in the insertion of forms of assent, such as, *Thou hast answered right, Thou hast said the truth.* Hence it is evident that to fuse only two of their narratives is a half measure, and that we must either regard all three as independent, or all three as identical: whence again we may observe the freedom which was used by the early Christian legend, in giving various forms to a single fact or idea,—the fundamental fact in the present case being, that, out of the whole Mosaic code, Jesus had selected the two commandments concerning the love of God and our neighbour as the most excellent [23].

We come now to the great anti-pharisaic discourse, which Matthew gives (xxiii.) as a sort of pitched battle after the skirmishing of the preceding disputations. Mark (xii. 38 ff.) and Luke (xx. 45 ff.) have also a discourse of Jesus against the *scribes,* γραμματεῖς, but extending no farther than a few verses. It is however highly probable, as our modern critics allow [24], that Jesus should launch out into fuller invectives against that body of men under the circumstances in which Matthew places that discourse, and it is almost certain that such sharp enunciations must have preceded the catastrophe; so that it is not admissible to control the account of the first evangelist by the meagre one of the two other synoptists [25], especially as the former is distinguished by connectedness and unity. It is true that much of what Matthew here presents as a continuous address, is assigned by Luke to various scenes and occasions, and it would hence follow that the former has, in this case again, blended the original elements of the discourse with kindred matter, belonging to the discourses of various periods [26], if it could be shown that the arrangement of Luke is

---

[23] Comp. De Wette, exeg. Handb., 1, 1, s. 186.
[24] Sieffert, über den Ursprung des ersten Ev., s. 117 f.
[25] Comp. De Wette, 1, 1, s. 189.
[26] Schulz, über das Abendmahl, s. 313 f.; Schneckenburger, über den Ursprung, s. 54.

the correct one: a position which must therefore be examined. Those parts of the anti-pharisaic harangue which Luke has in common with Matthew, are, excepting the couple of verses which he places in the same connexion as Matthew, introduced by him as concomitant with two entertainments to which he represents Jesus as being invited by Pharisees (xi. 37 ff.; xiv. 1 ff.)—a politeness on their part which appears in no other Gospel. The expositors of the present day, almost with one voice, concur in admiring the naturalness and faithfulness with which Luke has preserved to us the original occasions of these discourses [27]. It is certainly natural enough that, in the second entertainment, Jesus, observing the efforts of the guests to obtain the highest places for themselves, should take occasion to admonish them against assuming the precedence at feasts, even on the low ground of prudential considerations; and this admonition appears in a curtailed form, and without any special cause in the final anti-pharisaic discourse in Matthew, Mark, and even in Luke again (xx. 46). But it is otherwise with the discourse which Luke attaches to the earlier entertainment in the Pharisee's house. In the very commencement of this repast, Jesus not only speaks of the *ravening*, ἀρπαγη, and *wickedness*, πονηρία, with which the Pharisees fill the cup and platter, and honours them with the title of *fools*, ἄφρονες, but breaks forth into a denunciation of *woe*, οὐαὶ, against them and the scribes and doctors of the law, threatening them with retribution for all the blood that had been shed by their fathers, whose deeds they approved. We grant that Attic urbanity is not to be expected in a Jewish teacher, but even according to the oriental standard, such invectives uttered at table against the host and his guests, would be the grossest dereliction of what is due to hospitality. This was obvious to Schleiermacher's acute perception; and he therefore supposes that the meal passed off amicably, and that it was not until its close, when Jesus was again out of the house, that the host expressed his surprise at the neglect of the usual

[27] Schleiermacher, über den Lukas, s. 182, 196 f.; Olshausen, in loc., and the writers mentioned in the foregoing note.

ablutions by Jesus and his disciples, and that Jesus answered
with so much asperity [28]. But to assume that the writer has not
described the meal itself and the incidents that accompanied it,
and that he has noticed it merely for the sake of its connexion
with the subsequent discourse, is an arbitrary mode of over-
coming the difficulty. For the text runs thus : *And he went
in and sat down to meat. And when the Pharisee saw it, he
marvelled that he had not first washed before dinner.* And
the Lord said unto him, εἰσελθὼν δὲ ἀνέπεσεν· ὁ δὲ Φαρισαῖος ἰδὼν
ἐθαύμασεν, ὅτι οὐ πρῶτον ἐβαπτίσθη— εἶπε δὲ ὁ Κύριος πρὸς αὐτὸν.
It is manifestly impossible to thrust in between these sentences
the duration of the meal, and it must have been the intention of
the writer to attach *he marvelled* ἐθαύμασεν to *he · sat down to
meat* ἀνέπεσεν, and *he said* εἶπεν to *he marvelled* ἐθαύμασεν.
But if this could not really have been the case, unless Jesus
violated in the grossest manner the simplest dictates of civility,
there is an end to the vaunted accuracy of Luke in his allocation of this discourse : and we have only to inquire how he
could be led to give it so false a position. This is to be discovered by comparing the manner in which the two other
synoptists mention the offence of the Pharisees, at the omission
of the ablutions before meals by Jesus and his disciples : a circumstance to which they annex discourses different from those
given by Luke. In Matthew (xv. 1 ff.), scribes and Pharisees
from Jerusalem ask Jesus why his disciples do not observe the
custom of washing before meat ? It is thus implied that they
knew of this omission, as may easily be supposed, by report.
In Mark (vii. 1 ff.), they look on (ἰδόντες), while some disciples
of Jesus eat with unwashen hands, and call them to account for
this irregularity. Lastly, in Luke, Jesus himself dines with a
Pharisee, and on this occasion it is observed that he neglects
the usual washings. This is an evident climax : hearing,
witnessing, taking food together. Was it formed, in the descending gradation, from Luke to Matthew, or, in the ascending

[28] Ut sup. 180.

one, from Matthew to Luke ? From the point of view adopted by the recent critics of the first Gospel, the former mode will be held the most probable, namely, that the memory of the original scene, the repast in the Pharisee's house, was lost in the process of tradition, and is therefore wanting in the first Gospel. But, apart from the difficulty of conceiving that this discourse was uttered under the circumstances with which it is invested by Luke, it is by no means in accordance with the course of tradition, when once in possession of so dramatic a particular as a feast, to let it fall again, but rather to supply it, if lacking. The general tendency of the legend is to transform the abstract into the concrete, the mediate into the immediate, hearsay into vision, the spectator into the participator; and as the offence taken against Jesus by the Pharisees referred, among other things, to the usages of the table, nothing was more natural than for legend to associate the origin of the offence with a particular place and occasion, and for this purpose to imagine invitations given to Jesus by Pharisees—invitations which would be historically suspicious, if for no other reason than that Luke alone knows anything of them. Here, then, we again find Luke in his favourite employment of furnishing a frame to the discourses of Jesus which tradition had delivered to him ; a procedure much farther removed from historic faithfulness, than the effort of Matthew to give unity to discourses gathered from different periods, without adding matter of his own. The formation of the climax above displayed, can only be conceived, in accordance with the general relation between the synoptists, in the following manner : Mark, who in this instance evidently had Matthew before him, enriched his account with the dramatic expression ἰδόντες; while Luke, independent of both, has added a repast, δεῖπνον, whether presented to him by a more developed tradition, or invented by his own more fertile imagination. Together with this unhistorical position, the proportions themselves seem to be disfigured in Luke (xi. 39—41, 49.), and the observation of the lawyer, *Master, thus saying thou reproachest us also* (xi. 45), too much resembles an artificial transition

from the philippic against the Pharisees, to that against the
doctors of the law [29].

Another passage in this discourse has been the subject of
much discussion. It is that (v. 35) in which Jesus threatens
his cotemporaries, that all the innocent blood shed from that
of Abel to that of Zacharias, the son of Barachias, slain in the
temple, will be required of their generation. The Zacharias of
whom such an end is narrated 2 Chron. xxiv. 20 ff. was a son,
not of Barachias, but of Jehoiada. On the other hand, there
was a Zacharias, the son of Baruch, who came to a similar end
in the Jewish war [30]. Moreover, it appears unlikely that Jesus
would refer to a murder which took place 850 b. c. as the last.
Hence it was at first supposed that we have in v. 35 a prophecy,
and afterwards, a confusion of the earlier with the later event;
and the latter notion has been used as an accessory proof that
the first gospel is a posterior compilation [31]. It is, however,
equally probable, that the Zacharias, son of Jehoiada, whose
death is narrated in the Chronicles, has been confounded with
the prophet Zachariah, who was a son of Barachias (Zach. i. 1;
LXX.; Baruch, in Josephus, is not the same name) [32]; especially
as a Targum, evidently in consequence of a like confusion with
the prophet who was a grandson of Iddo, calls the murdered
Zachariah a son of Iddo [33]. The murder of a prophet, mentioned
by Jeremiah (xxvi. 23.), was doubtless subsequent to that of
Zachariah, but in the Jewish order of the canonical books,
Jeremiah precedes the Chronicles; and to oppose a murder
revealed in the first canonical book, to one recorded in the
last, was entirely in the style of Jewish parlance [34].

After having considered all the discourses of Jesus given by

---

[29] Comp. De Wette, exeg. Handb. 1, 1, s. 189. 1, 2, s. 67, 76.

[30] Joseph. b. j. iv. v. 4.

[31] Eichhorn, Einleitung in das N. T., 1, s. 510 ff.; Hug, Einl. in das N. T., 2, s.
10 ff.; Credner, Einl., 1, s. 207.

[32] Vid. Theile, über Zacharias Barachias Sohn, in Winer's und Engelhardt's neuem
krit. Journ., 2, s. 401 ff.; De Wette, in loc.

[33] Targum Thren. ii. 20, in Wetstein, s. 491.

[34] Comp. De Wette, in loc.

Matthew, and compared them with their parallels, with the exception of those which had come before us in previous discussions, or which have yet to come before us in our examination of single incidents in the public ministry, or of the history of the passion : it might appear requisite to the completeness of our criticism, that we should also give a separate investigation to the connexion in which the two other synoptists give the discourses of Jesus, and from this point review the parallels in Matthew. But we have already cast a comparative glance over the most remarkable discourses in Luke and Mark, and gone through the parables which are peculiar to each; and as to the remainder of what they offer in the form of discourses, it will either come under our future consideration, or if not, the point of view from which it is to be criticised, has been sufficiently indicated in the foregoing investigations.

CHAPTER VII.

DISCOURSES OF JESUS IN THE FOURTH GOSPEL.

§ 80.

THE first considerable specimen which the fourth Gospel gives of the teaching of Jesus, is his conversation with Nicodemus (iii. 1—21.). In the previous chapter (23—25.) it is narrated, that during the first passover attended by Jesus after his entrance on his public ministry, he had won many to faith in him by the *miracles*, σημεῖα, which he performed, but that he did not commit himself to them because he saw through them : he was aware, that is, of the uncertainty and impurity of their faith. Then follows in our present chapter, as an example, not only of the adherents whom Jesus had found even thus early, but also of the wariness with which he tested and received them, a more detailed account how Nicodemus, a ruler of the Jews and a Pharisee, applied to him, and how he was treated by Jesus.

It is through the Gospel of John alone that we learn anything of this Nicodemus, who in vii. 50 f. appears as the advocate of Jesus, so far as to protest against his being condemned without a hearing, and in xix. 39. as the partaker with Joseph of Arimathea of the care of interring Jesus. Modern criticism, with reason, considers it surprising that Matthew (with the other synoptists) does not even mention the name of this remarkable adherent of Jesus, and that we have to gather all our knowledge of him from the fourth Gospel; since the peculiar relation in which Nicodemus stood to Jesus, and his participation in the care of his interment, must have been as well known to Matthew as to John. This difficulty has been numbered among the arguments which are thought to prove that the first Gospel was not written by the apostle Matthew, but was the product of a tradition considerably more remote from the time and locality of Jesus[1]. But the fact is that the common fund of tradition on which all the synoptists drew had preserved no notice of this Nicodemus. With touching piety the Christian legend has recorded in the tablets of her memory, the names of all the others who helped to render the last honours to their murdered master—of Joseph of Arimathea and the two Marys (Matt. xxvii. 57—61 parall.); why then was Nicodemus the only neglected one—he who was especially distinguished among those who tended the remains of Jesus, by his nocturnal interview with the teacher sent from God, and by his advocacy of him among the chief priests and Pharisees? It is so difficult to conceive that the name of this man, if he had really assumed such a position, would have vanished from the popular evangelical tradition, without leaving a single trace, that one is induced to inquire whether the contrary supposition be not more capable of explanation: namely, that such a relation between Nicodemus and Jesus might have been fabricated by tradition, and adopted by the author of the fourth Gospel without having really subsisted.

John xii. 42, it is expressly said that *many among the chief rulers* believed on Jesus, but concealed their faith from dread of excommunication by the Pharisees, because *they loved the praise of men more than the praise of God*[2]. That towards

---

[1] Schulz, über das Abendmahl, s. 321.

[2] This " secret information" is very welcome to Dr. Paulus, because it gives a useful hint " as to many occurrences in the life of Jesus, the causes of which are not obvious" (L. J. 1, b. s. 141.); that is, Paulus, like Bahrdt and Venturini, though less openly, is fond of using such secret and influential allies as *deos ex machinâ*, for the explanation of much that is miraculous in the life of Jesus (the transfiguration, residence after the resurrection, &c.).

the end of his career *many* people of rank believed in Jesus, even in secret only, is not very probable, since no indication of it appears in the Acts of the Apostles; for that the advice of Gamaliel (Acts v. 34 ff.) did not originate in a positively favourable disposition towards the cause of Jesus, seems to be sufficiently demonstrated by the spirit of his disciple Saul. Moreover the synoptists make Jesus declare in plain terms that the secret of his Messiahship had been revealed only to *babes*, and hidden from the *wise* and *prudent* (Matt. xi. 25; Luke x. 21.), and Joseph of Arimathea is the only individual of the ruling class whom they mention as an adherent of Jesus. How, then, if Jesus did not really attach to himself any from the upper ranks, came the case to be represented differently at a later period? In John vii. 48 f. we read that the Pharisees sought to disparage Jesus by the remark that none of the rulers or of the Pharisees, but only the ignorant populace, believed on him; and even later adversaries of Christianity, for example, Celsus, laid great stress on the circumstance that Jesus had had as his disciples ἐπιρρήτους ἀνθρώπους, τελώνας καὶ ναύτας τοὺς πονηροτά-τους[a]. This reproach was a thorn in the side of the early church, and though as long as her members were drawn only from the people, she might reflect with satisfaction on the declarations of Jesus, in which he had pronounced the *poor*, πτωχοὺς, and *simple*, νηπίους, blessed: yet so soon as she was joined by men of rank and education, these would lean to the idea that converts like themselves had not been wanting to Jesus during his life. But, it would be objected, nothing had been hitherto known of such converts. Naturally enough, it might be answered; since fear of their equals would induce them to conceal their relations with Jesus. Thus a door was opened for the admission of any number of secret adherents among the higher class (John xii. 42 f.). But, it would be farther urged, how could they have intercourse with Jesus, un-observed? Under the veil of the night, would be the answer;

---

[a] Orig. c. Cels. i. 62.

and thus the scene was laid for the interviews of such men with Jesus (xix. 39.). This, however, would not suffice; a representative of this class must actually appear on the scene: Joseph of Arimathea might have been chosen, his name being still extant in the synoptical tradition; but the idea of him was too definite, and it was the interest of the legend to name more than one eminent friend of Jesus. Hence a new personage was devised, whose Greek name Νικόδημος seems to point him out significantly as the representative of the dominant class [4]. That this development of the legend is confined to the fourth Gospel, is to be explained, partly by the generally admitted lateness of its origin, and partly on the ground that in the evidently more cultivated circle in which it arose, the limitation of the adherents of Jesus to the common people would be more offensive, than in the circle in which the synoptical tradition was formed. Thus the reproach which modern criticism has cast on the first Gospel, on the score of its silence respecting Nicodemus, is turned upon the fourth, on the score of its information on the same subject.

These considerations, however, should not create any prejudice against the ensuing conversation, which is the proper object of our investigations. This may still be in the main genuine; Jesus may have held such a conversation with one of his adherents, and our evangelist may have embellished it no further than by making this interlocutor a man of rank. Neither will we, with the author of the Probabilia, take umbrage at the opening address of Nicodemus, nor complain, with him, that there is a want of connexion between that address and the answer of Jesus [5]. The requisition of a *new birth* (γεννηθῆναι ἄνωθεν), as a condition of entrance into the kingdom of heaven,

---

[4] Let the reader bear in mind the kindred names Nicolaus and Nicolaitans.

[5] Prob. p. 44. Bretschneider is right, however, in declaring against Kuinöl's method of supplying a connexion between the discourses in John, by the insertion of propositions and intermediate discourses, supposed to have been omitted. Lücke judiciously admits (1, p. 446) that if, in John, something appears to be wanting between two consecutive expressions of Jesus, we are yet to suppose that there was

does not differ essentially from the summons with which Jesus opens his ministry in the synoptical gospels, *Repent ye, for the kingdom of heaven is at hand.* New birth, or new creation, was a current image among the Jews, especially as denoting the conversion of an idolater into a worshipper of Jehovah. It was customary to say of Abraham, that when, according to the Jewish supposition, he renounced idolatry for the worship of the true God, he became a new creature (בריה חדשה)[6]. The proselyte, too, in allusion to his relinquishing all his previous associations, was compared to a new-born child[7]. That such phraseology was common among the Jews at that period, is shown by the confidence with which Paul applies, as if it required no explanation, the term *new creation, καινὴ κτίσις,* to those truly converted to Christ. Now, if Jesus required, even from the Jews, as a condition of entrance into the messianic kingdom, the *new birth* which they ascribed to their heathen proselytes, Nicodemus might naturally wonder at the requisition, since the Israelite thought himself, as such, unconditionally entitled to that kingdom : and this is the construction which has been put upon his question v. 4[8]. But Nicodemus does not ask, How canst thou say that a Jew, or a child of Abraham, must be born again? His ground of wonder is that Jesus appears to suppose it possible for a *man* to be born again, and that *when he is old.* It does not, therefore, astonish him that spiritual new birth should be expected in a Jew, but corporeal new birth in a man. How an oriental, to whom figurative speech in general—how a Jew, to whom the

---

an immediate connexion between them in the mind of the evangelist, and it is this connexion which it is the task of exegesis to ascertain. In truth the discourses in the 4th Gospel are never entirely wanting in connexion (apart from the exceptions to be noticed § 81), though that connexion is sometimes very latent.

[6] Bereschith R. sect. 39 f. xxxviii. 2. Bammidbar R. s. 11 f. ccxi. 2. Tanchuma f. v. 2, in Schöttgen, i. s. 704. Something similar is said of Moses, from Schemoth R. ib.

[7] Jevamoth f. lxii. 1. xcii. 1, in Lightfoot, p. 984.

[8] E. g. Knapp, Comm. in colloq. Christi cum Nicod. in loc.

image of the new birth in particular must have been familiar—
how especially a *master of Israel*, in whom the misconstruction
of figurative phrases cannot, as in the Apostles (e. g. Matt.
xv. 15 f.; xvi. 7.), be ascribed to want of education—could
understand this expression literally, has been matter of extreme
surprise to expositors of all parties, as well as to Jesus (v. 10).
Hence some have supposed that the Pharisee really understood
Jesus, and only intended by his question to test the ability of
Jesus to interpret his figurative expression into a simple proposition [9] : but Jesus does not treat him as a hypocrite, as in
that case he must have done—he continues to instruct him, as
one really *ignorant* οὐ γινώσκοντα (v. 10). Others give the
question the following turn : This cannot be meant in a physical
sense, how then otherwise [10] ? But the true drift of the question
is rather the contrary: By these words I can only understand
physical new birth, but how is this possible ? Our wonder at
the ignorance of the Jewish doctor, therefore, returns upon us ;
and it is heightened when, after the copious explanation of
Jesus (v. 5—8.), that the new birth which he required was a
spiritual birth, γεννηθῆναι ἐκ τοῦ πνεύματος, Nicodemus has made
no advance in comprehension, but asks with the same obtuseness as before (v. 9.), *How can these things be?* By this
last difficulty Lücke is so straitened, that, contrary to his
ordinary exegetical tact, he refers the continued amazement of
Nicodemus, (as other expositors had referred his original question,) to the circumstance that Jesus maintained the necessity
of new birth even for Israelites. But, in that case, Nicodemus
would have inquired concerning the necessity, not the possibility, of that birth ; instead of asking, *How can* these things
be ? he would have asked, *Why must* these things be ? This
inconceivable mistake in a Jewish doctor is not then to be
explained away, and our surprise must become strong suspicion
so soon as it can be shown, that legend or the evangelist had
inducements to represent this individual as more simple than

---

[9] Paulus, Comm. 4, s. 183. L. J. 1, a. s. 176.
[10] Lücke and Tholück, in loc.

he really was.   First, then, it must occur to us, that in all descriptions and recitals, contrasts are eagerly exhibited; hence in the representation of a colloquy in which one party is the teacher, the other the taught, there is a strong temptation to create a contrast to the wisdom of the former, by exaggerating the simplicity of the latter.   Further, we must remember the satisfaction it must give to a Christian mind of that age, to place a master of Israel in the position of an unintelligent person, by the side of the Master of the Christians.   Lastly it is, as we shall presently see more clearly, the constant method of the fourth evangelist in detailing the conversations of Jesus, to form the knot and the progress of the discussion, by making the interlocutors understand literally what Jesus intended figuratively.

In reply to the second query of Nicodemus, Jesus takes entirely the tone of the fourth evangelist's prologue (v. 11— 13 [11]).   The question hence arises, whether the evangelist borrowed from Jesus, or lent to him his own style.   A previous investigation has decided in favour of the latter alternative [12]. But this inquiry referred merely to the form of the discourses; in relation to their matter, its analogy with the ideas of Philo, does not authorize us at once to conclude that the writer here puts his Alexandrian doctrine of the Logos into the mouth of Jesus [13]; because the expressions, *We speak that we do know,* &c. ὃ οἴδαμεν λαλοῦμεν κ. τ. λ., and, *No man hath ascended up to heaven,* &c. οὐδεὶς ἀναβέβηκεν κ. τ. λ., have an analogy with Matt. xi. 27.; and the idea of the pre-existence of the Messiah which is here propounded, is, as we have seen, not foreign to the apostle Paul.

V. 14 and 15 Jesus proceeds from the more simple things of

---

[11] III. 11 : ὃ ἑωράκαμεν, μαρτυροῦμεν· καὶ τὴν μαρτυρίαν ἡμῶν οὐ λαμβάνετε. 13 : καὶ οὐδεὶς ἀναβέβηκεν εἰς τὸν οὐρανὸν, εἰ μὴ ὁ ἐκ τοῦ οὐρανοῦ καταβὰς, ὁ υἱὸς τοῦ ἀνθρώπου, ὁ ὢν ἐν τῷ οὐρανῷ.

[12] Sup. § 46.

[13] This is inferred in the Probabilia, p. 46.

I. 18 : θεὸν οὐδεὶς ἑώρακε πώποτε· ὁ μονογενὴς υἱὸς, ὁ ὢν εἰς τὸν κόλπον τοῦ πατρὸς, ἐκεῖνος ἐξηγήσατο. 11 : —καὶ οἱ ἴδιοι αὐτὸν οὐ παρέλαβον.

the earth, ἐπιγείοις, the communications concerning the new
birth, to the more difficult things of heaven, ἐπουρανίοις, the
announcement of the destination of the Messiah to a vicarious
death. The Son of Man, he says, must *be lifted up* (ὑψωθῆναι,
which, in John's phraseology, signifies crucifixion, with an
allusion to a glorifying exaltation), in the same way, and with
the same effect, as the brazen serpent Numb. xxi. 8, 9. Here
many questions press upon us. Is it credible, that Jesus already,
at the very commencement of his public ministry, foresaw his
death, and in the specific form of crucifixion? and that long
before he instructed his disciples on this point, he made a communication on the subject to a Pharisee? Can it be held consistent with the wisdom of Jesus as a teacher, that he should
impart such knowledge to Nicodemus? Even Lücke [14] puts
the question why, when Nicodemus had not understood the
more obvious doctrine, Jesus tormented him with the more
recondite, and especially with the secret of the Messiah's death,
which was then so remote? He answers: it accords perfectly
with the wisdom of Jesus as a teacher, that he should reveal
the sufferings appointed for him by God as early as possible,
because no instruction was better adapted to cast down false
worldly hopes. But the more remote the idea of the Messiah's death from the conceptions of his cotemporaries, owing
to the worldliness of their expectations, the more impres-
sively and unequivocally must Jesus express that idea, if he
wished to promulgate it; not in an enigmatical form which
he could not be sure that Nicodemus would understand. Lücke
continues: Nicodemus was a man open to instruction; one of
whom good might be expected. But in this very conversation,
his dulness of comprehension in *earthly things*, ἐπίγεια, had
evinced that he must have still less capacity for *heavenly things*,
ἐπουράνια; and, according to v. 12, Jesus himself despaired of
enlightening him with respect to them. Lücke, however,
observes, that it was a practice with Jesus to follow up easy

[14] Ut sup. p. 476.

doctrine which had not been comprehended, by difficult doctrine which was of course less comprehensible; that he purposed thus to give a spur to the minds of his hearers, and by straining their attention, engage them to reflect. But the examples which Lücke adduces of such proceeding on the part of Jesus, are all drawn from the fourth gospel. Now the very point in question is, whether that gospel correctly represents the teaching of Jesus; consequently Lücke argues in a circle. We have seen a similar procedure ascribed to Jesus in his conversation with the woman of Samaria, and we have already declared our opinion that such an overburthening of weak faculties with enigma on enigma, does not accord with the wise rule as to the communication of doctrine, which the same gospel puts into the mouth of Jesus, xvi. 12. It would not stimulate, but confuse, the mind of the hearer, who persisted in a misapprehension of the well-known figure of the new birth, to present to him the novel comparison of the Messiah and his death, to the brazen serpent and its effects; a comparison quite incongruous with his Jewish ideas [15]. In the first three gospels Jesus pursues an entirely different course. In these, where a misconstruction betrays itself on the part of the disciples, Jesus (except where he breaks off altogether, or where it is evident that the evangelist unhistorically associates a number of metaphorical discourses) applies himself with the assiduity of an earnest teacher to the thorough explanation of the difficulty, and not until he has effected this does he proceed, step by step, to convey further instruction (e. g. Matt. xiii. 10 ff. 36 ff.; xv. 16; xvi. 8 ff.) [16]. This is the method

---

[15] Comp. Bretschneider, ut sup.

[16] De Wette adduces as examples of a similar procedure on the part of Jesus in the synoptical gospels, Matt. xix. 21; xx. 22 f. But these two cases are of a totally different kind from the one under consideration in John. We have here to treat of a want of comprehension, in the face of which it is surprising that Jesus instead of descending to its level, chooses to elevate himself to a still less attainable altitude. In the passages quoted from the synoptists, on the other hand, we have examples of an excessive self-valuation, too high an estimate of their ability to promote the cause of Jesus, on the part of the rich young man and of the sons of Zebedee, and Jesus

of a wise teacher; on the contrary, to leap from one subject to
another, to overburthen and strain the mind of the hearer, a
mode of instruction which the fourth evangelist attributes to
Jesus, is wholly inconsistent with that character. To explain
this inconsistency, we must suppose that the writer of the fourth
gospel thought to heighten in the most effective manner the
contrast which appears from the first, between the wisdom of
the one party and the incapacity of the other, by representing
the teacher as overwhelming the pupil who put unintelligent
questions on the most elementary doctrine, with lofty and
difficult themes, beneath which his faculties are laid prostrate.

From v. 16, even those commentators who pretend to some
ability in this department, lose all hope of showing that the remainder of the discourse may have been spoken by Jesus. Not
only does Paulus make this confession, but even Olshausen,
with a concise statement of his reasons [17]. At the above verse,
any special reference to Nicodemus vanishes, and there is commenced an entirely general discourse on the destination of the
Son of God, to confer a blessing on the world, and on the
manner in which unbelief forfeits this blessing. Moreover,
these ideas are expressed in a form, which at one moment
appears to be a reminiscence of the evangelist's introduction,
and at another has a striking similarity with passages in the
first epistle of John [18]. In particular, the expression, *the only
begotten Son,* ὁ μονογενὴς υἱός, which is repeatedly (v. 16 and

with perfect propriety checks their egotistic ardour by the abrupt presentation of a
higher demand. These instances could only be parallel with that of Nicodemus, if
the latter had piqued himself on his enlightenment, and Jesus, by a sudden flight
into a higher region, had sought to convince him of his ignorance.

[17] Bibl. Comm. 2, s. 96.

[18] III. 19 : αὕτη δέ ἐστιν ἡ κρίσις,
ὅτι τὸ φῶς ἐλήλυθεν εἰς τὸν κόσμον, καὶ
ἠγάπησαν οἱ ἄνθρωποι μᾶλλον τὸ σκότος ἢ
τὸ φῶς.
III. 16 : οὕτω γὰρ ἠγάπησεν ὁ θεὸς τὸν
κόσμον, ὥστε τὸν υἱὸν αὐτοῦ τὸν μονογενῆ
ἔδωκεν, ἵνα πᾶς ὁ πιστεύων εἰς αὐτὸν, μὴ
ἀπόληται, ἀλλ᾽ ἔχῃ ζωὴν αἰώνιον.

I. 9 : ἦν τὸ φῶς τὸ ἀληθινὸν, τὸ φωτί-
ζον πάντα ἄνθρωπον, ἐρχόμενον εἰς τὸν κόσμον. 5 : καὶ τὸ φῶς ἐν τῇ σκοτίᾳ φαί-
νει, καὶ ἡ σκοτία αὐτὸ οὐ κατέλαβεν.
1 John iv. 9 : ἐν τούτῳ ἐφανερώθη ἡ
ἀγάπη τοῦ θεοῦ ἐν ἡμῖν, ὅτι τὸν υἱὸν αὐτοῦ
τὸν μονογενῆ ἀπέστειλεν ὁ θεὸς εἰς τὸν κόσμον, ἵνα ζήσωμεν δι᾽ αὐτοῦ.

18.) attributed to Jesus as a designation of his own person, is nowhere else found in his mouth, even in the fourth gospel; this circumstance, however, marks it still more positively as a favourite phrase of the evangelist (i. 14—18.), and of the writer of the Epistles (1 John iv. 9). Further, many things are spoken of as past, which at the supposed period of this conversation with Nicodemus were yet future. For even if the words, *he gave*, ἔδωκεν, refer not to the giving over to death, but to the sending of the Messiah into the world; the expressions, *men loved darkness* ἠγάπησαν οἱ ἄνθρωποι τὸ σκότος, and, *their deeds were evil*, ἦν πονηρὰ αὐτῶν τὰ ἔργα (v. 19.), as Lücke also remarks, could only be used after the triumph of darkness had been achieved in the rejection and execution of Jesus: they belong then to the evangelist's point of view at the time when he wrote, not to that of Jesus when on the threshold of his public ministry. In general the whole of this discourse attributed to Jesus, with its constant use of the third person to designate the supposed speaker; with its dogmatical terms *only begotten*, *light*, and the like, applied to Jesus; with its comprehensive view of the crisis and its results, which the appearance of Jesus produced, is far too objective for us to believe that it came from the lips of Jesus. Jesus could not speak thus of himself, but the evangelist might speak thus of Jesus. Hence the same expedient has been adopted, as in the case of the Baptist's discourse already considered, and it has been supposed that Jesus is the speaker down to v. 16, but that from that point the evangelist appends his own dogmatic reflections [19]. But there is again here no intimation of such a transition in the text; rather, the connecting word *for*, γὰρ (v. 16.), seems to indicate a continuation of the same discourse. No writer, and least of all the fourth evangelist (comp. vii. 39; xi. 51 f.; xii. 16; xxxiii. 37 ff.), would scatter his own observations thus undistinguishingly, unless he wished to create a misapprehension [20].

---

[19] Paulus and Olshausen, in loc.

[20] Tholuck (Glaubwürdigkeit, s. 335.) adduces as examples of a similar unobserved

If then it be established that the evangelist, from v. 16. to the end of the discourse, means to represent Jesus as the speaker, while Jesus can never have so spoken ; we cannot rest satisfied with the half measure adopted by Lücke, when he maintains that it is really Jesus who continues to speak from the above passage, but that the evangelist has inwoven his own explanations and amplifications more liberally than before. For this admission undermines all certainty as to how far the discourse belongs to Jesus, and how far to the evangelist; besides, as the discourse is distinguished by the closest uniformity of thought and style, it must be ascribed either wholly to Jesus or wholly to the evangelist. Of these two alternatives the former is, according to the above considerations, impossible; we are therefore restricted to the latter, which we have observed to be entirely consistent with the manner of the fourth evangelist.

But not only on the passage v. 16—21 must we pass this judgment: v. 14 has appeared to us out of keeping with the position of Jesus ; and the behaviour of Nicodemus, v. 4 and 9, altogether inconceivable. Thus in the very first sample, when compared with the observations which we have already made on John iii. 22 ff. ; iv. 1 ff., the fourth gospel presents to us all the peculiarities which characterize its mode of reporting the discourses of Jesus. They are usually commenced in the form of dialogue, and so far as this extends, the lever that propels the

fusion of a discourse quoted from a foreign source, with the writer's own matter, Gal. ii. 14 ff. Euseb. H. E. iii. 1, 39. Hieron. Comm. in Jes. 53. But such instances in an epistle, a commentary or an historical work interspersed with reasoning and criticism, are not parallel with those in an historical narrative of the nature of our fourth gospel. In works of the former kind, the reader expects the author to reason, and hence, when the discourse of another party has been introduced, he is prepared at the slightest pause to see the author again take up the argument. It is quite different with a work like our fourth gospel. The introduction, it is true, is put forth as the author's own reasoning, and it is there quite natural that after a brief quotation from the discourse of another, v. 15, he should, at v. 16, resume the character of speaker without any express intimation. But when once he has entered on his narrative, which is strictly a recital of what has been done, and what has been said, all that he annexes without any mark of distinction (as e. g. xii. 37.) to a discourse explicitly ascribed to another, must be considered as a continuation of that discourse.

conversation is the striking contrast between the spiritual sense and the carnal interpretation of the language of Jesus; generally, however, the dialogue is merged into an uninterrupted discourse, in which the writer blends the person of Jesus with his own, and makes the former use concerning himself, language which could only be used by John concerning Jesus.

§ 81.

THE DISCOURSES OF JESUS, JOHN V.—XII.

In the fifth chapter of John, a long discourse of Jesus is connected with a cure wrought by him on the sabbath (19—47). The mode in which Jesus at v. 17 defends his activity on the sabbath, is worthy of notice, as distinguished from that adopted by him in the earlier Gospels. These ascribe to him, in such cases, three arguments : the example of David, who ate the shew-bread ; the precedent of the sabbatical labours of the priests in the temple, quoted also in John vii. 23 (Matt. xii. 3 ff. parall.) ; and the course pursued with respect to an ox, sheep, or ass, that falls into the pit (Matt. xii. 11. parall.), or is led out to watering on the sabbath (Luke xiii. 18.): all which arguments are entirely in the practical spirit that characterizes the popular teaching of Jesus. The fourth evangelist, on the contrary, makes him argue from the uninterrupted activity of God, and reminds us by the expression which he puts into the mouth of Jesus, *My Father worketh hitherto,* ὁ πατὴρ ἕως ἄρτι ἐργάζεται, of a principle in the Alexandrian metaphysics, viz. *God never ceases to act,* ποιῶν ὁ θεὸς οὐδέποτε παύεται [1] : a metaphysical proposition more likely to be familiar to the author of the fourth gospel than to Jesus. In the synoptical gospels, miracles of healing on the sabbath are followed up by declarations respecting the nature and design of the sabbatical institution, a species of instruction of which the people were greatly in need ; but in the present passage, a digression is immediately made to the main theme of the

---

[1] Philo. Opp. ed. Mang. i. 44. apud Gfrörer, i. p. 122.

gospel, the person of Christ and his relation to the Father. The perpetual recurrence of this theme in the fourth gospel has led its adversaries, not without reason, to accuse it of a tendency purely theoretic, and directed to the glorification of Jesus. In the matter of the succeeding discourse there is nothing to create a difficulty, nothing that Jesus might not have spoken, for it treats, with the strictest coherence, of things which the Jews expected of the Messiah, or which Jesus attributed to himself, according to the synoptists also: as, for instance, the raising of the dead, and the office of judging the world. But this consistency in the matter, only heightens the difficulty connected with the form and phraseology in which it is expressed. For the discourse, especially its latter half (from v. 31), is full of the closest analogies with the first epistle of John, and with passages in the gospel in which either the author speaks, or John the Baptist[2]. One means of explaining

---

[2] Joh. v. 20 : ὁ γὰρ πατὴρ φιλεῖ τὸν υἱὸν καὶ πάντα δείκνυσιν αὐτῷ ἃ αὐτὸς ποιεῖ.

24 : ὁ τὸν λόγον μου ἀκούων—μεταβέβηκεν ἐκ τοῦ θανάτου εἰς τὴν ζωήν.

32 : καὶ οἶδα, ὅτι ἀληθής ἐστιν ἡ μαρτυρία, ἣν μαρτυρεῖ περὶ ἐμοῦ.

34 : ἐγὼ δὲ οὐ παρὰ ἀνθρώπου τὴν μαρτυρίαν λαμβάνω.

36 : ἐγὼ δὲ ἔχω μαρτυρίαν μείζω τοῦ Ἰωάννου.

37 : καὶ ὁ πέμψας με πατὴρ αὐτὸς μεμαρτύρηκε περὶ ἐμοῦ.

Ib. : οὔτε τὴν φωνὴν αὐτοῦ ἀκηκόατε πώποτε, οὔτε τὸ εἶδος αὐτοῦ ἑωράκατε.

38 : καὶ τὸν λόγον αὐτοῦ οὐκ ἔχετε μένοντα ἐν ὑμῖν.

40 : καὶ οὐ θέλετε ἐλθεῖν πρός με, ἵνα ζωὴν ἔχητε.

42 : ὅτι τὴν ἀγάπην τοῦ θεοῦ οὐκ ἔχετε ἐν ἑαυτοῖς.

44 : πῶς δύνασθε ὑμεῖς πιστεύειν, δόξαν παρὰ ἀλλήλων λαμβάνοντες, καὶ τὴν δόξαν τὴν παρὰ τοῦ μόνου θεοῦ οὐ ζητεῖτε ;

John iii. 35 (the Baptist) : ὁ γὰρ πατὴρ ἀγαπᾷ τὸν υἱὸν καὶ πάντα δίδωκεν ἐν τῇ χειρὶ αὐτοῦ.

1 Joh. iii. 14 : ἡμεῖς οἴδαμεν, ὅτι μεταβεβήκαμεν ἐκ τοῦ θανάτου εἰς τὴν ζωήν.

Joh. xix. 35 : καὶ ἀληθινή ἐστιν αὐτοῦ ἡ μαρτυρία, κἀκεῖνος οἶδεν, ὅτι ἀληθῆ λέγει.

Comp. xxi. 24. 1 Joh. 3, 12.

1 Joh. v. 9 : εἰ τὴν μαρτυρίαν τῶν ἀνθρώπων λαμβάνομεν, ἡ μαρτυρία τοῦ θεοῦ μείζων ἐστίν· ὅτι αὕτη ἐστιν ἡ μαρτυρία τοῦ θεοῦ, ἣν μεμαρτύρηκε περὶ τοῦ υἱοῦ αὐτοῦ.

Joh. i. 18 : θεὸν οὐδεὶς ἑώρακε πώποτε. Comp. 1 Joh. iv. 12.

1 Joh. i. 10 : καὶ ὁ λόγος αὐτοῦ οὐκ ἔστιν ἐν ὑμῖν.

1 Joh. v. 12 : ὁ μὴ ἔχων τὸν υἱὸν τοῦ θεοῦ ζωὴν οὐκ ἔχει.

1 Joh. ii. 15 : οὐκ ἔστιν ἡ ἀγάπη τοῦ πατρὸς ἐν αὐτῷ.

Joh. xi. 43 : ἠγάπησαν γὰρ τὴν δόξαν τῶν ἀνθρώπων μᾶλλον, ἤπερ τὴν δόξαν τοῦ θεοῦ.

the former resemblance is to suppose, that the evangelist formed his style by closely imitating that of Jesus.   That this is possible, is not to be disputed; but it is equally certain that it could proceed only from a mind destitute of originality and self-confidence,—a character which the fourth evangelist in nowise exhibits.   Farther, as in the other gospels Jesus speaks in a thoroughly different tone and style, it would follow, if he really spoke as he is represented to have done by John, that the manner attributed to him by the synoptists is fictitious. Now, that this manner did not originate with the evangelists is plain from the fact, that each of them is so little master of his matter.   Neither could the bulk of the discourses have been the work of tradition, not only because they have a highly original cast, but because they bear the impress of the alleged time and locality.   On the contrary, the fourth evangelist, by the ease with which he disposes his materials, awakens the suspicion that they are of his own production; and some of his favourite ideas and phrases, such as, *The Father showeth the Son all that himself doeth* [3], and those already quoted, seem to have sprung from an Hellenistic source, rather than from Palestine.   But the chief point in the argument is, that in this gospel John the Baptist speaks, as we have seen, in precisely the same strain as the author of the gospels, and his Jesus. It cannot be supposed, that not only the evangelist, but the Baptist, whose public career was prior to that of Jesus, and whose character was strongly marked, modelled his expressions with verbal minuteness on those of Jesus.   Hence only two cases are possible: either the Baptist determined the style of Jesus and the evangelist (who indeed appears to have been the Baptist's disciple); or the evangelist determined the style of the Baptist and Jesus.   The former alternative will be rejected by the orthodox, on the ground of the higher nature that dwelt in Christ; and we are equally disinclined to adopt it, for the reason that Jesus, even though he may have been excited to

---

[3] Vid. the passages compared by Gfrörer, 1, s. 194, from Philo, *de linguarum confusione.*

activity by the Baptist, yet appears as a character essentially distinct from him, and original; and for the still more weighty consideration, that the style of the evangelist is much too feeble for the rude Baptist,—too mystical for his practical mind. There remains, then, but the latter alternative, namely, that the evangelist has given his own style both to Jesus and to the Baptist: an explanation in itself more natural than the former, and supported by a multitude of examples from all kinds of historical writers. If however the evangelist is thus responsible for the form of this discourse, it is still possible that the matter may have belonged to Jesus, but we cannot pronounce to what extent this is the case, and we have already had proof that the evangelist, on suitable opportunities, very freely presents his own reflections in the form of a discourse from Jesus.

In chap. vi., Jesus represents himself, or rather his Father, v. 27 ff., as the giver of the spiritual manna. This is analogous to the Jewish idea above quoted, that the second Goël, like the first, would provide manna [4]; and to the invitation of Wisdom in the Proverbs, ix. 5, *Come, eat of my bread :* ἔλθετε, φάγετε τῶν ἐμῶν ἄρτων. But the succeeding declaration, that he is himself *the bread of life that cometh down from heaven,* ἄρτος ὁ ζῶν ὁ ἐκ τοῦ οὐρανοῦ καταβὰς (v. 33 and 35) appears to find its true analogy only in the idea of Philo, that the *divine word,* λόγος θεῖος, is *that which nourishes the soul,* τὸ τρέφον τὴν ψυχὴν [5]. From v. 51, the difficulty becomes still greater. Jesus proceeds to represent his flesh as the bread from heaven, which he will give for the life of the world, and *to eat the flesh of the Son of Man, and to drink his blood,* he pronounces to be the only means of attaining *eternal life.* The similarity of these expressions to the words which the synoptists and Paul attribute to Jesus, at the institution of the Lord's Supper, led the older commentators generally to understand this passage as

---

[4] Sup. § 14.

[5] De profugis, Opp. Mang., i. s. 566, Gfrörer, 1, s. 202. What is farther said of the λόγος : ἀφ' οὗ σῶσαι παιδεῖαι καὶ σοφίαι ῥέουσιν ἀέναοι may be compared with John iv. 14; vi. 35; vii. 38.

having reference to the Sacramental supper, ultimately to be appointed by Jesus [7]. The chief objection to this interpretation is, that before the institution of the supper, such an allusion would be totally unintelligible. Still the discourse might have some sense, however erroneous, for the hearers, as indeed it had, according to the narrator's statement; and the impossibility of being understood is not, in the fourth gospel, so shunned by Jesus, that that circumstance alone would suffice to render this interpretation improbable. It is certainly supported by the analogy between the expressions in the discourse, and the words associated with the institution of the supper, and this analogy has wrung from one of our recent critics the admission, that even if Jesus himself, in uttering the above expressions, did not refer to the supper, the evangelist, in choosing and conveying this discourse of Jesus, might have had that institution in his mind, and might have supposed that Jesus here gave a premonition of its import [8]. In that case, however, he could scarcely have abstained from modifying the language of Jesus; so that, if the choice of the expression *eat the flesh*, &c., can only be adequately explained on the supposition of a reference to the Lord's Supper, we owe it, without doubt, to the evangelist alone. Having once said, apparently in accordance with Alexandrian ideas, that Jesus had described himself as *the bread of life*, how could he fail to be reminded of the *bread*, which in the Christian community was partaken of as the body of Christ, together with a beverage, as his blood? He would the more gladly seize the opportunity of making Jesus institute the supper prophetically, as it were; because, as we shall hereafter see, he knew nothing definite of its historical institution by Jesus [9].

The discourse above considered, also bears the form of a dialogue, and it exhibits strikingly the type of dialogue which especially belongs to the fourth gospel: that, namely, in which language intended spiritually, is understood carnally. In the first

---

[7] See Lücke's History of the interpretation of this passage in his Comm. 2, Appendix B, p. 727 ff.

[8] Hase, L. J. § 99.   [9] Comp. Bretschneider, Probab. p. 56, 88 ff.

place (v. 34), the Jews (as the woman of Samaria in relation to the water) suppose that by *the bread which cometh down from heaven*, Jesus means some material food, and entreat him evermore to supply them with such. Such a misapprehension was certainly natural ; but one would have thought that the Jews, before they carried the subject farther, would have indignantly protested against the assertion of Jesus (v. 32), that Moses had not given them heavenly bread. When Jesus proceeds to call himself *the bread from heaven*, the Jews in the synagogue at Capernaum murmur that he, the son of Joseph, whose father and mother they knew, should arrogate to himself a descent from heaven (v. 41) ; a reflection which the synoptists with more probability attribute to the people of Nazareth, the native city of Jesus, and to which they assign a more natural cause. That the Jews should not understand (v. 53) how Jesus could give them his flesh to eat is very conceivable ; and for that reason, as we have observed, it is the less so that Jesus should express himself thus unintelligibly. Neither is it surprising that this *hard saying* σκληρὸς λόγος should cause many disciples to fall away from him, nor easy to perceive how Jesus could, in the first instance, himself give reason for the secession, and then, on its occurrence, feel so much displeasure as is implied in v. 61 and 67. It is indeed said, that Jesus wished to sift his disciples, to remove from his society the superficial believers, the earthly-minded, whom he could not trust ; but the measure which he here adopted was one calculated to alienate from him even his best and most intelligent followers. For it is certain that the twelve, who on other occasions knew not what was meant by the leaven of the Pharisees (Matt. xvi. 7), or by the opposition between what goes into the mouth, and what comes out of it (Matt. xv. 15), would not understand the present discourse ; and the *words of eternal life*, for the sake of which they remained with him (v. 68), were assuredly not the words of this sixth chapter [10].

[10] In relation to this chapter, I entirely approve the following remark in the Probabilia (p. 56): *videretur—Jesus ipse studuisse, ut verbis illuderet Judæis, nec*

The farther we read in the fourth gospel, the more striking is the repetition of the same ideas and expressions. The discourses of Jesus during the Feast of Tabernacles, ch. vii. and viii. are, as Lücke has remarked, mere repetitions and amplifications of the oppositions previously presented (especially in ch. v.), of the coming, speaking, and acting, of Jesus, and of God (vii. 17, 28 f.; viii. 28 f., 38, 40, 42. compare with v. 30, 43; vi. 38.); of being *from above,* εἶναι ἐκ τῶν ἄνω, and *from beneath,* ἐκ τῶν κάτω (viii. 23. comp. iii. 31.); of bearing witness of one's self, and receiving witness from God (viii. 13—19. comp. v. 31—37.); of light and darkness (viii. 12. comp. iii. 10 ff., also xii. 35 f.); of true and false judgment (viii. 15 f., comp. v. 30.). All that is new in these chapters, is quickly repeated, as the mention of the departure of Jesus whither the Jews cannot follow him (vii. 33 f., viii. 21.; comp. xiii. 33., xiv. 2 ff., xvi. 16 ff.); a declaration, to which are attached, in the first two instances, very improbable misapprehensions or perversions on the part of the Jews, who, although Jesus had said, *I go unto him that sent me,* are represented as imagining, at one time, that he purposed journeying to the *dispersed among the Gentiles,* at another, that he meditated suicide. How often, again, in this chapter are repeated the asseverations, that he seeks not his own honour, but the honour of the Father (vii. 17 f., viii. 50, 54); that the Jews neither know whence he came, nor the father who sent him (vii. 28; viii. 14, 19, 54); that whosoever believeth in him shall have eternal life, shall not see death, while whosoever believeth not must die in his sins, having no share in eternal life (viii. 21, 24, 51; comp. iii. 36, vi. 40.). —The ninth chapter, consisting chiefly of the deliberations of the Sanhedrim with the man born blind, whom Jesus had restored to sight, has of course the form of conversation, but as Jesus is less on the scene than heretofore, there is not the usual amount of artificial contrast; in its stead, however, there is, as

ab iis intelligeretur, sed reprobaretur. Ita vero nec egit, nec agere potuit, neque si ita docuisset, tanta effecisset, quanta illum effecisse historia testatur. Comp. De Wette, exeg. Handb., 1, 3, s. 6.

we shall presently find, another evidence of artistic design in the narrator.

The tenth chapter commences with the well-known discourse on the Good Shepherd ; a discourse which has been incorrectly called a parable [11]. Even the briefest among the other parables of Jesus, such as that of the leaven and of the mustard-seed, contain the outline of a history that developes itself, having a commencement, progress, and conclusion. Here, on the contrary, there is no historical development ; even the particulars that have an historical character are stated generally, as things that are wont to happen, not as things that once happened, and they are left without farther limitation ; moreover, the *door* usurps the place of the Shepherd, which is at first the principal image ; so that we have here, not a parable, but an allegory. Therefore this passage at least—(and we shall find no other, for the similitude of the vine, ch. xv., comes, as Lücke confesses, under the same category as the one in question)—furnishes no argument against the allegation by which recent critics have justified their suspicions as to the authenticity of the fourth gospel ; namely, that its author seems ignorant of the parabolic mode of teaching which, according to the other evangelists, was habitual with Jesus. It does not however appear totally unknown to the fourth evangelist that Jesus was fond of teaching by parables, for he attempts to give examples of this method, both in ch. x. and xv., the first of which he expressly styles a *parable, παροιμία*. But it is obvious that the parabolic form was not accordant with his taste, and that he was too deficient in the faculty of depicting external things, to abstain from the intermixture of reflections, whence the parable in his hand became an allegory.

The discourses of Jesus at the Feast of Tabernacles extend

---

[11] E. g. by Tholück and Lücke. The latter, however, allows that it is rather an incipient than a complete parable. Olshausen also remarks, that the discourses of the Shepherd and the Vine are rather comparisons than parables ; and Neander shows himself willing to distinguish the parable presented by the synoptists as a species, under the genus similitude, to which the παροιμίαι of John belong.

to x. 18. From v. 25, the evangelist professes to record sayings which were uttered by Jesus three months later, at the
Feast of Dedication. When, on this occasion, the Jews desire
from him a distinct declaration whether he be the Messiah, his
immediate reply is, that he has already told them this sufficiently, and he repeats his appeal to the testimony of the Father,
as given in the *works*, ἔργα, done by Jesus in his name (as in
v. 36.). Hereupon he observes that his unbelieving interro-
gators are not of his sheep, whence he reverts to the allegory of
the shepherd, which he had abandoned, and repeats part of it
word for word[12]. But Jesus had not recently abandoned this
allegory; for since its delivery three months are supposed to
have elapsed, and it is certain that in the interim much must
have been spoken, done, and experienced by Jesus, that would
thrust this figurative discourse into the background of his
memory, so that he would be very unlikely to recur to it, and
in no case would he be able to repeat it, word for word. He
who had just quitted the allegory was the evangelist, to whom
three months had not intervened between the inditing of the
first half of this chapter, and that of the second. He wrote at
once what, according to his statement, was chronologically separated by a wide interval; and hence the allegory of the shepherd might well leave so distinct an echo in his memory, though
not in that of Jesus. If any think that they can solve this
difficulty by putting only the *verbal* similarity of the later discourse to the earlier one to the account of the evangelist, such
an opinion cannot be interdicted to them. For others, this
instance, in connexion with the rest, will be a positive proof that
the discourses of Jesus in the fourth gospel are to a great
extent the free compositions of the evangelist.

---

[12] x. 27 : τὰ πρόβατα τὰ ἐμὰ τῆς   x. 3 : καὶ τὰ πρόβατα τῆς φωνῆς
φωνῆς μου ἀκούει,   αὐτοῦ ἀκούει·
κἀγὼ γινώσκω αὐτά·   14 : καὶ γινώσκω τὰ ἐμα
28 : καὶ ἀκολουθοῦσί μοι.   4 : καὶ τὰ πρόβατα αὐτῷ ἀκολουθεῖ.

Also κἀγὼ ζωὴν αἰώνιον δίδωμι αὐτοῖς corresponds to ἐγὼ ἦλθον, ἵνα ζωὴν ἔχωσι, v. 10,
and καὶ οὐχ ἁρπάσει τις αὐτὰ ἐκ τῆς χειρός μου is the counterpart of what is said v.
12 of the hireling who allows the sheep to be scattered.

The same conclusion is to be drawn from the discourse with which the fourth evangelist represents Jesus as closing his public ministry (xii. 44—50). This discourse is entirely composed of reminiscences out of previous chapters[13], and, as Paulus expresses it[14], is a mere echo of some of the principal apophthegms of Jesus occurring in the former part of the gospel. One cannot easily consent to let the ministry of Jesus close with a discourse so little original, and the majority of recent commentators are of opinion that it is the intention of the evangelist here to give us a mere epitome of the teaching of Jesus[15]. According to our view also, the evangelist is the real speaker; but we must contend that his introductory words, *Jesus cried and said*, Ἰησοῦς δὲ ἔκραξε καὶ εἶπεν, are intended to imply that what follows is an actual harangue, from the lips of Jesus. This commentators will not admit, and they can appeal, not without a show of reason, to the statement of the evangelist, v. 36, that Jesus withdrew himself from the public eye, and to his ensuing observations on the obstinate unbelief of the Jews, in which he seems to put a period to the public career of Jesus; whence it would be contrary to his plan to make Jesus again step forward to deliver a valedictory discourse. I will not, with the older expositors, oppose to these arguments the supposition that Jesus, after his withdrawal, returned to pronounce these words in the ears of the Jews; but I hold fast to the proposition, that by the introduction above quoted, the evangelist can only have intended to announce an actual harangue. It is said, indeed, that the aorist in ἔκραξε and εἶπε has the signification of the pluperfect, and that we have here a recapitulation of the previous discourses of Jesus, notwithstanding which the Jews had not given him credence. But to give this retrospective signification there ought to be a corresponding indication in the words themselves, or in the context, whereas this is far

---

[13] Comp. v. 44 with vii. 17; v. 46 with viii. 12; v. 47 with iii. 17; v. 48 with iii. 18; v. 45; v. 49 with viii. 28; v. 50 with vi. 40; vii. 17; viii. 28.

[14] L. J. b. s. 142.

[15] Lücke, Tholück, Paulus, in loc.

less the case than e. g. in John xviii. 24. Hence the most probable view of the question is this : John had indeed intended to close the narrative of the public ministry of Jesus at v. 36, but his concluding observations, v. 37 ff., with the categories of *faith, πίστις,* and *unbelief, ἀπιστία,* reminded him of discourses which he had already recorded, and he could not resist the temptation of making Jesus recapitulate them with additional emphasis in a parting harangue.

§ 82.

ISOLATED MAXIMS OF JESUS, COMMON TO THE FOURTH GOSPEL AND THE SYNOPTICAL ONES.

The long discourses of Jesus above examined are peculiar to the fourth gospel ; it has only a few brief maxims to which the synoptists present parallels. Among the latter, we need not give a special examination to those which are placed by John in an equally suitable connexion, with that assigned to them by the other evangelists (as xii. 25. comp. with Matt. x. 39 ; xvi. 25 ; and xiii. 16. comp. with Matt. x. 24.) ; and as the passage ii. 19 compared with Matt. xxvi. 61, must be reserved until we treat of the history of the Passion, there remain to us only three passages for our present consideration.

The first of these is iv. 44, where the evangelist, after having mentioned that Jesus departed from Samaria into Galilee, adds, *For Jesus himself testified that a prophet has no honour in his own country,* αὐτὸς γὰρ ὁ 'Ι. ἐμαρτύρησεν, ὅτι προφήτης ἐν τῇ ἰδίᾳ πατρίδι τιμὴν οὐκ ἔχει. We find the same idea in Matthew xiii. 57. (Mark vi. 4 ; Luke iv. 24.), *A prophet is not without honour, save in his own country and in his own house,* οὐκ ἔστι προφήτης ἄτιμος, εἰ μὴ ἐν τῇ πατρίδι αὐτοῦ καὶ ἐν τῇ οἰκίᾳ αὐτοῦ. But while in the latter case it stands in a highly appropriate connexion, as a remark prompted by the ungracious reception which Jesus met with in his native city, and which caused him to leave it again : in John, on the contrary, it is given as a motive for the return of Jesus into his own country, Galilee, where, moreover, he is immediately said to be warmly received. The

experience stated in the above sentence, would rather have disinclined than induced Jesus to undertake a journey into Galilee ;
hence the expedient of translating γὰρ by *although*, is the best
adapted to the necessity of the case, and has even been embraced
by Kuinöl, except that, unhappily, it is an open defiance of the
laws of language. Unquestionably, if Jesus knew that the prophet held this unfavourable position in his *native country*,
πατρὶς, it is not probable that he would regard it as a
reason for going thither. Some expositors [1], therefore, have
been induced to understand πατρὶς, not as the province, but in
a narrower sense, as the native city, and to supply, after the
statement that Jesus went into Galilee, the observation, which
they assume the evangelist to have omitted, that he avoided his
native city Nazareth, for the reason given in the ensuing verse.
But an ellipsis such as this explanation requires us to suppose,
belongs not less to the order of impossibilities than the transmutation of γὰρ into *though*. The attempt to introduce the
desiderated statement that Jesus did not visit his own πατρὶς
into the present passage has been therefore renounced : but it
has yet been thought possible to discover there an intimation
that he did not soon return thither; a delay for which the
maxim, οτι προφήτης κ. τ. λ. might consistently be quoted as a
reason [2]. But to render this interpretation admissible, the entire
period of the absence of Jesus from Galilee must have been
mentioned immediately before the notice of his return ; instead
of this, however, only the short time that Jesus had tarried in
Samaria is given (v. 45), so that in ludicrous disproportion of
cause and effect, the fear of the contempt of his fellow countrymen would, on the above supposition, be made the reason for
delaying his return into Galilee, not until after a residence of
some months in Judea, but until after the lapse of two days

---

[1] Cyril, Erasmus. Tholück's expedient, which Olshausen approves, is to give
ἐμαρτύρησεν the signification of the pluperfect, and to understand γὰρ as an expli-
cative. But I do not see how this can be of any avail, for γὰρ and οὖν (v. 45,)
would still form a relation of agreement between two propositions, which one would
have expected to be opposed to each other by μὲν and δὲ,

[2] Paulus, Comm. 4, s. 251, 56,

spent in Samaria. So long, therefore, as Galilee and Nazareth are admitted to be the πατρὶς of Jesus, the passage in question cannot be vindicated from the absurdity of representing, that Jesus was instigated to return thither by the contempt which he knew to await him. Consequently, it becomes the interest of the expositor to recollect, that Matthew and Luke pronounce Bethlehem to be the birthplace of Jesus, whence it follows that Judea was his native country, which he now forsook on account of the contempt he had there experienced [3]. But according to iv. 1. comp. ii. 23, iii. 26 ff., Jesus had won a considerable number of adherents in Judea, and could not therefore complain of a lack of *honour*, τιμὴ; moreover the enmity of the Pharisees, hinted at in iv. 1, was excited by the growing consequence of Jesus in Judea, and was not at all referrible to such a cause as that indicated in the maxim: ὅτι προφήτης κ. τ. λ. Further, the entrance into Galilee is not connected in our passage with a departure from Judea, but from Samaria; and as, according to the import of the text, Jesus departed from Samaria and went into Galilee, because he had found that a prophet has no honour in his own country, Samaria might rather seem to be pointed out as his native country, in conformity with the reproach cast on him by the Jews, viii. 48; though even this supposition would not give consistency to the passage, for in Samaria also Jesus is said, iv. 39, to have had a favourable reception. Besides, we have already seen [4] that the fourth evangelist knows nothing of the birth of Jesus in Bethlehem, but on all occasions presupposes him to be a Galilean and a Nazarene. From the above considerations we obtain only the negative result, that it is impossible to discover any consistent relation between the maxim in question and the context. A positive result,—namely, how the maxim came to occupy its actual position, notwithstanding this want of relation, will perhaps be obtained when we have

---

[3] This idea is so entirely in the spirit of the ancient harmonists, that I can scarcely believe Lücke to be the first to whom it had occurred (Comm. 1, s. 545 f.).

[4] Vid. sup. § 39.

examined the two other passages belonging to the present head of our inquiry.

The declaration xiii. 20, *He that receiveth you receiveth me, and he that receiveth me receiveth him that sent me,* has an almost verbal parallel in Matt. x. 40. In John, it is preceded by the prediction of the betrayal of Jesus, and his explanation to his disciples that he had told them this before it came to pass, in order that when his prediction was fulfilled, they might believe in him as the Messiah. What is the connexion between these subjects and the above declaration, or between the latter and its ensuing context, where Jesus recurs to his betrayer? It is said that Jesus wished to impress on his disciples the high dignity of a messianic missionary, a dignity which the betrayer thought lightly of losing [5]; but the negative idea of loss, on which this supposition turns, is not intimated in the text. Others are of opinion that Jesus, observing the disciples to be disheartened by the mention of the betrayer, sought to inspire them with new courage by representing to them their high value [6]; but in that case he would hardly have reverted immediately after to the traitor. Others, again, conjecture that some intermediate sentences have been omitted by the writer [7]; but this expedient is not much happier than that of Kuinöl, who supposes the passage to be a gloss taken from Matt. x. 40, united originally to v. 16 of chap. xiii. of John, but by some chance transposed to the end of the paragraph. Nevertheless, the indication of v. 16 is an useful way-mark. This verse, as well as v. 20, has a parallel in the discourse of instructions in Matthew (x. 24.); if a few fragments of this discourse had reached the author of the fourth gospel through the medium of tradition, it is very probable that one of them would bring the others to his recollection. In v. 16 there is mention of the *sent,* ἀπόστολος, and of *him who sent him,* πέμψας αὐτὸν; so in v. 20, of those whom Jesus will send, and of Him who sent Jesus. It is true,

[5] Paulus, L. J. 1, b, s. 158.
[6] Lücke, 2, s. 478.
[7] Tholück, in loc.

that the one passage has a humiliating, the other an encouraging tendency, and their affinity lies therefore, not in the sense, but in the words; so that as soon as the fourth evangelist puts down, from memory, traditional sayings of Jesus, we see him subject to the same law of association as the synoptists. It would have been the most natural arrangement to place v. 20 immediately after v. 16; but the thought of the traitor was uppermost in the mind of the writer, and he could easily postpone the insertion of an apophthegm that had only a verbal connexion with his previous matter.

Our third passage, xiv. 31, lies yet farther within the domain of the history of the Passion than the one last examined, but as, like this, it can be viewed quite independently, we shall not be anticipating if we include it in our present chapter. In the above passage, the words *Arise, let us go hence*, ἐγείρεσθε, ἄγωμεν ἐντεῦθεν, remind us of those by which Jesus, Matt. xxvi. 46, Mark xiv. 42, summons his disciples to join him in encountering the traitor: *Rise, let us be going*, ἐγείρεσθε ἄγωμεν. The position of the words in John is perplexing, because the summons to depart has no effect; Jesus, as if he had said nothing of the kind, immediately continues (xv. 1.), *I am the true vine*, &c., and does not take his departure with his disciples until after he has considerably prolonged his discourse. Expositors of every hue have been singularly unanimous in explaining the above words by the supposition, that Jesus certainly intended at the moment to depart and betake himself to Gethsemane, but love for his disciples, and a strong desire to impart to them still farther admonition and comfort, detained him; that hence, the first part of the summons, *Arise*, was executed, but that, standing in the room in which he had supped, he pursued his discourse, until, later, (xviii. 1.), he also put into effect the words, *let us go hence*[8]. It is possible that the circumstances were such; it is also possible that the image of this last evening, with all its details, might be en-

[8] Paulus, L. J. 1, b. s. 175; Lücke, Tholück, Olshausen, in loc.; Hug, Einl. in das N. T. 2, s. 209.

graven so deeply and accurately in the memory of a disciple, that he might narrate how Jesus arose, and how touchingly he lingered.   But one who wrote under the influence of a recollection thus lively, would note the particulars which were most apparent; the rising to depart and the delay,—not the mere words, which without the addition of those circumstances are altogether unintelligible.   Here again, then, the conjecture arises that a reminiscence of the evangelical tradition presented itself to the writer, and that he inserted it just where it occurred to him, not, as it happened, in the best connexion; and this conjecture assumes probability so soon as we discover what might have reminded him of the above expression.   In the synoptical parallels the command, *Rise, let us be going,* is connected with the announcement, *Behold the hour is at hand, and the Son of man is betrayed into the hands of sinners— behold he is at hand that doth betray me;* with the announcement, that is, of the hostile power which is approaching, before which, however, Jesus exhibits no fear, but goes to encounter the danger with the decision implied in that command.   In John's gospel, also, Jesus, in the passage under our notice, had been speaking of a hostile power when he said, *The prince of this world cometh and hath nothing in me.*   It makes little difference that in John it is the power that dwells in the betrayer, and in those led by him, while, in the synoptical gospels, it is the betrayer who is impelled by that power, that is said to approach.   If the author of the fourth gospel knew by tradition that Jesus had united with the announcement of an approaching danger the words, *Rise, let us be going,* this expression would be likely to occur to him on the mention of the prince of this world; and as in that stage of his narrative he had placed Jesus and his disciples in the city and within doors, so that a considerable change of place was necessary before they could encounter the enemy, he added to ἄγωμεν (*let us go*), ἐντεῦθεν (*hence*).   As, however, this traditional fragment had intruded itself unawares into the train of thought, which he designed to put as a farewell discourse into the mouth of Jesus, it was immediately lost sight of, and a free course was given to the stream of valedictory instruction, not yet exhausted.

If, from the point of view now attained, we glance back on our first passage, iv. 44, it is easy to see how the evangelist might be led to insert in so unsuitable a connexion the testimony of Jesus as to the treatment of a prophet in his own country. It was known to him traditionally, and he appears to have applied it to Galilee in general, being ignorant of any unfavourable contact of Jesus with the Nazarenes. As, therefore, he knew of no special scene by which this observation might have been prompted, he introduced it where the simple mention of Galilee suggested it, apparently without any definite idea of its bearing.

The result of the above investigation is this: the fourth evangelist succeeds in giving connectedness to his materials, when he presents his own thoughts in the form of discourses delivered by Jesus; but he often fails lamentably in that particular, when he has to deal with the real traditional sayings of Jesus. In the above instances, when he has the same problem before him as the synoptists, he is as unfortunate in its solution as they; nay, he is in a yet more evil case, for his narrative is not homogeneous with the common evangelical tradition, and presented few places where a genuine traditional relic could be inserted. Besides, he was accustomed to cast his metal, liquid from his own invention, and was little skilled in the art of adapting independent fragments to each other, so as to form an harmonious mosaic.

§ 83.

THE MODERN DISCUSSIONS ON THE AUTHENTICITY OF THE DISCOURSES IN THE GOSPEL OF JOHN.   RESULT.

The foregoing examination of the discourses of Jesus in the fourth gospel, has sufficiently prepared us to form a judgment on the controversy of which they have recently been the subject. Modern criticism views these discourses with suspicion, partly on account of their internal contexture, which is at variance with certain generally received rules of historical probability, and partly on account of their external relation to other discourses and narratives.   On the other hand, this gospel has had numerous defenders.

With respect to the internal contexture of the above discourses, there arises a twofold question : Does it correspond to the laws, first, of verisimilitude, and secondly, of memory ? It is alleged by the friends of the fourth gospel that its discourses are distinguished by a peculiar stamp of truth and credibility; that the conversations which it represents Jesus as holding with men of the most diverse disposition and capacity, are faithful delineations of character, satisfying the strictest demands of psychological criticism [1].   In opposition to this, it is maintained to be in the highest degree improbable, that Jesus should have adopted precisely the same style of teaching to persons differing widely in their degrees of cultivation ; that he should have spoken to the Galileans in the synagogue at Capernaum not more intelligibly than to a *master of Israel;* that the matter of his discourses should have turned almost entirely on one doctrine—the dignity of his person; and that their form should have been such, as to seem selected with a view to perplex and repel his hearers.   Neither, it is further urged, do the interlocutors express themselves in conformity with their position and character.   The most educated Pharisee has no advantage in intelligence over a Samaritan woman of the lowest grade ; the one, as well as the other, can only put a carnal interpretation on the discourse which Jesus intends spiritually; their misconstructions, too, are frequently so glaring, as to transcend all belief, and so uniform that they seem to belong to a standing set of features with which the author of the fourth gospel has chosen, for the sake of contrast, to depict those whom he brings into conversation with Jesus [2].

---

[1] Wegscheider, Einl. in das Evang. Joh. s. 271 ; Tholück Comm. s. 37 f.

[2] Thus Eckermann, theol. Beiträge, 5, 2, s. 228 ; (Vogel) der Evangelist Johannes und seine Ausleger vor dem jüngsten Gericht, 1, s. 28 ff., Wegscheider, s. 281. ; Bretschneider, Probabil. 33, 45, apud Wegscheider, ut sup. s. 281 ; Bretschneider, Probab. p. 33, 45.

Hence, I confess, I understand not what is the meaning of verisimilitude in the mind of those who ascribe it to the discourses of Jesus in the gospel of John.

As to the second point, regarding the powers of memory, it is pretty generally agreed that discourses of the kind peculiar to John's gospel,—in contradistinction to the apothegms and parables, either isolated or strung together, in the synoptical gospels,—namely, series of dependent propositions, or prolonged dialogues, are among the most difficult to retain and reproduce with accuracy[3]. Unless such discourses were reduced to writing at the moment of their delivery, all hope of their faithful reproduction must be abandoned. Hence Dr. Paulus once actually entertained the idea, that in the judgment-halls of the temple or the synagogues at Jerusalem, there were stationed a sort of shorthand writers, whose office it was to draw up verbal processes, and that from their records the Christians, after the death of Christ, made transcripts[4]. In like manner, Bertholdt was of opinion, that our evangelist, during the lifetime of Jesus, took down most of the discourses of Jesus in the Aramæan language, and made these notes the foundation of his gospel, composed at a much later period[5]. These modern hypotheses are clearly unhistorical[6]; nevertheless, their propounders were able to adduce many reasons in their support. The prophetic declarations of Jesus relative to his death and resurrection, said Bertholdt, are more indefinite in John than in the synoptical gospels, a sure sign that they were recorded before their fulfilment, for otherwise the writer's experience of the event would have reflected more clearness on the predictions. To this we may add the kindred argument, by which

---

[3] De Wette, Einl. in das N. T. § 105; Tholuck, Comm. z. Joh. s. 38 f.; Glaubwürdigkeit, s. 344 ff.; Lücke, 1, s. 198 f.

[4] Commentar. 4, s. 275 f.

[5] Verosimilia de origine evangelii Joannis, opusc. p. 1 ff. Einleit. in das N. T. s. 1302 ff. This opinion is approved by Wegscheider, ut sup. p. 270 ff. and also Hug. 2. 263 f. and Tholuck, Comm. p. 38, think the supposition of early notes not to be altogether rejected.

[6] Lücke, 1, s. 192 f.

Henke thought it possible to establish the genuineness of the discourses in John: namely, that the fourth Evangelist not seldom appends explanatory remarks, often indeed erroneous, to the obscure expressions of Jesus, thus proving that he was scrupulously conscientious in reporting the discourses, for otherwise he would have mingled his comments with their original matter [7]. But it is with justice objected, that the obscurity of the predictions in the fourth gospel is in perfect harmony with the mystical spirit that pervades the work, and as, besides, the author, together with his fondness for the obscure and enigmatical, indisputably possessed taste, he must have been conscious that a prophecy would only be the more piquant and genuine-looking, the more darkly it was delivered : hence, though he put those predictions into the mouth of Jesus long after the events to which they refer, he might yet choose to give them an indefinite form. This observation helps to explain why the evangelist, when elucidating some obscure expressions of Jesus, adds that his disciples did not understand them until after his resurrection, or after the outpouring of the Holy Spirit (ii. 22 ; vii. 39); for the opposition of the darkness in which the disciples at one time groped, to the light which ultimately arose on them, belongs to that order of contrasts with which this gospel abounds. Another argument, adopted by Bertholdt and approved by Tholück, is, that in the discourses of the fourth gospel there sometimes occur observations, which, having no precise meaning in themselves, nor any connexion with the rest of the discourse, must have been occasioned by some external circumstance, and can only be accounted for on the supposition of prompt, nay, of immediate reduction to writing; and among their examples the passage, *Arise, let us go hence* (xiv. 31), is one of the most important. But the origin of such digressive remarks has been above explained, in

---

[7] Henke, programm. quo illustratur Johannes apostolus nonnullorum Jesu apophthegmatum et ipse interpres.

[9] Bretschneider, Probab. p. 14 f.

a manner that renders the hypothesis of instantaneous note-taking superfluous.

Thus commentators had to excogitate some other means of certifying the genuineness of the discourses of Jesus in the fourth gospel. The general argument, so often adduced, founded on what a good memory might achieve, especially among men of simple lives, unused to writing, lies in the region of abstract possibility, where, as Lücke remarks [9], there may always be nearly as much said against as for a theory. It has been thought more effectual to adopt an argument resting on a narrower basis, and to appeal to the individual distinctions of the apostle John,—to his intimate and peculiar relation to Jesus as the favourite disciple,—to his enthusiasm for his master, which must surely have strengthened his memory, and have enabled him to preserve in the most lively recollection all that came from the lips of his divine friend [10]. Although this peculiar relation of John to Jesus rests on the authority of John's gospel alone, we might, without reasoning in a circle, draw from it conclusions as to the credibility of the discourses communicated by him, were the faults of which his gospel is accused only such as proceed from the inevitable fading of the memory; because the positive notices of that relation could never flow from this negative cause. As, however, the suspicion which has arisen to the prejudice of the fourth evangelist has gone far beyond those limits, even to the extent of taxing him with free invention, no fact resting on the word of John can be used in support of the discourses which he communicates. But neither the above relation, if admitted, nor the remark that John apparently attached himself to Jesus in early youth, when impressions sink deepest, and from the time of his master's death lived in a circle where the memory of his words and deeds was cherished [11], suffices to render it probable that John could retain

[9] Ut sup. p. 199.
[10] Wegscheider, p. 286 ; Lücke, p. 195 f.
[11] Wegscheider, p. 285 ; Lücke ut sup.

in his mind long series of ideas, and complicated dialogues, until the period in which the composition of his gospel must be placed. For critics are agreed that the tendency of the fourth gospel, its evident aim to spiritualize the common faith of Christians into the Gnosis, and thus to crush many errors which had sprung up, is a decisive attestation that it was composed at a period when the church had attained a degree of maturity, and consequently in the extreme old age of the apostle [12].

Hence the champions of the discourses in question are fain to bring forward, as a forlorn hope, the supernatural assistance of the Paraclete, which was promised to the disciples, and which was to restore all that Jesus had said to their remembrance. This is done by Tholück with great confidence [13], by Lücke with some diffidence [14], which Tholück's Anzeiger severely censures, but which we consider laudable, because it implies a latent consciousness of the circle that is made, in attempting to prove the truthfulness of the discourses in John, by a promise which appears nowhere but in those discourses [15]; and of the inadequacy of an appeal, in a scientific inquiry, to a popular notion, such as that of the aid of the Holy Spirit. The consciousness of this inadequacy shows itself indirectly in Tholück, for he ekes out the assistance of the Paraclete by early notes; and in Lücke also, for he renounces the verbal authenticity of the discourses in John, and only contends for their substantial veracity on grounds chiefly connected with the relation which they bear to other discourses.

The external relation of the discourses of Jesus in John's gospel is also twofold; for they may be compared both with those discourses which the synoptists put into the mouth of Jesus,

[12] Lücke, s. 124 f. 175.   Kern, über den Ursprung des Evang. Matthäi, in der Tüb. Zeitschrift, 1834, 2, s. 109.

[13] S. 39.

[14] S. 197.   "But lastly, why should we fear to adduce," &c.

[15] The aid promised to the disciples when brought before rulers and tribunals, Matt. x. 19 f., is quite distinct from a bringing to remembrance of the discourses of Jesus (John xiv. 26).

and with the manner in which the author of the fourth gospel expresses himself when he is avowedly the speaker.

As a result of the former comparison, critics have pointed out the important difference that exists between the respective discourses in their matter, as well as in their form. In the first three gospels, Jesus closely adapts his teaching to the necessities of his shepherdless people, contrasting, at one time, the corrupt institutions of the Pharisees with the moral and religious precepts of the Mosaic law; at another, the carnal messianic hopes of the age with the purely spiritual nature of his kingdom, and the conditions of entrance therein. In the fourth gospel, on the contrary, he is perpetually dilating, and often in a barren, speculative manner, on the doctrine of his person and higher nature : so that in opposition to the diversified doctrinal and practical materials of the synoptical discourses, we have in John a one-sided dogmatism [16]. That this opposition does not hold invariably, and that in the discourses of the synoptical gospels there are passages which have more affinity with those of John, and vice versâ, must be granted to judicious critics [17]; but the important preponderance of the dogmatical element on the one side, and of the practical on the other, is a difficulty that demands a thorough explanation. In answer to this requisition, it is common to adduce the end which John is supposed to have had in view in the composition of his gospel : namely, to furnish a supplement to the first three gospels, and to supply their omissions. But if Jesus taught first in one style, then in another, how was it that the synoptists selected almost exclusively the practical and popular, John, nearly without exception, the dogmatic and speculative portions of his discourse ? This is accounted for in a manner intrinsically probable. In the oral tradition, it is observed, on which the first three gospels were founded, the simple and popular, the concise and sententious discourses of Jesus, being the most easy of retention, would alone be propagated, while

[16] Bretschneider, Probab. p. 2, 3, 31 ff.
[17] De Wette, Einl. in das N. T. § 103 ; Hase, L. J. § 7.

his more profound, subtle and diffuse discourses would be lost [18]. But according to the above supposition, the fourth evangelist came as a gleaner after the synoptists: now it is certain that all the discourses of Jesus having a practical tendency had not been preserved by them; hence, that the former has almost invariably avoided giving any relic of such discourses, can only be explained by his preference for the dogmatic and speculative vein: a preference which must have had both an objective and a subjective source, the necessities of his time and circumstances, and the bent of his own mind. This is admitted even by critics who are favourable to the authenticity of the fourth gospel [19], with the reservation, that that preference betrays itself only negatively, by omission, not positively, by addition.

There is a further difference between the synoptical gospels and the fourth, as to the form of teaching adopted by Jesus; in the one, it is aphoristic and parabolic, in the other, dialectic [20]. We have seen that the parable is altogether wanting in the fourth gospel, and it is natural to ask why, since Luke, as well as Matthew, has many admirable parables peculiar to himself, John has not been able to make a rich gleaning, even after those two predecessors? It is true that isolated apothegms and sentences, similar to the synoptical ones, are not entirely absent from the fourth gospel: but, on the other hand, it must be admitted that the prevailing aphoristic and parabolic form of instruction, ascribed to Jesus by the synoptists, is more suited to the character of a popular teacher of Palestine, than the dialectic form which he is made to adopt by John [21].

But the relation of the discourses of Jesus in the gospel of John, to the evangelist's own style of thinking and writing, is decisive. Here we find a similarity [22], which, as it extends to the discourses of a third party, namely, the Baptist, cannot be

[18] Lücke, ut sup. p. 100. Kern, ut. sup.
[19] Tholück, ut sup.
[20] Bretschneider, ut sup.
[21] De Wette, ut sup. § 105.
[22] Comp. Schulze, der schriftst. Charakter und Werth des Johannes. 1803.

explained by supposing that the disciple had formed his style on that of the master [23], but requires us to admit that the evangelist has lent his own style to the principal characters in his narrative. The latest commentator on John has not only acknowledged this with regard to the colouring of the expression; he even thinks that in the matter itself he can here and there detect the explanatory amplifications of the evangelist, who, to use his own phrase, has had a hand in the composition of the longer and more difficult discourses [24]. But since the evangelist does not plainly indicate his additions, what is to assure us that they are not throughout interwoven with the ideas of Jesus, nay, that all the discourses which he communicates are not entirely his own productions? The style furnishes no guidance, for this is every where the same, and is admitted to be the evangelist's own; neither does the sense, for in it also there is no essential difference whether the evangelist speaks in his own name, or in that of Jesus: where then is the guarantee that the discourses of Jesus are not, as the author of the Probabilia maintains, free inventions of the fourth evangelist?

Lücke adduces some particulars, which on this supposition would be in his opinion inexplicable [25]. First, the almost verbal agreement of John with the synoptists in isolated sayings of Jesus. But as the fourth evangelist was within the pale of the Christian community, he must have had at his command a tradition, from which, though drawing generally on his own resources, he might occasionally borrow isolated, marked expressions, nearly unmodified. Another argument of Lücke is yet more futile. If, he says, John had really had the inclination and ability to invent discourses for Jesus, he would have been more liberal in long discourses; and the alternation of brief remarks with prolonged addresses, is not to be explained on the above supposition. But this would follow only if the author of

---

[23] Stronck—de doctrinâ et dictione Johannis apostoli, ad Jesu magistri doctrinam dictionemque exacte composita.   1797.

[24] Lücke, Comm. z. Joh. 1, p. 200.

[25] Ut. sup. p. 199.

the fourth gospel appeared to be a tasteless writer, whose perception did not tell him, that to one occasion a short discourse
was suitable, to another a long one, and that the alternation of
diffuse harangues with concise sentences was adapted to produce
the best impression. Of more weight is the observation of
Paulus, that if the fourth evangelist had given the rein to his
invention in attributing discourses to Jesus, he would have obtruded more of his own views, of which he has given an abstract
in his prologue; whereas the scrupulousness with which he
abstains from putting his doctrine of the Logos into the mouth
of Jesus, is a proof of the faithfulness with which he confined
himself to the materials presented by his memory or his authorities [26]. But the doctrine of the Logos is substantially contained in the succeeding discourse of Jesus; and that the form
in which it is propounded by the evangelist in his preface, does
not also reappear, is sufficiently explained by the consideration,
that he must have known that form to be altogether foreign to
the teaching of Jesus.

We therefore hold it to be established, that the discourses of
Jesus in John's gospel are mainly free compositions of the
evangelist; but we have admitted that he has culled several sayings of Jesus from an authentic tradition, and hence
we do not extend this proposition to those passages which are
countenanced by parallels in the synoptical gospels. In these
compilations we have an example of the vicissitudes which befal
discourses, that are preserved only in the memory of a second
party. Severed from their original connexion, and broken up
into smaller and smaller fragments, they present when reassembled the appearance of a mosaic, in which the connexion
of the parts is a purely external one, and every transition an
artificial juncture. The discourses of Jesus in John present
just the opposite appearance. Their gradual transitions, only
rendered occasionally obscure by the mystical depths of meaning in which they lie,—transitions in which one thought deve-

---

[26] In his review of the 2nd Ed. of Lücke's Commentar., in the Lit. Blatt der
allgem. Kirchenzeitung 1834, no. 18.

lops itself out of another, and a succeeding proposition is frequently but an explanatory amplification of the preceding [27],— are indicative of a pliable, unresisting mass, such as is never presented to a writer by the traditional sayings of another, but such as proceeds from the stores of his own thought, which he moulds according to his will. For this reason the contributions of tradition to these stores of thought, (apart from the sayings which are also found in the earlier gospels,) were not so likely to have been particular, independent dicta of Jesus, as rather certain ideas which formed the basis of many of his discourses, and which were modified and developed according to the bent of a mind of Alexandrian or Greek culture. Such are the correlative ideas of πατήρ and υἱός (*father* and *son*), φῶς and σκότος (*light* and *darkness*), ζωή and θάνατος (*life* and *death*), ἄνω and κάτω (*above* and *beneath*), σάρξ and πνεῦμα (*flesh* and *spirit*) ; also some symbolical expressions, as ἄρτος τῆς ζωῆς (*bread of life*), ὕδωρ ζῶν (*water of life*). These and a few other ideas, variously combined by an ingenious author, compose the bulk of the discourses attributed to Jesus by John ; a certain uniformity necessarily attending this elemental simplicity.

[27] This peculiarity of the discourses in John cannot be better described than by Erasmus in his Epist. ad Ferdinandum, prefatory to his Paraphrase : *habet Johannes suum quoddam dicendi genus, ita sermonem velut ansulis ex sese cohærentibus contexens, nonnunquam ex contrariis, nonnunquam ex similibus, nonnunquam ex iisdem, subinde repetitis,——ut orationis quodque membrum semper excipiat prius, sic ut prioris finis sit initium sequentis*, etc.

CHAPTER VIII.

EVENTS IN THE PUBLIC LIFE OF JESUS, EXCLUDING THE MIRACLES.

§ 84.

GENERAL COMPARISON OF THE MANNER OF NARRATION THAT DISTINGUISHES THE SEVERAL EVANGELISTS.

IF, before proceeding to the consideration of details, we compare the general character and tone of the historical narration in the various gospels, we find differences, first, between Matthew and the two other synoptists; secondly, between the three first evangelists collectively and the fourth.

Among the reproaches which modern criticism has heaped on the gospel of Matthew, a prominent place has been given to its want of individualized and dramatic life; a want which is thought to prove that the author was not an eye-witness, since an eye-witness is ordinarily distinguished by the precision and minuteness of his narration[1]. Certainly, when we read the indefinite designation of times, places and persons, the perpetually recurring τότε, *then*, παράγων ἐκεῖθεν, *departing from thence*, ἄνθρωπ:ς, *a man*, which characterize this gospel; when we recollect its wholesale statements, such as that Jesus went through all the cities and villages (ix. 35; xi. 1; comp. iv. 23); that they brought to him all sick people, and that he healed them all (iv. 24 f.; xiv. 35 f.; comp. xv. 29 ff.); and finally, the bareness and brevity of many isolated narratives: we cannot

[1] Schulz, über das Abendmahl, s. 303 ff. : Sieffert, über den Urspr. des ersten kanon. Evang. s. 58, 73, u. s. ; Schneckenburger, über den Urspr. s. 73.

disapprove the decision of this criticism, that Matthew's whole narrative resembles a record of events which, before they were committed to writing, had been long current in oral tradition, and had thus lost the impress of particularity and minuteness. But it must be admitted, that this proof, taken alone, is not absolutely convincing; for in most cases we may verify the remark, that even an eye-witness may be unable graphically to narrate what he has seen[2].

But our modern critics have not only measured Matthew by the standard of what is to be expected from an eye-witness, in the abstract; they have also compared him with his fellow-evangelists. They are of opinion, not only that John decidedly surpasses Matthew in the power of delineation, both in their few parallel passages and in his entire narrative, but also that the two other synoptists, especially Mark, are generally far clearer and fuller in their style of narration[3]. This is the actual fact, and it ought not to be any longer evaded. With respect to the fourth evangelist, it is true that, as one would have anticipated, he is not devoid of general, wholesale statements, such as, that Jesus during the feast did many miracles, that hence many believed on him (ii. 23), with others of a similar kind (iii. 22 ; vii. 1) : and he not seldom designates persons indecisively. Sometimes, however, he gives the names of individuals whom Matthew does not specify (xii. 3, 4 ; comp. with Matt. xxvi. 7, 8 ; and xviii. 10. with Matt. xxvi. 51 ; also vi. 5 ff. with Matt. xiv. 16 f.) ; and he generally lets us know the district or country in which an event happened. His careful chronology we have already noticed ; but the point of chief importance is that his narratives, (e. g. that of the man born blind, and that of the resurrection of Lazarus,) have a dramatic and life-like character, which we seek in vain in the first gospel. The two intermediate evangelists are not free from indecisive designations of time (e. g. Mark viii. 1 ; Luke v. 17 ; viii. 22); of place (Mark iii. 13 ; Luke vi. 12); and of

---

[2] Olshausen, b. Comm. 1, s. 15.

[3] See the above named critics, passim ; and Hug. Einl. in das N. T. 2, s. 212.

persons (Mark x. 17 ; Luke xiii. 23) ; nor from statements that
Jesus went through all cities, and healed all the sick (Mark
i. 32 ff. ; 38 f. ; Luke iv. 40 f.) ; but they often give us the
details of what Matthew has only stated generally. Not only
does Luke associate many discourses of Jesus with special
occasions concerning which Matthew is silent, but both he and
Mark notice the office or names of persons, to whom Matthew
gives no precise designation (Matt. ix. 18 ; Mark v. 22 ; Luke
viii. 41 ; Matth. xix. 16 ; Luke xviii. 18 ; Matth. xx. 30 ;
Mark x. 46). But it is chiefly in the lively description of particular incidents, that we perceive the decided superiority of
Luke, and still more of Mark, over Matthew. Let the reader
only compare the narrative of the execution of John the Baptist
in Matthew and Mark (Matth. xiv. 3 ; Mark vi. 17), and that of
the demoniac or demoniacs of Gadara (Matt. viii. 28 ff. parall.).

These facts are, in the opinion of our latest critics, a confirmation of the fourth evangelist's claim to the character of an
eye-witness, and of the greater proximity of the second and
third evangelists to the scenes they describe, than can be
attributed to the first. But, even allowing that one who
does not narrate graphically cannot be an eye-witness, this
does not involve the proposition that whoever does narrate
graphically must be an eye-witness. In all cases in which
there are extant two accounts of a single fact, the one full,
the other concise, opinions may be divided as to which of
them is the original [4]. When these accounts have been liable
to the modifications of tradition, it is important to bear in mind
that tradition has two tendencies : the one, to sublimate the concrete into the abstract, the individual into the general ; the other,
not less essential, to substitute arbitrary fictions for the historical reality which is lost [5]. If then we put the want of precision in the narrative of the first evangelist to the account of
the former function of the legend, ought we at once to regard
the precision and dramatic effect of the other gospels, as a proof

---

[4] Comp. Saunier, über die Quellen des Markus, s. 42 ff.

[5] Kern, über den Urspr. des Ev. Matth. ut sup. s. 70 f.

that their authors were eye-witnesses ? Must we not rather examine whether these qualities be not derived from the second function of the legend [6] ? The decision with which the other inference is drawn, is in fact merely an after-taste of the old orthodox opinion, that all our gospels proceed immediately from eye-witnesses, or at least through a medium incapable of error. Modern criticism has limited this supposition, and admitted the possibility that one or the other of our gospels may have been affected by oral tradition.   Accordingly it maintains, not without probability, that a gospel in which the descriptions are throughout destitute of colouring and life, cannot be the production of an eye-witness, and must have suffered from the effacing fingers of tradition.   But the counter proposition, that the other gospels, in which the style of narration is more detailed and dramatic, rest on the testimony of eye-witnesses, would only follow from the supposed necessity that this must be the case with some of our gospels.   For if such a supposition be made with respect to several narratives of both the above kinds, there is no question that the more graphic and vivid ones are with preponderant probability to be referred to eye-witnesses.   But this supposition has merely a subjective foundation.   It was an easier transition for commentators to make from the old notion that all the gospels were immediately or mediately autoptical narratives, to the limited admission that perhaps one may fall short of this character, than to the general admission that it may be equally wanting to all.   But, according to the rigid rules of consequence, with the orthodox view of the scriptural canon, falls the assumption of pure ocular testimony, not only for one or other of the gospels, but for all : the possibility of the contrary must be presupposed in relation to them all, and their pretensions must be estimated according to their internal character, compared with the external testimonies.   From this point of view—the only one that criticism can consistently

---

[6] I say, *examine whether*—not, *consider it decided that*—so that the accusation of opponents, that I use both the particularity and the brevity of narratives as proofs of their mythical character, falls to the ground of itself.

adopt—it is as probable, considering the nature of the external testimonies examined in our Introduction, that the three last evangelists owe the dramatic effect in which they surpass Matthew, to the embellishments of a more mature tradition, as that this quality is the result of a closer communication with eye-witnesses.

That we may not anticipate, let us, in relation to this question, refer to the results we have already obtained. The greater particularity by which Luke is distinguished from Matthew in his account of the occasions that suggested many discourses of Jesus, has appeared to us often to be the result of subsequent additions; and the names of persons in Mark (xiii. 3. comp. v. 37; Luke viii. 51.) have seemed to rest on a mere inference of the narrator. Now, however, that we are about to enter on an examination of particular narratives, we will consider, from the point of view above indicated, the constant forms of introduction, conclusion, and transition, already noticed, in the several gospels. Here we find the difference between Matthew and the other synoptists, as to their more or less dramatic style, imprinted in a manner that can best teach us how much this style is worth.

Matthew (viii. 16 f.) states in general terms, that on the evening after the cure of Peter's mother-in-law, many demoniacs were brought to Jesus, all of whom, together with others that were sick, he healed. Mark, (i. 32.) in a highly dramatic manner, as if he himself had witnessed the scene, tells, that on the same occasion, the whole city was gathered together at the door of the house in which Jesus was; at another time, he makes the crowd block up the entrance (ii. 2.); in two other instances, he describes the concourse as so great, that Jesus and his disciples could not take their food (iii. 20; vi. 31.); and Luke on one occasion states, that the people even gathered together in innumerable multitudes so that *they trode one upon another.* (xii. 1.). All highly vivid touches, certainly: but the want of them can hardly be prejudicial to Matthew, for they look thoroughly like strokes of imagination, such as abound in

Mark's narrative, and often, as Schleiermacher observes [7], give it almost an apocryphal appearance. In detailed narratives, of which we shall presently notice many examples, while Matthew simply tells what Jesus said on a certain occasion, the two other evangelists are able to describe the glance with which his words were accompanied (Mark iii. 5; x. 21; Luke vi. 10). On the mention of a blind beggar of Jericho, Mark is careful to give us his name, and the name of his father (x. 46). From these particulars we might already augur, what the examination of single narratives will prove: namely, that the copiousness of Mark and Luke is the product of the second function of the legend, which we may call the function of embellishment. Was this embellishment gradually wrought out by oral tradition, or was it the arbitrary addition of our evangelists? Concerning this, there may be a difference of opinion, and a degree of probability in relation to particular passages is the nearest approach that can be made to a decision. In any case, not only must it be granted, that a narrative adorned by the writer's own additions is more remote from primitive truth than one free from such additions; but we may venture to pronounce that the earlier efforts of the legend are rapid sketches, tending to set off only the leading points whether of speech or action, and that at a later period it aims rather to give a symmetrical effect to the whole, including collateral incidents; so that, in either view, the closest approximation to truth remains on the side of the first gospel.

While the difference as to the more or less dramatic style of concluding and connecting forms, lies chiefly between Matthew and the other synoptists; another difference with respect to these forms, exists between all the synoptists and John. While most of the synoptical anecdotes from the public life of Jesus are wound up by a panegyric, those of John generally terminate, so to speak, polemically. It is true that the three first evangelists sometimes mention, by way of conclusion, the

---

[7] Ueber den Lukas, s. 74, and elsewhere.

offence that Jesus gave to the narrow-hearted, and the machinations of his enemies against him (Matt. viii. 34; xii. 14; xxi. 46; xxvi. 3 f.; Luke iv. 28 f.; xi. 53 f.); and, on the other hand, the fourth evangelist closes some discourses and miracles by the remark, that in consequence of them, many believed on Jesus (ii. 23; iv. 39. 53; vii. 31. 40 f.; viii. 30; x. 42; xi. 45). But in the synoptical gospels, throughout the period previous to the residence of Jesus in Jerusalem, we find forms implying that the fame of Jesus had extended far and wide (Matt. iv. 24; ix. 26. 31; Mark i. 28. 45; v. 20; vii. 36; Luke iv. 37; v. 15; vii. 17; viii. 39); that the people were astonished at his doctrine (Matt. vii. 28; Mark i. 22; xi. 18; Luke xix. 48), and miracles (Matt. viii. 27; ix. 8; xiv. 33; xv. 31), and hence followed him from all parts (Matt. iv. 25; viii. 1; ix. 36; xii. 15; xiii. 2; xiv. 13). In the fourth gospel, on the contrary, we are continually told that the Jews sought to kill Jesus (v. 18; vii. 1); the Pharisees wish to take him, or send out officers to seize him (vii. 30. 32. 44; comp. viii. 20; x. 39); stones are taken up to cast at him (viii. 59; x. 31); and even in those passages where there is mention of a favourable disposition on the part of the people, the evangelist limits it to one portion of them, and represents the other as inimical to Jesus (vii. 11—13). He is especially fond of drawing attention to such circumstances, as that before the final catastrophe all the guile and power of the enemies of Jesus were exerted in vain, because his hour was not yet come (vii. 30; viii. 20); that the emissaries sent out against him, overcome by the force of his words, and the dignity of his person, retired without fulfilling their errand (vii. 32. 44 ff.); and that Jesus passed unharmed through the midst of an exasperated crowd (viii. 59; x. 39; comp. Luke iv. 30). The writer, as we have above remarked, certainly does not intend us in these instances to think of a natural escape, but of one in which the higher nature of Jesus, his invulnerability so long as he did not choose to lay down his life, was his protection. And this throws some light on the object which the fourth evangelist had in view, in giving prominence to such traits as those just enumerated: they helped him to add to the number of the contrasts, by which, throughout his works, he aims to exalt the person of Jesus. The profound wisdom of Jesus, as the divine Logos, appeared the more resplendent, from its opposition to the rude unapprehensiveness of the Jews; his goodness wore a more touching aspect, confronted with the inveterate malice of his enemies; his appearance gained in impressiveness, by the strife he excited among the people; and his power, as that of one who had life in himself, commanded the more reverence, the oftener his enemies and their instruments tried to seize him, and, as if restrained by a higher power, were not able to lay hands on him,—the more marvellously he passed through the ranks of adversaries prepared to take away his life. It has been made matter of praise to the fourth evangelist, that he alone presents the opposition of the pharisaic party to Jesus, in its rise and gradual progress: but there are reasons for questioning whether the course of events described by him, be not rather fictitious than real. Partially fictitious, it evidently is; for he appeals to the supernatural for a reason why the Pharisees so long effected nothing against Jesus: whereas the synoptists preserve the natural sequence of the facts by stating as a cause, that the Jewish hierarchy feared the people, who were attached to Jesus as a prophet (Matt. xxi. 46; Mark xii. 12; Luke xx. 19). If then the fourth evangelist was so far guided by his dogmatical interest, that for the escape of Jesus from the more early snares and assaults of his enemies, he invented such a reason as best suited his purpose; what shall assure us that he has not also, in consistency with the characteristics which we have already discerned in him, fabricated, for the sake of that interest, entire scenes of the kind above noticed? Not that we hold it improbable, that many futile plots and attacks of the enemies of Jesus preceded the final catastrophe of his fate:—we are only dubious whether these attempts were precisely such as the gospel of John describes.

§ 85.

In conformity with the aim of our criticism, we shall here confine our attention to those narratives, in which the influence of the legend may be demonstrated. The strongest evidence of this influence is found where one narrative is blended with another, or where the one is a mere variation of the other: hence, chronology having refused us its aid, we shall arrange the anecdotes about to be considered according to their mutual affinity.

To begin with the more simple form of legendary influence: Schulz has already complained, that Matthew mentions two instances, in which a league with Beelzebub was imputed to Jesus, and a sign demanded from him; circumstances which in Mark and Luke happen only once[1]. The first time the imputation occurs (Matt. ix. 32 ff.), Jesus has cured a dumb demoniac; at this the people marvel, but the Pharisees observe, *He casts out demons through the prince* ($ἄρχων$) *of the demons.* Matthew does not here say that Jesus returned any answer to this accusation. On the second occasion (xii. 22 ff.), it is a blind and dumb demoniac whom Jesus cures; again the people are amazed, and again the Pharisees declare that the cure is effected by the help of Beelzebub, the $ἄρχων$ of the demons, whereupon Jesus immediately exposes the absurdity of the accusation. That it should have been alleged against Jesus more than once when he cast out demons, is in itself probable. It is however suspicious that the demoniac who gives occasion to the assertion of the Pharisees, is in both instances dumb (in the second only, blindness is added). Demoniacs were of many kinds, every variety of malady being ascribed to the influence of evil spirits; why, then, should the above imputation be not once attached to the cure of another kind of demoniac, but twice

[1] Ut. sup s. 311.

to that of a dumb one? The difficulty is heightened if we compare the narrative of Luke (xi. 14 f.), which, in its introductory description of the circumstances, corresponds not to the second narrative in Matthew, but to the first; for as there, so in Luke, the demoniac is only dumb, and his cure and the astonishment of the people are told with precisely the same form of expression:—in all which points, the second narrative of Matthew is more remote from that of Luke. But with this cure of the dumb demoniac, which Matthew represents as passing off in silence on the part of Jesus, Luke connects the very discourse which Matthew appends to the cure of the one both blind and dumb; so that Jesus must on both these successive occasions, have said the same thing. This is a very unlikely repetition, and united with the improbability, that the same accusation should be twice made in connexion with a dumb demoniac, it suggests the question, whether legend may not here have doubled one and the same incident? How this can have taken place, Matthew himself shows us, by representing the demoniac as, in the one case, simply dumb, in the other, blind also. Must it not have been a striking cure which excited, on the one hand, the astonishment of the people, on the other, this desperate attack of the enemies of Jesus? Dumbness alone might soon appear an insufficient malady for the subject of the cure, and the legend, ever prone to enhance, might deprive him of sight also. If then, together with this new form of the legend, the old one too was handed down, what wonder that a compiler, more conscientious than critical, such as the author of the first gospel, adopted both as distinct histories, merely omitting on one occasion the discourse of Jesus, for the sake of avoiding repetition[2].

[2] Schleiermacher (s. 175), does not perceive the connexion of the discourse on the blasphemy against the Holy Ghost, in Matthew (xii. 31 f.), though it links on excellently to the foregoing expression, ἐγὼ ἐν πνεύματι θεοῦ ἐκβάλλω τὰ δαιμόνια (v. 28). It is more easy, however, to understand this difficulty, than that he should think (s. 185 f.) that discourse better introduced in Luke (xii. 10). For here, between the preceding proposition, that whosoever denies the Son of man before men, shall be denied before the angels of God, and the one in question, the only con-

Matthew, having omitted (ix. 34) the discourse of Jesus, was obliged also to defer the demand of a sign, which required a previous rejoinder on the part of Jesus, until his second narration of the charge concerning Beelzebub; and in this point again the narrative of Luke, who also attaches the demand of a sign to the accusation, is parallel with the later passage of Matthew[3]. But Matthew not only has, with Luke, a demand of a sign in connexion with the above charge; he has also another,

nexion is that the expression ἀρνεῖσθαι τὸν υἱὸν τοῦ ἀνθρώπου brought to the writer's recollection the words εἰπεῖν λόγον εἰς τὸν υἱὸν τοῦ ἀνθρώπου. One proof of this is that between the latter passage and the succeeding declaration, that the necessary words would be given to the disciples, when before the tribunal, by the πνεῦμα ἅγιον, the connexion consists just as superficially in the expression πνεῦμα ἅγιον. What follows in Matthew (v. 33—37), had been partly given already in the sermon on the mount, but stands here in a better connexion than Schleiermacher is willing to admit.

[3] Luke makes the demand of a sign follow immediately on the accusation, and then gives in succession the answers of Jesus to both. This representation modern criticism holds to be far more probable than that of Matthew, who gives first the accusation and its answer, then the demand of a sign and its refusal; and this judgment is grounded on the difficulty of supposing, that after Jesus had given a sufficiently long answer to the accusation, the very same people who had urged it would still demand a sign (Schleiermacher, s. 175; Schneckenburger, über den Urspr. s. 52 f.) But on the other hand, it is equally improbable that Jesus, after having some time ago delivered a forcible discourse on the more important point, the accusation concerning Beelzebub, and even after an interruption which had led him to a totally irrelevant declaration (Luke xi. 27 f.), should revert to the less important point, namely, the demand of a sign. The discourse on the departure and return of the unclean spirit, is in Matthew (v. 43—45) annexed to the reply of Jesus to this demand; but in Luke (xi. 24 ff.) it follows the answer to the imputation of a league with Beelzebub, and this may at first seem to be a more suitable arrangement. But on a closer examination, it will appear very improbable that Jesus should conclude a defence, exacted from him by his enemies, with so calm and purely theoretical a discourse, which supposes an audience, if not favourably prepossessed, at least open to instruction ; and it will be found that here again there is no further connexion than that both discourses treat of the expulsion of demons. By this single feature of resemblance, the writer of the third gospel was led to sever the connexion between the answer to the oft-named accusation, and that to the demand of a sign, which accusation and demand, as the strongest proofs of the malevolent unbelief of the enemies of Jesus, seem to have been associated by tradition. The first evangelist refrained from this violence, and reserved the discourse on the return of the unclean spirit, which was suggested by the suspicion cast on the expulsion of demons by Jesus, until he had communicated the answer by which Jesus parries the demand of a sign.

after the second feeding of the multitude (xvi. 1 ff.), and this second demand Mark also has (viii. 11 f.), while he omits the first. Here the Pharisees come to Jesus (according to Matthew, in the unlikely companionship of Sadducees), and tempt him by asking for *a sign from heaven*, σημεῖον ἐκ τοῦ οὐρανοῦ. To this Jesus gives an answer, of which the concluding proposition, *a wicked and adulterous generation seeketh after a sign; and there shall no sign be given unto it, but the sign of the prophet Jonas*, γενεὰ πονηρὰ καὶ μοιχαλὶς σημεῖον ἐπιζητεῖ, καὶ σημεῖον οὐ δοθήσεται αὐτῇ, εἰ μὴ τὸ σημεῖον Ἰωνᾶ τοῦ προφήτου, in Matthew, agrees word for word with the opening of the earlier refusal. It is already improbable enough, that Jesus should have twice responded to the above requisition with the same enigmatical reference to Jonah; but the words (v. 2, 3) which, in the second passage of Matthew, precede the sentence last quoted, are totally unintelligible. For why Jesus, in reply to the demand of his enemies that he would show them a sign from heaven, should tell them that they were indeed well versed in the natural signs of the heavens, but were so much the more glaringly ignorant of the spiritual signs of the messianic times, is so far from evident, that the otherwise unfounded omission of v. 2 and 3, seems to have arisen from despair of finding any connexion for them[4]. Luke, who also has, (xii. 54 f.), in words only partly varied, this reproach of Jesus that his cotemporaries understood better the signs of the weather than of the times, gives it another position, which might be regarded as the preferable one; since after speaking of the fire which he was to kindle, and the divisions which he was to cause, Jesus might very aptly say to the people; You take no notice of the unmistakeable prognostics of this great revolution which is being prepared by my means, so ill do you understand the signs of the times[5]. But on a closer examination, Luke's arrangement appears just as abrupt here, as in the case of the two parables

---

[4] Vid. Griesbach, Comm. crit. in loc.
[5] Comp. Schleiermacher, s. 190 f.

(xiii. 18) [6]. If from hence we turn again to Matthew, we easily see how he was led to his mode of representation. He may have been induced to double the demand of a sign, by the verbal variation which he met with, the required sign being at one time called simply a σημεῖον, at another a σημεῖον ἐκ τοῦ οὐρανοῦ. And if he knew that Jesus had exhorted the Jews to study the signs of the times, as they had hitherto studied the appearance of the heavens, the conjecture was not very remote, that the Jews had given occasion for this admonition by demanding a *sign from heaven,* σημεῖον ἐκ τοῦ οὐρανοῦ. Thus Matthew here presents us, as Luke often does elsewhere, with a fictitious introduction to a discourse of Jesus; a proof of the proposition, advanced indeed, but too little regarded by Sieffert [7]: that it is in the nature of traditional records, such as the three first gospels, that one particular should be best preserved in this narrative, another in that; so that first one, and then the other, is at a disadvantage, in comparison with the rest.

§ 86.

VISIT OF THE MOTHER AND BRETHREN OF JESUS.   THE WOMAN WHO PRONOUNCES
THE MOTHER OF JESUS BLESSED.

All the synoptists mention a visit of the mother and brethren of Jesus, on being apprised of which Jesus points to his disciples, and declares that they who do the will of God are his mother and his brethren (Matt. xii. 46 ff.; Mark iii. 31 ff.; Luke viii. 19 ff.). Matthew and Luke do not tell us the object of this visit, nor, consequently, whether this declaration of Jesus, which appears to imply a disowning of his relatives, was occasioned by any special circumstance. On this subject Mark gives us unexpected information: he tells us (v. 21) that while Jesus was teaching among a concourse of people, who even prevented him from taking food, his relatives, under the idea that he was beside himself, went out to seize him, and take him

[6] De Wette, exeg. Handb. i. 1, s. 139.
[7] Ueber den Urspr. s. 115.

into the keeping of his family[1]. In describing this incident, the evangelist makes use of the expression, ἔλεγον ὅτι ἐξέστη, (*they said, he is beside himself*), and it was merely this expression, apparently, that suggested to him what he next proceeds to narrate: οἱ γραμματεῖς ἔλεγον, ὅτι Βεελζεβοὺλ ἔχει κ. τ. λ. (*the scribes said, he hath Beelzebub*, &c., comp. John x. 20). With this reproach, which however he does not attach to an expulsion of demons, he connects the answer of Jesus; he then recurs to the relatives, whom he now particularizes as the mother and brethren of Jesus, supposing them to have arrived in the meantime; and he makes their announcement call forth from Jesus the answer of which we have above spoken.

These particulars imparted by Mark are very welcome to commentators, as a means of explaining and justifying the apparent harshness of the answer which Jesus returns to the announcement of his nearest relatives, on the ground of the perverted object of their visit. But, apart from the difficulty that, on the usual interpretation of the accounts of the childhood of Jesus, it is not to be explained how his mother could, after the events therein described, be thus mistaken in her son, it is very questionable whether we ought to accept this information of Mark's. In the first place, it is associated with the obvious exaggeration, that Jesus and his disciples were prevented even from taking food by the throng of people; and in the second place, it has in itself a strange appearance, from its want of relation to the context. If these points are considered, it will scarcely be possible to avoid agreeing with the opinion of Schleiermacher, that no explanation of the then existing relations of Jesus with his family is to be sought in this addition; that it rather belongs to those exaggerations to which Mark is so prone, as well in his introductions to isolated incidents, as in his general statements[2]. He wished to make it understood why Jesus returned an ungracious answer to the announcement of his relatives; for this purpose he thought it necessary to give

---

[1] For the proof of this interpretation, see Fritzsche, comm. in Marc. p. 97 ff.
[2] Ueber den Lukas, s. 121.

their visit an object of which Jesus did not approve, and as he knew that the Pharisees had pronounced him to be under the influence of Beelzebub, he attributed a similar opinion to his relatives.

If we lay aside this addition of Mark's, the comparison of the three very similar narratives presents no result as it regards their matter[3]; but there is a striking difference between the connexions in which the evangelists place the event. Matthew and Mark insert it after the defence against the suspicion of diabolical aid, and before the parable of the sower; whereas Luke makes the visit considerably prior to that imputation, and places the parable even before the visit. It is worthy of notice, however, that Luke has, after the defence against the accusation of a league with Beelzebub, in the position which the two other evangelists give to the visit of the relatives of Jesus, an incident which issues in a declaration, precisely similar to that which the announcement calls forth. After the refutation of the Pharisaic reproach, and the discourse on the return of the unclean spirit, a woman in the crowd is filled with admiration, and pronounces the mother of Jesus blessed, on which Jesus, as before on the announcement of his mother, replies ; *Yea, rather blessed are they who hear the word of God and keep it!*[4] Schleiermacher

---

[3] Schneckenburger, (über den Ur s. 54), finds an attempt at dramatic effect in the εἰπέ τις, and the ἐκτείνας τὴν χεῖρα of Matthew, as compared with the εἶπον and περιβλεψάμενος κύκλῳ of Mark. This is a remarkable proof of the partial acumen which plays so distinguished a part to the disadvantage of Matthew in modern criticism. For who does not see that if Matthew had εἶπον, it would be numbered among the proofs that his narrative is wanting in dramatic life? As for the words ἐκτείνας τὴν χεῖρα, there is nothing to be discovered in them which could give to them more than to the περιβλεψάμενος of Mark, the stamp of artificiality : we might as well attribute the latter expression to Mark's already discovered fondness for describing the action of the eyes, and consequently regard it as an addition of his own.

[4] Answer to the announcement, viii.
21: μήτηρ μοῦ καὶ ἀδελφοί μοῦ οὗτοί εἰσιν οἱ τὸν λόγον τοῦ θεοῦ ἀκούντες καὶ ποιοῦντες αὐτόν.

Answer to the woman, xi. 28 :
μενοῦνγε μακάριοι (sc. οὐχ ἡ μήτηρ μοῦ, ἀλλ') οἱ ἀκούοντες τὸν λόγον τοῦ θεοῦ καὶ φυλάσσοντες αὐτόν.

here again prefers the account of Luke: he thinks this little
digression on the exclamation of the woman, especially evinces
a fresh and lively recollection, which has inserted it in its real
place and circumstances; whereas Matthew, confounding the
answer of Jesus to the ejaculation of the woman, with the very
similar one to the announcement of his relatives, gives to the
latter the place of the former, and thus passes over the scene
with the woman[5]. But how the woman could feel herself hur-
ried away into so enthusiastic an exclamation, precisely on
hearing the abstruse discourse on the return of the expelled
demons, or even the foregoing reprehensive reply to the Pharisees, it is difficult to understand, and the contrary conjecture
to that of Schleiermacher might rather be established; namely,
that in the place of the announcement of the relatives, the writer
of the third gospel inserted the scene with the woman, from its
having a like termination. The evangelical tradition, as we
see from Matthew and Mark, whether from historical or merely
accidental motives, had associated the above visit and the saying
about the spiritual relatives, with the discourse of Jesus on the
accusation of a league with Beelzebub, and on the return of the
unclean spirit; and Luke also, when he came to the conclusion
of that discourse, was reminded of the anecdote of the visit and
its point—the extolling of a spiritual relationship to Jesus. But
he had already mentioned the visit[6]; he therefore seized on the
scene with the woman, which presented a similar termination.
From the strong resemblance between the two anecdotes, I can
scarcely believe that they are founded on two really distinct incidents; rather, it is more likely that the memorable declaration
of Jesus, that he preferred his spiritual before his bodily rela-

---

[5] Ut sup. s. 177 f.

[6] That which decided the evangelist to place the visit after the parable of the
sower, was probably not, as Schleiermacher thinks, a real chronological connexion.
On the contrary, we recognize the usual characteristic of his arrangement, in the
transition from the concluding sentence in the explanation of the parable : *these are
they who having heard the word, keep it, and bring forth fruit with patience,* to the
similar expression of Jesus on the occasion of the visit : *those who hear the word of
God and do it.*

tives, had in the legend received two different settings or frames. According to one, it seemed the most natural that such a depreciation of his kindred should be united with an actual rejection of them; to another, that the exaltation of those who were spiritually near to him, should be called forth by a blessing pronounced on those who were nearest to him in the flesh. Of these two forms of the legend, Matthew and Mark give only the first: Luke, however, had already disposed of this on an earlier occasion; when, therefore, he came to the passage where, in the common evangelical tradition, that anecdote occurred, he was induced to supply its place by the second form.

§ 87.

CONTENTIONS FOR PRE-EMINENCE AMONG THE DISCIPLES.   THE LOVE OF JESUS FOR
CHILDREN.

The three first evangelists narrate several contentions for pre-eminence which arose among the disciples, with the manner in which Jesus composed these differences. One such contention, which is said to have arisen among the disciples after the transfiguration, and the first prediction of the passion, is common to all the gospels (Matt. xviii. 1 ff.; Mark ix. 33 ff.; Luke ix. 46 ff.). There are indeed divergencies in the narratives, but the identity of the incident on which they are founded is attested by the fact, that in all of them, Jesus sets a little child before his disciples as an example; a scene which, as Schleiermacher remarks[1], would hardly be repeated. Matthew and Mark concur in mentioning a dispute about pre-eminence, which was excited by the two sons of Zebedee. These disciples (according to Mark), or their mother for them (according to Matthew), petitioned for the two first places next to Jesus in the messianic kingdom (Matt. xx. 20 ff.; Mark x. 35 ff.)[2]. Of such a re-

[1] Ut. sup. s. 152.
[2] Schulz (üb. d. Abendm. s. 320) speaks consistently with the tone of the recent criticism on Matthew when he asserts, that he does not doubt *for a moment* that every *observant* reader will, *without hesitation*, prefer the representation of Mark, who, without mentioning the mother, confines the whole transaction to Jesus and the

quest on the part of the sons of Zebedee, the third evangelist
knows nothing; but apart from this occasion, there is a further
contention for pre-eminence, on which discourses are uttered,
similar to those which the two first evangelists have connected
with the above petition.   At the last supper of which Jesus partook with his disciples before his passion, Luke makes the latter
fall into a φιλονεικία (*dispute*) which among them shall be
the greatest; a dispute which Jesus seeks to quell by the same
reasons, and partly with the same words, that Matthew and
Mark give in connexion with the ἀγανάκτησις (*indignation*),
excited in the disciples generally by the request of the sons of
Zebedee.   Luke here reproduces a sentence which he, in common with Mark, had previously given almost in the same
form, as accompanying the presentation of the child; and which
Matthew has, not only on the occasion of Salome's prayer, but
also in the great anti-pharisaic discourse (comp. Luke xxii. 26;
Mark ix. 35; Luke ix. 48; Matt. xx. 26 f., xxiii. 11).   However credible it may be that with the worldly messianic hopes
of the disciples, Jesus should often have to suppress disputes
among them on the subject of their future rank in the Messiah's kingdom, it is by no means probable that, for example,
the sentence, *Whosoever will be great among you, let him be
the servant of all:* should be spoken, 1st, on the presentation
of the child; 2ndly, in connexion with the prayer of the sons of
Zebedee; 3rdly, in the anti-pharisaic discourse, and 4thly, at
the last supper.   There is here obviously a traditional confusion, whether it be (as Sieffert in such cases is fond of supposing) that several originally distinct occurrences have been
assimilated by the legend, i. e. the same discourse erroneously
repeated on various occasions; or that out of one incident the

two apostles.   But so far as historical probability is concerned, I would ask, why
should not a woman, who was one of the female companions of Jesus (Matt. xxvii.
56), have ventured on such a petition?   As regards psychological probability, the
sentiment of the church, in the choice of the passage for St. James's day, has usually
decided in favour of Matthew; for so solemn a prayer, uttered on the spur of the
moment, is just in character with a woman, and more especially a mother devoted to
her sons.

legend has made many, i. e. has invented various occasions for
the same discourse. Our decision between these two possibili-
ties must depend on the answer to the following question :
Have the various facts, to which the analogous discourses on
humility are attached, the dependent appearance of mere frames
to the discourses, or the independent one of occurrences that
carry their truth and significance in themselves ?

It will not be denied that the petition of the sons of Zebedee,
is in itself too specific and remarkable to be a mere background
to the ensuing discourse ; and the same judgment must be
passed on the scene with the child : so that we have already two
cases of contention for pre-eminence subsisting in themselves.
If we would assign to each of these occurrences its appropriate
discourses, the declarations which Matthew connects with the
presentation of the child : *Unless ye become as this child,* &c.,
and *Whosoever shall humble himself as this child,* &c., evidently belong to this occasion. On the other hand, the
sentences on ruling and serving in the world and in the kingdom of Jesus, seem to be a perfectly suitable comment on the
petition of the sons of Zebedee, with which Matthew associates
them : also the saying about the first and the last, the
greatest and the least, which Mark and Luke give so early as
at the scene with the child, Matthew seems rightly to have reserved for the scene with the sons of Zebedee. It is otherwise
with the contention spoken of by Luke (xxii. 24 ff.). This
contention originates in no particular occasion, nor does it
issue in any strongly marked scene, (unless we choose to insert here the washing of the disciples' feet, described by John,
who, for the rest, mentions no dispute ;—of which scene, however, we cannot treat until we come to the history of the Passion.) On the contrary, this contention is ushered in merely
by the words, ἐγένετο δὲ καὶ φιλονεικία ἐν αὐτοῖς,—nearly the
same by which the first contention is introduced, ix. 46,—and
leads to a discourse from Jesus, which, as we have already
noticed, Matthew and Mark represent him to have delivered in
connexion with the earlier instances of rivalry ; so that this

passage of Luke has nothing peculiarly its own, beyond its position, at the last supper. This position, however, is not very secure; for that immediately after the discourse on the betrayer, so humiliating to the disciples, pride should so strongly have taken possession of them, is as difficult to believe, as it is easy to discover, by a comparison of v. 23 and 24, how the writer might be led, without historical grounds, to insert here a contention for pre-eminence. It is clear that the words καὶ αὐτοὶ ἤρξαντο συζητεῖν πρὸς ἑαυ- τοὺς, τὸ, τίς ἄρα εἴη ἐξ αὐτῶν ὁ τοῦτο μέλλων πράσσειν; suggested to him the similar ones, ἐγένετο δὲ καὶ φιλονεικία ἐν αὐτοῖς, τὸ, τίς αὐτῶν δοκεῖ εἶναι μείζων; that is, the disputes about the be- trayer called to his remembrance the disputes about pre-emi- nence. One such dispute indeed, he had already mentioned, but had only connected with it, one sentence excepted, the discourses occasioned by the exhibition of the child; he had yet in reserve those which the two first evangelists attach to the petition of the sons of Zebedee, an occasion which seems not to have been present to the mind of the third evangelist, whence he introduces the discourses pertaining to it here, with the general statement that they originated in a contention for pre-eminence, which broke out among the disciples. Mean- while the chronological position, also, of the two first-named disputes about rank, has very little probability; for in both in- stances, it is after a prediction of the passion, which, like the prediction of the betrayal, would seem calculated to suppress such thoughts of earthly ambition[3]. We therefore welcome the indication which the evangelical narrative itself presents, of the manner in which the narrators were led unhistorically to such an arrangement. In the answer of Jesus to the prayer of Salome, the salient point was the suffering that awaited him and his disciples; hence by the most natural association of ideas, the ambition of the two disciples, the antidote to which was the announcement of approaching trial, was connected with the prediction of the passion. Again, on the first occasion of

---

[3] Compare Schleiermacher, ut sup. s. 283.

rivalry, the preceding prediction of the passion leads in Mark and Luke to the observation, that the disciples did not understand the words of Jesus, and yet feared to ask him concerning them, whence it may be inferred that they debated and disputed on the subject among themselves; here, then, the association of ideas caused the evangelists to introduce the contention for preeminence, also carried on in the absence of Jesus. This explanation is not applicable to the narrative of Matthew, for there, between the prediction of the passion and the dispute of the disciples, the anecdote of the coin angled for by Peter, intervenes.

With the above contentions for pre-eminence, another anecdote is indirectly connected by means of the child which is put forward on one of those occasions. Children are brought to Jesus that he may bless them; the disciples wish to prevent it, but Jesus speaks the encouraging words, *Suffer little children to come unto me*, and adds that only for children, and those who resemble children, is the kingdom of heaven destined (Matt. xix. 13 ff.; Mark x. 13 ff.; Luke xviii. 15 ff.). This narrative has many points of resemblance to that of the child placed in the midst of the disciples. 1stly, in both, Jesus presents children as a model, and declares that only those who resemble children can enter the kingdom of God; 2ndly, in both, the disciples appear in the light of opposition to children; and, 3rdly, in both, Mark says, that Jesus took the children in his arms (ἐναγκαλισάμενος.) If these points of resemblance be esteemed adequate ground for reducing the two narratives to one, the latter must, beyond all question, be retained as the nearest to truth, because the saying of Jesus, *Suffer little children*, &c. which, from its retaining this original form in all the narratives, bears the stamp of genuineness, could scarcely have been uttered on the other occasion; whereas, the sentences on children as patterns of humility, given in connection with the contention about rank, might very well have been uttered under the circumstances above described, in retrospective allusion to previous contentions about rank. Nevertheless, this might rather be the place for supposing an assimilation of originally diverse occurrences, since it is at least evident, that Mark has inserted the expression ἐναγκαλισάμενος in both, simply on account of the resemblance between the two scenes.

§ 88.

THE PURIFICATION OF THE TEMPLE.

Jesus, during his first residence in Jerusalem, according to John (ii. 14 ff.), according to the synoptists, during his last (Matt. xxi. 12 ff. parall.), undertook the purification of the temple. The ancient commentators thought, and many modern ones still think [1], that these were separate events, especially as, besides the chronological difference, there is some divergency between the three first evangelists and the fourth in their particulars. While, namely, the former, in relation to the conduct of Jesus, merely speak in general terms of an *expulsion*, ἐκβάλλειν, John says that he made a *scourge of small cords*, φραγέλλιον ἐκ σχοινίων, for this purpose: again, while according to the former, he treats all the sellers alike, he appears, according to John, to make some distinction, and to use the sellers of doves somewhat more mildly; moreover, John does not say that he drove out the buyers, as well as the sellers. There is also a difference as to the language used by Jesus on the occasion; in the synoptical gospels, it is given in the form of an exact quotation from the Old Testament; in John, merely as a free allusion. But, above all, there is a difference as to the result: in the fourth gospel, Jesus is immediately called to account; in the synoptical gospels, we read nothing of this, and according to them, it is not until the following day that the Jewish authorities put to Jesus a question, which seems to have reference to the purification of the Temple (Matt. xxi. 23 ff.), and to which Jesus replies quite otherwise than to the remonstrance in the fourth gospel. To explain the repetition of such a

---

[1] Paulus and Tholuck, in loc.; Neander, L. J. Chr., s. 388, Anm.

measure, it is remarked that the abuse was not likely to cease on the first expulsion, and that on every revival of it, Jesus would feel himself anew called on to interfere; that, moreover, the temple purification in John is indicated to be an earlier event than that in the synoptical gospels, by the circumstance, that the fourth evangelist represents Jesus as being immediately called to account, while his impunity in the other case appears a natural consequence of the heightened consideration which he had in the meantime won.

But allowing to these divergencies their full weight, the agreement between the two narratives preponderates. We have in both the same abuse, the same violent mode of checking it, by *casting out* ($\dot{\epsilon}\varkappa\beta\acute{a}\lambda\lambda\epsilon\iota\nu$) the people, and *overthrowing* ($\dot{a}\nu\alpha\sigma\tau\rho\acute{\epsilon}\varphi\epsilon\iota\nu$) the tables; nay, virtually, the same language in justification of this procedure, for in John, as well as in the other gospels, the words of Jesus contain a reference, though not a verbally precise one, to Isai. lvi. 7; Jer. vii. 11. These important points of resemblance must at least extort such an admission as that of Sieffert[2], namely, that the two occurrences, originally but little alike, were assimilated by tradition, the features of the one being transferred to the other. But thus much seems clear; the synoptists know as little of an earlier event of this kind, as in fact of an earlier visit of Jesus to Jerusalem: and the fourth evangelist seems to have passed over the purification of the temple after the last entrance of Jesus into the metropolis, not because he presumed it to be already known from the other gospels, but because he believed that he must give an early date to the sole act of the kind with which he was acquainted. If then each of the evangelists knew only of one purification of the temple, we are not warranted either by the slight divergencies in the description of the event, or by the important difference in its chronological position, to suppose that there were two; since chronological differences are by no means rare in the gospels, and are quite natural in writings of traditional origin. It is therefore with justice that our most

[2] Ueber den Urspr. s. 108 ff.

modern interpreters have, after the example of some older ones, declared themselves in favour of the identity of the two histories [3].

On which side lies the error? We may know beforehand how the criticism of the present day will decide on this question: namely, in favour of the fourth gospel. According to Lücke, the scourge, the diversified treatment of the different classes of traders, the more indirect allusion to the Old Testament passage, are so many indications that the writer was an eye and ear witness of the scene he describes; while as to chronology, it is well known that this is in no degree regarded by the synoptists, but only by John, whence, according to Sieffert [4], to surrender the narrative of the latter to that of the former, would be to renounce the certain for the uncertain. As to John's dramatic details, we may match them by a particular peculiar to Mark, *And they would not suffer that any man should carry any vessel through the temple* (v. 16), which besides has a support in the Jewish custom which did not permit the court of the temple to be made a thoroughfare [5]. If, nevertheless, this particular is put to the account of Mark's otherwise ascertained predilection for arbitrary embellishment [6], what authorizes us to regard similar artistic touches from the fourth evangelist, as necessary proofs of his having been an eyewitness? To appeal here to his character of eye-witness as a recognized fact [7], is too glaring a *petitio principii*, at least in the point of view taken by a comparative criticism, in which the decision as to whether the artistic details of the fourth evangelist are mere embellishments, must depend solely on intrinsic probability. Although the different treatment of the different classes of men is in itself a probable feature, and the freer allusion to the Old Testament is at least an indifferent one; it

[3] Lücke, 1. s. 435 ff.; De Wette, exeg. Handb. i. 1, s. 174 f.; i. 3, s. 40.

[4] Ut sup. s. 109; comp. Schneckenburger, s. 26 f.

[5] Lightfoot, s. 632, from Bab. Jevamoth, f. vi. 2.

[6] Lücke, s. 438.

[7] Lücke, s. 437; Sieffert, s. 110.

is quite otherwise with the most striking feature in the narrative of John. Origen has set the example of objecting to the twisting and application of the scourge of small cords, as far too violent and disorderly a procedure [8]. Modern interpreters soften the picture by supposing that Jesus used the scourge merely against the cattle [9] (a supposition, however, opposed to the text, which represents *all* πάντας as being driven out by the scourge); yet still they cannot avoid perceiving the use of a scourge at all to be unseemly in a person of the dignity of Jesus, and only calculated to aggravate the already tumultuary character of the proceeding [10]. The feature peculiar to Mark is encumbered with no such difficulties, and while it is rejected, is this of John to be received? Certainly not, if we can only find an indication in what way the fourth evangelist might be led to the free invention of such a particular. Now it is evident from the quotation v. 17, which is peculiar to him, that he looked on the act of Jesus as a demonstration of holy zeal—a sufficient temptation to exaggerate the traits of zealousness in his conduct.

In relation to the chronological difference, we need only remember how the fourth evangelist antedates the acknowledgment of Jesus as the Messiah by the disciples, and the conferring of the name of Peter on Simon, to be freed from the common assumption of his pre-eminent chronological accuracy, which is alleged in favour of his position of the purification of the temple. For this particular case, however, it is impossible to show any reason why the occurrence in question would better suit the time of the first, than of the last passover visited by Jesus, whereas there are no slight grounds for the opposite opinion. It is true that nothing in relation to chronology is to be founded on the improbability that Jesus should so early have referred to his death and resurrection, as he must have done, according to John's interpretation of the saying about the

---

[8] Comm. in Joh. tom. 10, § 17; Opp. 1, p. 322, ed. Lommatzsch.
[9] Kuinöl, in loc.
[10] Bretschneider, Probab. p. 43.

destruction and rebuilding of the temple [11]; for we shall see, in the proper place, that this reference to the death and resurrection, owes its introduction into the declaration of Jesus to the evangelist alone.   But it is no inconsiderable argument against John's position of the event, that Jesus, with his prudence and tact, would hardly have ventured thus early on so violent an exercise of his messianic authority [12].   For in that first period of his ministry he had not given himself out as the Messiah, and under any other than messianic authority, such a step could then scarcely have been hazarded; moreover, he in the beginning rather chose to meet his cotemporaries on friendly ground, and it is therefore hardly credible that he should at once, without trying milder means, have adopted an appearance so antagonistic.   But to the last week of his life such a scene is perfectly suited.   Then, after his messianic entrance into Jerusalem, it was his direct aim in all that he did and said, to assert his messiahship, in defiance of the contradiction of his enemies; then, all lay so entirely at stake, that nothing more was to be lost by such a step.

As regards the nature of the event, Origen long ago thought it incredible, that so great a multitude should have unresistingly submitted to a single man,—one, too, whose claims had ever been obstinately contested: his only resource in this exigency is to appeal to the superhuman power of Jesus, by virtue of which he was able suddenly to extinguish the wrath of his enemies, or to render it impotent; and hence Origen ranks this expulsion among the greatest miracles of Jesus [13].   Modern expositors decline the miracle [14], but Paulus is the only one among them

[11] English Commentators, ap. Lücke, 1, s. 435 f. Anm.

[12] Eng. Comm. ap. Lücke.   According to Neander (s. 387, anm.), Jesus, after his last entrance into Jerusalem, when the enthusiasm of the populace was on his side, must have shunned every act that could be interpreted into a design of using external force, and thus creating disturbances.   But he must equally have shunned this at the beginning, as at the end, of his career, and the proceeding in the temple was rather a provocation of external force against himself, than a use of it for his own purposes.

[13] Comm. in Joh. Tom. 10. 16. p. 321 f. ed. Lommatzsch.

[14] Lücke, in loc.

who has adequately weighed Origen's remark, that in the
ordinary course of things the multitude would have opposed
themselves to a single person.   Whatever may be said of the
surprise caused by the suddenness of the appearance of Jesus [15]
(if, as John relates, he made himself a scourge of cords, he
would need some time for preparation), of the force of right
on his side [16] (on the side of those whom he attacked, however,
there was established usage); or, finally, of the irresistible
impression produced by the personality of Jesus [17] (on usurers
and cattle-dealers—on brute-men, as Paulus calls them?):
still, such a multitude, certain as it might be of the protection
of the priesthood, would not have unresistingly allowed themselves to be driven out of the temple by a single man.   Hence
Paulus is of opinion that a number of others, equally scandalized by the sacrilegious traffic, made common cause with Jesus,
and that to their united strength the buyers and sellers were
compelled to yield [18].   But this supposition is fatal to the entire
incident, for it makes Jesus the cause of an open tumult; and
it is not easy either to reconcile this conduct with his usual
aversion to every thing revolutionary, or to explain the omission
of his enemies to use it as an accusation against him.   For that
they held themselves bound in conscience to admit that the
conduct of Jesus was justifiable in this case, is the less credible,
since, according to a rabbinical authority [19], the Jews appear to
have been so far from taking umbrage at the market in the court
of the Gentiles (and this is all we are to understand by the word
ἱερὸν) [20], that the absence of it seemed to them like a melancholy
desolation of the temple.   According to this, it is not surprising
that Origen casts a doubt on the historical value of this narrative, by the expression, εἴγε καὶ αὐτὴ γεγένηται, (*if it really
happened*), and at most admits that the evangelist, in order to

[15] Lücke, s. 413.
[16] Ib. and Tholuck, in loc.
[17] Olshausen, 1. s. 785.
[18] Comm. 4, s. 164.
[19] Hieros. Joh. tobh. f. lxi. 3, ap. Lightfoot, p. 411.
[20] Lücke, Comm. 1, s. 410.

present an idea allegorically, καὶ γεγενημένῳ συνέχρήσατο πράγματι (*also borrowed the form of an actual occurrence*)[21].

But in order to contest the reality of this history, in defiance of the agreement of all the four evangelists, the negative grounds hitherto adduced must be seconded by satisfactory positive ones, from whence it might be seen how the primitive Christian legend could be led to the invention of such a scene, apart from any historical foundation. But these appear to be wanting. For our only positive data in relation to this occurrence are the passages cited by the synoptists from Isaiah and Jeremiah, prohibiting that the temple should be made a den of robbers; and the passage from Malachi, iii. 1—3, according to which it was expected that in the messianic times Jehovah would suddenly come to his temple, that no one would stand before his appearing, and that he would undertake a purification of the people and the worship. Certainly these passages seem to have some bearing on the irresistible reforming activity of Jesus in the temple, as described by our evangelists; but there is so little indication that they had reference in particular to the market in the outer court of the temple, that it seems necessary to suppose an actual opposition on the part of Jesus to this abuse, in order to account for the fulfilment of the above prophecies by him being represented under the form of an expulsion of buyers and sellers.

§ 89.

NARRATIVES OF THE ANOINTING OF JESUS BY A WOMAN.

An occasion on which Jesus was anointed by a woman as he sat at meat, is mentioned by all the evangelists (Matt. xxvi. 6 ff.; Mark xiv. 3 ff.; Luke vii. 36 ff.; John xii. 1 ff.), but with some divergencies, the most important of which lie between Luke and the other three. First, as to the chronology; Luke places the incident in the earlier period of the life of Jesus, before his departure from Galilee, while the other three assign it

[21] Ut sup. comp. also Woolston, Disc. 1.

to the last week of his life; secondly, as to the character of the woman who anoints Jesus: she is, according to Luke, a *woman who was a sinner,* γυνὴ ἁμαρτωλὸς; according to the two other synoptists, a person of unsullied reputation; according to John, who is more precise, Mary of Bethany. From the second point of difference it follows, that in Luke the objection of the spectators turns on the admission of so infamous a person, in the other gospels, on the wastefulness of the woman; from both, it follows, that Jesus in his defence dwells, in the former, on the grateful love of the woman, as contrasted with the haughty indifference of the Pharisees, in the latter, on his approaching departure, in opposition to the constant presence of the poor. There are yet the minor differences, that the place in which the entertainment and the anointing occur, is by the two first and the fourth evangelists called Bethany (which according to John xi. 1, was a κώμη *town*), by Luke a πόλις (*city*), without any more precise designation; further, that the objection, according to the three former, proceeds from the disciples, according to Luke, from the entertainer. Hence the majority of commentators distinguish two anointings, of which one is narrated by Luke, the other by the three remaining evangelists [1].

But it must be asked, if the reconciliation of Luke with the other three evangelists is despaired of, whether the agreement of the latter amongst themselves is so decided, and whether we must not rather proceed, from the distinction of two anointings, to the distinction of three, or even four? To four certainly it will scarcely extend; for Mark does not depart from Matthew, except in a few touches of his well-known dramatic manner; but between these two evangelists on the one side, and John on the other, there are differences which may fairly be compared with those between Luke and the rest. The first difference relates to the house in which the entertainment is said to have been given; according to the two first evangelists, it was the house of Simon

---

[1] Thus Paulus, exeg. Handb. 1, b. s. 766; L. J. 1, a, s. 292; Tholück, Lücke, Olshausen, in loc.; Hase, L. J. § 96 Anm.

the leper, a person elsewhere unnoticed; the fourth does not, it is true, expressly name the host, but since he mentions Martha as the person who waited on the guests, and her brother Lazarus as one of those who sat at meat, there is no doubt that he intended to indicate the house of the latter as the locality of the repast [2]. Neither is the time of the occurrence precisely the same, for according to Matthew and Mark the scene takes place after the solemn entrance of Jesus into Jerusalem, only two days at the utmost before the passover; according to John, on the other hand, before the entrance, as early as six days prior to the passover [3]. Further, the individual whom John states to be that Mary of Bethany so intimately united to Jesus, is only known to the two first evangelists as *a woman γυνὴ;* [4] neither do they represent her as being, like Mary, in the house, and one of the host's family, but as coming, one knows not whence, to Jesus, while he reclined at table. Moreover the act of anointing is in the fourth gospel another than in the two first. In the latter, the woman pours her ointment of spikenard on the head of Jesus; in John, on the contrary, she anoints his feet, and dries them with her hair [5], a difference which gives the whole scene a new character. Lastly, the two synoptists are not aware that it was Judas who gave utterance to the censure against the woman; Matthew attributing it to the disciples, Mark, to the spectators generally [6].

Thus between the narrative of John, and that of Matthew and Mark, there is scarcely less difference than between the account of these three collectively, and that of Luke: whoever supposes two distinct occurrences in the one case, must, to be consistent, do so in the other; and thus, with Origen hold, at

---

[2] This difference struck Origen, who has given a critical comparison of these four narratives, to which, in point of acumen, there is no parallel in more modern commentaries. See his *in Matth. Commentarior. series,* Opp. ed. de la Rue, 3, s. 892 ff.

[3] Origenes, ut sup.

[4] Ib.

[5] Ib.

[6] Ib.

least conditionally, that there were three separate anointings. So soon, however, as this consequence is more closely examined, it must create a difficulty, for how improbable is it that Jesus should have been expensively anointed three times, each time at a feast, each time by a woman, that woman being always a different one; that moreover Jesus should, in each instance, have had to defend the act of the woman against the censures of the spectators [7]! Above all, how is it to be conceived that after Jesus, on one and even on two earlier occasions, had so decidedly given his sanction to the honour rendered to him, the disciples, or one of them, should have persisted in censuring it [8]?

These considerations oblige us to think of reductions, and it is the most natural to commence with the narratives of the two first synoptists and of John, for these agree not only in the place, Bethany, but also, generally, in the time of the event, the last week of the life of Jesus; above all, the censure and the reply are nearly the same on both sides. In connexion with these similarities the differences lose their importance, partly from the improbability that an incident of this kind should be repeated; partly from the probability, that in the traditional propagation of the anecdote such divergencies should have insinuated themselves. But if in this case the identity of the occurrences be admitted, in consideration of the similarities, and in spite of the dissimilarities; then, on the other hand, the divergencies peculiar to the narrative of Luke, can no longer hinder us from pronouncing it to be identical with that of the three other evangelists, provided that there appear to be only a few important points of resemblance between the two. And such really exist, for Luke now strikingly accords with Matthew and Mark, in opposition to John; now, with the latter, in opposition to the former. Luke gives the entertainer the same name as the two first synoptists, namely, Simon, the only difference being, that the former calls him *a pharisee*, while the

[7] Comp. Schleiermacher, über den Lukas, s. 111.

[8] Origenes and Schleiermacher.   Winer, N. T. Gramm. s. 149.

latter style him *the leper*.   Again, Luke agrees with the other synoptists in opposition to John, in representing the woman who anoints Jesus as a nameless individual, not belonging to the house; and further, in making her appear with a *box of ointment*, ἀλάβαστρον μύρου, while John speaks only of a *pound of ointment*, λίτρα μύρου, without specifying the vessel.   On the other hand, Luke coincides in a remarkable manner with John, and differs from the two other evangelists, as to the mode of the anointing.   While, namely, according to the latter, the ointment is poured on the head of Jesus, according to Luke, the woman, *who was a sinner*, as, according to John, Mary, anoints the feet of Jesus; and even the striking particular, that she dried them with her hair [9], is given by both in nearly the same words; excepting that in Luke, where the woman is described as a sinner, it is added that she bathed the feet of Jesus with her tears, and kissed them.   Thus, without doubt, we have here but one history under three various forms; and this seems to have been the real conclusion of Origen, as well as recently of Schleiermacher.

In this state of the case, the effort is to escape as cheaply as possible, and to save the divergencies of the several evangelists at least from the appearance of contradiction.   First, with regard to the differences between the two first evangelists and the last, it has been attempted to reconcile the discrepant dates by the supposition, that the meal at Bethany was held really, as John informs us, six days before Easter; but that Matthew, after whom Mark wrote, has no contradictory date; that rather he has no date at all; for though he inserts the narrative of the meal and the anointing after the declaration of Jesus, *that after two days is the feast of the Passover*, ὅτι μετὰ δύο ἡμέρας τὸ πάσχα γίνεται, this does not prove that he intended to place it later as to time, for it is probable that he gave it this position simply because he wished to note here, before coming to the betrayal by Judas, the occasion on which the traitor first em-

---

[9] Luke vii. 38 : τοὺς πόδας αὐτοῦ— ταῖς θριξὶ τῆς κεφαλῆς αὐτῆς ἐξέμασσε.   John xii. 3 : ἐξέμαξε ταῖς θριξὶν αὐτῆς τοὺς πόδας αὐτοῦ.

braced his black resolve, namely, the repast at which he was in-
censed by Mary's prodigality, and embittered by the rebuke of
Jesus [10]. But in opposition to this, modern criticism has shown
that, on the one hand, in the mild and altogether general reply
of Jesus there could lie nothing personally offensive to Judas ;
and that, on the other hand, the two first gospels do not name
Judas as the party who censured the anointing, but the disciples or the bystanders generally : whereas, if they had noted
this scene purely because it was the motive for the treachery of
Judas, they must have especially pointed out the manifestation
of his feeling [11]. There remains, consequently, a chronological
contradiction in this instance between the two first synoptists
and John : a contradiction which even Olshausen admits [12].

It has been attempted in a variety of ways to evade the farther difference as to the person of the host. As Matthew and
Mark speak only of the *house of Simon the leper*, οἰκία Σίμωνος
τοῦ λεπροῦ, some have distinguished the owner of the house,
Simon, from the giver of the entertainment, who doubtless was
Lazarus, and have supposed that hence, in both cases without
error, the fourth evangelist mentions the latter, the two first
synoptists the former [13]. But who would distinguish an entertainment by the name of the householder, if he were not in any
way the giver of the entertainment ? Again, since John does
not expressly call Lazarus the host, but merely one of the
συνανακειμένων (*those sitting at the table*), and since the inference that he was the host is drawn solely from the circumstance that his sister Martha *served*, διηκόνει ; others have regarded Simon as the husband of Martha, either separated on
account of his leprosy, or already deceased, and have supposed
that Lazarus then resided with his widowed sister [14] : an hypothesis which it is more easy to reconcile with the narratives than

---

[10] Kuinöl, Comm. in Matt. p. 687.
[11] Sieffert, über den Ursprung, s. 125 f.
[12] Bibl. Comm. 2, s. 277.
[13] Vid. Kuinöl, ut sup. p. 688 ; also Tholück, s. 228.
[14] Paulus, exeg. Handb. 2, s. 582. ; 3, b. s. 466.

the former, but which is unsupported by any certain information.

We come next to the divergency relative to the mode of anointing; according to the two first evangelists, the ointment was poured on the head of Jesus; according to the fourth, on his feet. The old, trivial mode of harmonizing the two statements, by supposing that both the head and the feet were anointed, has recently been expanded into the conjecture that Mary indeed intended only to anoint the feet of Jesus (John), but that as she accidentally broke the vessel ($\sigma\upsilon\nu\tau\rho\iota\psi\alpha\sigma\alpha$, Mark), the ointment flowed over his head also (Matt.) [15]. This attempt at reconciliation falls into the comic, for as we cannot imagine how a woman who was preparing to anoint the feet of Jesus could bring the vessel of ointment over his head, we must suppose that the ointment spirted upwards like an effervescing draught. So that here also the contradiction remains, and not only between Matthew and John, where it is admitted even by Schneckenburger, but also between the latter evangelist and Mark.

The two divergencies relative to the person of the woman who anoints Jesus, and to the party who blames her, were thought to be the most readily explained. That what John ascribes to Judas singly, Matthew and Mark refer to all the disciples or spectators, was believed to be simply accounted for by the supposition, that while the rest manifested their disapprobation by gestures only, Judas vented his in words [16].

---

[15] Schneckenburger, über den Ursprung, u. s. f. s. 60. There is no trace in Mark's account that the words $\sigma\upsilon\nu\tau\rho\iota\psi\alpha\sigma\alpha$ $\tau\grave{o}$ $\grave{\alpha}\lambda\acute{\alpha}\beta\alpha\sigma\tau\rho\nu$ signify an accidental fracture; nor, on the other hand can they, without the harshest ellipsis, be understood to imply merely the removal of that which stopped the opening of the vessel, as Paulus and Fritzsche maintain. Interpreted without violence, they can only mean a breaking of the vessel itself. Is it asked with Paulus (ex. handb. 3. b. s. 471): To what purpose destroy a costly vessel? or with Fritzsche (in Marc. p. 602): To what purpose risk wounding her own hand, and possibly the head of Jesus also? These are questions which have a bearing on the matter considered as the act of the woman, but not as a narrative of Mark; for that to him, the destruction of a precious vessel should appear suited to the noble prodigality of the woman, is in perfect accordance with the exaggerating style which we have often observed in him.

[16] Kuinöl, in Matth. p. 689.

We grant that the word ἔλεγον, (*they said*) preceded as it is in Mark, by the words ἀγανακτοῦντες πρὸς ἑαυτοὺς (*having indignation within themselves*), and followed, as in Matthew, by the words γνοὺς δὲ ὁ Ἰησοῦς (*but Jesus knowing*), does not necessarily imply that all the disciples gave audible expression to their feelings ; as, however, the two first evangelists immediately after this meal narrate the betrayal by Judas, they would certainly have named the traitor on the above occasion, had he, to their knowledge, made himself conspicuous in connexion with the covetous blame which the woman's liberality drew forth. That John particularizes the woman, whose name is not given by the synoptists, as Mary of Bethany, is, in the ordinary view, only an example how the fourth evangelist supplies the omissions of his predecessors [17]. But as the two first synoptists attach so much importance to the deed of the woman, that they make Jesus predict the perpetuation of her memory on account of it—a particular which John has not—they would assuredly have also given her name had they known it; so that in any case we may conclude thus much : they knew not who the woman was, still less did they conceive her to be Mary of Bethany.

Thus if the identity only of the last evangelist's narrative with that of the two first be acknowledged, it must be confessed that we have, on the one side or the other, an account which is inaccurate, and disfigured by tradition. It is, however, not only between these, but also between Luke and his fellow evangelists collectively, that they who suppose only one incident to be the foundation of their narratives, seek to remove as far as possible the appearance of contradiction. Schleiermacher, whose highest authority is John, but who will on no account renounce Luke, comes in this instance, when the two so widely diverge, into a peculiar dilemma, from which he must have thought that he could extricate himself with singular dexterity, since he has not evaded it, as he does others of a similar kind, by the supposition of two fundamental occurrences. It is true that he

[17] Paulus, exeg. Handb. 3 b. s. 466, and many others.

finds himself constrained to concede, in favour of John, that
Luke's informant could not in this case have been an eye-
witness; whence minor divergencies, as for instance those relative to the locality, are to be explained. On the other hand,
the apparently important differences that, according to Luke,
the woman is a sinner, according to John, Mary of Bethany;
that according to the former, the host, according to the latter,
the disciples, make objections; and that the reply of Jesus is in
the respective narrations totally different—these, in Schleiermacher's opinion, have their foundation in the fact that the occurrence may be regarded from two points of view. The one
aspect of the occurrence is the murmuring of the disciples, and
this is given by Matthew; the other, namely, the relations of
Jesus with the pharisaic host, is exhibited by Luke; and John
confirms both representations. The most decided impediment
to the reconciliation of Luke with the other evangelists, his
designation of the woman as *a sinner*, ἁμαρτωλὸς, Schleiermacher invalidates, by calling it a false inference of the narrator
from the address of Jesus to Mary, *Thy sins are forgiven thee*,
ἀφέωνταί σοι αἱ ἁμαρτίαι. This Jesus might say to Mary
in allusion to some error, unknown to us, but such as the
purest are liable to, without compromising her reputation with
the spectators, who were well acquainted with her character;
and it was only the narrator who erroneously concluded from
the above words of Jesus, and from his further discourse, that
the woman concerned was a sinner in the ordinary sense of the
word, whence he has incorrectly amplified the thoughts of the
host, v. 39 [18]. It is not, however, simply of *sins*, ἁμαρτίαι,
but of *many sins*, πολλαῖ ἁμαρτίαι, that Jesus speaks in rela
tion to the woman; and if this also be an addition of the narrator, to be rejected as such because it is inconsistent with the
character of Mary of Bethany, then has the entire speech of
Jesus from v. 40—48, which turns on the opposition between
forgiving and loving little and much, been falsified or mis-
represented by the evangelist: and on the side of Luke espe-

[18] Ueber den Lukas, s. 111 ff.

cially, it is in vain to attempt to harmonize the discordant narratives.

If, then, the four narratives can be reconciled only by the supposition that several of them have undergone important traditional modifications : the question is, which of them is the nearest to the original fact ? That modern critics should unanimously decide in favour of John, cannot surprise us after our previous observations; and as little can the nature of the reasoning by which their judgment is supported. The narrative of John, say they, (reasoning in a circle,) being that of an eyewitness, must be at once supposed the true one [19], and this conclusion is sometimes rested for greater security on the false premiss, that the more circumstantial and dramatic narrator is the more accurate reporter—the eye-witness [20]. The breaking of the box of ointment, in Mark, although a dramatic particular, is readily rejected as a mere embellishment; but does not John's statement of the quantity of spikenard as a pound, border on exaggeration ? and ought not the extravagance which Olshausen, in relation to this disproportionate consumption of ointment, attributes to Mary's love, to be rather referred to the evangelist's imagination, which would then also have the entire credit of the circumstance, that *the house was filled with the odour of the ointment ?* It is worthy of notice, that the estimate of the value of the perfume at 300 denarii, is given by John and Mark alone ; as also at the miraculous feeding of the multitude, it is these two evangelists who rate the necessary food at 200 denarii. If Mark only had this close estimate, how quickly would it be pronounced, at least by Schleiermacher, a gratuitous addition of the narrator ! What then is it that, in the actual state of the case, prevents the utterance of this opinion, even as a conjecture, but the prejudice in favour of the fourth gospel ? Even the anointing of the head, which is attested by two of the synoptists, is, because John mentions the feet instead of the head, rejected as unusual, and incompatible

[19] Sieffert, ut sup. s. 123 f.
[20] Schulz, ut sup. s. 320 f.

with the position of Jesus at a meal [21] : whereas the anointing
of the feet with precious oil was far less usual ; and this the
most recent commentator on the fourth gospel admits [22].

But peculiar gratitude is rendered to the eye-witness John,
because he has rescued from oblivion the names, both of the
anointing woman, and of the censorious disciple [23]. It has
been supposed that the synoptists did in fact know the name of
the woman, but withheld it from the apprehension that danger
might possibly accrue to the family of Lazarus, while John,
writing later, was under no such restraint [24] ; but this expedient
rests on mere assumptions.   Our former conclusion therefore
subsists, namely, that the earlier evangelists knew nothing of
the name of the woman ; and the question arises, how was this
possible ?   Jesus having expressly promised immortal renown
to the deed of the woman, the tendency must arise to per-
petuate her name also, and if this were identical with the known
and oft repeated name of Mary of Bethany, it is not easy to
understand how the association of the deed and the name could
be lost in tradition, and the woman who anointed Jesus become
nameless. It is perhaps still more incomprehensible, supposing
the covetous blame cast upon the woman to have been really
uttered by him who proved the betrayer, that this should be
forgotten in tradition, and the expression of blame attributed
to the disciples generally.   When a fact is narrated of a person
otherwise unknown, or even when the person being known, the
fact does not obviously accord with his general character, it is
natural that the name should be lost in tradition ; but when
the narrated word or work of a person agrees so entirely with his
known character, as does the covetous and hypocritical blame
in question with the character of the traitor, it is difficult to
suppose that the legend would sever it from his name.   Moreover, the history in which this blame occurs, verges so nearly

[21] Schneckenburger, ut sup. s. 60.
[22] Lücke, 2, s. 417 ; comp. Lightfoot, horæ, p. 468, 1081.
[23] Schulz, ut sup.
[24] Thus Grotius and Herder.

on the moment of the betrayal, (especially according to the position given to it by the two first evangelists,) that had the blame really proceeded from Judas, the two facts would have been almost inevitably associated. Nay, even if that expression of latent cupidity had not really belonged to Judas, there must have been a temptation eventually to ascribe it to him, as a help to the delineation of his character, and to the explanation of his subsequent treachery. Thus the case is reversed, and the question is whether, instead of praising John that he has preserved to us this precise information, we ought not rather to give our approbation to the synoptists, that they have abstained from so natural but unhistorical a combination. We can arrive at no other conclusion with respect to the designation of the woman who anoints Jesus as Mary of Bethany. On the one hand, it is inconceivable that the deed, if originally hers, should be separated from her celebrated name; on the other, the legend, in the course of its development, might naturally come to attribute to one whose spiritual relations with Jesus had, according to the third and fourth gospels, early obtained great celebrity in the primitive church, an act of devoted love towards him, which originally belonged to another and less known person.

But from another side also we find ourselves induced to regard the narratives of Matthew and Mark, who give no name to the woman, rather than that of John, who distinguishes her as Mary of Bethany, as the parent stem of the group of anecdotes before us. Our position of the identity of all the four narratives must, to be tenable, enable us also to explain how Luke's representation of the facts could arise. Now, supposing the narrative of John to be the nearest to the truth, it is not a little surprising that in the legend, the anointing woman should doubly descend from the highly honoured Mary, sister of Lazarus, to an unknown, nameless individual, and thence even to a notorious sinner; it appears far more natural to give the intermediate position to the indifferent statement of the synoptists, out of whose equivocal nameless woman might equally be made, either in an ascending scale, a Mary ; or, in a descending one, a sinner.

The possibility of the first transformation has been already shown : it must next be asked, where could be an inducement, without historical grounds, gradually to invest the anointing woman with the character of a sinner ? In the narrative itself our only clue is a feature which the two first synoptists have not, but which John has in common with Luke ; namely, that the woman anointed the feet of Jesus. To the fourth evangelist, this tribute of feeling appeared in accordance with the sensitive, devoted nature of Mary, whom he elsewhere also (xi. 32), represents as falling at the feet of Jesus ; but by another it might be taken, as by Luke, for the gesture of contrition ; an idea which might favour the conception of the woman as a sinner.—Might *favour*, we say, not *cause :* for a cause, we must search elsewhere.

§ 90.

THE NARRATIVES OF THE WOMAN TAKEN IN ADULTERY, AND OF MARY AND MARTHA.

In the Gospel of John (viii. 1—11), the Pharisees and scribes bring a woman taken in adultery to Jesus, that they may obtain his opinion as to the procedure to be observed against her ; whereupon Jesus, by appealing to the consciences of the accusers, liberates the woman, and dismisses her with an admonition. The genuineness of this passage has been strongly contested, nay, its spuriousness might be regarded as demonstrated, were it not that even the most thorough investigations of the subject [1] indirectly betray a design, which Paulus openly avows, of warding off the dangerous surmises as to the origin of the fourth gospel, which are occasioned by the supposition that this passage, encumbered as it is with improbabilities, is a genuine portion of that gospel. For in the first place, the scribes say to Jesus : *Moses in the law commanded us that*

---

[1] Ap. Wetstein, Paulus, Lücke, in loc.

such should be stoned: now in no part of the Pentateuch is this punishment prescribed for adultery, but simply death, the mode of inflicting it being left undetermined (Lev. xx. 10; Deut. xxii. 22); nor was stoning for adultery a later institution of the Talmud, for according to the canon: *omne mortis supplicium, in scripturâ absolutè positum, esse strangulationem*[2], the punishment appointed for this offence in the Talmud is strangulation[3]. Further, it is difficult to discover what there was to ensnare Jesus in the question proposed to him[4]; the scribes quoted to him the commandment of the law, as if they would warn him, rather than tempt him, for they could not expect that he would decide otherwise than agreeably to the law. Again, the decision of Jesus is open to the stricture, that if only he who is conscious of perfect purity were authorized to judge and punish, all social order would be at an end. The circumstance of Jesus writing on the ground has a legendary and mystical air, for even if it be not correctly explained by the gloss of Jerome: *eorum videlicet, qui accusabant, et omnium mortalium peccata,* it yet seems to imply something more mysterious than a mere manifestation of contempt for the accusers. Lastly, it is scarcely conceivable that every one of those men who dragged the woman before Jesus, zealous for the law, and adverse to his cause as they are supposed to be, should have had so tender a conscience, as on the appeal of Jesus to retire without prosecuting their design, and leave the woman behind them uninjured; this rather appears to belong merely to the legendary or poetical embellishment of the scene. Yet however improbable it may appear, from these observations, that the occurrence happened precisely as it is here narrated, this, as Bretschneider justly maintains[5], proves nothing against the genuineness of the passage, since it is arguing in a circle to assume the apostolic composition of the fourth gospel, and the consequent

[2] Maimonides on Sanhedr. 7, 1.

[3] Mischna, tr. Sanhedr. c. 10.

[4] For a thorough discussion of this and the following points, vid. Paulus and Lücke, in loc.

[5] Probab. p. 72 ff.

impossibility that a narrative containing contradictions should form a portion of it, prior to an examination of its several parts. Nevertheless, on the other hand, the absence of the passage in the oldest authorities is so suspicious, that a decision on the subject cannot be hazarded.

In any case, the narrative of an interview between Jesus and a woman of the above character must be very ancient, since, according to Eusebius, it was found in the gospel of the Hebrews, and in the writings of Papias [6]. It was long thought that the woman mentioned in the Hebrew gospel and by Papias was identical with the adulteress in John; but against this it has been justly observed, that one who had the reproach of *many* sins, must be distinct from her who was detected in the *one* act of adultery [7]. I wonder, however, that no one has, to my knowledge, thought, in connexion with the passage of Eusebius, of the woman in Luke of whom Jesus says that her *many sins, ἁμαρτίαι πολλαὶ*, are forgiven. It is true that the word διαβληθείσης does not fully agree with this idea, for Luke does not speak of actual expressions of the Pharisee in disparagement of the woman, but merely of the unfavourable thoughts which he had concerning her; and in this respect the passage in Eusebius would agree better with the narrative of John, which has an express denunciation, a διαβάλλειν.

Thus we are led on external grounds, by the doubt whether an ancient notice refer to the one or the other of the two narratives, to a perception of their affinity [8], which is besides evident from internal reasons. In both we have a woman, a sinner, before Jesus; in both, this woman is regarded with an evil eye by Pharisaic sanctimoniousness, but is taken into protection by Jesus, and dismissed with a friendly πορεύου, *go*. These were precisely the features, the origin of which

---

[6] Euseb. H. E. iii. 39 : ἐκτέθειται δὲ (ὁ Παπίας) καὶ ἄλλην ἱστορίαν περὶ γυναικὸς ἐπὶ πολλαῖς ἁμαρτίαις διαβληθείσης ἐπὶ τοῦ Κυρίου, ἣν τὸ καθ' Ἑβραίους εὐαγγέλιον περιέχει.

[7] Lücke, 2, s. 217. Paulus, Comm. 4, s. 410.

[8] Elsewhere also the two were confounded, vid. Fabricii Cod. apocryph. N. T. 1, s. 357. not.

we could not understand in the narrative of Luke, viewed as a mere variation of the history of the anointing given by the other evangelists. Now, what is more natural than to suppose that they were transferred into Luke's history of the anointing, from that of the forgiven sinner ? If the Christian legend possessed, on the one side, a woman who had anointed Jesus, who was on this account reproached, but was defended by Jesus; and on the other side, a woman who was accused before him of many sins, but whom he pardoned ; how easily, aided by the idea of an anointing of the feet of Jesus, which bears the interpretation of an act of penitence, might the two histories flow together— the anointing woman become also a sinner, and the sinner also an anointer ? Then, that the scene of the pardon was an entertainment, was a feature also drawn from the history of the anointing : the entertainer must be a Pharisee, because the accusation of the woman ought to proceed from a Pharisaic party, and because, as we have seen, Luke has a predilection for Pharisaic entertainments. Lastly, the discourse of Jesus may have been borrowed, partly from the original narrative of the woman who was a sinner, partly from analogous occasions. If these conjectures be correct, the narratives are preserved unmixed, on the one hand, by the two first evangelists ; on the other, by the fourth, or whoever was the author of the passage on the adulteress ; for if the latter contains much that is legendary, it is at least free from any admixture of the history of the anointing.

Having thus accounted for one modification of the narrative concerning the anointing woman, namely, her degradation into a sinner, by the influence of another and somewhat similar anecdote, which was current in the first age of Christianity, we may proceed to consider experimentally, whether a like external influence may not have helped to produce the opposite modification of the unknown into Mary of Bethany : a modification which, for the rest, we have already seen to be easy of explanation. Such an influence could only proceed from the sole notice of Mary (with the exception of her appearance at the resurrection of Lazarus) which has been preserved to us, and which is rendered memorable by the declaration of Jesus, *One thing is needful, and Mary hath chosen,* &c. (Luke x. 38 ff.). We have, in fact, here as well as there, Martha occupied in serving (John xii. 2, καὶ ἡ Μάρθα διηκόνει ; Luke x. 40, ἡ δὲ Μάρθα περιεσπᾶτο περὶ πολλὴν διακονίαν) ; here, Mary sitting at the feet of Jesus, there, anointing his feet; here, blamed by her sister, there by Judas, for her useless conduct, and in both cases, defended by Jesus.   It is surely unavoidable to say ; if once the narrative of the anointing of Jesus by a woman were current together with that of Mary and Martha, it was very natural, from the numerous points of resemblance between them, that they should be blended in the legend, or by some individual, into one story ; that the unknown woman who anointed the feet of Jesus, who was blamed by the spectators, and vindicated by Jesus, should be changed into Mary, whom tradition had depicted in a similar situation ; the task of serving at the meal with which the anointing was connected attributed to Mary's sister, Martha ; and finally, her brother Lazarus made a partaker of the meal :—so that here the narrative of Luke on the one side, and that of the two synoptists on the other, appear to be pure anecdotes, that of John a mixed one.

Further, in Luke's narrative of the visit of Jesus to the two sisters, there is no mention of Lazarus, with whom, however, according to John (xi. and xii.), Mary and Martha appear to have dwelt; nay, Luke speaks precisely as if the presence or existence of this brother, whom indeed neither he nor either of the other synoptists anywhere notices, were entirely unknown to him.   For had he known anything of Lazarus, or had he thought of him as present, he could not have said : *A certain woman, named Martha, received him into her house ;* he must at least have named her brother also, especially as, according to John, the latter was an intimate friend of Jesus. This silence is remarkable, and commentators have not succeeded in finding a better explanation of it than that given in the natural history of the prophet of Nazareth, where the shortly subsequent death of Lazarus is made available for the supposition that he was, about the time of that visit of Jesus, on a journey for the benefit of his health [9]. Not less striking is another point relative to the locality of this scene. According to John, Mary and Martha dwelt in Bethany, a small town in the immediate vicinity of Jerusalem; whereas Luke, when speaking of the visit of Jesus to these sisters, only mentions a *certain town*, κώμην τινὰ, which is thought, however, to be easily reconciled with the statement of John, by the observation, that Luke assigns the visit to the journey of Jesus to Jerusalem, and to one travelling thither out of Galilee, Bethany would lie in the way. But it would lie quite at the end of this way, so that the visit of Jesus must fall at the close of his journey, whereas Luke places it soon after the departure out of Galilee, and separates it from the entrance into Jerusalem by a multitude of incidents filling eight entire chapters. Thus much then is clear : the author or editor of the third Gospel was ignorant that that visit was paid in Bethany, or that Mary and Martha dwelt there, and it is only that evangelist who represents Mary as the anointing woman, who also names Bethany as the home of Mary : the same place where, according to the two first synoptists, the anointing occurred. If Mary were once made identical with the anointing woman, and if the anointing were known to have happened in Bethany, it would naturally follow that this town would be represented as Mary's home. Hence it is probable that the anointing woman owes her name to the current narrative of the visit of Jesus to Martha and Mary, and that Mary owes her home to the narrative of the meal at Bethany.

We should thus have a group of five histories, among which the narrative given by the two first synoptists of the anointing of Jesus by a woman, would form the centre, that in John of the adulteress, and that in Luke of Mary and Martha, the extremes, while the anointing by the sinner in Luke, and that by Mary in John, would fill the intermediate places. It is true

[9] 3, s. 379 f.

that all the five narratives might with some plausibility be
regarded as varied editions of one historical incident; but from
the essential dissimilarity between the three to which I have assigned the middle and extreme places, I am rather of opinion
that these are each founded on a special incident, but that the
two intermediate narratives are secondary formations which owe
their existence to the intermixture of the primary ones by tradition.

CHAPTER IX.

§ 91.

THAT the Jewish people in the time of Jesus expected miracles from the Messiah is in itself natural, since the Messiah was a second Moses and the greatest of the prophets, and to Moses and the prophets the national legend attributed miracles of all kinds : by later Jewish writings it is rendered probable [1]; by our gospels, certain. When Jesus on one occasion had (without natural means) cured a blind and dumb demoniac, the people were hereby led to ask : *Is not this the son of David ?* (Matt. xii. 23,) a proof that a miraculous power of healing was regarded as an attribute of the Messiah. John the Baptist, on hearing of the *works* of Jesus, (ἔργα), sent to him with the inquiry, *Art thou he that should come,* (ἐρχόμενος)? Jesus, in proof of the affirmative, merely appealed again to his miracles (Matt. xi. 2 ff. parall.). At the Feast of Tabernacles, which was celebrated by Jesus in Jerusalem, many of the people believed on him, saying, in justification of their faith, *When*

---

[1] See the passages quoted in the first volume, Introd. § 14, notes 9, 10, to which may be added 4 Esdr. xiii. 50, (Fabric. Cod. pseudepigr. V. T. ii. p. 286,) and Sohar Exod. fol. iii. col. 12, (Schöttgen, horæ, ii. p. 541, also in Bertholdt's Christol. § 33, note 1.)

Christ cometh, will he do more miracles than these which this man hath done (John vii. 31) ?

But not only was it predetermined in the popular expectation that the Messiah should work miracles in general,—the particular kinds of miracles which he was to perform were fixed, also in accordance with Old Testament types and declarations. Moses dispensed meat and drink to the people in a supernatural manner (Exod. xvi. 17): the same was expected, as the rabbins explicitly say, from the Messiah. At the prayer of Elisha, eyes were in one case closed, in another, opened supernaturally (2 Kings vi.): the Messiah also was to open the eyes of the blind. By this prophet and his master, even the dead had been raised (1 Kings xvii.; 2 Kings iv.): hence to the Messiah also power over death could not be wanting [2]. Among the prophecies, Isai. xxxv. 5, 6 (comp. xlii. 7) was especially influential in forming this portion of the messianic idea. It is here said of the messianic times : *Then shall the eyes of the blind be opened and the ears of the deaf unstopped; then shall the lame man leap as a hart, and the tongue of the dumb shall sing.* These words, it is true, stand in Isaiah in a figurative connexion, but they were early understood literally, as is evident from the circumstance that Jesus describes his miracles to the messengers of John (Matt. xi. 5) with an obvious allusion to this prophetic passsage.

Jesus, in so far as he had given himself out and was believed to be the Messiah, or even merely a prophet, had to meet this expectation when, according to several passages already considered (Matt. xii. 38; xvi. 1. parall.), his Pharisaic enemies required *a sign* from him; when, after the violent expulsion of the traders and money-changers from the Temple, the Jews desired from him *a sign* that should legitimate such an assumption of authority (John ii. 18); and when the people in the synagogue at Capernaum, on his requiring faith in himself as the sent of God, made it a condition of this faith that he should show them *a sign* (John vi. 30).

According to the Gospels, Jesus more than satisfied this

[2] See the rabbinical passages quoted in the 1st vol. ut sup.

demand made by his cotemporaries on the Messiah. Not only
does a considerable part of the evangelical narratives consist of
descriptions of his miracles; not only did his disciples after his
death especially call to their own remembrance and to that of
the Jews the δυνάμεις (*miracles*) σημεῖα (*signs*) and τέρατα
(*wonders*) wrought by him (Acts ii. 22; comp. Luke xxiv. 19):
but the people also were, even during his life, so well satisfied
with this aspect of his character that many believed on him in
consequence (John ii. 23; comp vi. 2), contrasted him with
the Baptist who gave no sign (John x. 41), and even believed
that he would not be surpassed in this respect by the future
Messiah (John vii. 31). The above demands of a sign do not
appear to prove that Jesus had performed no miracles, especially
as several of them occur immediately after important miracles,
e. g., after the cure of a demoniac, Matt. xii. 38; and after the
feeding of the five thousand, John vi. 30. This position indeed
creates a difficulty, for how the Jews could deny to these two
acts the character of proper *signs* it is not easy to understand;
the power of expelling demons, in particular, being rated very
highly (Luke x. 17). The sign demanded on these two occasions must therefore be more precisely defined according to
Luke xi. 16 (comp. Matt. xvi. 1; Mark viii. 11), as a *sign
from heaven*, σημεῖον ἐξ οὐρανοῦ, and we must understand it to be
the specifically messianic *sign of the Son of Man in heaven*,
σημεῖον τοῦ υἱοῦ τοῦ ἀνθρώπου ἐν τῷ οὐρανῷ (Matt. xxiv. 30). If
however it be preferred to sever the connexion between these
demands of a sign and the foregoing miracles, it is possible
that Jesus may have wrought numerous miracles, and yet that
some hostile Pharisees, who had not happened to be eye-
witnesses of any of them, may still have desired to see one for
themselves.

That Jesus censures the seeking for miracles (John iv. 48)
and refuses to comply with any one of the demands for a sign,
does not in itself prove that he might not have voluntarily
worked miracles in other cases, when they appeared to him to
be more seasonable. When in relation to the demand of the
Pharisees, Mark viii. 12, he declares that there shall be no sign

given *to this generation* τῇ γενεᾷ ταύτῃ, or Matt. xii. 39 f.;
xvi. 4 ; Luke xi. 29 f., that there shall no sign be given to it
but *the sign of Jonah the prophet*, it would appear that by
this *generation* γενεὰ, which in Matthew and Luke he characterizes as *evil and adulterous*, he could only mean the Pharisaic
part of his cotemporaries who were hostile to him, and that he
intended to declare, that to these should be granted either no
sign at all, or merely the sign of Jonas, that is, as he interprets
it in Matthew, the miracle of his resurrection, or as modern
expositors think, the impressive manifestation of his person
and teaching.   But if we take the words οὐ δοθήσεται αὐτῇ in
the sense that his enemies were to obtain no sign from him, we
encounter two difficulties : on the one hand, things must have
chanced singularly if among the many miracles wrought by
Jesus in the greatest publicity, not one fell under the observation of Pharisees (moreover Matt. xii. 24 f. parall. contradicts
this, for there Pharisees are plainly supposed to be present at
the cure of the blind and dumb demoniac) : on the other hand,
if signs personally witnessed are here intended, the enemies of
Jesus certainly did not see his resurrection, or his person after
he was risen.   Hence the above declaration cannot well mean
merely that his enemies should be excluded from an actual sight
of his miracles.   There is yet another expedient, namely, to suppose that the expression οὐ δοθήσεται αὐτῇ refers to a sign which
should conduce to the good of the subject of which it is predicated : but all the miracles of Jesus happened equally with his
original mission and his resurrection at once for the benefit of
that subject and the contrary, namely, in their object for its
benefit, in their result not so.   Nothing therefore remains but
to understand the γενεὰ of the cotemporaries of Jesus generally,
and the δίδοσθαι to refer to observation generally, mediate or
immediate : so that thus Jesus would appear to have here repudiated the working of miracles in general.

This is not very consistent with the numerous narratives of
miracles in the Gospels, but it accords fully with the fact that
in the preaching and epistles of the apostles, a couple of general

notices excepted (Acts ii. 22; x. 38 f.), the miracles of Jesus appear to be unknown, and everything is built on his resurrection : on which the remark may be ventured that it could neither have been so unexpected nor could it have formed so definite an epoch, if Jesus had previously raised more than one dead person, and had wrought the most transcendent miracles of all kinds. This then is the question : Ought we, on account of the evangelical narratives of miracles, to explain away that expression of Jesus, or doubt its authenticity; or ought we not, rather, on the strength of that declaration, and the silence of the apostolic writings, to become distrustful of the numerous histories of miracles in the Gospels ?

This can only be decided by a close examination of these narratives, among which, for a reason that will be obvious hereafter, we give the precedence to the expulsions of demons.

§ 92.

THE DEMONIACS, CONSIDERED GENERALLY.

While in the fourth gospel, the expressions δαιμόνιον ἔχειν *to have a demon*, and δαιμονιζόμενος, *being a demoniac*, appear nowhere except in the accusations of the Jews against Jesus, and as parallels to μαίνεσθαι, *to be mad* (viii. 48 f.; x. 20 f.; comp. Mark iii. 22, 30 ; Matt. xi. 18) : the synoptists may be said to represent demoniacs as the most frequent objects of the curative powers of Jesus. When they describe the commencement of his ministry in Galilee, they give the demoniacs δαιμονιζομένους [1] a prominent place among the sufferers whom Jesus healed (Matt. iv. 24 ; Mark i. 34), and in all their summary notices of the ministry of Jesus in certain districts, demoniacs play a chief part (Matt. viii. 16 f. ; Mark i. 39 ; iii. 11 f. ; Luke vi. 18). The power to cast out devils is before any

---

[1] That the σεληνιαζόμενοι associated with them by Matthew are only a particular species of demoniacs, whose malady appeared to be governed by the changes of the moon, is proved by Matt. xvii. 14 ff. where a δαιμόνιον is expelled from a σεληνιαζόμενος.

thing else imparted by Jesus to his disciples (Matt. x. 1, 8 ; Mark iii. 15 ; vi. 7 ; Luke ix. 1), who to their great joy succeed in using it according to their wishes (Luke x. 17, 20 ; Mark vi. 13).

Besides these summary notices, however, several cures of demoniacs are narrated to us in detail, so that we can form a tolerably accurate idea of their peculiar condition. In the one whose cure in the synagogue at Capernaum is given by the evangelists as the first of this kind (Mark i. 23 ff. ; Luke iv. 33 ff.), we find, on the one hand, a disturbance of the self-consciousness, causing the possessed individuals to speak in the person of the demon, which appears also in other demoniacs, as for example, the Gadarenes (Matt. viii. 29 f. parall.) ; on the other hand, spasms and convulsions with savage cries. This spasmodic state has, in the demoniac who is also called a lunatic (Matt. xvii. 14 ff. parall.), reached the stage of manifest epilepsy ; for sudden falls, often in dangerous places, cries, gnashing of the teeth, and foaming, are known symptoms of that malady[2]. The other aspect of the demoniacal state, namely, the disturbance of the self-consciousness, amounts in the demoniac of Gadara, by whose lips a demon, or rather a plurality of these evil spirits, speaks as a subject, to misanthropic madness, with attacks of maniacal fury against himself and others[3]. Moreover, not only the insane and epileptic, but the dumb (Matt. ix. 32 ; Luke xi. 14 ; Matt. xii. 22, the *dumb demoniac* is also *blind*) and those suffering from a gouty contraction of the body (Luke xiii. 11 ff.), are by the evangelists designated more or less precisely as demoniacs.

The idea of these sufferers presupposed in the gospels and shared by their authors, is that a wicked, unclean spirit ($\delta\alpha\iota\mu\acute{o}\nu\iota\sigma\nu$, $\pi\nu\epsilon\tilde{\upsilon}\mu\alpha$ $\dot{\alpha}\kappa\acute{\alpha}\theta\alpha\rho\tau\sigma\nu$) or several, have taken possession of them (hence their condition is described by the expressions $\delta\alpha\iota\mu\acute{o}\nu\iota\sigma\nu$ $\ddot{\epsilon}\chi\epsilon\iota\nu$, $\delta\alpha\iota\mu\sigma\nu\acute{\iota}\zeta\epsilon\sigma\theta\alpha\iota$, *to have a demon, to be a demoniac*), speak

---

[2] Compare the passages of ancient physicians, ap. Winer, bibl. Realwörterb. 1, s. 191.

[3] Rabbinical and other passages, ap. Winer, ut sup. s. 192.

through their organs, (thus Matt. viii. 31, οἱ δαίμονες παρεκάλουν αὐτὸν λέγοντες,) and put their limbs in motion at pleasure, (thus Mark ix. 20, τὸ πνεῦμα ἐσπάραξεν αὐτὸν,) until, forcibly expelled by a cure, they depart from the patient (ἐκβάλλειν, ἐξέρχεσθαι). According to the representation of the evangelists, Jesus also held this view of the matter. It is true that when, as a means of liberating the possessed, he addresses the demons within them (as in Mark ix. 25; Matt. viii. 32; Luke iv. 35), we might with Paulus [4] regard this as a mode of entering into the fixed idea of these more or less insane persons, it being the part of a psychical physician, if he would produce any effect, to accommodate himself to this idea, however strongly he may in reality be convinced of its groundlessness. But this is not all; Jesus, even in his private conversations with his disciples, not only says nothing calculated to undermine the notion of demoniacal possession, but rather speaks repeatedly on a supposition of its truth; as e. g. in Matt. x. 8, where he gives the commission, *Cast out devils;* in Luke x. 18 ff.; and especially in Matt. xvii. 21, parall., where he says, *This kind goeth not out but by prayer and fasting.* Again, in a purely theoretical discourse, perhaps also in the more intimate circle of his disciples, Jesus gives a description quite accordant with the idea of his cotemporaries of the departure of the unclean spirit, his wandering in the wilderness, and his return with a reinforcement (Matt. xii. 43 ff.). With these facts before us, the attempt made by generally unprejudiced inquirers, such as Winer [5], to show that Jesus did not share the popular opinion on demoniacal possession, but merely accommodated his language to their understanding, appears to us a mere adjustment of his ideas by our own. A closer examination of the last-mentioned passage will suffice to remove every thought of a mere accommodation on the part of Jesus. It is true that commentators have sought to evade all that is conclusive in this passage, by inter-

---

[4] Exeg. Handb. 1, b. s. 475; comp. Hase, L. J. s. 60.
[5] Ut sup. s. 191.

preting it figuratively, or even as a parable [6], in every explanation of which (if we set aside such as that given by Olshausen [7] after Calmet,) the essential idea is, that superficial conversion to the cause of Jesus is followed by a relapse into aggravated sin [8]. But, I would fain know, what justifies us in abandoning the literal interpretation of this discourse? In the propositions themselves there is no indication of a figurative meaning, nor is it rendered probable by the general style of teaching used by Jesus, for he nowhere else presents moral relations in the garb of demoniacal conditions; on the contrary, whenever he speaks, as here, of the departure of evil spirits, e. g. in Matt. xvii. 21, he evidently intends to be understood literally. But does the context favour a figurative interpretation? Luke (xi. 24 ff.) places the discourse in question after the defence of Jesus against the Pharisaic accusation, that he cast out devils by Beelzebub: a position which is undoubtedly erroneous, as we have seen, but which is a proof that he at least understood Jesus to speak literally—of real demons. Matthew also places the discourse near to the above accusation and defence, but he inserts between them the demand of a sign, together with its refusal, and he makes Jesus conclude with the application, *Even so shall it be also unto this wicked generation.* This addition, it is true, gives the discourse a figurative application to the moral and religious condition of his cotemporaries, but only thus: Jesus intended the foregoing description of the expelled and returning demon literally, though he made a secondary use of this event as an image of the moral condition of his cotemporaries. At any rate Luke, who has not the same addition, gives the discourse of Jesus, to use the expression of Paulus, as a warning against demoniacal relapses. That the majority of theologians in the present day, without decided support on the

---

[6] Gratz, Comm. z. Matth. 1, s. 615.

[7] B. Comm. 1, s. 424. According to this, the passage relates to the Jewish people, who before the exile were possessed by the devil in the form of idolatry, and afterwards in the worse form of Pharisaism.

[8] Thus Fritzsche, in Matt. p. 447.

part of Matthew, and in decided contradiction to Luke, advocate the merely figurative interpretation of this passage, appears to be founded in an aversion to ascribe to Jesus so strongly developed a demonology, as lies in his words literally understood. But this is not to be avoided, even leaving the above passage out of consideration. In Matt. xii. 25 f. 29, Jesus speaks of a kingdom and household of the devil, in a manner which obviously outsteps the domain of the merely figurative; but above all, the passage already quoted, Luke x. 18—20, is of such a nature as to compel even Paulus, who is generally so fond of lending to the hallowed personages of primitive Christian history the views of the present age, to admit that the kingdom of Satan was not merely a symbol of evil to Jesus, and that he believed in actual demoniacal possession. For he says very justly, that as Jesus here speaks, not to the patient or to the people, but to those who themselves, according to his instructions, cured demoniacs, his words are not to be explained as a mere accommodation, when he confirms their belief that *the spirits are subject* unto them, and describes their capability of curing the malady in question, as a power over the *power of the enemy* [9]. In answer also to the repugnance of those with whose enlightenment a belief in demoniacal possession is inconsistent, to admit that Jesus held that belief, the same theologian justly observes that the most distinguished mind may retain a false idea, prevalent among his cotemporaries, if it happen to lie out of his peculiar sphere of thought [10].

Some light is thrown on the evangelical conception of the demoniacs, by the opinions on this subject which we find in writers more or less cotemporary. The general idea that evil spirits had influence on men, producing melancholy, insanity, and epilepsy, was early prevalent among the Greeks [11] as well

[9] Exeg. Handb. 2, s. 566.
[10] Ut sup. 1, b. s. 483. 2, s. 96.
[11] Hence the words δαιμονᾷν. κακοδαιμονᾷν were used as synonymous with μελαγχολᾷν, μαίνεσθαι. Hippocrates had to combat the opinion that epilepsy was the effect of demoniacal influence. Vid. Wetstein, s. 282 ff.

as the Hebrews [12]: but the more distinct idea that evil spirits entered into the human body and took possession of its members was not developed until a considerably later period, and was a consequence of the dissemination of the oriental, particularly the Persian pneumatology among both Hebrews and Greeks [13]. Hence we find in Josephus the expressions δαιμόνια τοῖς ζῶσιν εἰσδυόμενα [14], εγκαθεζόμενα [15] (*demons entering into the living, settling themselves there*), and the same ideas in Lucian [16] and Philostratus [17].

Of the nature and origin of these spirits nothing is expressly stated in the gospels, except that they belong to the household of Satan (Matt. xii. 26 ff. parall.), whence the acts of one of them are directly ascribed to Satan (Luke xiii. 16.). But from Josephus [18], Justin Martyr [19] and Philostratus [20], with whom rabbinical writings agree [21], we learn that these demons were the disembodied souls of wicked men; and modern theologians have not scrupled to attribute this opinion on their origin to the New Testament also [22]. Justin and the Rabbins more

---

[12] Let the reader compare the רוּחַ רָעָה מֵאֵת יְהוָֹה, which made Saul melancholy, 1 Sam. xvi. 14. Its influence on Saul is expressed by בְּעַתַּתּוּ

[13] Vid. Creuzer, Symbolik, 3, s. 69 f. ; Baur, Apollonius von Tyana und Christus, s. 144.

[14] Bell. jud. vii. vi. 3.

[15] Antiq. vi. xi. 2.   On the state of Saul.

[16] Philopseud. 16.

[17] Vitæ Apollon. iv. 20, 25. comp. Baur, ut sup. s. 38 f. 42.   Even Aristotle speaks of δαίμονί τινι γενομένοις κατόχοις. de mirab. 166, ed. Bekk.

[18] Ut sup. bell. j. : τὰ γὰρ καλούμενα δαιμόνια—πονηρῶν ἐστιν ἀνθρώπων πνεύματα, τοῖς ζῶσιν εἰσδυόμενα καὶ κτείνοντα τοὺς βοηθείας μὴ τυγχάνοντας.

[19] Apoll. i. 18.

[20] Ut sup. iii. 38.

[21] Vid. Eisenmenger, entdecktes Judenthum, 2, s. 427.

[22] Paulus, exeg. Handb. 2, s. 39; L. J. 1. a. s. 217. He appeals in support of this to Matt. xiv. 2, where Herod, on hearing of the miracles of Jesus, says: *It is John the Baptist, he is risen from the dead.*   In this expression Paulus finds the rabbinical opinion of the עִיבּוּר, which is distinct from that of the גִלְגּוּל, or transmigration of souls properly so called, (that is, the passage of disembodied souls into the bodies of infants, while in the process of formation,) and according to which the soul of a dead person might unite itself to that of a living one, and add to its power

nearly particularize, as spirits that torment the living, the souls of the giants, the offspring of those angels who allied themselves to the daughters of men; the rabbins further add the souls of those who perished in the deluge, and of those who participated in building the tower of Babel [23]; and with this agree the Clementine Homilies, for according to them also, these souls of the giants, having become demons, seek to attach themselves, as the stronger, to human souls, and to inhabit human bodies [24]. As, however, in the continuation of the passage first cited, Justin endeavours to convince the heathens of immortality from their own ideas, the opinion which he there expresses, of demons being the souls of the departed in general, can scarcely be regarded as his, especially as his pupil Tatian expressly declares himself against it [25]; while Josephus affords no criterion as to the latent idea of the New Testament, since his Greek education renders it very uncertain whether he presents the doctrine of demoniacal possession in its original Jewish, or in a Grecian form. If it must be admitted that the Hebrews owed their doctrine of demons to Persia, we know that the Deves of the Zend mythology were originally and essentially wicked beings, existing prior to the human race; of these two characteristics, Hebraism as such might be induced to expunge the former, which pertained to Dualism, but could have no reason for rejecting the latter. Accordingly, in the Hebrew view, the demons were the fallen angels of Gen. vi., the souls of their offspring the giants, and of the great criminals before and immediately after the deluge, whom the popular imagination

(vid. Eisenmenger 2, s. 85 ff.) But, as Fritzsche and others have shown, the word ἠγέρθη refers to an actual resurrection of the Baptist, and not to this rabbinical notion; which, moreover, even were it implied, is totally different from that of demoniacal possession. Here it would be a good spirit who had entered into a prophet for the strengthening of his powers, as according to a later Jewish idea the soul of Seth was united to that of Moses, and again the souls of Moses and Aaron to that of Samuel (Eisenmenger, ut sup.); but from this it would by no means follow, that it was possible for wicked spirits to enter into the living.

[23] Justin. Apol. ii. 5. Eisenmenger, ut sup.
[24] Homil. viii. 18 f.; ix. 9 f.
[25] Orat. contra Græcos, 16.

gradually magnified into superhuman beings. But in the ideas of the Hebrews, there lay no motive for descending beyond the circle of these souls, who might be conceived to form the court of Satan. Such a motive was only engendered by the union of the Græco-roman culture with the Hebraic : the former had no Satan, and consequently no retinue of spirits devoted to his service, but it had an abundance of Manes, Lemures, and the like, —all names for disembodied souls that disquieted the living. Now, the combination of these Græco-roman ideas with the above-mentioned Jewish ones, seems to have been the source of the demonology of Josephus, of Justin, and also of the later rabbins : but it does not follow that the same mixed view belongs to the New Testament. Rather, as this Græcised form of the doctrine in question is nowhere positively put forth by the evangelical writers, while on the contrary the demons are in some passages represented as the household of Satan : there is nothing to contravene the inference to be drawn from the unmixedly Jewish character of thought which reigns in the synoptical gospels on all other subjects (apart from Christian modifications) ; namely, that we must attribute to them the pure and original Jewish conception of the doctrine of demons.

It is well known that the older theology, moved by a regard for the authority of Jesus and the evangelists, espoused the belief in the reality of demoniacal possession. The new theology, on the contrary, especially since the time of Semler [26], in consideration of the similarity between the condition of the demoniacs in the New Testament and many naturally diseased subjects of our own day, has begun to refer the malady of the former also to natural causes, and to ascribe the evangelical supposition of supernatural causes, to the prejudices of that age. In modern days, on the occurrence of epilepsy, insanity, and even a dis-

---

[26] See his *Commentatio de dæmoniacis quorum in N. T. fit mentio,* and his minute consideration of demoniacal cases. So early as the time of Origen, physicians gave natural explanations of the state of those supposed to be possessed. Orig. in Matth. xvii. 15.

turbance of the self-consciousness resembling the condition of
the possessed described in the New Testament, it is no longer
the custom to account for them by the supposition of demoniacal influence: and the reason of this seems to be, partly that
the advancement in the knowledge of nature and of mind has
placed at command a wider range of facts and analogies, which
may serve to explain the above conditions naturally; partly
that the contradiction, involved in the idea of demoniacal possession, is beginning to be at least dimly perceived. For,—apart
from the difficulties which the notion of the existence of a devil
and demons entails,—whatever theory may be held as to the relation between the self-consciousness and the bodily organs, it
remains absolutely inconceivable how the union between the
two could be so far dissolved, that a foreign self-consciousness
could gain an entrance, thrust out that which belonged to the
organism, and usurp its place. Hence for every one who at
once regards actual phenomena with enlightened eyes, and the
New Testament narratives with orthodox ones, there results
the contradiction, that what now proceeds from natural causes,
must in the time of Jesus have been caused supernaturally.

In order to remove this inconceivable difference between the
conditions of one age and another, avoiding at the same time
any imputation on the New Testament, Olshausen, whom we
may fairly take as the representative of the mystical theology
and philosophy of the present day, denies both that all states
of the kind in question have now a natural cause, and that they
had in the time of Jesus invariably a supernatural cause.
With respect to our own time he asks, if the apostles were to
enter our mad-houses, how would they name many of the inmates [27]? We answer, they would to a certainty name many
of them demoniacs, by reason of their participation in the ideas
of their people and their age, not by reason of their apostolic
illumination; and the official who acted as their conductor
would very properly endeavour to set them right: whatever
names therefore they might give to the inmates of our asylums,

[27] B. Comm. 1, s. 296. Anm.

our conclusions as to the naturalness of the disorders of those inmates would not be at all affected. With respect to the time of Jesus, this theologian maintains that the same forms of disease were, even by the Jews, in one case held demoniacal, in another not so, according to the difference in their origin : for example, one who had become insane through an organic disorder of the brain, or dumb through an injury of the tongue, was not looked on as a demoniac, but only those, the cause of whose condition was more or less psychical. Of such a distinction in the time of Jesus, Olshausen is manifestly bound to give us instances. Whence could the Jews of that age have acquired their knowledge of the latent natural causes of these conditions—whence the criterion by which to distinguish an insanity or imbecility originating in a malformation of the brain, from one purely psychical ?   Was not their observation limited to outward phenomena, and those of the coarsest character ? The nature of their distinctions seems to be this : the state of an epileptic with his sudden falls and convulsions, or of a maniac in his delirium, especially if, from the reaction of the popular idea respecting himself he speaks in the person of another, seems to point to an external influence which governs him ; and consequently, so soon as the belief in demoniacal possession existed among the people, all such states were referred to this cause, as we find them to be in the New Testament: whereas in dumbness and gouty contraction or lameness, the influence of an external power is less decidedly indicated, so that these afflictions were at one time ascribed to a possessing demon, at another not so.   Of the former case we find an example in the dumb persons already mentioned, Matt. ix. 32 ; xii. 22, and in the woman who was *bowed down*, Luke xiii. 11 ; of the latter, in the man *who was deaf and had an impediment* in his speech, Mark vii. 32 ff., and in the many paralytics mentioned in the gospels. The decision for the one opinion or the other was however certainly not founded on an investigation into the origin of the disease, but solely on its external symptoms. If then the Jews, and with them the evangelists, referred the two chief classes of these conditions to demoniacal influence, there remains for him who believes himself bound by their opinion, without choosing to shut out the lights of modern science, the glaring inconsistency of considering the same diseases as in one age natural, in another supernatural.

But the most formidable difficulty for Olshausen, in his attempted mediation between the Judaical demonology of the New Testament and the intelligence of our own day, arises from the influence of the latter on his own mind—an influence which renders him adverse to the idea of personal demons. This theologian, initiated in the philosophy of the present age, endeavours to resolve the host of demons, which in the New Testament are regarded as distinct individuals, into a system of emanations, forming the continuity of a single substance, which indeed sends forth from itself separate powers, not, however to subsist as independent individuals, but to return as accidents into the unity of the substance.   This cast of thought we have already observed in the opinions of Olshausen concerning angels, and it appears still more decidedly in his demonology. Personal demons are too repugnant, and as Olshausen himself expresses it [28], the comprehension of two subjects in one individual is too inconceivable, to find a ready acceptance.   Hence it is everywhere with vague generality that a kingdom of evil and darkness is spoken of; and though a personal prince is given to it, its demons are understood to be mere effluxes and operations, by which the evil principle manifests itself.   But the most vulnerable point of Olshausen's opinion concerning demons is this: it is too much for him to believe that Jesus asked the name of the demon in the Gadarene; since he himself doubts the personality of those emanations of the kingdom of darkness, it cannot, he thinks, have been thus decidedly supposed by Christ;—hence he understands the question, *What is thy name?* (Mark v. 9.) to be addressed, not to the demon, but to the man [29], plainly in opposition to the whole

[28] S. 295 f.
[29] S. 302, after the example of Paulus, exeg. Handb. 1, b. s. 474.

context, for the answer, *Legion*, appears to be in no degree the result of a misunderstanding, but the right answer—the one expected by Jesus.

If, however, the demons are, according to Olshausen's opinion, impersonal powers, that which guides them and determines their various functions is the law which governs the kingdom of darkness in relation to the kingdom of light.   On this theory, the worse a man is morally, the closer must be the connexion between him and the kingdom of evil, and the closest conceivable connexion—the entrance of the power of darkness into the personality of the man, i. e. possession—must always occur in the most wicked.   But historically this is not so : the demoniacs in the gospels appear to be sinners only in the sense that all sick persons need forgiveness of sins ; and the greatest sinners (Judas for example) are spared the infliction of possession.   The common opinion, with its personal demons, escapes this contradiction.   It is true that this opinion also, as we find for instance in the Clementine Homilies, firmly maintains it to be by sin only that man subjects himself to the ingress of the demon [30]; but here there is yet scope for the individual will of the demon, who often, from motives not to be calculated, passes by the worst, and holds in chase the less wicked [31].   On the contrary, if the demons are considered, as by Olshausen, to be the actions of the power of evil in its relation to the power of goodness ; this relation being regulated by laws, every thing arbitrary and accidental is excluded.   Hence it evidently costs that theologian some pains to disprove the consequence, that according to his theory the possessed must always be the most wicked.   Proceeding from the apparent contest of two powers in the demoniacs, he adopts the position that the state of demoniacal possession does not appear in those who entirely give themselves up to evil, and thus maintain an

---

[30] Homil. viii. 19.

[31] Thus Asmodeus chooses Sara and her husband as objects of torment and destruction, not because either the former or the latter were particularly wicked, but because Sara's beauty attracted him. Tob. vi. 12—15.

internal unity of disposition, but only in those in whom there exists a struggle against sin [32]. In that case, however, the above state, being reduced to a purely moral phenomenon, must appear far more frequently; every violent inward struggle must manifest itself under this form, and especially those who ultimately give themselves up to evil must, before arriving at this point, pass through a period of conflict, that is of possession. Olshausen therefore adds a physical condition, namely, that the preponderance of evil in the man must have weakened his corporeal organization, particularly the nervous system, before he can become susceptible of the demoniacal state. But since such disorders of the nervous system may occur without any moral fault, who does not see that the state which it is intended to ascribe to demoniacal power as its proper source, is thus referred chiefly to natural causes, and that therefore the argument defeats its own object? Hence Olshausen quickly turns away from this side of the question, and lingers on the comparison of the δαιμονιζόμενος (*demoniac*) with the πονηρὸς (*wicked*); whereas he ought rather to compare the former with the epileptic and insane, for it is only by this means that any light can be thrown on the nature of possession. This shifting of the question from the ground of physiology and psychology to that of morality and religion, renders the discussion concerning the demoniacs, one of the most useless which Olshausen's work contains [33].

Let us then relinquish the ungrateful attempt to modernize the New Testament conception of the demoniacs, or to judaize our modern ideas;—let us rather, in relation to this subject, understand the statements of the New Testament as simply as they are given, without allowing our investigations to be restricted by the ideas therein presented, which belonged to the age and nation of its writers [34].

[32] S. 294.

[33] It fills s. 289—298.

[34] I have endeavoured to present helps towards a scientific conception of the states in question in several essays, which are now incorporated in my Charakteristiken u. Kritiken. Comp. Wirth, Theorie des Somnambulismus. S. 311 ff.

The method adopted for the cure of the demoniacal state was, especially among the Jews, in conformity with what we have ascertained to have been the idea of its nature. The cause of the malady was not supposed to be, as in natural diseases, an impersonal object or condition, such as an impure fluid, a morbid excitement or debility, but a self-conscious being; hence it was treated, not mechanically or chemically, but logically, i. e. by words. The demon was enjoined to depart; and to give effect to this injunction, it was coupled with the names of beings who were believed to have power over demons. Hence the main instrument against demoniacal possession was conjuration [35], either in the name of God, or of angels, or of some other potent being, e. g. the Messiah (Acts xix. 13), with certain forms which were said to be derived from Solomon [36]. In addition to this, certain roots [37], stones [38], fumigations and amulets [39] were used, in obedience to traditions likewise believed to have been handed down from Solomon. Now as the cause of the malady was not seldom really a psychical one, or at least one lying in the nervous system, which may be acted on to an incalculable extent by moral instrumentality, this psychological treatment was not altogether illusory; for by exciting in the patient the belief that the demon by which he was possessed, could not retain his hold before a form of conjuration, it might often effect the removal of the disorder. Jesus himself admits that the Jewish exorcists sometimes succeeded in working such cures (Matt. xii. 27). But we read of Jesus that without conjuration by any other power, and without the appliance of any further means, he expelled the demons by his word. The most remarkable cures of this kind, of which the gospels inform us, we are now about to examine.

[35] See note 16, the passage quoted from Lucian.
[36] Joseph. Antiq. viii. ii. 5.
[37] Joseph. ut sup.
[38] Gittin, f. lxvii. 2.
[39] Justin. Mart. dial. c. Tryph. lxxxv.

§ 93.

CASES OF THE EXPULSION OF DEMONS BY JESUS, CONSIDERED SINGLY.

Among the circumstantial narratives which are given us in the three first gospels of cures wrought by Jesus on demoniacs, three are especially remarkable : the cure of a demoniac in the synagogue at Capernaum, that of the Gadarenes possessed by a multitude of demons, and lastly, that of the lunatic whom the disciples were unable to cure.

In John, the conversion of water into wine is the first miracle performed by Jesus after his return from the scene of his baptism into Galilee; but in Mark (i. 23 ff.) and Luke (iv. 33 ff.) the cure of a demoniac in the synagogue of Capernaum has this position. Jesus had produced a deep impression by his teaching, when suddenly, a demoniac who was present, cried out in the character of the demon that possessed him, that he would have nothing to do with him, that he knew him to be the Messiah who was come to destroy them—the demons ; whereupon Jesus commanded the demon to hold his peace and come out of the man, which happened amid cries and convulsions on the part of the demoniac, and to the great astonishment of the people at the power thus exhibited by Jesus.

Here we might, with rationalistic commentators, represent the case to ourselves thus : the demoniac, during a lucid interval, entered the synagogue, was impressed by the powerful discourse of Jesus, and overhearing one of the audience speak of him as the Messiah, was seized with the idea, that the unclean spirit by which he was possessed, could not maintain itself in the presence of the holy Messiah ; whence he fell into a paroxysm, and expressed his awe of Jesus in the character of the demon. When Jesus perceived this, what was more natural than that he should make use of the man's persuasion of his power, and command the demon to come out of him, thus laying hold of the maniac by his fixed idea ; which, according to the laws of mental hygiène, might very probably have a favourable effect. It is under this view that Paulus regards the occasion as that on which the thought of using his messianic fame as a means of curing such sufferers, first occurred to Jesus [1].

But many difficulties oppose themselves to this natural conception of the case. The demoniac is supposed to learn that Jesus was the Messiah from the people in the synagogue. On this point the text is not merely silent, but decidedly contradicts such an opinion. The demon speaking through the man evidently proclaims his knowledge of the Messiahship of Jesus, in the words, οἶδά σε τίς εἶ κ. τ. λ., not as information casually imparted by man, but as an intuition of his demoniacal nature. Further, when Jesus cries, *Hold thy peace!* he refers to what the demon had just uttered concerning his messiahship; for it is related of Jesus that he suffered not the demons to speak because they knew him (Mark i. 34; Luke iv. 41), or because they made him known (Mark iii. 12.). If then Jesus believed that by enjoining silence on the demon he could hinder the promulgation of his messiahship, he must have been of opinion, not that the demoniac had heard something of it from the people in the synagogue, but contrariwise that the latter might learn it from the demoniac; and this accords with the fact, that at the time of the first appearance of Jesus, in which the evangelists place the occurrence, no one had yet thought of him as the Messiah.

If it be asked, how the demoniac could discover that Jesus was the Messiah, apart from any external communication, Olshausen presses into his service the preternaturally heightened activity of the nervous system, which, in demoniacs as in somnambules, sharpens the presentient power, and produces a kind of clear-sightedness, by means of which such a man might very well discern the importance of Jesus as regarded the whole realm of spirits. The evangelical narrative, it is true, does not ascribe that knowledge to a power of the patient, but of the demon dwelling within him, and this is the only view consistent with the Jewish ideas of that period. The Messiah was to appear,

---

[1] Exeg. Handb. i. 6. s. 422; L. J. 1, a. s. 128.

in order to overthrow the demoniacal kingdom (ἀπολέσαι ἡμᾶς,
comp. 1 John iii. 8 ; Luke x. 18 f.)[2] and to cast the devil and
his angels into the lake of fire (Matt. xxv. 41 ; Rev. xx. 10.) [3] :
it followed of course that the demons would recognize him who
was to pass such a sentence on them [4]. This, however, might
be deducted, as an admixture of the opinion of the narrator,
without damage to the rest of the narrative; but it must first be
granted admissible to ascribe so extensive a presentient power to
demoniacal subjects. Now, as it is in the highest degree improbable that a nervous patient, however intensely excited, should
recognize Jesus as the Messiah, at a time when he was not believed to be such by any one else, perhaps not even by himself;
and as on the other hand this recognition of the Messiah by
the demon so entirely agrees with the popular ideas ;—we must
conjecture that on this point the evangelical tradition is not in
perfect accordance with historical truth, but has been attuned
to those ideas [5]. There was the more inducement to this, the
more such a recognition of Jesus on the part of the demons
would redound to his glory. As when adults disowned him,
praise was prepared for him out of the mouth of babes (Matt.
xxi. 16.)—as he was convinced that if men were silent, the
very stones would cry out (Luke xix. 40.): so it must appear
fitting, that when his people whom he came to save would not
acknowledge him, he should have the involuntary homage of
demons, whose testimony, since they had only ruin to expect
from him, must be impartial, and from their higher spiritual
nature, was to be relied on.

---

[2] Bibl. Comm. i. 296.

[3] Comp. Bertholdt, Christol. Jud. §§ 36—41.

[4] According to Pesikta in Jalkut Schimoni ii. f. lvi. 3. (s. Bertholdt, p. 185.)
Satan recognizes in the same manner the pre-existing Messiah at the foot of the
throne of God with terror, as he *qui me et omnes gentiles in infernum præcipita-
turus est.*

[5] Fritzsche, in Marc. p. 35 : *In multis evangeliorum locis homines legas a pravis
dæmonibus agitatos, quum primum conspexerint Jesum, eum Messiam esse, a nemine
unquam de hac re commonitos, statim intelligere. In qua re hac nostri scriptores
ducti sunt sententia, consentaneum esse. Satanæ satellites facile cognovisse Messiam,
quippe insignia de se supplicia aliquando sumturum.*

In the above history of the cure of a demoniac, we have a case of the simplest kind; the cure of the possessed Gadarenes on the contrary (Matt. viii. 28 ff.; Mark v. 1 ff.; Luke viii. 26 ff.) is a very complex one, for in this instance we have, together with several divergencies of the evangelists, instead of one demon, many, and instead of a simple departure of these demons, their entrance into a herd of swine.

After a stormy passage across the sea of Galilee to its eastern shore, Jesus meets, according to Mark and Luke, a demoniac who lived among the tombs [6], and was subject to outbreaks of terrific fury against himself [7] and others; according to Matthew, there were two.   It is astonishing how long harmonists have resorted to miserable expedients, such as that Mark and Luke mention only one because he was particularly distinguished by wildness, or Matthew two, because he included the attendant who guarded the maniac [8], rather than admit an essential difference between the two narratives.   Since this step has been gained, the preference has been given to the statement of the two intermediate evangelists, from the consideration that maniacs of this class are generally unsociable; and the addition of a second demoniac by Matthew has been explained by supposing that the plurality of the demons spoken of in the narratives, became in his apprehension a plurality of demoniacs [9]. But the impossibility that two maniacs should in reality associate themselves, or perhaps be associated merely in the original legend, is not so decided as to furnish in itself a ground for preferring the narrative in Mark and Luke to that in Matthew. At least if it be asked, which of the two representations could

---

[6] A favourite resort of maniacs, vid. Lightfoot and Schöttgen, in loc., and of unclean spirits, vid. rabbinical passages, ap. Wetstein.

[7] The notion that the cutting himself with stones which Mark ascribes to the demoniac, was an act of penance in lucid moments, belongs to the errors to which Olshausen is led by his false opinion of a moral and religious point of view in relation to these phenomena.   It is well known, however, that the paroxysms of such disorders are precisely the occasions on which a self-destructive fury is manifested.

[8] Vid. the collection of such explanations, ap. Fritzsche, in Matt. p. 327.

[9] Thus Schulz, über das Abendmahl, s. 309; Paulus, in loc. Hase, L. J. § 75.

the most easily have been formed from the other by tradition, the probability on both sides will be found equal. For if according to the above supposition, the plurality of demons might give rise to the idea of a plurality of demoniacs, it may also be said, conversely: the more accurate representation of Matthew, in which a plurality of demoniacs as well as of demons was mentioned, did not give prominence to the specifically extraordinary feature in the case, namely, that one man was possessed by many demons; and as, in order to exhibit this, the narrative when reproduced must be so expressed as to make it clear that many demons inhabited one man, this might easily occasion by degrees the opposition of the demoniac in the singular to the plural number of the demons. For the rest, the introduction of Matthew's narrative is concise and general, that of the two others circumstantially descriptive; another difference from which the greater originality of the latter has been deduced[10]. But it is quite as probable that the details which Luke and Mark have in common, namely, that the possessed would wear no clothing, broke all fetters, and wounded himself with stones, are an arbitrary enlargement on the simple characteristic, *exceeding fierce*, which Matthew gives, with the consequence that no one could pass by that way,—as that the latter is a vague abridgment of the former.

This scene between Jesus and the demoniac or demoniacs opens, like the other, with a cry of terror from the latter, who, speaking in the person of the possessing demon, exclaims that he wishes to have nothing to do with Jesus, the Messiah, from whom he has to expect only torment. Two hypotheses have been framed, to explain how the demoniac came at once to recognise Jesus as the Messiah: according to one, Jesus was even then reputed to be the Messiah on the Peræan shore[11]; according to the other, some of those who had come across the sea with Jesus had said to the man (whom on account of his fierceness no one could come near!) that the Messiah had just

[10] Schulz, ut sup.
[11] Schleiermacher, über den Lukas, s. 127.

landed at such a spot[12]: but both are alike groundless, for it is
plain that in this narrative, as in the former, the above feature
is a product of the Jewish-Christian opinion respecting the
relation of the demons to the Messiah[13]. Here however another
difference meets us. According to Matthew, the possessed,
when they see Jesus, cry: *What have we to do with thee?
Art thou come to torment us?* — according to Luke, the
demoniac falls at the feet of Jesus and says beseechingly,
Torment me not; and lastly, according to Mark, he runs from
a distance to meet Jesus, falls at his feet and adjures him by
God not to torment him. Thus we have again a climax: in
Matthew, the demoniac, stricken with terror, deprecates the
unwelcome approach of Jesus; in Luke, he accosts Jesus, when
arrived, as a suppliant; in Mark, he eagerly runs to meet Jesus,
while yet at a distance. Those commentators who here take
Mark's narrative as the standard one, are obliged themselves to
admit, that the hastening of a demoniac towards Jesus whom
he all the while dreaded, is somewhat of a contradiction; and
they endeavour to relieve themselves of the difficulty, by the
supposition that the man set off to meet Jesus in a lucid moment, when he wished to be freed from the demon, but being
heated by running[14], or excited by the words of Jesus[15], he fell
into the paroxysm in which, assuming the character of the
demon, he entreated that the expulsion might be suspended.
But in the closely consecutive phrases of Mark, *Seeing—he
ran—and worshipped—and cried—and said* ἰδὼν—ἔδραμε—
καὶ προσεκύνησε—καὶ κράξας—εἶπε· there is no trace of a change
in the state of the demoniac, and the improbability of his representation subsists, for one really possessed, if he had recognised
the Messiah at a distance, would have anxiously avoided, rather
than have approached him; and even setting this aside, it is
impossible that one who believed himself to be possessed by a

---

[12] Paulus, L. J. 1, a. s. 232.
[13] Vid. Fritzsche, in Matth. p. 329.
[14] Natürliche Geschichte, 2, 174.
[15] Paulus, exeg. Handb. 1,   473 ; Olshausen, s. 302.

demon inimical to God, should adjure Jesus by God, as Mark makes the demoniac do [16].   If then his narrative cannot be the original one, that of Luke which is only so far the simpler that it does not represent the demoniac as running towards Jesus and adjuring him, is too closely allied to it to be regarded as the nearest to the fact.   That of Matthew is without doubt the purest, for the terror-stricken question, *Art thou come to destroy us before the time?* is better suited to a demon, who, as the enemy of the Messiah's kingdom, could expect no forbearance from the Messiah, than the entreaty for clemency in Mark and Luke; though Philostratus, in a narrative which might be regarded as an imitation of this evangelical one, has chosen the latter form [17].

From the course of the narratives hitherto, it would appear that the demons, in this as in the first narrative, addressed Jesus in the manner described, before anything occurred on his part; yet the two intermediate evangelists go on to state, that Jesus had commanded the unclean spirit to come out of the man.   When did Jesus do this?   The most natural answer would be: before the man spoke to him.   Now in Luke the address of the demoniac is so closely connected with the word προσέπεσε, *he fell down,* and then again with ἀνακράξας, *having cried out,* that it seems necessary to place the command of Jesus before the cry and the prostration, and hence to consider it as their cause.   Yet Luke himself rather gives the mere sight of Jesus as the cause of those demonstrations on the part of the demoniac, so that his representation leaves us in perplexity as to where the command of Jesus should find its place.   The case is still worse in Mark, for here a similar dependence of the successive phrases thrusts back the command of Jesus even before the word ἔδραμε, *he ran,* so that we should have to imagine rather strangely that Jesus cried to the demon, ἔξελθε, *Come out,* from a distance.

---

[16] This even Paulus, s. 474, and Olshausen, s. 303, find surprising.

[17] It is the narrative of the manner in which Apollonius of Tyana unmasked a demon (empusa), vit. Ap. iv. 35; ap. Baur, s. 145.

Thus the two intermediate evangelists are in an error with regard either to the consecutive particulars that precede the command or to the command itself, and our only question is, where may the error be most probably presumed to lie ?   Here Schleiermacher himself admits, that if in the original narrative an antecedent command of Jesus had been spoken of, it would have been given in its proper place, before the prayer of the demons, and as a quotation of the precise words of Jesus ; whereas the supplementary manner in which it is actually inserted, with its abbreviated and indirect form (in Luke ; Mark changes it after his usual style, into a direct address), is a strong foundation for the opinion that it is an explanatory addition furnished by the narrator from his own conjecture [18]. And it is an extremely awkward addition, for it obliges the reader to recast his conception of the entire scene.   At first the pith of the incident seems to be, that the demoniac had instantaneously recognised and supplicated Jesus ; but the narrator drops this original idea, and reflecting that the prayer of the demon must have been preceded by a severe command from Jesus, he corrects his previous omission, and remarks that Jesus had given his command in the first instance.

To their mention of this command, Mark and Luke annex the question put by Jesus to the demon: *What is thy name ?* In reply, a multitude of demons make known their presence, and give as their name, *Legion.*   Of this episode Matthew has nothing. In the above addition we have found a supplementary explanation of the former part of the narrative : what if this question and answer were an anticipatory introduction to the sequel, and likewise the spontaneous production of the legend or the narrator ?   Let us examine the reasons that render it probable : the wish immediately expressed by the demons to

---

[18] Ut sup. s. 128.   When, however, he accounts for this incorrect supplement of Luke's by supposing that his informant, being engaged in the vessel, had remained behind, and thus had missed the commencement of the scene with the demoniac, this is too laboured an exercise of ingenuity, and pre-supposes the antiquated opinion, that there was the most immediate relation possible between the evangelical histories and the facts which they report.

enter the herd of swine, does not in Matthew pre-suppose a multitude of demons in each of the two possessed, since we cannot know whether the Hebrews were not able to believe that even two demons only could possess a whole herd of swine : but a later writer might well think it requisite to make the number of the evil spirits equal the number of the swine. Now, what a herd is in relation to animals, an army or a division of an army is in relation to men, and superior beings, and as it was required to express a large division, nothing could more readily suggest itself than the Roman legion, which term in Matt. xxvi. 53, is applied to angels, as here to demons. But without further considering this more precise estimate of the evangelists, we must pronounce it inconceivable that several demons had set up their habitation in one individual. For even if we had attained so far as to conceive how one demon by a subjection of the human consciousness could possess himself of a human organization, imagination would still fail us to conceive that many personal demons could at once possess one man. For as possession means nothing else, than that the demon constitutes himself the subject of the consciousness, and as consciousness can in reality have but one focus, one central point : it is under every condition absolutely inconceivable that several demons should at the same time take possession of one man. Manifold possession could only exist in the sense of an alternation of possession by various demons, and not as here in that of a whole army of them dwelling at once in one man, and at once departing from him.

All the narratives agree in this, that the demons (in order, as Mark says, not to be sent out of the country, or according to Luke, into the *deep*,) entreated of Jesus permission to enter into the herd of swine feeding near ; that this was granted them by Jesus ; and that forthwith, owing to their influence, the whole herd of swine (Mark, we must not ask on what authority, fixes their number at about two thousand) were precipitated into the sea and drowned. If we adopt here the point of view taken in the gospel narratives, which throughout suppose the existence of real demons, it is yet to be asked : how can demons, admitting even that they can take possession of men,—how, we say, can they, being at all events intelligent spirits, have and obtain the wish to enter into brutal forms ? Every religion and philosophy which rejects the transmigration of souls, must, for the same reason, also deny the possibility of this passage of the demons into swine ; and Olshausen is quite right in classing the swine of Gadara in the New Testament with Balaam's ass in the Old, as a similar *scandal and stumbling block* [19]. This theologian, however, rather evades than overcomes the difficulty, by the observation that we are here to suppose, not an entrance of the individual demons into the individual swine, but merely an influence of all the evil spirits on the swine collectively. For the expression, εἰσελθεῖν εἰς τοὺς χοίρους, *to enter into the swine*, as it stands opposed to the expression, ἐξελθεῖν ἐκ τοῦ ἀνθρώπου, *to go out of the man*, cannot possibly mean otherwise than that the demons were to assume the same relation to the swine which they had borne to the possessed man ; besides, a mere influence could not preserve them from banishment out of the country or into the deep, but only an actual habitation of the bodies of the animals : so that the scandal and stumbling block remain. Thus the prayer in question cannot possibly have been offered by real demons, though it might by Jewish maniacs, sharing the ideas of their people. According to these ideas it is a torment to evil spirits to be destitute of a corporeal envelopement, because without a body they cannot gratify their sensual desires [20]; if therefore they were driven out of men they must wish to enter into the bodies of brutes, and what was better suited to an impure spirit πνεῦμα ἀκάθαρτον, than an impure animal ζῶον ἀκάθαρτον, like a swine [21] ? So far, therefore, it is possible that the evangelists might correctly represent the fact,

[19] S. 305, Anm.

[20] Clem. Hom. ix. 10.

[21] Fritzsche, in Matth. p. 332. According to Eisenmenger, 2, 447 ff., the Jews held that demons generally had a predilection for impure places, and in Jalkut Rubeni f. x. 2. (Wetstein) we find this observation : *Anima idololatrarum, quæ venit a spiritu immundo, vocatur porcus.*

only, in accordance with their national ideas, ascribing to the
demons what should rather have been referred to the madness
of the patient. But when it is further said that the demons
actually entered the swine, do not the evangelists affirm an
evident impossibility ? Paulus thinks that the evangelists here
as everywhere else identify the possessed men with the possessing demons, and hence attribute to the latter the entrance into
the swine, while in fact it was only the former, who, in obedience
to their fixed idea, rushed upon the herd [22]. It is true that
Matthew's expression ἀπῆλθον εἰς τοὺς χοίρους, taken alone,
might be understood of a mere rushing towards the swine ; not
only however, as Paulus himself must admit, does the word
εἰσελθόντες in the two other evangelists distinctly imply a real
entrance into the swine; but also Matthew has like them before
the word ἀπῆλθον, *they entered,* the expression ἐξελθόντες οἱ
δαίμονες, *the demons coming out* (sc. ἐκ τῶν ἀνθρώπων *out of the
men*) : thus plainly enough distinguishing the demons who
entered the swine from the men [23]. Thus our evangelists do not
in this instance merely relate what actually happened, in the
colours which it took from the false lights of their age; they
have here a particular, which cannot possibly have happened in
the manner they allege.

A new difficulty arises from the effect which the demons are
said to have produced in the swine. Scarcely had they entered
them, when they compelled the whole herd to precipitate themselves into the sea. It is reasonably asked, what then did the
demons gain by entering into the animals, if they immediately
destroyed the bodies of which they had taken possession, and
thus robbed themselves of the temporary abode for which they
had so earnestly entreated [24] ? The conjecture, that the design
of the demons in destroying the swine, was to incense the
minds of their owners against Jesus, which is said to have been

[22] Ut sup. s. 474, 485.   Winer, b. Realw. 1, s. 192.
[23] Fritzsche, in Matth. s. 330.
[24] Paulus, ut sup. s. 475 f.

the actual result [25], is too far-fetched; the other conjecture that the demoniacs, rushing with cries on the herd, together with the flight of their keepers, terrified the swine and chased them into the water [26],—even if it were not opposed as we have seen to the text,—would not suffice to explain the drowning of a herd of swine amounting to 2,000, according to Mark; or only a numerous herd, according to the general statement of Matthew. The expedient of supposing, that in truth it was only a part of the herd that was drowned [27], has not the slightest foundation in the evangelical narrative. The difficulties connected with this point are multiplied by the natural reflection that the drowning of the herd would involve no slight injury to the owners, and that of this injury Jesus was the mediate author. The orthodox, bent on justifying Jesus, suppose that the permission to the demons to enter into the swine was necessary to render the cure of the demoniac possible, and, they argue, brutes are assuredly to be killed that man may live [28]; but they do not perceive that they thus, in a manner most inconsistent with their point of view, circumscribe the power of Jesus over the demoniacal kingdom. Again, it is supposed, that the swine probably belonged to Jews, and that Jesus intended to punish them for their covetous transgression of the law [29], that he acted with divine authority, which often sacrifices individual good to higher objects, and by lightning, hail and inundations causes destruction to the property of many men [30], in which case, to accuse God of injustice would be absurd [31]. But to adopt this expedient is to confound, in a way the most inadmissible on the orthodox system, Christ's state of humiliation with his state of exaltation: it is to depart, in a spirit of mysticism, from the

[25] Olshausen, s. 307.
[26] Paulus, s. 474.
[27] Paulus, s. 485 ; Winer, ut sup.
[28] Olshausen, ut sup.
[29] Ibid.
[30] Ullmann, über die Unsündlichkeit Jesu, in seinen Studien, 1, 1, s. 51 f.
[31] Olshausen, ut sup.

wise doctrine of Paul, that he was *made under the law*, γενό-
μενος ὑπὸ νόμον (Gal. iv. 4.), and that he *made himself of no
reputation* ἑαυτὸν ἐκένωσε (Phil. ii. 7): it is to make Jesus a
being altogether foreign to us, since in relation to the moral
estimate of his actions, it lifts him above the standard of
humanity. Nothing remains therefore, but to take the naturalistic supposition of the rushing of the demoniacs among the
swine, and to represent the consequent destruction of the latter,
as something unexpected by Jesus, for which therefore he is
not responsible [32]: in the plainest contradiction to the evangelical account, which makes Jesus, even if not directly cause
the issue, foresee it in the most decided manner [33]. Thus there
appears to attach to Jesus the charge of an injury done to the
property of another, and the opponents of Christianity have
long ago made this use of the narrative [3] . It must be admitted
that Pythagoras in a similar case acted far more justly, for when
he liberated some fish from the net, he indemnified the fishermen who had taken them [35].

Thus the narrative before us is a tissue of difficulties, of
which those relating to the swine are not the slightest. It is
no wonder therefore that commentators began to doubt the
thorough historical truth of this anecdote earlier than that of
most others in the public life of Jesus, and particularly to sever
the connexion between the destruction of the swine and the
expulsion of the demons by Jesus. Thus Krug thought that
tradition had reversed the order of these two facts. The swine
according to him were precipitated into the sea before the landing of Jesus, by the storm which raged during his voyage, and
when Jesus subsequently wished to cure the demoniac, either
he himself or one of his followers persuaded the man that his
demons were already gone into those swine and had hurled them
into the sea; which was then believed and reported to be the

---

[32] Paulus.
[33] Ullmann.
[34] E. g. Woolston, Disc. 1, p. 32 ff.
[35] Jamblich. vita Pythag. no. 36. ed. Kiessling.

fact[36]. K. Ch. L. Schmidt makes the swine-herds go to meet
Jesus on his landing; during which interim many of the un-
tended swine fall into the sea; and as about this time Jesus had
commanded the demon to depart from the man, the bystanders
imagine that the two events [37] stood in the relation of cause and
effect. The prominent part which is played in these endeavours
at explanation, by the accidental coincidence of many circumstances, betrays that maladroit mixture of the mythical system
of interpretation with the natural which characterizes the
earliest attempts, from the mythical point of view. Instead of
inventing a natural foundation, for which we have nowhere any
warrant, and which in no degree explains the actual narrative
in the gospels, adorned as it is with the miraculous; we must
rather ask, whether in the probable period of the formation of
the evangelical narratives, there are not ideas to be found from
which the story of the swine in the history before us might be
explained?

We have already adduced one opinion of that age bearing on
this point, namely, that demons are unwilling to remain without
bodies, and that they have a predilection for impure places,
whence the bodies of swine must be best suited to them: this
does not however explain why they should have precipitated the
swine into the water. But we are not destitute of information,
that will throw light on this also. Josephus tells us of a Jewish
conjuror who cast out demons by forms and means derived from
Solomon, that in order to convince the bystanders of the reality
of his expulsions, he set a vessel of water in the neighbourhood of the possessed person, so that the departing demon must
throw it down and thus give ocular proof to the spectators that
he was out of the man [38]. In like manner it is narrated of
Apollonius of Tyana, that he commanded a demon which
possessed a young man, to depart with a visible sign, where-

---

[36] In the Abhandlung über Genetische oder formelle Erklärungsart der Wunder,
in Henke's Museum, 1, 3, s. 410 ff.

[37] Exeg. Beiträge, 2, 109 ff.

[38] Antiq. viii. ii. 5.

upon the demon entreated that he might overturn a statue that stood near at hand; which to the great astonishment of the spectators actually ensued, in the very moment that the demon went out of the youth [39]. If then the agitation of some near object, without visible contact, was held the surest proof of the reality of an expulsion of demons: this proof could not be wanting to Jesus; nay, while in the case of Eleazar, the object being only *a little* ($\mu\iota\kappa\varrho\grave{o}\nu$) removed from the exorciser and the patient, the possibility of deception was not altogether excluded, Matthew notices in relation to Jesus, more emphatically than the two other evangelists, the fact that the herd of swine was feeding a *good way off* ($\mu\alpha\kappa\varrho\grave{a}\nu$), thus removing the last remnant of such a possibility. That the object to which Jesus applied this proof, was from the first said to be a herd of swine, immediately proceeded from the Jewish idea of the relation between unclean spirits and animals, but it furnished a welcome opportunity for satisfying another tendency of the legend. Not only did it behove Jesus to cure ordinary demoniacs, such as the one in the history first considered; he must have succeeded in the most difficult cures of this kind. It is the evident object of the present narrative, from the very commencement, with its startling description of the fearful condition of the Gadarene, to represent the cure as one of extreme difficulty. But to make it more complicated, the possession must be, not simple, but manifold, as in the case of Mary Magdalene, *out of whom were cast seven demons* (Luke viii. 2.), or in the demoniacal relapse in which the expelled demon returns with seven worse than himself (Matt. xii. 45); whence the number of the demons was here made, especially by Mark, to exceed by far the probable number of a herd. As in relation to an inanimate object, as a vessel of water or a statue, the influence of the expelled demons could not be more clearly manifested by any means, than by its falling over contrary to the law of gravity; so in animals it could not be more surely attested in any way, than by their drowning themselves contrary to their instinctive desire of life.

[39] Philostr. v. Ap. iv. 20; ap. Baur, ut sup. s. 39.

Only by this derivation of our narrative from the confluence of various ideas and interests of the age, can we explain the above noticed contradiction, that the demons first petition for the bodies of the swine as a habitation, and immediately after of their own accord destroy this habitation. The petition grew, as we have said, out of the idea that demons shunned incorporeality, the destruction, out of the ordinary test of the reality of an exorcism;—what wonder if the combination of ideas so heterogeneous produced two contradictory features in the narrative?

The third and last circumstantially narrated expulsion of a demon has the peculiar feature, that in the first instance the disciples in vain attempt the cure, which Jesus then effects with ease. The three synoptists (Matt. xvii. 14 ff. ; Mark ix. 14 ff. ; Luke ix. 37 ff.) unanimously state that Jesus, having descended with his three most confidential disciples from the Mount of the Transfiguration, found his other disciples in perplexity, because they were unable to cure a possessed boy, whom his father had brought to them.

In this narrative also there is a gradation from the greatest simplicity in Matthew, to the greatest particularity of description in Mark ; and here again this gradation has led to the conclusion that the narrative of Matthew is the farthest from the fact, and must be made subordinate to that of the two other evangelists [40]. In the introduction of the incident in Matthew, Jesus, having descended from the mountain, joins the multitude, ($\ddot{o}\chi\lambda o\varsigma$) whereupon the father of the boy approaches, and on his knees entreats Jesus to cure his child ; in Luke, the *multitude* ($\ddot{o}\chi\lambda o\varsigma$) meet Jesus ; lastly, in Mark, Jesus sees around the disciples a great multitude, among whom were scribes disputing with them ; the people, when they see him, run towards him and salute him, he inquires what is the subject of dispute, and on this the father of the boy begins to speak. Here we have a climax in relation to the conduct of the people : in Matthew, Jesus appears to join them by accident; in Luke,

[40] Schulz, s. 319.

they come to meet him; and in Mark, they run towards him to salute him. The last evangelist has the singular remark: *And straightway all the people, when they saw him, were greatly amazed.* What could there possibly be so greatly to amaze the people in the arrival of Jesus with some disciples? This remains, in spite of all the other means of explanation that have been devised, so thorough a mystery, that I cannot find so absurd as Fritzsche esteems it, the idea of Euthymius, that Jesus, having just descended from the Mount of Transfiguration, some of the heavenly radiance which had there shone around him was still visible, as on Moses when he came down from Sinai (Exod. xxxiv. 29 f.). That among this throng of people there were scribes who arraigned the disciples on the ground of their failure, and involved them in a dispute, is in and by itself quite natural; but connected as it is with the exaggerations concerning the behaviour of the multitude, this feature also becomes suspicious, especially as the other two evangelists have it not; so that if it can be shown how the narrator might be led to insert it by a mental combination of his own, we shall have sufficient warrant for renouncing it. Shortly before (viii. 11.), on the occasion of the demand of a sign from Jesus by the Pharisees, Mark says, *ἤρξαντο συζητεῖν αὐτῷ, they began to question with him,* apparently on the subject of his ability to work miracles; and so here when the disciples show themselves unable to perform a miracle, he represents the scribes, (the majority of whom belonged to the Pharisaic sect,) as *συζητοῦντας τοῖς μαθηταῖς, questioning with the disciples.* In the succeeding description of the boy's state there is the same gradation as to particularity, except that Matthew is the one who alone has the expression *σεληνιάζεται (is lunatic)*, which it is unfair to make a reproach to him [41], since the reference of periodical disorders to the moon was not uncommon in the time of Jesus [42]. Mark alone calls the spirit that possessed the

---

[41] As Schulz appears to do, ut sup.

[42] See the passages quoted by Paulus, exeg. Handb. 1, b. s. 569, and by Winer, 1, s. 191 f.

dumb boy (v. 17), and *deaf* (v. 25). The emission of inarticulate sounds by epileptics during their fits, might be regarded as the dumbness of the demon, and their incapability of noticing any words addressed to them, as his deafness.

When the father has informed Jesus of the subject of dispute and of the inability of the disciples to relieve the boy, Jesus breaks forth into the exclamation, *O faithless and perverse generation*, &c. On a comparison of the close of the narrative in Matthew, where Jesus, when his disciples ask him why they could not cast out the demon, answers: *Because of your unbelief*, and proceeds to extol the power of faith, even though no larger than a grain of mustard seed, as sufficient to remove mountains (v. 19 ff.): it cannot be doubted that in this expression of dissatisfaction Jesus apostrophizes his disciples, in whose inability to cast out the demon, he finds a proof of their still deficient faith [43]. This concluding explanation of the want of power in the disciples, by their unbelief, Luke omits: and Mark not only imitates him in this, but also interweaves (v. 21 —24), a by-scene between Jesus and the father, in which he first gives an amplified description of the symptoms of the child's malady, drawn partly from Matthew, partly from his own resources, and then represents the father, on being required to believe, as confessing with tears the weakness of his faith, and his desire that it may be strengthened. Taking this together with the mention of the disputative scribes, we cannot err in supposing the speech of Jesus, *O faithless generation*, &c., in Mark and also in Luke to refer to the people, as distinguished from the disciples; in Mark, more particularly to the father, whose unbelief is intimated to be an impediment to the cure, as in another case (Matt. ix. 2.), the faith of relatives appears to further the desired object. As however both the evangelists give this aspect to the circumstances, because they do not here give the explanation of the inefficiency of the disciples by their unbelief, together with the declaration concerning the power of faith to remove mountains :· we must inquire whether the con-

[43] Thus Fritzsche, in loc.

nexion in which they place these discourses is more suitable
than this in which they are inserted by Matthew. In Luke the
declaration: *If ye have faith as a grain of mustard seed*, &c.,
(neither he nor Mark has, *Because of your unbelief*,) occurs
xvii. 5, 6, with only the slight variation, that instead of the
mountain a tree is named; but it is here destitute of any connexion either with the foregoing or the following context, and
has the appearance of a short, stray fragment, with an introduction, no doubt fictitious (of the same kind as Luke xi. 1 ; xiii.
23.), in the form of an entreaty from the disciples: *Lord, increase our faith*. Mark gives the sentence on the faith which
removes mountains as the moral of the history of the cursed fig
tree, where Matthew also has it a second time. But to this
history the declaration is totally unsuitable, as we shall presently see ; and if we are unwilling to content ourselves with
ignorance of the occasion on which it was uttered, we must accept its connexion in Matthew as the original one, for it is perfectly appropriate to a failure of the disciples in an attempted
cure. Mark has sought to make the scene more effective by
other additions, besides this episode with the father; he tells us
that the people ran together that they might observe what was
passing, that after the expulsion of the demon the boy was *as
one dead, insomuch that many said, he is dead ;* but that Jesus,
taking him by the hand, as he does elsewhere with the dead
(Matt. ix. 25), lifts him up and restores him to life.

After the completion of the cure, Luke dismisses the narrative with a brief notice of the astonishment of the people; but
the two first synoptists pursue the subject by making the disciples, when alone with Jesus, ask him why they were not able to
cast out the demon ? In Matthew, the immediate reply of
Jesus accounts for their incapability by their unbelief; but in
Mark, his answer is, *This kind goeth not out but by prayer
and fasting,* which Matthew also adds after the discourse on
unbelief and the power of faith. This seems to be an unfortunate connexion of Matthew's ; for if fasting and praying were
necessary for the cure, the disciples, in case they had not pre-

viously fasted, could not have cast out the demon even if they
had possessed the firmest faith [44].   Whether these two reasons
given by Jesus for the inability of the disciples can be made
consistent by the observation, that fasting and prayer are means
of strengthening faith [45]; or whether we are to suppose with
Schleiermacher an association of two originally unrelated passages, we will not here attempt to decide.   That such a spiritual and corporeal discipline on the part of the exorcist should
have effect on the possessed, has been held surprising: it has
been thought with Porphyry [46], that it would rather be to the
purpose that the patient should observe this discipline, and
hence it has been supposed that the προσευχὴ καὶ νηστεία, *prayer
and fasting*, were prescribed to the demoniac as a means of
making the cure radical [47].   But this is evidently in contradiction to the text.   For if fasting and praying on the part of the
patient were necessary for the success of the cure, it must have
been gradual and not sudden, as all cures are which are attributed to Jesus in the gospels, and as this is plainly enough
implied to be by the words, καὶ ἐθεραπεύθη ὁ παῖς ἀπὸ τῆς ὥρας
ἐκείνης, *and the child was cured from that very hour*, in Matthew, and the word ἰάσατο *he cured*, placed between ἐπετίμησε
κ. τ. λ. *Jesus rebuked the unclean spirit*, and ἀπέδωκε κ. τ. λ.
delivered him again to his father, in Luke.   It is true, Paulus
turns the above expression of Matthew to his advantage,
for he understands it to mean that from that time forward the
boy, by the application of the prescribed discipline, gradually
recovered.   But we need only observe the same form of expression where it elsewhere occurs as the final sentence in narratives of cures, to be convinced of the impossibility of such an
interpretation.   When, for example, the story of the woman
who had an issue of blood closes with the remark (Matt. ix.
22.) καὶ ἐσώθη ἡ γυνὴ ἀπὸ τῆς ὥρας ἐκείνης, this will hardly be

[44] Schleiermacher, s. 150.
[45] Köster, Immanuel, s. 197; Fritzsche, in loc.
[46] De abstinent. ii. p. 204 and 417 f.; Vid. Winer, 1, s. 191.
[47] Paulus, exeg. Handb. 2, s. 471 f.

translated, *et exinde mulier paulatim servabatur* : it can only
mean : *servata est* (*et servatam se præbuit*) *ab illo temporis mo-
mento*. Another point to which Paulus appeals as a proof that
Jesus here commenced a cure which was to be consummated by
degrees, is the expression of Luke, ἀπέδωκεν αὐτὸν τῷ πατρὶ
αὐτοῦ, *he delivered him again to his father*, which, he argues,
would have been rather superfluous, if it were not intended to
imply a recommendation to special care. But the more immediate signification of ἀποδίδωμι is not to deliver or give up, but
to give back ; and therefore in the above expression the only
sense is : *puerum, quem sanandum acceperat, sanatum
reddidit*, that is, the boy who had fallen into the hands of a
strange power—of the demon—was restored to the parents as
their own. Lastly, how arbitrary is it in Paulus to take the ex
pression ἐκπορεύεται, *goeth out*, (Matt. v. 21) in the closer signification of a total departure, and to distinguish this from the
preliminary departure which followed on the bare word of Jesus (v. 18) ! Thus in this case, as in every other, the gospels
present to us, not a cure which was protracted through days
and weeks, but a cure which was instantaneously completed by
one miracle : hence the *fasting and prayer* cannot be regarded
as a prescription for the patient.

With this whole history must be compared an analogous narrative in 2 Kings iv. 29 ff. Here the prophet Elisha attempts
to bring a dead child to life, by sending his staff by the hands
of his servant Gehazi, who is to lay it on the face of the child ;
but this measure does not succeed, and Elisha is obliged in his
own person to come and call the boy to life. The same relation
that exists in this Old Testament story between the prophet and
his servant, is seen in the New Testament narrative between the
Messiah and his disciples : the latter can do nothing without
their master, but what was too difficult for them, he effects with
certainty. Now this feature is a clue to the tendency of both
narratives, namely, to exalt their master by exhibiting the distance between him and his most intimate disciples ; or, if we
compare the evangelical narrative before us with that of the

demoniacs of Gadara, we may say : the latter case was made to appear one of extreme difficulty in itself; the former, by the relation in which the power of Jesus, which is adequate to the occasion, is placed to the power of the disciples, which, however great in other instances, was here insufficient.

Of the other more briefly narrated expulsions of demons, the cure of a dumb demoniac and of one who was blind also, has been already sufficiently examined in connexion with the accusation of a league with Beelzebub : as also the cure of the woman who was bowed down, in our general considerations on the demoniacs. The cure of the possessed daughter of the Canaanitish woman (Matt. xv. 22 ff.; Mark vii. 25 ff.) has no further peculiarity than that it was wrought by the word of Jesus at a distance: a point of which we shall speak later.

According to the evangelical narratives, the attempt of Jesus to expel the demon succeeded in every one of these cases. Paulus remarks that cures of this kind, although they contributed more than any thing else to impress the multitude with veneration for Jesus, were yet the easiest in themselves, and even De Wette sanctions a psychological explanation of the cures of demoniacs, though of no others [48]. With these opinions we cannot but agree; for if we regard the real character of the demoniacal state as a species of madness accompanied by a convulsive tendency of the nervous system, we know that psychical and nervous disorders are most easily wrought upon by psychical influence ;—an influence to which the surpassing dignity of Jesus as a prophet, and eventually even as the Messiah himself, presented all the requisite conditions. There is, however, a marked gradation among these states, according as the psychical derangement has more or less fixed itself corporeally, and the disturbance of the nervous system has become more or less habitual, and shared by the rest of the organization. We may therefore lay down the following rule : the more strictly the malady was confined to mental derangement, on which

[48] Paulus, exeg. Handb. 1, b. s. 488; L. J. 1, a. s. 223; De Wette, bibl. Dogm. § 222, Anm. c.

the word of Jesus might have an immediate moral influence, or in a comparatively slight disturbance of the nervous system, on which he would be able to act powerfully through the medium of the mind, the more possible was it for Jesus *by his word* λόγῳ (Matt. viii. 16.), and *instantly* παραχρῆμα (Luke xiii. 13.), to put an end to such states : on the other hand, the more the malady had already confirmed itself, as a bodily disease, the more difficult is it to believe that Jesus was able to relieve it in a purely psychological manner and at the first moment. From this rule results a second : namely, that to any extensive psychological influence on the part of Jesus the full recognition of his dignity as a prophet was requisite ; whence it follows that at times and in districts where he had long had that reputation, he could effect more in this way than where he had it not.

If we apply these two measures to the cures in the gospels, we shall find that the first, viz. that of the demoniac in the synagogue at Capernaum, is not, so soon as we cease to consider the evangelist's narrative of it circumstantially correct, altogether destitute of probability. It is true that the words attributed to the demon seem to imply an intuitive knowledge of Jesus ; but this may be probably accounted for by the supposition that the widely-spread fame of Jesus in that country, and his powerful discourse in the synagogue, had impressed the demoniac with the belief, if not that Jesus was the Messiah, as the evangelists say, at least that he must be a prophet : a belief that would give effect to his words. As regards the state of this demoniac we are only told of his fixed idea, (that he was possessed,) and of his attacks of convulsions ; his malady may therefore have been of the less rooted kind, and accessible to psychological influence. The cure of the Gadarenes is attended with more difficulty in both points of view. Firstly, Jesus was comparatively little known on the eastern shore ; and secondly, the state of these demoniacs is described as so violent and deep-seated a mania, that a word from Jesus could hardly suffice to put

an end to it.   Here therefore the natural explanation of Paulus
will not suffice, and if we are to regard the narrative as having
any foundation in fact, we must suppose that the description of
the demoniac's state, as well as other particulars, has been exaggerated by the legend.   The same judgment must be passed
in relation to the cure of the boy who was lunatic, since an
epilepsy which had existed from infancy (Mark v. 21) and the
attacks of which were so violent and regular, must be too
deeply rooted in the system for the possibility of so rapid and
purely psychological a cure to be credible.   That even dumbness and a contraction of many years' duration, which we cannot with Paulus explain as a mere insane imagination that
speech or an erect carriage was not permitted [49],—that these
afflictions should disappear at a word, no one who is not committed to dogmatical opinions can persuade himself.   Lastly,
least of all is it to be conceived, that even without the imposing
influence of his presence, the miracle-worker could effect a cure
at a distance, as Jesus is said to have done on the daughter of
the Canaanitish woman.

Thus in the nature of things there is nothing to prevent the
admission, that Jesus cured many persons who suffered from
supposed demoniacal insanity or nervous disorder, in a psychical manner, by the ascendancy of his manner and words (if
indeed Venturini [50] and Kaiser [51] are not right in their conjecture, that patients of this class often believed themselves to be
cured, when in fact the crisis only of their disorder had been
broken by the influence of Jesus ; and that the evangelists state
them to have been cured because they learned nothing further
of them, and thus knew nothing of their probable relapse).
But while granting the possibility of many cures, it is evident
that in this field the legend has not been idle, but has confounded the easier cases, which alone could be cured psycho-

[49] Exeg. Handb. in loc.
[50] Natürliche Geschichte, 2, s. 429.
[51] Bibl. Theol. 1, s. 196.

logically, with the most difficult and complicated, to which such a treatment was totally inapplicable [52]. Is the refusal of a sign on the part of Jesus reconcileable with such a manifestation of power as we have above defined,—or must even such cures as can be explained psychologically, but which in his age must have seemed miracles, be denied in order to make that refusal comprehensible? We will not here put this alternative otherwise than as a question.

If in conclusion we cast a glance on the gospel of John, we find that it does not even mention demoniacs and their cure by Jesus. This omission has not seldom been turned to the advantage of the apostle John, the alleged author, as indicating a superior degree of enlightenment [53]. If however this apostle did not believe in the reality of possession by devils, he must have had, as the author of the fourth gospel, according to the ordinary view of his relation to the synoptical writers, the strongest motives for rectifying their statements, and preventing the dissemination of what he held to be a false opinion, by setting the cures in question in a true light. But how could the apostle John arrive at the rejection of the opinion that the above diseases had their foundation in demoniacal possession? According to Josephus it was at that period a popular Jewish opinion, from which a Jew of Palestine who, like John, did not visit a foreign land until late in life, would hardly be in a condition to liberate himself; it was, according to the nature of things and the synoptical accounts, the opinion of Jesus himself, John's adored master, from whom the favourite disciple certainly would not be inclined to swerve even a hair's breadth. But if John shared with his cotemporaries and with Jesus himself the notion of real demoniacal possession, and if the cure of demoniacs formed the principal part, nay, perhaps the true

---

[52] Among the transient disorders on which Jesus may have acted psychologically, we may perhaps number the fever of Peter's mother-in-law, which Jesus is said to have cured Matt. viii. 14 ff. parall.

[53] It is so more or less by Eichhorn, in the allg. Bibliothek, 4, s. 435; Herder, von Gottes Sohn u. s. f., s. 20; Wegscheider, Einl. in das Evang. Joh. s. 313; De Wette, bibl. Dogm. § 269.

foundation of the alleged miraculous powers of Jesus: how comes it that the apostle nevertheless makes no mention of them in his gospel? That he passed over them because the other evangelists had collected enough of such histories, is a supposition that ought by this time to be relinquished, since he repeats more than one history of a miracle which they had already given; and if it be said that he repeated these because they needed correction,—we have seen, in our examination of the cures of demoniacs, that in many, a reduction of them to their simple historical elements would be very much in place. There yet remains the supposition that, the histories of demoniacs being incredible or offensive to the cultivated Greeks of Asia Minor, among whom John is said to have written, he left them out of his gospel for the sake of accommodating himself to their ideas. But we must ask, could or should an apostle, out of mere accommodation to the refined ears of his auditors, withhold so essential a feature of the agency of Jesus? Certainly this silence, supposing the authenticity of the three first gospels, rather indicates an author who had not been an eye-witness of the ministry of Jesus; or, according to our view, at least one who had not at his command the original tradition of Palestine, but only a tradition modified by Hellenistic influence, in which the expulsions of demons, being less accordant with the higher culture of the Greeks, were either totally suppressed or kept so far in the background that they might have escaped the notice of the author of the gospel.

§ 94.

CURES OF LEPERS.

Among the sufferers whom Jesus healed, the leprous play a prominent part, as might have been anticipated from the tendency of the climate of Palestine to produce cutaneous disease. When, according to the synoptical writers, Jesus directs the attention of the Baptist's messengers to the actual proofs which he had given of his Messiahship (Matt. ix. 5), he adduces, among these, the cleansing of lepers; when, on the first mission of the disciples, he empowers them to perform all kinds of miracles, the cleansing of lepers is numbered among the first (Matt. x. 8.), and two cases of such cures are narrated to us in detail.

One of these cases is common to all the synoptical writers, but is placed by them in two different connexions: namely, by Matthew, immediately after the delivery of the sermon on the mount (viii. 1 ff.); by the other evangelists, at some period, not precisely marked, at the beginning of the ministry of Jesus in Galilee (Mark i. 40 ff.; Luke v. 12 ff.). According to the narratives, a leper comes towards Jesus, and falling on his knees, entreats that he may be cleansed; this Jesus effects by a touch, and then directs the leper to present himself to the priest in obedience to the law, that he may be pronounced clean (Lev. xiv. 2 ff.). The state of the man is in Matthew and Mark described simply by the word λεπρὸς, *a leper;* but in Luke more strongly, by the words, πλήρης λέπρας, *full of leprosy.* Paulus, indeed, regards the being thus replete with leprosy as a symptom that the patient was curable (the eruption and peeling of the leprosy on the entire skin being indicative of the healing crisis); and accordingly, that commentator represents the incident to himself in the following manner. The leper applied to Jesus in his character of Messiah for an opinion on his state, and, the result being favourable, for a declaration that he was clean (εἰ θέλεις, δύνασαί με καθαρίσαι), which might either spare him an application to the priest, or at all events give him a consolatory hope in making that application. Jesus expressing himself ready to make the desired examination, (θέλω,) stretched out his hand, in order to feel the patient, without allowing too near an approach while he was possibly still capable of communicating contagion; and after a careful examination, he expressed, as its result, the conviction that the patient was no longer in a contagious state (καθαρίσθητι), whereupon quickly and easily (εὐθέως) the leprosy actually disappeared [1].

---

[1] Exeg. Handb., 1, b, s. 698 ff.

Here, in the first place, the supposition that the leper was precisely at the crisis of healing is foreign to the text, which in the two first evangelists speaks merely of leprosy, while the πλήρης λέπρας of the third can mean nothing else than the Old Testament expression מְצֹרָע כַּשֶּׁלֶג, (Exod. iv. 6; Num. xii. 10; 2 Kings v. 27.), which, according to the connexion in every instance, signifies the worst stage of leprosy. That the word καθαρίζειν in the Hebraic and Hellenistic use of the Greek language, might also mean merely *to pronounce clean* is not to be denied, only it must retain the signification throughout the passage. But that after having narrated that Jesus had said, *Be thou clean*, καθαρίσθητι, Matthew should have added καὶ εὐθέως ἐκαθαρίσθη κ. τ. λ. in the sense that thus the sick man was actually pronounced clean by Jesus, is, from the absurd tautology such an interpretation would introduce, so inconceivable, that we must here, and consequently throughout the narrative, understand the word καθαρίζεσθαι of actual cleansing. It is sufficient to remind the reader of the expressions λεπροὶ καθαρίζονται, *the lepers are cleansed*, (Matt. xi. 5,) and λεπροὺς καθαρίζετε *cleanse the lepers* (Matt. x. 8.), where neither can the latter word signify merely to pronounce clean, nor can it have another meaning than in the narrative before us. But the point in which the natural interpretation the most plainly betrays its weakness, is the disjunction of θέλω, *I will*, from καθαρίσθητι, *be thou clean*. Who can persuade himself that these words, united as they are in all the three narratives, were separated by a considerable pause—that θέλω was spoken during or more properly before the manipulation, καθαρίσθητι after, when all the evangelists represent the two words as having been uttered by Jesus without separation, whilst he touched the leper? Surely, if the alleged sense had been the original one, at least one of the evangelists, instead of the words, ἥψατο αὐτοῦ ὁ Ἰησοῦς λέγων· θέλω, καθαρίσθητι, *Jesus touched him, saying, I will, be thou clean*, would have substituted the more accurate expression ὁ Ἰ. ἀπεκρίνατο· θέλω, καὶ ἁψάμενος αὐτοῦ εἶπε· καθαρίσθητι. *Jesus answered, I will; and having touched him, said: be thou clean*. But if καθαρίσθητι was spoken in one breath with θέλω, so that Jesus announces the cleansing simply as a result of his will without any intermediate examination, the former word cannot possibly signify a mere declaration of cleanness, to which a previous examination would be requisite, and it must signify an actual making clean. It follows, therefore, that the word ἄπτεσθαι in this connexion is not to be understood of an exploratory manipulation, but, as in all other narratives of the same class, of a curative touch.

In support of his natural explanation of this incident, Paulus appeals to the rule, that invariably the ordinary and regular is to be presupposed in a narrative where the contrary is not expressly indicated [2]. But this rule shares the ambiguity which is characteristic of the entire system of natural interpretation, since it leaves undecided what is ordinary and regular in our estimation, and what was so in the ideas of the author whose writings are to be explained. Certainly, if I have a Gibbon before me, I must in his narratives presuppose only natural causes and occurrences when he does not expressly convey the contrary, because to a writer of his cultivation, the supernatural is at the utmost only conceivable as a rare exception. But the case is altered when I take up an Herodotus, in whose mode of thought the intervention of higher powers is by no means unusual and out of rule; and when I am considering a collection of anecdotes which are the product of Jewish soil, and the object of which is to represent an individual as a prophet of the highest rank—as a man in the most intimate connexion with the Deity, to meet with the supernatural is so completely a thing of course, that the rule of the rationalists must here be reversed, and we must say: where, in such narratives, importance is attached to results which, regarded as natural, would have no importance whatever,—*there*, supernatural causes must be expressly excluded, if we are not to presuppose it the opinion of the narrator that such causes were in action. Moreover, in the history before us, the extraordinary character of the incident is sufficiently indicated by the statement, that the

[2] Ut sup s. 705, and elsewhere.

leprosy left the patient immediately on the word of Jesus. Paulus, it is true, contrives, as we have already observed, to interpret this statement as implying a gradual, natural healing, on the ground that εὐθέως, the word by which the evangelists determine the time of the cure, signifies, according to the different connexions in which it may occur, in one case *immediately*, in another merely *soon*, and *unobstructedly*. Granting this, are we to understand the words εὐθέως ἐξέβαλεν αὐτὸν, which follow in close connexion in Mark (v. 43), as signifying that soon and without hindrance Jesus sent the cleansed leper away? Or is the word to be taken in a different sense in two consecutive verses?

We conclude, then, that in the intention of the evangelical writers the instantaneous disappearance of the leprosy in consequence of the word and touch of Jesus, is the fact on which their narratives turn. Now to represent the possibility of this to one's self is quite another task than to imagine the instantaneous release of a man under the grasp of a fixed idea, or a permanently invigorating impression on a nervous patient. Leprosy, from the thorough derangement of the animal fluids of which it is the symptom, is the most obstinate and malignant of cutaneous diseases; and that a skin corroded by this malady should by a word and touch instantly become pure and healthy, is, from its involving the immediate effectuation of what would require a long course of treatment, so inconceivable [3], that every one who is free from certain prejudices (as the critic ought always to be) must involuntarily be reminded by it of the realm of fable. And in the fabulous region of oriental and more particularly of Jewish legend, the sudden appearance and disappearance of leprosy presents itself the first thing. When Jehovah endowed Moses, as a preparation for his mission into Egypt, with the power of working all kinds of signs, amongst other tokens of this gift he commanded him to put his hand into his bosom, and when he drew it out again, it was covered with leprosy; again he was commanded to put it

[3] Compare Hase, L. J. § 86.

into his bosom, and on drawing it out a second time it was once more clean (Exod. iv. 6, 7.). Subsequently, on account of an attempt at rebellion against Moses, his sister Miriam was suddenly stricken with leprosy, but on the intercession of Moses was soon healed (Num. xii. 10 ff.). Above all, among the miracles of the prophet Elisha the cure of a leper plays an important part, and to this event Jesus himself refers (Luke iv. 27.). The Syrian General Naaman, who suffered from leprosy, applied to the Israelitish prophet for his aid; the latter sent to him the direction to wash seven times in the river Jordan, and on Naaman's observance of this prescription the leprosy actually disappeared, but was subsequently transferred by the prophet to his deceitful servant Gehazi (2 Kings v.). I know not what we ought to need beyond these Old Testament narratives to account for the origin of the evangelical anecdotes. What the first Goël was empowered to do in the fulfilment of Jehovah's commission, the second Goël must also be able to perform, and the greatest of prophets must not fall short of the achievements of any one prophet. If then, the cure of leprosy was without doubt included in the Jewish idea of the Messiah; the Christians, who believed the Messiah to have really appeared in the person of Jesus, had a yet more decided inducement to glorify his history by such traits, taken from the mosaic and prophetic legend; with the single difference that, in accordance with the mild spirit of the New Covenant (Luke ix. 55 f.) they dropped the punitive side of the old miracles.

Somewhat more plausible is the appeal of the rationalists to the absence of an express statement, that a miraculous cure of the leprosy is intended in the narrative of the ten lepers, given by Luke alone (xvii. 12 ff.). Here neither do the lepers expressly desire to be cured, their words being only, *Have mercy on us;* nor does Jesus utter a command directly referring to such a result, for he merely enjoins them to show themselves to the priests: and the rationalists avail themselves of this indirectness in his reply, as a help to their supposition, that Jesus, after ascertaining the state of the patients, encouraged them to subject themselves to the examination of the priests, which resulted in their being pronounced clean, and the Samaritan returning to thank Jesus for his encouraging advice [4]. But mere advice does not call forth so ardent a demonstration of gratitude as is here described by the words ἔπεσεν ἐπὶ πρόσωπον, *he fell down on his face;* still less could Jesus desire that because his advice had had a favourable issue, all the ten should have returned, and returned to glorify God—for what? that he had enabled Jesus to give them such good advice? No: a more real service is here presupposed; and this the narrative itself implies, both in attributing the return of the Samaritan to his discovery that he was healed (ἰδὼν ὅτι ἰάθη), and in making Jesus indicate the reason why thanks were to be expected from all, by the words: οὐχὶ οἱ δέκα ἐκαθαρίσθησαν; *Were there not ten cleansed?* Both these expressions can only by an extremely forced interpretation be made to imply, that because the lepers saw the correctness of the judgment of Jesus in pronouncing them clean, one of them actually returned to thank him, and the others ought to have returned. But that which is most decisive against the natural explanation is this sentence: *And as they went they were cleansed,* ἐν τῷ ὑπάγειν αὐτοὺς ἐκαθαρίσθησαν. If the narrator intended, according to the above interpretation, merely to say: the lepers having gone to the priest, and showed themselves to him, were pronounced clean; he must at least have said: πορευθέντες ἐκαθαρίσθησαν, *having made the journey, they were cleansed,* whereas the deliberate choice of the expression ἐν τῷ ὑπάγειν (*while in the act of going*), incontestably shows that a healing effected during the journey is intended. Thus here also we have a miraculous cure of leprosy, which is burdened with the same difficulties as the former anecdote; the origin of which is, however, as easily explained.

But in this narrative there is a peculiarity which distinguishes it from the former. Here there is no simple cure, nay, the cure does not properly form the main object of the narra-

[4] Paulus, L. J. 1, b. s. 68.

tive: this lies rather in the different conduct of the cured, and the question of Jesus, *were there not ten cleansed*, &c., (v. 17.) forms the point of the whole, which thus closes altogether morally, and seems to have been narrated for the sake of the instruction conveyed [5]. That the one who appears as a model of thankfulness happens to be a Samaritan, cannot pass without remark, in the narrative of the evangelist who alone has the parable of the Good Samaritan. As there two Jews, a priest and a Levite, show themselves pitiless, while a Samaritan, on the contrary, proves exemplarily compassionate: so here, nine unthankful Jews stand contrasted with one thankful Samaritan. May it not be then (in so far as the sudden cure of these lepers cannot be historical) that we have here, as well as there, a parable pronounced by Jesus, in which he intended to represent gratitude, as in the other case compassion, in the example of a Samaritan? It would then be with the present narrative as some have maintained it to be with the history of the temptation. But in relation to this we have both shown, and given the reason, that Jesus never made himself immediately figure in a parable, and this he must have done if he had given a narrative of ten lepers once healed by him. If then we are not inclined to relinquish the idea that something originally parabolic is the germ of our present narrative, we must represent the case to ourselves thus: from the legends of cures performed by Jesus on lepers, on the one hand; and on the other, from parables in which Jesus (as in that of the compassionate Samaritan) presented individuals of this hated race as models of various virtues, the Christian legend wove this narrative, which is therefore partly an account of a miracle and partly a parable.

§ 95.

CURES OF THE BLIND.

One of the first places among the sufferers cured by Jesus is filled (also agreeably to the nature of the climate [1]) by the

---

[5] Schleiermacher, über den Lukas, s. 215.

[1] Vid. Winer, Realw. Art. Blinde.

blind, of whose cure again we read not only in the general descriptions which are given by the evangelists (Matt. xv. 30 f.; Luke vii. 21.), and by Jesus himself (Matt. xi. 5.), of his messianic works, but also in some detailed narratives of particular cases.   We have indeed more of these cures than of the kind last noticed, doubtless because blindness, as a malady affecting the most delicate and complicated of organs, admitted a greater diversity of treatment.   One of these cures of the blind is common to all the synoptical writers; the others (with the exception of the blind and dumb demoniac in Matthew, whom we need not here reconsider) are respectively peculiar to the first, second, and fourth evangelists.

The narrative common to all the three synoptical writers is that of a cure of blindness wrought by Jesus at Jericho, on his last journey to Jerusalem (Matt. xx. 29. parall.): but there are important differences both as to the object of the cure, Matthew having two blind men, the two other evangelists only one; and also as to its locality, Luke making it take place on the entrance of Jesus into Jericho, Matthew and Mark on his departure out of Jericho.   Moreover the touching of the eyes, by which, according to the first evangelist, Jesus effected the cure, is not mentioned by the two other narrators.   Of these differences the latter may be explained by the observation, that though Mark and Luke are silent as to the touching, they do not therefore deny it: the first, relative to the number cured, presents a heavier difficulty.   To remove this it has been said by those who give the prior authority to Matthew, that one of the two blind men was possibly more remarkable than the other, on which account he alone was retained in the first tradition; but Matthew, as an eye-witness, afterwards supplied the second blind man.   On this supposition Luke and Mark do not contradict Matthew, for they nowhere deny that another besides their single blind man was healed; neither does Matthew contradict them, for where there are two, there is also one [2].   But when the simple narrator speaks of one individual

---

[2] Gratz. Comm. z. Matth. 2, s. 323.

in whom something extraordinary has happened, and even, like Mark, mentions his name, it is plain that he tacitly contradicts the statement that it happened in two individuals—to contradict it expressly there was no occasion. Let us turn then to the other side and, taking the singular number of Mark and Luke as the original one, conjecture that the informant of Matthew (the latter being scarcely on this hypothesis an eye-witness) probably mistook the blind man's guide for a second blind man [3]. Hereby a decided contradiction is admitted, while to account for it an extremely improbable cause is superfluously invented. The third difference relates to the place ; Matthew and Mark have ἐκπορευομένων ἀπὸ, *as they departed from*, Luke, ἐν τῷ ἐγγίζειν εἰς Ἱεριχὼ, *as they came nigh to Jericho*. If there be any whom the words themselves fail to convince that this difference is irreconcileable, let them read the forced attempts to render these passages consistent with each other which have been made by commentators from Grotius down to Paulus.

Hence it was a better expedient which the older harmonists [4] adopted, and which has been approved by some modern critics [5]. In consideration of the last-named difference, they here distinguished two events, and held that Jesus cured a blind man first on his entrance into Jericho (according to Luke), and then again on his departure from that place (according to Matthew and Luke). Of the other divergency, relative to the number, these harmonists believed that they had disencumbered themselves by the supposition that Matthew connected in one event the two blind men, the one cured on entering and the other on leaving Jericho, and gave the latter position to the cure of both. But if so much weight is allowed to the statement of Matthew relative to the locality of the cure, as to make it, in conjunction with that of Mark, a reason for supposing two cures, one at each extremity of the town, I know not why equal credit should not be given to his numerical statement, and Storr appears to

[3] Paulus, exeg. Handb. 3, a. s. 44.
[4] Schulz, Anmerkungen zu Michaelis, 2, s. 105.
[5] Sieffert, ut sup. s. 104.

me to proceed more consistently when, allowing equal weight to both differences, he supposes that Jesus on his entrance into Jericho, cured one blind man (Luke) and subsequently on his departure, two (Matthew)[6]. The claim of Matthew is thus fully vindicated, but on the other hand that of Mark is denied. For if the latter be associated with Matthew, as is here the case, for the sake of his locality, it is necessary to do violence to his numerical statement, which taken alone would rather require him to be associated with Luke; so that to avoid impeaching either of his statements, which on this system of interpretation is not admissible, his narrative must be equally detached from that of both the other evangelists.   Thus we should have three distinct cures of the blind at Jericho: 1st, the cure of one blind man on the entrance of Jesus, 2nd, that of another on his departure, and 3rd, the cure of two blind men, also during the departure; in all, of four blind men.   Now to separate the second and third cases is indeed difficult.   For it will not be maintained that Jesus can have gone out by two different gates at the same time, and it is nearly as difficult to imagine that having merely set out with the intention of leaving Jericho, he returned again into the town, and not until afterwards took his final departure.   But, viewing the case more generally, it is scarcely an admissible supposition, that three incidents so entirely similar thus fell together in a group.   The accumulation of cures of the blind is enough to surprise us; but the behaviour of the companions of Jesus is incomprehensible; for after having seen in the first instance, on entering Jericho, that they had acted in opposition to the designs of Jesus by rebuking the blind man for his importunity, since Jesus called the man to him, they nevertheless repeated this conduct on the second and even on the third occasion.   Storr, it is true, is not disconcerted by this repetition in at least two incidents of this kind, for he maintains that no one knows whether those who had enjoined silence on going out of Jericho were not altogether different persons from those who had done the like on entering

[6] Ueber den Zweck der evang. Geschichte und der Briefe Joh. s. 345.

the town : indeed, supposing them to be the same, such a repetition of conduct which Jesus had implicitly disapproved, how ever unbecoming, was not therefore impossible, since even the disciples who had been present at the first miraculous feeding, yet asked, before the second, whence bread could be had for such a multitude?—but this is merely to argue the reality of one impossibility from that of another, as we shall presently see when we enter on the consideration of the two miraculous feedings.   Further, not only the conduct of the followers of Jesus, but also almost every feature of the incident must have been repeated in the most extraordinary manner.   In the one case as in the other, the blind men cry, *Have mercy upon us,* (or *me,*) *thou son of David;* then (after silence has been enjoined on them by the spectators) Jesus commands that they should be brought to him : he next asks what they will that he should do to them ; they answer, that we may receive our sight ; he complies with their wish, and they gratefully follow him.   That all this was so exactly repeated thrice, or even twice, is an improbability amounting to an impossibility ; and we must suppose, according to the hypothesis adopted by Sieffert in such cases, a legendary assimilation of different facts, or a traditionary variation of a single occurrence.   If, in order to arrive at a decision, it be asked : what could more easily happen, when once the intervention of the legend is presupposed, than that one and the same history should be told first of one, then of several, first of the entrance, then of the departure ? it will not be necessary to discuss the other possibility, since this is so incomparably more probable that there cannot be even a momentary hesitation in embracing it as real.   But in thus reducing the number of the facts, we must not with Sieffert stop short at two, for in that case not only do the difficulties with respect to the repetition of the same incident remain, but we fall into a want of logical sequency in admitting one divergency (in the number) as unessential, for the sake of removing another (in the locality).   If it be further asked, supposing only one incident to be here narrated, which of the several narratives is the original one ? the statements as to the locality will not aid us in coming to a decision ; for Jesus might just as well meet a blind man on entering as on leaving Jericho. The difference in the number is more likely to furnish us with a basis for a decision, and it will be in favour of Mark and Luke, who have each only one blind man ; not, it is true, for the reason alleged by Schleiermacher [7], namely, that Mark by his mention of the blind man's name, evinces a more accurate acquaintance with the circumstances ; for Mark, from his propensity to individualize out of his own imagination, ought least of all to be trusted with respect to names which are given by him alone. Our decision is founded on another circumstance.

It seems probable that Matthew was led to add a second blind man by his recollection of a previous cure of two blind men narrated by him alone (ix. 27 ff). Here, likewise when Jesus is in the act of departure,—from the place, namely, where he had raised the ruler's daughter,—two blind men follow him, (those at Jericho are sitting by the way side,) and in a similar manner cry for mercy of the Son of David, who here also, as in the other instance, according to Matthew, immediately cures them by touching their eyes. With these similarities there are certainly no slight divergencies ; nothing is here said of an injunction to the blind men to be silent, on the part of the companions of Jesus ; and, while at Jericho Jesus immediately calls the blind men to him, in the earlier case, they come in the first instance to him when he is again in the house ; further, while there he asks them, what they will have him to do to them ? here he asks, if they believe him able to cure them ? Lastly, the prohibition to tell what had happened, is peculiar to the earlier incident. The two narratives standing in this relation to each other, an assimilation of them might have taken place thus : Matthew transferred the two blind men and the touch of Jesus from the first anecdote to the second ; the form of the appeal from the blind men, from the second to the first.

---

[7] Ut sup. s. 237.

The two histories, as they are given, present but few data for a natural explanation. Nevertheless the rationalistic commentators have endeavoured to frame such an explanation. When Jesus in the earlier occurrence asked the blind men whether they had confidence in his power, he wished, say they, to ascertain whether their trust in him would remain firm during the operation, and whether they would punctually observe his further prescriptions [8]; having then entered the house, in order to be free from interruption, he examined, for the first time, their disease, and when he found it curable, (according to Venturini [9] it was caused by the fine dust of that country,) he assured the sufferers that the result should be according to the measure of their faith.   Hereupon Paulus merely says briefly, that Jesus removed the obstruction to their vision; but he also must have imagined to himself something similar to what is described in detail by Venturini, who makes Jesus anoint the eyes of the blind men with a strong water prepared beforehand, and thus cleanse them from the irritating dust, so that in a short time their sight returned.   But this natural explanation has not the slightest root in the text; for neither can the *faith* ($\pi i \varsigma \tau \iota \varsigma$) required from the patient imply anything else than, as in all similar cases, trust in the miraculous power of Jesus, nor can the word ἥψατο *he touched*, signify a surgical operation, but merely that touch which appears in so many of the evangelical curative miracles, whether as a sign or a conductor of the healing power of Jesus ; of further prescriptions for the completion of the cure there is absolutely nothing. It is not otherwise with the cure of the blind at Jericho, where, moreover, the two middle evangelists do not even mention the touching of the eyes.

If then, according to the meaning of the narrators, the blind instantaneously receive their sight as a consequence of the simple word or touch of Jesus, there are the same difficulties to be encountered here as in the former case of the lepers. For a disease of the eyes, however slight, as it is only engendered

---

[8] Paulus, L. J. 1, a. s. 249.

[9] Natürl. Gesch. des Propheten von Nag. 2, s. 216.

gradually by the reiterated action of the disturbing cause, is still less likely to disappear on a word or a touch; it requires very complicated treatment, partly surgical, partly medical, and this must be pre-eminently the case with blindness, supposing it to be of a curable kind. How should we represent to ourselves the sudden restoration of vision to a blind eye by a word or a touch? as purely miraculous and magical? That would be to give up thinking on the subject. As magnetic? There is no precedent of magnetism having influence over a disease of this nature. Or, lastly, as psychical? But blindness is something so independent of the mental life, so entirely corporeal, that the idea of its removal at all, still less of its sudden removal by means of a mental operation is not to be entertained. We must therefore acknowledge that an historical conception of these narratives is more than merely difficult to us; and we proceed to inquire whether we cannot show it to be probable that legends of this kind should arise unhistorically.

We have already quoted the passage in which, according to the first and third gospels, Jesus in reply to the messengers of the Baptist who had to ask him whether he were the ἐρχόμενος, (*he that should come,*) appeals to his works. Now he here mentions in the very first place the cure of the blind, a significant proof that this particular miracle was expected from the Messiah, his words being taken from Is. xxxv. 5, a prophecy interpreted messianically; and in a rabbinical passage above cited, among the wonders which Jehovah is to perform in the messianic times, this is enumerated, that he *oculos cæcorum aperiet, id quod per Elisam fecit* [10]. Now Elisha did not cure a positive blindness, but merely on one occasion opened the eyes of his servant to a perception of the supersensual world, and on another, removed a blindness which had been inflicted on his enemies in consequence of his prayer (2 Kings vi. 17—20). That these deeds of Elisha were conceived, doubtless with reference to the passage of Isaiah, as a real opening

[10] Vid. Vol. I. p. 81, note.

of the eyes of the blind, is proved by the above rabbinical passage, and hence cures of the blind were expected from the Messiah [11]. Now if the Christian community, proceeding as it did from the bosom of Judaism, held Jesus to be the messianic personage, it must manifest the tendency to ascribe to him every messianic predicate, and therefore the one in question.

The narrative of the cure of a blind man at Bethsaida, and that of the cure of *a man that was deaf and had an impediment in his speech*, which are both peculiar to Mark, (viii. 22 ff.; vii. 32 ff.), and which we shall therefore consider together, are the especial favourites of all rationalistic commentators. If, they exclaim, in the other evangelical narratives of cures, the accessory circumstances by which the facts might be explained were but preserved as they are here, we could prove historically that Jesus did not heal by his mere word, and profound investigators might discover the natural means by which his cures were effected [12]! And in fact chiefly on the ground of these narratives, in connexion with particular features in other parts of the second gospel, Mark has of late been represented, even

---

[11] Elsewhere also we find proof that in those times the power of effecting miraculous cures, especially of blindness, was commonly ascribed to men who were regarded as favourites of the Deity. Thus Tacitus, Hist. iv. 81, and Suetonius, Vespas. vii. tell us, that in Alexandria a blind man applied to Vespasian, shortly after he was made emperor, alleging that he did so by the direction of the god Serapis, with the entreaty that he would cure him of his blindness by wetting his eyes with his spittle. Vespasian complied, and the result was that the blind man immediately had his sight restored. As Tacitus attests the truth of this story in a remarkable manner, Paulus is probably not wrong in regarding the affair as the contrivance of adulatory priests, who to procure for the emperor the fame of a miracle-worker, and by this means to secure his favour on behalf of their god by whose counsel the event was occasioned, hired a man to simulate blindness. Ex. Handb. 2, s. 56 f. However this may be, we see from the narrative what was expected, even beyond the limits of Palestine, of a man who, as Tacitus here expresses himself concerning Vespasian, enjoyed *favor e cælis* and an *inclinatio numinum*.

[12] These are nearly the words of Paulus, exeg. Handb. 2, s. 312, 391.

by theologians who do not greatly favour this method of interpretation, as the patron of the naturalistic system [13].

In the two cures before us, it is at once a good augury for the rationalistic commentators that Jesus takes both the patients apart from the multitude, for no other purpose, as they believe, than that of examining their condition medically, and ascertaining whether it were susceptible of relief. Such an examination is, according to these commentators, intimated by the evangelist himself, when he describes Jesus as putting his fingers into the ears of the deaf man, by which means he discovered that the deafness was curable, arising probably from the hardening of secretions in the ear, and hereupon, also with the finger, he removed the hindrance to hearing. Not only are the words, *he put his fingers into his ears,* ἔβαλε τοὺς δακτύλους εἰς τὰ ὦτα, interpreted as denoting a surgical operation, but the words, *he touched his tongue* ἥψατο τῆς γλώσσης, are supposed to imply that Jesus cut the ligament of the tongue in the degree necessary to restore the pliancy which the organ had lost. In like manner, in the case of the blind man, the words, *when he had put his hands upon him,* ἐπιθεὶς τὰς χεῖρας αὐτῷ, are explained as probably meaning that Jesus by pressing the eyes of the patient removed the crystalline lens which had become opaque. A further help to this mode of interpretation is found in the circumstance that both to the tongue of the man who had an impediment in his speech, and to the eyes of the blind man, Jesus applied spittle. Saliva has in itself, particularly in the opinion of ancient physicians [14], a salutary effect on the eyes; as, however, it in no case acts so rapidly as instantaneously to cure blindness and a defect in the organs of speech, it is conjectured, with respect to both instances, that Jesus used the saliva to moisten some medicament, probably a caustic

---

[13] De Wette, Beitrag zur Charakteristik des Evangelisten Markus, in Ullmann's und Umbreit's Studien, 1, 4, 789 ff. Comp. Köster, Immanuel, s. 72. On the other hand : comp. De Wette's exeg. Handb. 1, 2, s. 148 f.

[14] Pliny, H. N. xxviii. 7, and other passages in Wetstein.

powder; that the blind man only heard the spitting and saw nothing of the mixture of the medicaments, and that the deaf man, in accordance with the spirit of the age, gave little heed to the natural means, or that the legend did not preserve them. In the narrative of the deaf man the cure is simply stated, but that of the blind man is yet further distinguished, by its representing the restoration of his sight circumstantially, as gradual. After Jesus had touched the eyes of the patient as above mentioned, he asked him *if he saw aught;* not at all, observes Paulus, in the manner of a miracle-worker, who is sure of the result, but precisely in the manner of a physician, who after performing an operation endeavours to ascertain if the patient is benefited. The blind man answers that he sees, but first indistinctly, so that men seem to him like trees. Here apparently the rationalistic commentator may triumphantly ask the orthodox one: if divine power for the working of cures stood at the command of Jesus, why did he not at once cure the blind man perfectly? If the disease presented an obstacle which he was not able to overcome, is it not clear from thence that his power was a finite, ordinarily human power? Jesus once more puts his hands on the eyes of the blind man, in order to aid the effect of the first operation, and only then is the cure completed [15].

The complacency of the rationalistic commentators in these narratives of Mark, is liable to be disturbed by the frigid observation, that, here also, the circumstances which are requisite to render the natural explanation possible are not given by the evangelists themselves, but are interpolated by the said commentators. For in both cures Mark furnishes the saliva only; the efficacious powder is infused by Paulus and Venturini: it is they alone who make the introduction of the fingers into the ears first a medical examination and then an operation; and it is they alone who, contrary to the signification of language, explain the words ἐπιτιθέναι τὰς χεῖρας ἐπὶ

[15] Paulus, ut sup. s. 312 f. 392 ff.; Natürliche Geschichte, 3. s. 31 ff. 216 f.; Köster, Immanuel, s. 188 ff.

τοὺς ὀφθαλμοὺς, *to lay the hands upon the eyes*, as implying a surgical operation on those organs. Again, the circumstance that Jesus takes the blind man aside, is shown by the context (vii. 36 ; viii. 26.) to have reference to the design of Jesus to keep the miraculous result a secret, not to the desire to be undisturbed in the application of natural means: so that all the supports of the rationalistic explanation sink beneath it, and the orthodox one may confront it anew. This regards the touch and the spittle either as a condescension towards the sufferers, who were thereby made more thoroughly sensible to whose power they owed their cure ; or as a conducting medium for the spiritual power of Christ, a medium with which he might nevertheless have dispensed [16]. That the cure was gradual, is on this system accounted for by the supposition, that Jesus intended by means of the partial cure to animate the faith of the blind man, and only when he was thus rendered worthy was he completely cured [17]; or it is conjectured that, owing to the malady being deep-seated, a sudden cure would perhaps have been dangerous [18].

But by these attempts to interpret the evangelical narratives, especially in the last particular, the supranaturalistic theologians, who bring them forward, betake themselves to the same ground as the rationalists, for they are equally open to the charge of introducing into the narratives what is not in the remotest degree intimated by the text. For where, in the procedure of Jesus towards the blind man, is there a trace that his design in the first instance was to prove and to strengthen the faith of the patient ? In that case, instead of the expression, *He asked him if he saw aught,* which relates only to his external condition, we must rather have read, as in Matt. ix. 28, *Believe ye that I am able to do this ?* But what shall we say to the conjecture that a sudden cure might have been injurious!

---

[16] For the former explanation, Hess, Geschichte Jesu, 1, s. 390 f. ; for the latter, Olshausen, b. Comm. 1. s. 510.

[17] Kuinöl, in Marc. p. 110.

[18] Olshausen, s. 509.

The curative act of a worker of miracles is (according to Olshausen's own opinion) not to be regarded as the merely negative one of the removal of a disease, but also as the positive one of an impartation of new life and fresh strength to the organ affected, whence the idea of danger from an instantaneous cure when wrought by miraculous agency, is not to be entertained. Thus no motive is to be discovered which could induce Jesus to put a restraint on the immediate action of his miraculous power, and it must therefore have been restricted, independently of his volition, by the force of the deep-seated malady. This, however, is entirely opposed to the idea of the gospels, which represent the miraculous power of Jesus as superior to death itself; it cannot therefore have been the meaning of our evangelist. If we take into consideration the peculiar characteristics of Mark as an author, it will appear that his only aim is to give dramatic effect to the scene. Every sudden result is difficult to bring before the imagination: he who wishes to give to another a vivid idea of a rapid movement, first goes through it slowly, and a quick result is perfectly conceivable only when the narrator has shown the process in detail. Consequently a writer whose object it is to assist as far as may be the imagination of his reader, will wherever it is possible exhibit the propensity to render the immediate mediate, and when recording a sudden result, still to bring forward the successive steps that led to it [19]. So here Mark, or his informant, supposed that he was contributing greatly to the dramatic effect, when he inserted between the blindness of the man and the entire restoration of his sight, the partial cure, or the seeing men as trees, and every reader will say, from his own feeling, that this object is fully achieved. But herein, as others also have remarked, [20] Mark is so far from manifesting an inclination to the natural conception of such miracles, that he, on the contrary, not seldom labours to aggrandize the miracle, as we have partly seen in the case of the Gadarene, and shall yet have fre-

[19] Comp. De Wette, Kritik der Mosaischen Geschichte, s. 36 f.
[20] Fritzsche Comm. in Marc. p. xliii.

quent reason to remark.   In a similar manner may also be explained why Mark in these narratives which are peculiar to him (and elsewhere also, as in vi. 13, where he observes that the disciples anointed the sick with oil), mentions the application of external means and manifestations in miraculous cures. That these means, the saliva particularly, were not in the popular opinion of that age naturally efficacious causes of the cure, we may be convinced by the narrative concerning Vespasian quoted above, as also by passages of Jewish and Roman authors, according to which saliva was believed to have a magical potency, especially against diseases of the eye[21]. Hence Olshausen perfectly reproduces the conception of that age when he explains the touch, saliva, and the like, to be conductors of the superior power resident in the worker of miracles. We cannot indeed make this opinion ours, unless with Olshausen we proceed upon the supposition of a parallelism between the miraculous power of Jesus and the agency of animal magnetism : a supposition which, for the explanation of the miracles of Jesus, especially of the one before us, is inadequate and therefore superfluous.   Hence we put this means merely to the account of the evangelist.   To him also we may then doubtless refer the taking aside of the blind man, the exaggerated description of the astonishment of the people, (ὑπερπερισσῶς ἐξεπλήσσοντο ἅπαντες, vii. 37,) and the strict prohibition to tell any man of the cure. This secrecy gave the affair a mysterious aspect, which, as we may gather from other passages, was pleasing to Mark. We have another trait belonging to the mysterious in the narratives of the cure of the deaf man, where Mark says, *And looking up to heaven he sighed*, (vii. 34).   What cause was there for sighing at that particular moment?   Was it the misery of the human race[22], which must have been long known to Jesus from many melancholy examples ?   Or shall we evade the difficulty, by explaining the expression as implying nothing further than silent prayer or

[21] Vid. ap. Wetstein and Lightfoot, John ix. 6.
[22] Thus Fritzche, after Euthymius, in Marc. p. 304.

audible speech [23] ? Whoever knows Mark will rather recognise the exaggerating narrator in the circumstance that he ascribes to Jesus a deep emotion, on an occasion which could not indeed have excited it, but which, being accompanied by it, had a more mysterious appearance. But above all, there appears to me to be an air of mystery in this, that Mark gives the authoritative word with which Jesus opened the ears of the deaf man in its original Syriac form, ἐφφαθά, as on the resuscitation of the daughter of Jairus, this evangelist alone has the words ταλιθὰ κοῦμι (v. 41.). It is indeed said that these expressions are anything rather than magical forms [24]; but that Mark chooses to give these authoritative words in a language foreign to his readers, to whom he is obliged at the same time to explain them, nevertheless proves that he must have attributed to this original form a special significance, which, as it appears from the context, can only have been a magical one. This inclination to the mysterious we may now retrospectively find indicated in the application of those outward means which have no relation to the result; for the mysterious consists precisely in the presentation of infinite power through a finite medium, in the combination of the strongest effect with apparently inefficacious means.

If we have been unable to receive as historical the simple narrative given by all the synoptical writers of the cure of the blind man at Jericho, we are still less prepared to award this character to the mysterious description, given by Mark alone, of the cure of a blind man at Bethsaida, and we must regard it as a product of the legend, with more or less addition from the evangelical narrator. The same judgment must be pronounced on his narrative of the cure of the deaf man who had an impediment in his speech κωφὸς μογιλάλος; for, together with the negative reasons already adduced against its historical credibility, there are not wanting positive causes for its mythical origin, since the prophecy relating to the messianic times,

[23] The former is the supposition of Kuinöl, the latter of Schott.
[24] Hess, Gesch. Jesu, 1, s. 391, Anm. 1.

τότε ὦτα κωφῶν ἀκούσονται—τρανὴ δὲ ἔσται γλῶσσα μογιλάλων, *the ears of the deaf shall be unstopped, the tongue of the dumb shall sing* (Isai. xxxv. 5, 6.) was in existence, and according to Matt. xi. 5, was interpreted literally.

If the narratives of Mark which we have just considered, seem at the first glance to be favourable to the natural explanation, the narrative of John, chap. ix. must, one would think, be unfavourable and destructive to it; for here the question is not concerning a blind man, whose malady having originated accidentally, might be easier to remove, but concerning a man born blind. Nevertheless, as the expositors of this class are sharp-sighted, and do not soon lose courage, they are able even here to discover much in their favour. In the first place, they find that the condition of the patient is but vaguely described, however definite the expression *blind from his birth* τυφλὸν ἐκ γενετῆς may seem to sound. The statement of time which this expression includes, Paulus, it is true, refrains from overthrowing (though his forbearance is unwilling and in fact incomplete): hence he has the more urgent necessity for attempting to shake the statement as to quality. Τυφλὸς is not to signify total blindness, and as Jesus tells the man *to go* to the pool of Siloam, not to get himself led thither, he must have still had some glimmering of eye-sight, by means of which he could himself find the way thither. Still more help do the rationalistic commentators find for themselves in the mode of cure adopted by Jesus. He says before-hand (v. 4) he must work the works of him that sent him *while it is day,* ἕως ἡμέρα ἐστίν, for in the night no man can work; a sufficient proof that he had not the idea of curing the blind man by a mere word, which he might just as well have uttered in the night—that, on the contrary, he intended to undertake a medical or surgical operation, for which certainly daylight was required. Farther, the clay, πηλὸς, which Jesus made with his spittle, and with which he anointed the eyes of the blind man, is still more favourable to the natural explanation than the expression πτύσας *having spit,* in a former case, and hence it is a fertile

source of questions and conjectures. Whence did John know
that Jesus took nothing more than spittle and dust to make his
eye-salve ? Was he himself present, or did he understand it
merely from the narrative of the cured blind man ? The latter
could not, with his then weak glimmering of sight, correctly
see what Jesus took : perhaps Jesus while he mixed a salve out
of other ingredients accidentally spat upon the ground, and the
patient fell into the error of supposing that the spittle made
part of the salve. Still more : while or before Jesus put something on the eyes, did he not also remove something by extraction or friction, or otherwise effect a change in the state of
these organs ? This would be an essential fact which might
easily be mistaken by the blind man and the spectators for a
merely accessory circumstance. Lastly, the washing in the
pool of Siloam which was prescribed to the patient was perhaps
continued many days — was a protracted cure by means of
the bath—and the words ἦλθε βλέπων *he came seeing,* do not
necessarily imply that he came thus after his first bath, but that
at a convenient time after the completion of his cure, he came
again seeing [25].

But, to begin at the beginning, the meaning here given to
ἡμέρα and νὺξ is too shallow even for Venturini [26], and especially
clashes with the context (v. 5), which throughout demands an
interpretation of the words with reference to the speedy departure of Jesus [27]. As to the conjecture that the clay was
made of medicinal ingredients of some kind or other, it is the
more groundless, since it cannot be said here, as in the former
case, that only so much is stated as the patient could learn by
his hearing or by a slight glimmering of light, for, on this
occasion, Jesus undertook the cure, not in private, but in the
presence of his disciples. Concerning the farther supposition
of previous surgical operations, by which the anointing and
washing, alone mentioned in the text, are reduced to mere

[25] Paulus, Comm. 4, s. 472.
[26] Natürliche Gesch. 3. s. 215.
[27] Vid. Tholuck and Lücke, in loc.

accessories, nothing more is to be said, than that by this example we may see how completely the spirit of natural explanation despises all restraints, not scrupling to pervert the clearest words of the text in support of its arbitrary combinations. Further, when, from the circumstance that Jesus ordered the blind man to go to the pool of Siloam, it is inferred that he must have had a share of light, we may remark, in opposition to this, that Jesus merely told the patient *whither* he should go (ὑπάγειν); *how* he was to go, whether alone or with a guide, he left to his own discretion. Lastly, when the closely connected words *he went his way, therefore, and washed and came seeing,* ἀπῆλθεν οὖν καὶ ἐνίψατο καὶ ἦλθε βλέπων (v. 7; comp. v. 11) are stretched out into a process of cure lasting several weeks, it is just as if the words *veni, vidi, vici* were translated thus: After my arrival I reconnoitred for several days, fought battles at suitable intervals, and finally remained conqueror.

Thus here also the natural explanation will not serve us, and we have still before us the narrative of a man born blind, miraculously cured by Jesus. That the doubts already expressed as to the reality of the cures of the blind, apply with increased force to the case of a man born blind, is self-evident. And they are aided in this instance by certain special critical reasons. Not one of the three first evangelists mentions this cure. Now, if in the formation of the apostolic tradition, and in the selection which it made from among the miracles of Jesus, any kind of reason was exercised, it must have taken the shape of the two following rules: first, to choose the greater miracles before those apparently less important; and secondly, those with which edifying discourses were connected, before those which were not thus distinguished. In the first respect, it is plain that the cure of a man blind from his birth, as the incomparably more difficult miracle, was by all means to be chosen rather than that of a man in whom blindness had supervened, and it is not to be conceived why, if Jesus really gave sight to a man born blind, nothing of this should have entered into the evangelical tradition, and from thence into the synoptical gospels. It is true that with this consideration of the magnitude of the miracles, a regard to the edifying nature of the discourses connected with them might not seldom come into collision, so that a less striking, but from the conversations which it caused, a more instructive miracle, might be preferred to one more striking, but presenting less of the latter kind of interest. But the cure of the blind man in John is accompanied by very remarkable conversations, first, of Jesus with the disciples, then, of the cured man with the magistrates, and lastly of Jesus with the cured man, such as there is no trace of in the synoptical cures of the blind; conversations in which, if not the entire course of the dialogue, at least some aphoristic pearls (as v. 4, 5, 39,) were admirably suited to the purpose of the three first evangelists. These writers therefore, could not have failed to introduce the cure of the man born blind into their histories, instead of their less remarkable and less edifying cures of the blind, if the former had made a part of the evangelical tradition whence they drew. It might possibly have remained unknown to the general christian tradition, if it had taken place at a time and under circumstances which did not favour its promulgation—if it had been effected in a remote corner of the country, without further witnesses. But Jesus performed this miracle in Jerusalem, in the circle of his disciples; it made a great sensation in the city, and was highly offensive to the magistracy, hence the affair must have been known if it had really occurred; and as we do not find it in the common evangelical tradition, the suspicion arises that it perhaps never did occur.

But it will be said, the writer who attests it is the apostle John. This, however, is too improbable, not only on account of the incredible nature of the contents of the narrative, which could thus hardly have proceeded from an eye-witness, but also from another reason. The narrator interprets the name of the pool, Siloam, by the Greek ἀπεσταλμένος (v. 7) ; a false explanation, for one who is sent is called שָׁלוּחַ, whereas שִׁלֹחַ according to the most probable interpretation signifies a water-fall [28]. The evangelist, however, chose the above interpretation, because he sought for some significant relation between the name of the pool, and the sending thither of the blind man, and thus seems to have imagined that the pool had by a special providence received the name of *Sent*, because at a future time the Messiah, as a manifestation of his glory, was to send thither a blind man [29]. Now, we grant that an apostle might give a grammatically incorrect explanation, in so far as he is not held to be inspired, and that even a native of Palestine might mistake the etymology of Hebrew words, as the Old Testament itself shows; nevertheless, such a play upon words looks more like the laboured attempt of a writer remote from the event, than of an eye-witness. The eye-witness would have had enough of important matters in the miracle which he had beheld, and the conversation to which he had listened; only a remote narrator could fall into the triviality of trying to extort a significant meaning from the smallest accessory circumstance. Tholuck and Lücke are highly revolted by this allegory, which, as the latter expresses himself, approaches to absolute folly, hence they are unwilling to admit that it proceeded from John, and regard it as a gloss. As, however, all critical authorities, except one of minor importance, present this particular, such a position is sheer arbitrariness, and the only choice left us is either, with Olshausen, to edify ourselves by this interpretation as an apostolic one [30], or, with the author of the Probabilia, to number it among the indications that the fourth gospel had not an apostolic origin [31].

The reasons which might prevent the author of the fourth gospel, or the tradition whence he drew, from resting contented with the cures of the blind narrated by the synoptical writers,

---

[28] Vid. Paulus and Lücke, in loc.

[29] Thus Euthymius and Paulus, in loc.

[30] B. Comm. 2, s. 230, where, however, he refers the ἀπεσταλμένος to the outflow of the spirit proceeding from God.

[31] S. 93.

and thus induce the one or the other to frame the history before us, are already pointed out by the foregoing remarks. The observation has been already made by others, that the fourth evangelist has fewer miracles than the synoptical writers, but that this deficiency in number is compensated by a superiority in magnitude [32]. Thus while the other evangelists have simple paralytics cured by Jesus, the fourth gospel has one who had been lame thirty-eight years; while, in the former, Jesus resuscitates persons who had just expired, in the latter, he calls back to life one who had lain in the grave four days, in whom therefore it might be presumed that decomposition had begun; and so here, instead of a cure of simple blindness, we have that of a man born blind,—a heightening of the miracle altogether suited to the apologetic and dogmatic tendency of this gospel. In what way the author, or the particular tradition which he followed, might be led to depict the various details of the narrative, is easily seen. The act of spitting, πτύειν, was common in magical cures of the eyes; clay, πηλὸς, was a ready substitute for an eye-salve, and elsewhere occurs in magical proceedings [33]; the command to wash in the pool of Siloam may have been an imitation of Elisha's order, that the leper Naaman should bathe seven times in the river Jordan. The conversations connected with the cure partly proceed from the tendency of the gospel of John already remarked by Storr, namely, to attest and to render as authentic as possible both the cure of the man, and the fact of his having been born blind, whence the repeated examination of the cured man, and even of his parents; partly they turn upon the symbolical meaning of the expressions, *blind* and *seeing, day* and *night,*—a meaning which it is true is not foreign to the synoptical writers, but which specifically belongs to the circle of images in favour with John.

[32] Köster, Immanuel, s. 79; Bretschneider, Probab. s. 122.
[33] Wetstein, in loc.

§ 96.

An important feature in the history of the cure of the man born blind has been passed over, because it can only be properly estimated in connexion with a corresponding one in the synoptical narratives of the cure of a paralytic (Matt. ix. 1 ff.; Mark ii. 1 ff.; Luke v. 17 ff.), which we have in the next place to consider. Here Jesus first declares to the sick man: ἀφέωνταί σοί αἱ ἁμαρτίαι σου, *thy sins are forgiven thee*, and then as a proof that he had authority to forgive sins, he cures him. It is impossible not to perceive in this a reference to the Jewish opinion, that any evil befalling an individual, and especially disease, was a punishment of his sins; an opinion which, presented in its main elements in the Old Testament, (Lev. xxvi. 14 ff.; Deut. xxviii. 15 ff.; 2 Chron. xxi. 15. 18 f.) was expressed in the most definite manner by the later Jews [1]. Had we possessed that synoptical narrative only, we must have believed that Jesus shared the opinion of his cotemporary fellow-countrymen on this subject, since he proves his authority to forgive sins (as the cause of disease) by an example of his power to cure disease (the consequence of sin). But, it is said, there are other passages where Jesus directly contradicts this Jewish opinion; whence it follows, that what he then says to the paralytic was a mere accommodation to the ideas of the sick man, intended to promote his cure [2].

The principal passage commonly adduced in support of this position, is the introduction to the history of the man born blind, which was last considered (John ix. 1—3.). Here the disciples, seeing on the road the man whom they knew to have been blind from his birth, put to Jesus the question, whether his blindness was the consequence of his own sins, or of those

---

[1] Nedarim f. xli. 1. (Schöttgen, 1, p. 93.): *Dixit R. Chija fil. Abba: nullus aegrotus a morbo suo sanatur, donec ipsi omnia peccata remissa sint.*

[2] Hase, L. J. § 73. Fritzsche, in Matt. p. 335.

of his parents? The case was a peculiarly difficult one on the
Jewish theory of retribution. With respect to diseases which
attach themselves to a man in his course through life, an
observer who has once taken a certain bias, may easily discover
or assume some peculiar delinquencies on the part of this man
as their cause. With respect to inborn diseases, on the contrary, though the old Hebraic opinion (Exod. xx. 5; Deut. v. 9;
2 Sam. iii. 29.), it is true, presented the explanation that by
these the sins of the fathers were visited on their posterity:
yet as, for human regulation, the Mosaic law itself ordained
that each should suffer for his own sins alone (Deut. xxiv. 16;
2 Kings xiv. 6); and as also, in relation to the penal justice of
the Divine Being, the prophets predicted a similar dispensation
(Jer. xxxi. 30; Ezek. xviii. 19 f.); rabbinical acumen resorted
to the expedient of supposing, that men so afflicted might probably have sinned in their mother's womb [3], and this was doubtless the notion which the disciples had in view in their question
v. 2. Jesus says, in answer, that neither for his own sin nor
for that of his parents, did this man come into the world blind;
but in order that by the cure which he, as the Messiah, would
effect in him, he might be an instrument in manifesting the
miraculous power of God. This is generally understood as if Jesus
repudiated the whole opinion, that disease and other evils were
essentially punishments of sin. But the words of Jesus are
expressly limited to the case before him; he simply says, that
this particular misfortune had its foundation, not in the guilt of
the individual, but in higher providential designs. The supposition that his expressions had a more general sense, and
included a repudiation of the entire Jewish opinion, could only
be warranted by other more decided declarations from him to
that effect. As, on the contrary, according to the above
observations, a narrative is found in the synoptical gospels

[3] Sanhedr. f. xci. 2, and Bereschith Rabba f. xxxviii. 1. (Lightfoot p. 1050.) :
Antoninus interrogavit Rabbi (Judam) : a quonam tempore incipit malus affectus
praevalere in homine? an a tempore formationis ejus (in utero), an a tempore pro-
cessionis ejus (ex utero) ? Dicit ei Rabbi : a tempore formationis ejus.

which, simply interpreted, implies the concurrence of Jesus in
the prevalent opinion, the question arises: which is easier, to
regard the expression of Jesus in the synoptical narratives as
an accommodation, or that in John as having relation solely to
the case immediately before him?—a question which will be
decided in favour of the latter alternative by every one who, on
the one hand, knows the difficulties attending the hypothesis of
accommodation as applied to the expressions of Jesus in the
gospels, and on the other, is clear-sighted enough to perceive,
that in the passage in question in the fourth gospel, there is not
the slightest intimation that the declaration of Jesus had a
more general meaning.

It is true that according to correct principles of interpretation, one evangelist ought not to be explained immediately by
another, and in the present case it is very possible that while
the synoptical writers ascribe to Jesus the common opinion of
his age, the more highly cultivated author of the fourth gospel
may make him reject it: but that he also confined the rejection
of the current opinion on the part of Jesus to that single case,
is proved by the manner in which he represents Jesus as speaking on another occasion. When, namely, Jesus says to the
man who had been lame thirty-eight years (John v.) and had
just been cured, μηκέτι ἁμάρτανε, ἵνα μὴ χεῖρόν τί σοι γένηται
(v. 14), *Sin no more, lest a worse thing come unto thee;*
this is equivalent to his saying to the paralytic whom he was
about to cure, ἀφέωνταί σοι αἱ ἁμαρτίαι σου, *thy sins are forgiven thee:* in the one case disease is removed, in the other
threatened, as a punishment of sin. But here again the expositors, to whom it is not agreeable that Jesus should hold an
opinion which they reject, find a means of evading the direct
sense of the words. Jesus, say they, perceived that the particular disease of this man was a natural consequence of certain
excesses, and warned him from a repetition of these as calculated to bring on a more dangerous relapse [4]. But an insight

---

[4] Paulus Comm. 4, s. 264 ; Lücke, 2, s. 22.

into the natural connexion between certain excesses and certain diseases as their consequence, is far more removed from the mode of thinking of the age in which Jesus lived, than the notion of a positive connexion between sin in general and disease as its punishment; hence, if we are nevertheless to ascribe the former sense to the words of Jesus, it must be very distinctly conveyed in the text. But the fact is that in the whole narrative there is no intimation of any particular excess on the part of the man; the words μηκέτι ἁμάρτανε, relate only to sin in general, and to supply a conversation of Jesus with the sick man, in which he is supposed to have acquainted the former with the connexion between his sufferings and a particular sin [5], is the most arbitrary fiction. What exposition! for the sake of evading a result which is dogmatically unwelcome, to extend the one passage (John ix.) to a generality of meaning not really belonging to it, to elude the other (Matt. ix.) by the hypothesis of accommodation, and forcibly to affix to a third (John v.) a modern idea; whereas if the first passage be only permitted to say no more than it actually says, the direct meaning of the other two may remain unviolated!

But another passage, and that a synoptical one, is adduced in vindication of the superiority of Jesus to the popular opinion in question. This passage is Luke xiii. 1 ff., where Jesus is told of the Galileans whom Pilate had caused to be slain while they were in the act of sacrificing, and of others who were killed by the falling of a tower. From what follows, we must suppose the informants to have intimated their opinion that these calamities were to be regarded as a divine visitation for the peculiar wickedness of the parties so signally destroyed. Jesus replied that they must not suppose those men to have been especially sinful; they themselves were in no degree better, and unless they repented would meet with a similar destruction. Truly it is not clear how in these expressions of Jesus a repudiation of the popular notion can be found. If Jesus wished to give his voice in opposition to this, he must either have said : you are equally great sinners, though you may not perish bodily in the

[5] This is done by Tholuck, in loc.

same manner; or: do you believe that those men perished on account of their sins? No! the contrary may be seen in you, who, notwithstanding your wickedness, are not thus smitten with death. On the contrary, the expressions of Jesus as given by Luke can only have the following sense: that those men have already met with such calamities is no evidence of their peculiar wickedness, any more than the fact that you have been hitherto spared the like, is an evidence of your greater worth; on the contrary, earlier or later, similar judgments falling on you will attest your equal guilt:—whereby the supposed law of the connexion between the sin and misfortune of every individual is confirmed, not overthrown. This vulgar Hebrew opinion concerning sickness and evil, is indeed in contradiction with that esoteric view, partly Essene, partly Ebionite, which we have found in the introduction to the sermon on the mount, the parable of the rich man, and elsewhere, and according to which the righteous in this generation are the suffering, the poor and the sick; but both opinions are clearly to be seen in the discourses of Jesus by an unprejudiced exegesis, and the contradiction which we find between them authorizes us neither to put a forced construction on the one class of expressions, nor to deny them to have really come from Jesus, since we cannot calculate how he may have solved for himself the opposition between two ideas of the world, presented to him by different sides of the Jewish culture of that age.

As regards the above-mentioned cure, the synoptical writers make Jesus in his reply to the messengers of the Baptist, appeal to the fact that the lame walked (Matt. xi. 5), and at another time the people wonder when, among other miracles, they see *the maimed to be whole and the lame to walk* (Matt. xv. 31). In the place of the *lame, χωλοὶ, paralytics, παραλυτικοὶ,* are elsewhere brought forward (Matt. iv. 24), and especially in the detailed histories of cures relating to this kind of sufferers, (as Matt. ix. 1 ff. parall. viii. 5, parall.) *παραλυτικοὶ,* and not *χωλοὶ,* are named. The sick man at the pool of Bethesda (John v. 5) belongs probably to the *χωλοῖς* spoken of in v. 3; there also *ξηροὶ, withered,* are mentioned, and in Matt. xii. 9 ff. parall. we find the cure of a man who had a withered hand.   As however the three last named cures will return to us under different heads, all that remains here for our examination is the cure of the paralytic Matt. ix. 1 ff. parall.

As the definitions which the ancient physicians give of paralysis, though they all show it to have been a species of lameness, yet leave it undecided whether the lameness was total or partial[6]; and as, besides, no strict adherence to medical technicalities is to be expected from the evangelists, we must gather what they understand by paralytics from their own descriptions of such patients.   In the present passage, we read of the paralytic that he was borne on a *bed* κλίνη, and that to enable him to arise and carry his bed was an unprecedented wonder παράδοξον, whence we must conclude that he was lame, at least in the feet.   While here there is no mention of pains, or of an acute character of disease, in another narrative (Matt. viii. 6) these are evidently presupposed when the centurion says that his servant is *sick* of the *palsy, grievously tormented,* βέβληται —παραλυτικὸς, δεινῶς βασανιζόμενος; so that under paralytics in the gospels we have at one time to understand a lameness without pain, at another a painful, gouty disease of the limbs[7].

In the description of the scene in which the paralytic, (Matt. ix. 1 ff. parall.) is brought to Jesus, there is a remarkable gradation in the three accounts.   Matthew says simply, that as Jesus, after an excursion to the opposite shore, returned to Capernaum, there was brought to him a paralytic, stretched on a bed.   Luke describes particularly how Jesus, surrounded by a great multitude, chiefly Pharisees and scribes, taught and healed in a certain house, and how the bearers, because on account of the press they could not reach Jesus, let the sick man down to him through the roof.   If we call to mind the structure of oriental houses, which had a flat roof, to which an opening led from the upper story[8]; and if we add to this the

---

[6] See the examples in Wetstein, N. T. 1, s. 284, and in Wahl's Clavis.

[7] Comp. Winer, Realw. and Fritzsche, in Matt. p. 194.

[8] Winer, ut sup. Art. Dach.

rabbinical manner of speaking, in which to the *via per portam*
(דרך פתחים) was opposed the *via per tectum* (דרך גגין) as a no
less ordinary way for reaching the ὑπερῷον *upper story* or
chamber[9], we cannot under the expression καθιέναι διὰ τῶν
κεράμων, *to let down through the tiling*, understand anything
else than that the bearers—who, either by means of stairs
leading thither directly from the street, or from the roof of a
neighbouring house, gained access to the roof of the house in
which Jesus was,—let down the sick man with his bed, apparently by cords, through the opening already existing in the
roof.   Mark, who, while with Matthew he places the scene at
Capernaum, agrees with Luke in the description of the great
crowd and the consequent ascent to the roof, goes yet farther
than Luke, not only in determining the number of the bearers
to be four, but also in making them, regardless of the opening
already existing, uncover the roof and let down the sick man
through an aperture newly broken.

If we ask here also in which direction, upwards or down-
wards, the climax may most probably have been formed, the
narrative of Mark, which stands at the summit, has so many
difficulties that it can scarcely be regarded as nearest the truth.
For not only have opponents asked, how could the roof be
broken open without injury to those beneath[10]? but Olshausen
himself admits that the disturbance of the roof, covered with
tiles, partakes of the extravagant[11].   To avoid this, many expositors suppose that Jesus taught either in the inner court[12], or in
the open air in front of the house[13], and that the bearers only
broke down a part of the parapet in order to let down the sick
man more conveniently.   But both the phrase, διὰ τῶν κεράμων,
in Luke, and the expressions of Mark, render this conception of
the thing impossible, since here neither can στέγη mean parapet,

[9] Lightfoot, p. 601.
[10] Woolston, Disc. 4.
[11] 1, s. 310 f.
[12] Köster, Immanuel, s. 166, Anm. 66.
[13] This appears to be the meaning of Paulus, L. J. 1, a. s. 238.   Otherwise
exeg. Handb. 1, b. s. 505.

nor ἀποστεγάζω the breaking of the parapet, while ἐξορύττω can only mean the breaking of a hole. Thus the disturbance of the roof subsists, but this is further rendered improbable on the ground that it was altogether superfluous, inasmuch as there was a door in every roof. Hence help has been sought in the supposition that the bearers indeed used the door previously there, but because this was too narrow for the bed of the patient, they widened it by the removal of the surrounding tiles [14]. Still, however, there remains the danger to those below, and the words imply an opening actually made, not merely widened.

But dangerous and superfluous as such a proceeding would be in reality, it is easy to explain how Mark, wishing further to elaborate the narrative of Luke, might be led to add such a feature. Luke had said that the sick man was let down, so that he descended in the midst before Jesus, ἔμπροσθεν τοῦ Ἰησοῦ. How could the people precisely hit upon this place, unless Jesus accidentally stood under the door of the roof, except by breaking open the roof above the spot where they knew him to be (ἀπεστέγασαν τὴν στέγην ὅπου ἦν) [15]? This trait Mark the more gladly seized because it was adapted to place in the strongest light the zeal which confidence in Jesus infused into the people, and which was to be daunted by no labour. This last interest seems to be the key also to Luke's departure from Matthew. In Matthew, who makes the bearers bring the paralytic to Jesus in the ordinary way, doubtless regarding the laborious conveyance of the sick man on his bed as itself a proof of their faith, it is yet less evident wherein Jesus sees their faith. If the original form of the history was that in which it appears in the first gospel, the temptation might easily arise to make the bearers devise a more conspicuous means of evincing their faith, which, since the scene was already described as happening in a great crowd, might appear to be most suitably found in the uncommon way in which they contrived to bring their sick man to Jesus.

[14] Thus Lightfoot, Kuinöl, Olshausen, in loc.
[15] Vid. Fritzsche, in Marc. p. 52.

But even the account of Matthew we cannot regard as a true narrative of a fact. It has indeed been attempted to represent the result as a natural one, by explaining the state of the man to be a nervous weakness, the worst symptom of which was the idea of the sick man that his disease must continue as a punishment of his sin [16]; reference has been made to analogous cases of a rapid psychical cure of lameness [17]; and a subsequent use of long-continued curative means has been supposed [18]. But the first and last expedients are purely arbitrary; and if in the alleged analogies there may be some truth, yet it is always incomparably more probable that histories of cures of the lame and paralytic in accordance with messianic expectation, should be formed by the legend, than that they should really have happened. In the passage of Isaiah already quoted (xxxv. 6), it was promised in relation to the messianic time: *then shall the lame man leap as a hart,* τότε ἀλεῖται ὡς ἔλαφος ὁ χωλός, and in the same connexion, v. 3, the prophet addresses to the *feeble knees* γόνατα παραλελυμένα the exhortation, *Be strong,* ἰσχύσατε, which, with the accompanying particulars, must have been understood literally, of a miracle to be expected from the Messiah, since Jesus, as we have already mentioned, among other proofs that he was the ἐρχόμενος adduced this : χωλοὶ περιπατοῦσι, *the lame walk.*

§ 97.

INVOLUNTARY CURES.

Occasionally in their general statements concerning the curative power of Jesus, the synoptical writers remark, that all kinds of sick people only sought to touch Jesus, or to lay hold on the hem of his garment, in order to be healed, and that immediately on this slight contact, a cure actually followed (Matt. xiv. 36 ; Mark iii. 10, vi. 56 ; Luke vi. 19). In these cases

---

[16] Paulus, exeg. Handb. 1, b. s. 498, 501.

[17] Bengel, Gnomon, 1, 245, ed. 2.   Paulus, s. 502, again takes an obvious fable in Livy ii. 36 for a history, capable of a natural explanation.

[18] Paulus, ut sup. s. 501.

Jesus operated, not, as we have hitherto always seen, with a precise aim towards any particular sufferer, but on entire masses, without taking special notice of each individual; his power of healing appears not here, as elsewhere, to reside in his will, but in his body and its coverings ; he does not by his own voluntary act dispense its virtues, but is subject to have them drawn from him without his consent.

Of this species of cure again a detailed example is preserved to us, in the history of the woman who had an issue of blood, which all the synoptical writers give, and interweave in a peculiar manner with the history of the resuscitation of the daughter of Jairus, making Jesus cure the woman on his way to the ruler's house (Matt. ix. 20 ff. ; Mark v. 25 ff. ; Luke viii. 43 ff.). On comparing the account of the incident in the several evangelists, we might in this instance be tempted to regard that of Luke as the original, because it seems to offer an explanation of the uniform connexion of the two histories. As, namely, the duration of the woman's sufferings is fixed by all the narrators at twelve years, so Luke, whom Mark follows, gives twelve years also as the age of the daughter of Jairus ; a numerical similarity which might be a sufficient inducement to associate the two histories in the evangelical tradition. But this reason is far too isolated by itself to warrant a decision, which can only proceed from a thorough comparison of the three narratives in their various details. Matthew describes the woman simply as γυνὴ αἱμορροοῦσα δώδεκα ἔτη, which signifies that she had for twelve years been subject to an important loss of blood, probably in the form of excessive menstruation. Luke, the reputed physician, shows himself here in no degree favourable to his professional brethren, for he adds that the woman had spent all her living on physicians without obtaining any help from them. Mark, yet more unfavourable, says that she had *suffered many things of many physicians, and was nothing bettered, but rather grew worse.* Those who surround Jesus when the woman approaches him are, according to Matthew, his disciples, according to Mark and Luke, a thronging multitude.   After all the narrators have described how the woman, as timid as she was believing, came behind Jesus and touched the hem of his garment, Mark and Luke state that she was immediately healed, but that Jesus, being conscious of the egress of curative power, asked *who touched me?* The disciples, astonished, ask in return, how he can distinguish a single touch amidst so general a thronging and pressure of the crowd. According to Luke, he persists in his assertion ; according to Mark, he looks inquiringly around him in order to discover the party who had touched him : then, according to both these evangelists, the woman approaches trembling, falls at his feet and confesses all, whereupon Jesus gives her the tranquillizing assurance that her faith has made her whole.   Matthew has not this complex train of circumstances ; he merely states that after the touch Jesus looked round, discovered the woman, and announced to her that her faith had wrought her cure.

This difference is an important one, and we need not greatly wonder that it induced Storr to suppose two separate cures of women afflicted in the same manner [1].   To this expedient he was yet more decidedly determined by the still wider divergencies in the narrative of the resuscitation of the daughter of Jairus, a narrative which is interlaced with the one before us ; it is, however, this very interlacement which renders it totally impossible to imagine that Jesus, twice, on both occasions when he was on his way to restore to life the daughter of a Jewish ruler ($\ddot{\alpha}\rho\chi\omega\nu$), cured a woman who had had an issue of blood twelve years.   While, on this consideration, criticism has long ago decided for the singleness of the fact on which the narratives are founded, it has at the same time given the preference to those of Mark and Luke as the most vivid and circumstantial [2].   But, in the first place, if it be admitted that Mark's addition $\dot{\alpha}\lambda\lambda\dot{\alpha}\ \mu\ddot{\alpha}\lambda\lambda\omega\nu\ \epsilon\dot{\imath}\varsigma\ \tau\dot{o}\ \chi\epsilon\tilde{\imath}\rho\omega\nu\ \dot{\epsilon}\lambda\theta\omega\tilde{\upsilon}\sigma\alpha$, *but rather grew worse,* is merely a finishing touch from his own imagination to the expression $\omega\dot{\upsilon}\kappa\ \ddot{\imath}\sigma\chi\upsilon\sigma\epsilon\nu\ \dot{\upsilon}\pi'\ \omega\dot{\upsilon}\delta\epsilon\nu\dot{o}\varsigma\ \theta\epsilon\rho\alpha\pi\epsilon\upsilon\theta\tilde{\eta}\nu\alpha\iota$ *neither could be*

[1] Ueber den Zweck der evang. Geschichte und der Briefe Joh. s. 351 f.
[2] Schulz, ut sup. s. 317 ; Olshausen, 1, s. 322.

healed of any, which he found in Luke ; there seems to be the
same reason for regarding this particular of Luke's as an inference of his own by which he has amplified the simple statement
αἱμορροοῦσα δώδεκα ἔτη, which Matthew gives without any addition. If the woman had been ill twelve years, she must, it was
thought, during that period have frequently had recourse to
physicians; and as, when contrasted with the inefficiency of
the physicians, the miraculous power of Jesus, which instantaneously wrought a cure, appeared in all the more brilliant a
light; so in the legend, or in the imagination of the narrators,
there grew up these additions. What if the same observation
applied to the other differences? That the woman according
to Matthew also, only touched Jesus from behind, implied the
effort and the hope to remain concealed ; that Jesus immediately
looked round after her, implied that he was conscious of her
touch. This hope on the part of the woman became the more
accountable, and this consciousness on the part of Jesus the
more marvellous, the greater the crowd that surrounded Jesus
and pressed upon him ; hence the companionship of the disciples in Matthew is by the other two evangelists changed into
a *thronging* of the *multitude* (βλέπεις τὸν ὄχλον συνθλίβοντά σε).
Again, Matthew mentions that Jesus looked round after the
woman touched him; on this circumstance the supposition
might be founded that he had perceived her touch in a peculiar
manner ; hence the scene was further worked up, and we are
shown how Jesus, though pressed on all sides, had yet a special
consciousness of that particular touch by the healing power which
it had drawn from him ; while the simple feature ἐπιστραφεὶς καὶ
ἰδὼν αὐτὴν, *he turned him about, and when he saw her,* in Matthew, is transformed into an inquiry and a searching glance
around upon the crowd to discover the woman, who then is represented as coming forward, trembling, to make her confession.
Lastly, on a comparison of Matt. xiv. 36, the point of this narrative, even as given in the first gospel, appears to lie in the fact that
simply to touch the clothes of Jesus had in itself a healing efficacy. Accordingly, in the propagation of this history, there

was a continual effort to make the result follow immediately on the touch, and to represent Jesus as remaining, even after the cure, for some time uncertain with respect to the individual who had touched him, a circumstance which is in contradiction with that superior knowledge elsewhere attributed to Jesus. Thus, under every aspect, the narrative in the first gospel presents itself as the earlier and more simple, that of the second and third as a later and more embellished formation of the legend.

As regards the common substance of the narratives, it has in recent times been a difficulty to all theologians, whether orthodox or rationalistic, that the curative power of Jesus should have been exhibited apart from his volition. Paulus and Olshausen agree in the opinion[3], that the agency of Jesus is thus reduced too completely into the domain of physical nature; that Jesus would then be like a magnetiser who in operating on a nervous patient is conscious of a diminution of strength, or like a charged electrical battery, which a mere touch will discharge. Such an idea of Christ, thinks Olshausen, is repugnant to the Christian consciousness, which determines the fullness of power resident in Jesus to have been entirely under the governance of his will; and this will to have been guided by a knowledge of the moral condition of the persons to be healed. It is therefore supposed that Jesus fully recognized the woman even without seeing her, and considering that she might be spiritually won over to him by this bodily succour, he consciously communicated to her an influx of his curative power; but in order to put an end to her false shame and constrain her to a confession, he behaved as if he knew not who had touched him. But the Christian consciousness, in cases of this kind, means nothing else than the advanced religious culture of our age, which cannot appropriate the antiquated ideas of the Bible. Now this consciousness must be neutral where we are concerned, not with the dogmatical appropriation, but purely with the exegetical discovery of the biblical ideas. The

---

[3] Exeg. Handb. 1. b. s. 524 f.; bibl. Comm. 1, s. 324 f; comp. Köster, Immanuel, s. 201 ff.

interference of this alleged Christian consciousness is the secret of the majority of exegetical errors, and in the present instance it has led the above named commentators astray from the evident sense of the text. For the question of Jesus in both the more detailed narratives τίς ὁ ἀψάμενός μου; *who touched me?* repeated as it is in Luke, and strengthened as it is in Mark by a searching glance around, has the appearance of being meant thoroughly in earnest; and indeed it is the object of these two evangelists to place the miraculous nature of the curative power of Jesus in a particularly clear light by showing that the mere touching of his clothes accompanied by faith, no previous knowledge on his part of the person who touched, nor so much as a word from him, being requisite, was sufficient to obtain a cure. Nay, even originally, in the more concise account of Matthew, the expressions προσελθοῦσα ὄπισθεν ἥψατο *having come behind him, she touched,* and ἐπιστραφεὶς καὶ ἰδὼν αὐτὴν *he turned him about, and when he saw her,* clearly imply that Jesus knew the woman only after she had touched him. If then, it is not to be proved that Jesus had a knowledge of the woman previous to her cure and a special will to heal her; nothing remains for those who will not admit an involuntary exhibition of curative power in Jesus, but to suppose in him a constant general will to cure, with which it was only necessary that faith on the part of the diseased person should concur, in order to produce an actual cure. But that, notwithstanding the absence of a special direction of the will to the cure of this woman on the part of Jesus, she was restored to health, simply by her faith, without even touching his clothes, is assuredly not the idea of the evangelists. On the contrary, it is their intention to substitute for an individual act of the will on the part of Jesus, the touch on the part of the sick person; this it is which, instead of the former, brings into action the latent power of Jesus: so that the materialistic character of the representation is not in this way to be avoided.

A step farther was necessary to the rationalistic interpretation, which not only with modern supranaturalism regards as incredible the unconscious efflux of curative power from Jesus, but also denies in general any efflux of such power, and yet wishes to preserve unattainted the historical veracity of the evangelists. According to this system, Jesus was led to ask who touched him, solely because he felt himself held back in his progress; the assertion that consciousness of a departure of power, δύναμις ἐξελθοῦσα, was the cause of his question, is a mere inference of the two narrators, of whom the one, Mark, actually gives it as his own observation; and it is only Luke who incorporates it with the question of Jesus. The cure of the woman was effected by means of her exalted confidence, in consequence of which when she touched the hem of Jesus she was seized with a violent shuddering in her whole nervous system, which probably caused a sudden contraction of the relaxed vessels; at the first moment she could only believe, not certainly know that she was cured, and only by degrees, probably after the use of means recommended to her by Jesus, did the malady entirely cease [4]. But who can represent to himself the timid touch of a sick woman whose design was to remain concealed, and whose faith rendered her certain of obtaining a cure by the slightest touch, as a grasp which arrested the progress of Jesus, pressed upon as he was, according to Mark and Luke, by the crowd? Farther, what a vast conception of the power of confidence is demanded by the opinion, that it healed a disease of twelve years' duration without the concurrence of any real force on the part of Jesus! Lastly, if the evangelists are supposed to have put into the mouth of Jesus an inference of their own (that healing efficacy had gone out of him)—if they are supposed to have described a gradual cure as an instantaneous one; then, with the renunciation of these particulars all warrant for the historical reality of the entire narrative falls to the ground, and at the same time all necessity for troubling ourselves with the natural interpretation.

[4] Paulus, exeg. Handb. 1, b. s. 524 f. 530.   L. J. 1, a. s. 244 f.; Venturini, 2, s. 204 ff. ; Köster, ut sup.

In fact, if we only examine the narrative before us somewhat more closely, and compare it with kindred anecdotes, we cannot remain in doubt as to its proper character. As here and in some other passages it is narrated of Jesus, that the sick were cured by the bare touch of his clothes: so in the Acts we are told that the *handkerchiefs σουδάρια* and *aprons σιμικίνθια* of Paul cured all kinds of sick persons to whom they were applied (xix. 11 f.), and that the very shadow of Peter was believed to have the same efficacy (v. 15) ; while the apocryphal gospels represent a mass of cures to have been wrought by means of the swaddling bands of the infant Jesus, and the water in which he was washed [5]. In reading these last histories, every one knows that he is in the realm of fiction and legend ; but wherein are the cures wrought by the pocket-handkerchiefs of Paul to be distinguished from those wrought by the swaddling bands of Jesus, unless it be that the latter proceeded from a child, the former from a man ? It is certain that if the story relative to Paul were not found in a canonical book, every one would deem it fabulous, and yet the credibility of the narratives should not be concluded from the assumed origin of the book which contains them, but on the contrary, our judgment of the book must be founded on the nature of its particular narratives. But again, between these cures by the pocket-handkerchiefs and those by the touch of the hem of the garment, there is no essential distinction. In both cases we have the contact of objects which are in a merely external connexion with the worker of the miracle ; with the single difference, that this connexion is with regard to the pocket-handkerchiefs an interrupted one, with regard to the clothes a continuous one ; in both cases again, results which, even according to the orthodox view, are only derived from the spiritual nature of the men in question, and are to be regarded as acts of their will in virtue of its union with the divine, are reduced to physical effects and effluxes. The subject thus descends from the religious and

---

[5] Vid. Evangelium infantiæ arabicum, ap. Fabricius and Thilo.

theological sphere to the natural and physical, because a man with a power of healing resident in his body, and floating as an atmosphere around him, would belong to the objects of natural science, and not of religion. But natural science is not able to accredit such a healing power by sure analogies or clear definitions; hence these cures, being driven from the objective to the subjective region, must receive their explanation from psychology. Now psychology, taking into account the power of imagination and of faith, will certainly allow the possibility that without a real curative power in the reputed miracle-worker, solely by the strong confidence of the diseased person that he possesses this power, bodily maladies which have a close connexion with the nervous system may be cured : but when we seek for historical vouchers for this possibility, criticism, which must here be called to aid, will soon show that a far greater number of such cures has been invented by the faith of others, than has been performed by the parties alleged to be concerned. Thus it is in itself by no means impossible, that through strong faith in a healing power residing even in the clothes and handkerchiefs of Jesus and the apostles, many sick persons on touching these articles were conscious of real benefit : but it is at least equally probable, that only after the death of these men, when their fame in the church was ever on the increase, anecdotes of this kind were believingly narrated, and it depends on the nature of the accounts, for which of the two alternatives we are to decide.   In the general statement in the Gospels and the Acts, which speak of whole masses having been cured in the above way, this accumulation at any rate is traditional.   As to the detailed history which we have been examining, in its representation that the woman had suffered twelve years from a very obstinate disease, and one the least susceptible of merely psychical influence, and that the cure was performed by power consciously emitted from Jesus, instead of by the imagination of the patient: so large a portion betrays itself to be mythical that we can no longer discern any historical elements, and must regard the whole as legendary.

It is not difficult to see what might give rise to this branch of the evangelical miraculous legend, in distinction from others. The faith of the popular mind, dependent on the senses, and incapable of apprehending the divine through the medium of thought alone, strives perpetually to draw it down into material existence. Hence, according to a later opinion, the saint must continue to work miracles when his bones are distributed as relics, and the body of Christ must be present in the transubstantiated host ; hence also, according to an idea developed much earlier, the curative power of the men celebrated in the New Testament must be attached to their body and its coverings. The less the church retained of the words of Jesus, the more tenaciously she clung to the efficacy of his mantle, and the farther she was removed from the free spiritual energy of the apostle Paul, the more consolatory was the idea of carrying home his curative energy in a pocket-handkerchief.

§ 98.

CURES AT A DISTANCE.

The cures performed at a distance are, properly speaking, the opposite of these involuntary cures. The latter are effected by mere corporeal contact without a special act of the will ; the former solely by the act of the will without corporeal contact, or even local proximity. But there immediately arises this objection : if the curative power of Jesus was so material that it dispensed itself involuntarily at a mere touch, it cannot have been so spiritual that the simple will could convey it over considerable distances ; or conversely, if it was so spiritual as to act apart from bodily presence, it cannot have been so material as to dispense itself independently of the will. Since we have pronounced the purely physical mode of influence in Jesus to be improbable, free space is left to us for the purely spiritual, and our decision on the latter will therefore depend entirely on the examination of the narratives and the facts themselves.

As proofs that the curative power of Jesus acted thus at a

distance, Matthew and Luke narrate to us the cure of the sick servant of a centurion at Capernaum, John that of the son of a *nobleman* βασιλικὸς, at the same place (Matt. viii. 5 ff. ; Luke vii. 1 ff. ; John iv. 46 ff.) ; and again Matthew (xv. 22 ff.), and Mark (vii. 25 ff.), that of the daughter of the Canaanitish woman. Of these examples, as in the summary narration of the last there is nothing peculiar, we have here to consider the two first only. The common opinion is, that Matthew and Luke do indeed narrate the same fact, but John one distinct from this, since his narrative differs from that of the two others in the following particulars : firstly, the place from which Jesus cures, is in the synoptical gospels the place where the sick man resides, Capernaum,—in John a different one, namely, Cana ; secondly, the time at which the synoptists lay the incident, namely, when Jesus is in the act of returning home after his sermon on the mount, is different from that assigned to it in the fourth gospel, which is immediately after the return of Jesus from the first passover and his ministry in Samaria; thirdly, the sick person is according to the former the slave, according to the latter the son of the suppliant; but the most important divergencies are those which relate, fourthly, to the suppliant himself, for in the first and third gospels he is a military person (an ἑκατόνταρχος), in the fourth a person in office at court (βασιλικὸς), according to the former (Matt. v. 10 ff.), a Gentile, according to the latter without doubt a Jew; above all, the synoptists make Jesus eulogize him as a pattern of the most fervent, humble faith, because, in the conviction that Jesus could cure at a distance, he prevented him from going to his house ; whereas in John, on the contrary, he is blamed for his weak faith which required signs and wonders, because he thought the presence of Jesus in his house necessary for the purpose of the cure [1].

These divergencies are certainly important enough to be a reason, with those who regard them from a certain point of view, for maintaining the distinction of the fact lying at the

---

[1] See the observations of Paulus, Lücke, Tholuck, and Olshausen, in loc.

foundation of the synoptical narratives from that reported by
John: only this accuracy of discrimination must be carried
throughout, and the diversities between the two synoptical narratives themselves must not be overlooked. First, even in the
designation of the person of the patient they are not perfectly
in unison ; Luke calls him δοῦλος ἔντιμος, *a servant who was
dear* to the centurion ; in Matthew, the latter calls him ὁ παῖς
μοῦ, which may equally mean either a *son* or a *servant,* and as
the centurion when speaking (v. 9) of his servant, uses the
word δοῦλος, while the cured individual is again (v. 13) spoken
of as ὁ παῖς αὐτοῦ, it seems most probable that the former sense
was intended. With respect to his disease, the man is described by Matthew as παραλυτικὸς δεινῶς βασανιζόμενος *a paralytic grievously tormented ;* Luke is not only silent as to this
species of disease, but he is thought by many to presuppose a
different one, since after the indefinite expression κακῶς ἔχων,
being ill, he adds, ἤμελλε τελευτᾶν, *was ready to die,* and paralysis is not generally a rapidly fatal malady [2]. But the most
important difference is one which runs through the entire narrative, namely, that all which according to Matthew the centurion
does in his own person, is in Luke done by messengers, for here
in the first instance he makes the entreaty, not personally, as in
Matthew, but through the medium of the Jewish elders, and
when he afterwards wishes to prevent Jesus from entering his
house, he does not come forward himself, but commissions some
friends to act in his stead. To reconcile this difference, it is
usual to refer to the rule : *quod quis per alium facit,* etc. [3].
If then it be said, and indeed no other conception of the matter
is possible to expositors who make such an appeal,—Matthew
well knew that between the centurion and Jesus everything was
transacted by means of deputies, but for the sake of brevity, he
employed the figure of speech above alluded to, and represented
him as himself accosting Jesus : Storr is perfectly right in his

[2] Schleiermacher, über den Lukas, s. 92.

[3] Augustin, de consens. evang. i. 20 ; Paulus, exeg. Handb. 1, b. s. 709 ; Köster,
Immanuel, s. 63.

opposing remark, that scarcely any historian would so perse-
veringly carry that metonymy through an entire narrative, especially in a case where, on the one hand, the figure of speech
is by no means so obvious as when, for example, that is ascribed to a general which is done by his soldiers; and where,
on the other hand, precisely this point, whether the person acted
for himself or through others, is of some consequence to a full
estimate of his character [4]. With laudable consistency, therefore, Storr, as he believed it necessary to refer the narrative of
the fourth gospel to a separate fact from that of the first and
third, on account of the important differences; so, on account
of the divergencies which he found between the two last, pronounces these also to be narratives of two separate events. If
any one wonder that at three different times so entirely similar
a cure should have happened at the same place, (for according
to John also, the patient lay and was cured at Capernaum):
Storr on his side wonders how it can be regarded as in the
least improbable that in Capernaum at two different periods two
centurions should have had each a sick servant, and that again
at another time a nobleman should have had a sick son at the
same place; that the second centurion (Luke) should have
heard the history of the first, have applied in a similar manner
to Jesus, and sought to surpass his example of humility, as the
first centurion (Matthew), to whom the earlier history of the
nobleman (John) was known, wished to surpass the weak faith
of the latter; and lastly, that Jesus cured all the three patients
in the same manner at a distance. But the incident of a distinguished official person applying to Jesus to cure a dependent
or relative, and of Jesus at a distance operating on the latter
in such a manner, that about the time in which Jesus pronounced the curative word, the patient at home recovered, is
so singular in its kind that a threefold repetition of it may be
regarded as impossible, and even the supposition that it occurred twice only, has difficulties; hence it is our task to ascertain

---

[4] Ueber den Zweck Jesu, u. s. f., s. 351.

whether the three narratives may not be traced to a single root.

Now the narrative of the fourth evangelist which is most generally held to be distinct, has not only an affinity with the synoptical narratives in the outline already given; but in many remarkable details either one or the other of the synoptists agrees more closely with John than with his fellow synoptist. Thus, while in designating the patient as παῖς, Matthew may be held to accord with the υἱὸς of John, at least as probably as with the δοῦλος of Luke; Matthew and John decidedly agree in this, that according to both the functionary at Capernaum applies in his own person to Jesus, and not as in Luke by deputies. On the other hand, the account of John agrees with that of Luke in its description of the state of the patient; in neither is there any mention of the paralysis of which Matthew speaks, but the patient is described as near death, in Luke by the words ἤμελλε τελευτᾶν, in John by ἤμελλεν ἀποθνήσκειν, in addition to which it is incidentally implied in the latter v. 52 that the disease was accompanied by a *fever*, πυρετὸς. In the account of the manner in which Jesus effected the cure of the patient, and in which his cure was made known, John stands again on the side of Matthew in opposition to Luke. While namely, the latter has not an express assurance on the part of Jesus that the servant was healed, the two former make him say to the officer, in very similar terms, the one, ὕπαγε, καὶ ὡς ἐπίστευσας γενηθήτω σοι, *Go thy way, and as thou hast believed so shall it be done unto thee*, the other, πορεύου, ὁ υἱὸς σου ζῇ, *Go thy way, thy son liveth;* and the conclusion of Matthew also, καὶ ἰάθη ὁ παῖς αὐτοῦ ἐν τῇ ὥρᾳ ἐκείνη, has at least in its form more resemblance to the statement of John, that by subsequent inquiry the father ascertained it to be ἐν ἐκείνῃ τῇ ὥρᾳ, *at the same hour* in which Jesus had spoken the word that his son had begun to amend, than to the statement of Luke, that the messengers when they returned found the sick man restored to health. In another point of this conclusion, however, the agreement with John is transferred from Matthew again to Luke. In both Luke and John, namely, a kind of embassy is spoken of, which towards the close of the narrative comes out of the house of the officer; in the former it consists of the centurion's friends, whose errand it is to dissuade Jesus from giving himself unnecessary trouble; in the latter, of servants who rejoicingly meet their master and bring him the news of his son's recovery. Unquestionably where three narratives are so thoroughly entwined with each other as these, we ought not merely to pronounce two of them identical and allow one to stand for a distinct fact, but must rather either distinguish all, or blend all into one. The latter course was adopted by Semler, after older examples [5], and Tholuck has at least declared it possible. But with such expositors the next object is so to explain the divergencies of the three narratives, that no one of the evangelists may seem to have said any thing false. With respect to the rank of the applicant, they make the βασιλικὸς in John a military officer, for whom the ἑκατόνταρχος of the two others would only be a more specific designation; as regards the main point, however, namely the conduct of the applicant, it is thought that the different narrators may have represented the event in different periods of its progress; that is, John may have given the earlier circumstance, that Jesus complained of the originally weak faith of the suppliant, the synoptists only the later, that he praised its rapid growth. We have already shown how it has been supposed possible, in a yet easier manner, to adjust the chief difference between the two synoptical accounts relative to the mediate or immediate entreaty. But this effort to explain the contradictions between the three narratives in a favourable manner is altogether vain. There still subsist these difficulties: the synoptists thought of the applicant as a centurion, the fourth evangelist as a courtier; the former as strong, the latter as weak in faith; John and Matthew imagined that he applied in his own person to Jesus; Luke, that out of modesty he sent deputies [6].

[5] Vid. Lücke, 1, s. 552.

[6] Fritzsche, in Matth. p. 310 : *discrepat autem Lucas ita a Matthaei narratione, ut centurionem non ipsum venisse ad Jesum, sed per legatos cum eo egisse tradat ; quibus dissidentibus pacem obtrudere, boni nego interpretis esse.*

Which then represents the fact in the right way, which in the wrong? If we take first the two synoptists by themselves, expositors with one voice declare that Luke gives the more correct account. First of all, it is thought improbable that the patient should have been as Matthew says, a paralytic, since in the case of a disease so seldom fatal the modest centurion would scarcely have met Jesus to implore his aid immediately on his entrance into the city[7]: as if a very painful disease such as is described by Matthew did not render desirable the quickest help, and as if there were any want of modesty in asking Jesus before he reached home to utter a healing word. Rather, the contrary relation between Matthew and Luke seems probable from the observation, that the miracle, and consequently also the disease of the person cured miraculously, is never diminished in tradition but always exaggerated; hence the tormented paralytic would more probably be heightened into one *ready to die*, μέλλων τελευτᾷν, than the latter reduced to a mere sufferer. But especially the double message in Luke is, according to Schleiermacher, a feature very unlikely to have been invented. How if, on the contrary, it very plainly manifested itself to be an invention? While in Matthew the centurion, on the offer of Jesus to accompany him, seeks to prevent him by the objection: *Lord, I am not worthy that thou shouldest come under my roof,* in Luke he adds by the mouth of his messenger, *wherefore neither thought I myself worthy to come unto thee,* by which we plainly discover the conclusion on which the second embassy was founded. If the man declared himself unworthy that Jesus should come to him, he cannot, it was thought, have held himself worthy to come to Jesus; an exaggeration of his humility by which the narrative of Luke again betrays its secondary character. The first embassy seems to have originated in the desire to introduce a previous recommendation of the centurion as a motive for the promptitude with which Jesus offered to enter the house of a Gentile. The

---

[7] Schleiermacher, ut sup. s. 92 f.

Jewish elders after having informed Jesus of the case of disease, add, *that he was worthy for whom he should do this, for
he loveth our nation and has built us a synagogue:* a recommendation the tenor of which is not unlike what Luke (Acts
x. 22) makes the messengers of Cornelius say to Peter to induce him to return with them, namely, that the centurion was a
*just man, and one that feareth God, and in good report among
all the nation of the Jews.* That the double embassy cannot
have been original, appears the most clearly from the fact, that
by it the narrative of Luke loses all coherence.   In Matthew
all hangs well together: the centurion first describes to Jesus
the state of the sufferer, and either leaves it to Jesus to decide
what he shall next do, or before he prefers his request Jesus
anticipates him by the offer to go to his house, which the centurion declines in the manner stated.   Compare with this his
strange conduct in Luke: he first sends to Jesus by the Jewish
elders the request that he will come and heal his servant, but
when Jesus is actually coming, repents that he has occasioned
him to do so, and asks only for a miraculous word from Jesus.
The supposition that the first request proceeded solely from the
elders and not from the centurion [8] runs counter to the express
words of the evangelist, who by the expressions: ἀπέστειλε—
πρεσβυτέρους—ἐρωτῶν αὐτὸν, *he sent—the elders—beseeching
him* represents the prayer as coming from the centurion himself; and that the latter by the word ἐλθὼν meant only that
Jesus should come into the neighbourhood of his house, but
when he saw that Jesus intended actually to enter his house,
declined this as too great a favour,—is too absurd a demeanour
to attribute to a man who otherwise appears sensible, and
of whom for this reason so capricious a change of mind as
is implied in the text of Luke, was still less to be expected.
The whole difficulty would have been avoided, if Luke had put
into the mouth of the first messengers, as Matthew in that of
the centurion, only the entreaty, direct or indirect, for a cure in

---

[8] Kuinöl, in Matt. p. 221 f.

general; and then after Jesus had offered to go to the house where the patient lay, had attributed to the same messengers the modest rejection of this offer. But on the one hand, he thought it requisite to furnish a motive for the resolution of Jesus to go into the Gentile's house; and on the other, tradition presented him with a deprecation of this personal trouble on the part of Jesus: he was unable to attribute the prayer and the deprecation to the same persons, and he was therefore obliged to contrive a second embassy. Hereby, however, the contradiction was only apparently avoided, since both embassies are sent by the centurion. Perhaps also the centurion who was unwilling that Jesus should take the trouble to enter his house, reminded Luke of the messenger who warned Jairus not to trouble the master to enter his house, likewise after an entreaty that he would come into the house; and as the messenger says to Jairus, according to him and Mark, μὴ σκύλλε τὸν διδάσκαλον. *trouble not the master* (Luke viii. 49.), so here he puts into the mouth of the second envoys, the words, κύριε μὴ σκύλλου, *Lord, trouble not thyself,* although such an order has a reason only in the case of Jairus, in whose house the state of things had been changed since the first summons by the death of his daughter, and none at all in that of the centurion whose servant still remained in the same state.

Modern expositors are deterred from the identification of all the three narratives, by the fear that it may present John in the light of a narrator who has not apprehended the scene with sufficient accuracy, and has even mistaken its main drift [9]. Were they nevertheless to venture on a union, they would as far as possible vindicate to the fourth gospel the most original account of the facts; a position of which we shall forthwith test the security, by an examination of the intrinsic character of the narratives. That the suppliant is according to the fourth evangelist a βασιλικὸς, while according to the two others he is an ἑκατόνταρχος, is an indifferent particular from which we can

[9] Tholuck, in loc. Hase, § 68. Anm 2.

draw no conclusion on either side; and it may appear to be the same with the divergency as to the relation of the diseased person to the one who entreats his cure. If however, it be asked with reference to the last point, from which of the three designations the other two could most easily have arisen? it can scarcely be supposed that the υἱὸς of John became in a descending line, first the doubtful term παῖς, and then δοῦλος; and even the reverse ascending order is here less probable than the intermediate alternative, that out of the ambiguous παῖς (= בַּעַר) there branched off in one direction the sense of *servant*, as in Luke; in the other, of *son*, as in John. We have already remarked, that the description of the patient's state in John, as well as in Luke, is an enhancement on that in Matthew, and consequently of later origin. As regards the difference in the locality, from the point of view now generally taken in the comparative criticism of the gospels, the decision would doubtless be, that in the tradition from which the synoptical writers drew, the place from which Jesus performed the miracles was confounded with that in which the sick person lay, the less noted Cana being absorbed in the celebrated Capernaum; whereas John, being an eye-witness, retained the more correct details. But the relation between the evangelists appear to stand thus only when John is assumed to have been an eye-witness; if the critic seeks, as he is bound to do, to base his decision solely on the intrinsic character of the narratives, he will arrive at a totally different result. Here is a narrative of a cure performed at a distance, in which the miracle appears the greater, the wider the distance between the curer and the cured. Would oral tradition in propagating this narrative, have the tendency to diminish that distance, and consequently the miracle, so that in the account of John, who makes Jesus perform the cure at a place from which the nobleman does not reach his son until the following day, we should have the original narrative, in that of the synoptists on the contrary, who represent Jesus as being in the same town with the sick servant, the one modified by tradition? Only the converse of

this supposition can be held accordant with the nature of the
legend, and here again the narrative of John manifests itself
to be a traditional one. Again, the preciseness with which
the hour of the patient's recovery is ascertained in the fourth
gospel has a highly fictitious appearance. The simple expression of Matthew, usually found at the conclusion of histories of cures : *he was healed in the self-same hour,* is dilated
into an inquiry on the part of the father as to the hour in
which the son began to amend, an answer from the servants
that yesterday at the seventh hour the fever left him, and
lastly the result, that in the very hour in which Jesus had
said, Thy son liveth, the recovery took place. This is a solicitous accuracy, a tediousness of calculation, that seems to bespeak
the anxiety of the narrator to establish the miracle, rather than to
show the real course of the event. In representing the βασιλικὸς
as conversing personally with Jesus, the fourth gospel has preserved the original simplicity of the narrative better than the
third ; though as has been remarked, the servants who come
to meet their master in the former seem to be representatives
of Luke's second embassy. But in the main point of difference, relative to the character of the applicant, it might be
thought that, even according to our own standard, the preference must be given to John before the two other narrators.
For if that narrative is the more legendary, which exhibits
an effort at aggrandizement or embellishment, it might be
said that the applicant whose faith is in John rather weak, is
in Luke embellished into a model of faith. It is not, however,
on embellishment in general that legend or the inventive narrator is bent, but on embellishment in subservience to their
grand object, which in the gospels is the glorification of Jesus ;
and viewed in this light, the embellishment will in two respects
be found on the side of John. First, as this evangelist continually aims to exhibit the pre-eminence of Jesus, by presenting a contrast to it in the weakness of all who are brought into
communication with him, so here this purpose might be served
by representing the suppliant as weak rather than strong in

faith. The reply, however, which he puts into the mouth of Jesus, *Unless ye see signs and wonders ye will not believe*, has proved too severe, for which reason it reduces most of our commentators to perplexity. Secondly, it might seem unsuitable that Jesus should allow himself to be diverted from his original intention of entering the house in which the patient was, and thus appear to be guided by external circumstances; it might be regarded as more consistent with his character that he should originally resolve to effect the cure at a distance instead of being persuaded to this by another. If then, as tradition said, the suppliant did nevertheless make a kind of remonstrance, this must have had an opposite drift to the one in the synoptical gospels, namely, to induce Jesus to a journey to the house where the patient lay.

In relation to the next question, the possibility and the actual course of the incident before us, the natural interpretation seems to find the most pliant material in the narrative of John. Here, it is remarked, Jesus nowhere says that he will effect the patient's cure, he merely assures the father that his son is out of danger, (ὁ υἱὸς σου ζῇ), and the father, when he finds that the favourable turn of his son's malady coincides with the time at which he was conversing with Jesus, in no way draws the inference that Jesus had wrought the cure at a distance. Hence, this history is only a proof that Jesus by means of his profound acquaintance with semeiology, was able, on receiving a description of the patient's state, correctly to predict the course of his disease; that such a description is not here given is no proof that Jesus had not obtained it; while further this proof of knowledge is called a σημεῖον (v. 54) because it was a sign of a kind of skill in Jesus which John had not before intimated, namely, the ability to predict the cure of one dangerously ill [10]. But, apart from the misinterpretation of the word σημεῖον, and the interpolation of a conversation not intimated in the text; this view of the matter would place the character and even the

---

[10] Paulus, Comm. 4, s. 253 f.; Venturini, 2, s. 140 ff.; comp. Hase, § 68.

understanding of Jesus in the most equivocal light. For if we should pronounce a physician imprudent, who in the case of a patient believed to be dying of fever, should even from his own observation of the symptoms, guarantee a cure, and thus risk his reputation: how much more rashly would Jesus have acted, had he, on the mere description of a man who was not a physician, given assurance that a disease was attended with no danger? We cannot ascribe such conduct to him, because it would be in direct contradiction with his general conduct, and the impression which he left on his cotemporaries. If then Jesus merely predicted the cure without effecting it, he must have been assured of it in a more certain manner than by natural reasoning,—he must have known it in a supernatural manner. This is the turn given to the narrative by one of the most recent commentators on the gospel of John. He puts the question, whether we have here a miracle of knowledge or of power ; and as there is no mention of an immediate effect from the words of Jesus, while elsewhere in the fourth gospel the superior knowledge of Jesus is especially held up to our view, he is of opinion that Jesus, by means of his higher nature, merely knew that at that moment the dangerous crisis of the disease was past[11]. But if our gospel frequently exhibits the superior knowledge of Jesus, this proves nothing to the purpose, for it just as frequently directs our attention to his superior power. Further, where the supernatural knowledge of Jesus is concerned, this is plainly stated (as i. 49, ii. 25, vi. 64,) and hence if a supernatural cognizance of the already effected cure of the boy had been intended, John would have made Jesus speak on this occasion as he did before to Nathanael, and tell the father that he already saw his son on his bed in an ameliorated state. On the contrary, not only is there no intimation of the exercise of superior knowledge, but we are plainly enough given to understand that there was an exercise of miraculous power. When the sudden cure of one *at the point of death* is spoken of, the

---

[11] Lücke, 1, s. 550 f.

immediate question is, What brought about this unexpected change ? and when a narrative which elsewhere makes miracles follow on the word of its hero, puts into his mouth an assurance that the patient lives, it is only the mistaken effort to diminish the marvellous, which can prevent the admission, that in this assurance the author means to give the cause of the cure.

In the case of the synoptical narratives, the supposition of a mere prediction will not suffice, since here the father (Matt. v. 8) entreats the exercise of healing power, and Jesus (v. 13,) accedes to this entreaty.   Hence every way would seem to be closed to the natural interpretation (for the distance of Jesus from the patient made all physical or psychical influence impossible), if a single feature in the narrative had not presented unexpected help. This feature is the comparison which the centurion institutes between himself and Jesus.   As he need only speak a word in order to see this or that command performed by his soldiers and servants, so, he concludes, it would cost Jesus no more than a word to restore his servant to health.   Out of this comparison it has been found possible to extract an intimation that as on the side of the centurion, so on that of Jesus, human proxies were thought of.   According to this, the centurion intended to represent to Jesus, that he need only speak a word to one of his disciples, and the latter would go with him and cure his servant, which is supposed to have forthwith happened [12]. But as this would be the first instance in which Jesus had caused a cure to be wrought by his disciples, and the only one in which he commissions them immediately to perform a particular cure, how could this peculiar circumstance be silently presupposed in the otherwise detailed narrative of Luke ? Why, since this narrator is not sparing in spinning out the rest of the messenger's speech, does he stint the few words which would have explained all—the simple addition after εἰπὲ λόγῳ, *speak the word*, of ἑνὶ τῶν μαθητῶν, *to one of thy disciples*, or something similar ? But, above all, at the close of the narrative, where the result is

---

[12] Paulus, exeg. Handb. 1, b. s. 710 f.; Natürliche Geschichte, 2, s. 285 ff.

told, this mode of interpretation falls into the greatest perplexity, not merely through the silence of the narrator, but through his positive statement. Luke, namely, concludes with the information that when the friends of the centurion returned into the house, they found the servant already recovered. Now, if Jesus had caused the cure by sending with the messengers one or more of his disciples, the patient could only begin gradually to be better after the disciples had come into the house with the messengers ; he could not have been already well on their arrival. Paulus indeed supposes that the messengers lingered for some time listening to the discourse of Jesus, and that thus the disciples arrived before them ; but how the former could so unnecessarily linger, and how the evangelist could have been silent on this point as well as on the commission of the disciples, he omits to explain. Whether instead of the disciples, we hold that which corresponds on the side of Jesus to the soldiers of the centurion to be demons of disease [13], ministering angels [14], or merely the word and the curative power of Jesus [15] ; in any case there remains to us a miracle wrought at a distance.

This kind of agency on the part of Jesus is, according to the admission even of such commentators as have not generally any repugnance to the miraculous, attended with special difficulty, because from the want of the personal presence of Jesus, and its beneficial influence on the patient, we are deprived of every possibility of rendering the cure conceivable by means of an analogy observable in nature [16]. According to Olshausen, indeed, this distant influence has its analogies ; namely, in animal magnetism [17]. I will not directly contest this, but only point out the limits within which, so far as my knowledge extends, this phenomenon confines itself in the domain of animal magnetism. According to our experience hitherto, the cases in which one

[13] Clem. homil. ix. 21 ; Fritzsche, in Matth. 313.
[14] Wetstein, N. T. 1, p. 349 ; comp. Olshausen, in loc.
[15] Köster, Immanuel, s. 195. Anm.
[16] Lücke, 1, s. 550.
[17] Bibl. Comm. 1, s. 268.

person can exert an influence over another at a distance are
only two : first, the magnetizer or an individual in magnetic
relation to him can act thus on the somnambule, but this distant action must always be preceded by immediate contact,—a
preliminary which is not supposed in the relation of Jesus to
the patient in our narrative ; secondly, such an influence is
found to exist in persons who are themselves somnambules, or
otherwise under a disordered state of the nerves : neither of
which descriptions can apply to Jesus.   If thus such a cure of
distant persons as is ascribed to Jesus in our narratives, far
outsteps the extreme limits of natural causation, as exhibited in
magnetism and the kindred phenomena ; then must Jesus have
been, so far as the above narratives can lay claim to historical
credit, a supernatural being.   But before we admit him to have
been so really, it is worth our while as critical inquirers, to examine whether the narrative under consideration could not have
arisen without any historical foundation ; especially as by the
very fact of the various forms which it has taken in the different
gospels it shows itself to contain legendary ingredients.   And
here it is evident that the miraculous cures of Jesus by merely
touching the patient, such as we have examples of in that of
the leper, Matt. viii. 3, and in that of the blind men, Matt.
ix. 29, might by a natural climax rise, first into the cure
of persons when in his presence, by a mere word, as in the
case of the demoniacs, of the lepers Luke xvii. 14, and
other sufferers ; and then into the cure even of the absent by a
word ; of which there is a strongly marked precedent in the
Old Testament.   In 2 Kings v. 9 ff. we read that when the
Syrian general Naaman came before the dwelling of the prophet
Elisha that he might be cured of his leprosy, the prophet came
not out to meet him, but sent to him by a servant the direction
to wash himself seven times in the river Jordan.   At this the
Syrian was so indignant that he was about to return home
without regarding the direction of the prophet.   He had
expected, he said, that the prophet would come to him,
and calling on his God, strike his hand over the leprous

place; that without any personal procedure of this kind, the prophet merely directed him to go to the river Jordan and wash, discouraged and irritated him, since if water were the thing required, he might have had it better at home than here in Israel. By this Old Testament history we see what was ordinarily expected from a prophet, namely, that he should be able to cure when present by bodily contact; that he could do so without contact, and at a distance, was not presupposed. Elisha effected the cure of the leprous general in the latter manner (for the washing was not the cause of cure here, any more than in John ix., but the miraculous power of the prophet, who saw fit to annex its influence to this external act), and hereby proved himself a highly distinguished prophet: ought then the Messiah in this particular to fall short of the prophet? Thus our New Testament narrative is manifested to be a necessary reflection of that Old Testament story. As, there, the sick person will not believe in the possibility of his cure unless the prophet comes out of his house; so, here, according to one edition of the story, the applicant likewise doubts the possibility of a cure, unless Jesus will come into his house; according to the other editions, he is convinced of the power of Jesus to heal even without this; and all agree that Jesus, like the prophet, succeeded in the performance of this especially difficult miracle.

§ 99.

CURES ON THE SABBATH.

Jesus, according to the gospels, gave great scandal to the Jews by not seldom performing his curative miracles on the sabbath. One example of this is common to the three synoptical writers, two are peculiar to Luke, and two to John.

In the narrative common to the three synoptical writers, two cases of supposed desecration of the sabbath are united; the plucking of the ears of corn by the disciples (Matt. xii. 1. parall.), and the cure of the man with the withered hand by Jesus (v. 9 ff. parall.). After the conversation which was occa-

z 2

sioned by the plucking of the corn, and which took place in the fields, the two first evangelists continue as if Jesus went from this scene immediately into the synagogue of the same place, to which no special designation is given, and there, on the occasion of the cure of the man with the withered hand, again held a dispute on the observance of the sabbath. It is evident that these two histories were originally united only on account of the similarity in their tendency; hence it is to the credit of Luke, that he has expressly separated them chronologically by the words ἐν ἑτέρῳ σαββάτῳ, *on another sabbath* [1]. The further inquiry, which narrative is here the more original? we may dismiss with the observation, that if the question which Matthew puts into the mouth of the Pharisees, *Is it lawful to heal on the sabbath days?* is held up as a specimen of invented dialogue [2]; we may with equal justice characterize in the same way the question lent to Jesus by the two intermediate evangelists; while their much praised [3] description of Jesus calling to the man to stand forth in the midst, and then casting reproving glances around, may be accused of having the air of dramatic fiction.

The narratives all agree in representing the affliction under which the patient laboured, as a χεὶρ ξηρὰ, or ἐξηραμμένη. Indefinite as this expression is, it is treated too freely when it is understood, as by Paulus, to imply only that the hand was injured by heat [4], or even by a sprain, according to Venturini's supposition [5]. For when, in order to determine the signification in which this term is used in the New Testament we refer, as it is proper to do, to the Old Testament, we find (1 Kings, xiii. 4.) a hand which, on being stretched out, ἐξηράνθη (וַתִּיבַשׁ), described as incapable of being drawn back again, so that we must understand a lameness and rigidity of the hand; and on a comparison of Mark ix. 18, where the expression ξηραίνεσθαι

[1] Schleiermacher, über den Lukas, s. 80 f.
[2] Schneckenburger, über den Ursprung, u. s. f. s. 50.
[3] Schleiermacher, ut sup.
[4] Exeg. Handb. 2, s. 48 ff.
[5] Natürliche Geschichte, 2, s. 421.

to be withered or wasted away is applied to an epileptic, a drying up and shrinking of that member [6]. Now from the narrative before us a very plausible argument may be drawn in favour of the supposition, that Jesus employed natural means in the treatment of this and other diseases. Only such cures, it is said, were prohibited on the sabbath as were attended with any kind of labour; thus, if the Pharisees, as it is here said, expected Jesus to transgress the sabbatical laws by effecting a cure, they must have known that he was not accustomed to cure by his mere word, but by medicaments and surgical operations [7]. As, however, a cure merely by means of a conjuration otherwise lawful, was forbidden on the sabbath, a fact which Paulus himself elsewhere adduces [8]; as moreover there was a controversy between the schools of Hillel and Schammai, whether it were permitted even to administer consolation to the sick on the sabbath [9]; and as again, according to an observation of Paulus, the more ancient rabbins were stricter on the point of sabbatical observance than those whose writings on this subject have come down to us [10]; so the cures of Jesus, even supposing that he used no natural means, might by captious Pharisees be brought under the category of violations of the sabbath. The principal objection to the rationalistic explanation, namely, the silence of the evangelists as to natural means, Paulus believes to be obviated in the present case by conceiving the scene thus: at that time, and in the synagogue, there was indeed no application of such means; Jesus merely caused the hand to be shown to him, that he might see how far the remedies hitherto prescribed by him (which remedies however are still a bare assumption) had been serviceable, and he then found that it was completely cured; for the expression ἀποκατεστάθη, used by all the narrators, implies a cure completed previously, not one suddenly effected in the passing moment. It is true

[6] Winer, b. Realw. 1, s. 796.
[7] Paulus, ut sup. s. 49, 54 ; Köster, Immanuel, s. 185 f.
[8] Ut sup. s. 83, ex Tract. Schabbat.
[9] Schabbat, f. 12, ap. Schöttgen, i. p. 123.
[10] See the passage last cited.

that the context seems to require this interpretation, since the
outstretching of the hand prior to the cure would appear to be
as little possible, as in 1 Kings xiii. 4. the act of drawing it
back : nevertheless the evangelists give us only the word of
Jesus as the source of the cure, not natural means, which are
the gratuitous addition of expositors [11].

Decisive evidence, alike for the necessity of viewing this as a
miraculous cure, and for the possibility of explaining the origin
of the anecdote, is to be obtained by a closer examination of
the Old Testament narrative already mentioned, 1 Kings xiii.
1 ff. A prophet out of Judah threatened Jeroboam, while
offering incense on his idolatrous altar, with the destruction of
the altar and the overthrow of his false worship; the king with
outstretched hand commanded that this prophet of evil should
be seized, when suddenly his hand dried up so that he could
not draw it again towards him, and the altar was rent.   On the
entreaty of the king, however, the prophet besought Jehovah for
the restoration of the hand, and its full use was again granted [12].
Paulus also refers to this narrative in the same connexion, but
only for the purpose of applying to it his natural method of explanation ; he observes that Jeroboam's anger may have produced a transient convulsive rigidity of the muscles and so
forth, in the hand just stretched out with such impetuosity.
But who does not see that we have here a legend designed to
glorify the monotheistic order of prophets, and to hold up to
infamy the Israelitish idolatry in the person of its founder
Jeroboam ?   The man of God denounces on the idolatrous altar
quick and miraculous destruction ; the idolatrous king im-
piously stretches forth his hand against the man of God ; the
hand is paralyzed, the idolatrous altar falls asunder into the

---

[11] Fritzsche, in Matt. p. 427 ; in Marc. p. 79.

[12] 1 Kings xiii. 4, LXX: καὶ ἰδοὺ
ἐξηράνθη ἡ χεὶρ αὐτοῦ.

6 : καὶ ἐπίστρεψε τὴν χεῖρα τοῦ
βασιλίως πρὸς αὐτὸν, καὶ ἐγίνιτο καθὼς
τὸ πρότιρον.

Matth. xii. 10 : καὶ ἰδοὺ ἄνθρωπος
ἦν τὴν χεῖρα ἔχων ξηράν (Mark.
ἐξηραμμίνην).

13 : τότε λίγει τῷ ἀνθρώπῳ· ἔκτινον
τὴν χεῖρά σού· καὶ ἐξίτεινε· καὶ ἀποκατε-
σταθη ὑγιὴς ὡς ἡ ἄλλη.

dust, and only on the intercession of the prophet is the king restored. Who can argue about the miraculous and the natural in what is so evidently a mythus? And who can fail to perceive in our evangelical narrative an imitation of this Old Testament legend, except that agreeably to the spirit of Christianity the withering of the hand appears, not as a retributive miracle, but as a natural disease, and only its cure is ascribed to Jesus; whence also the outstretching of the hand is not, as in the case of Jeroboam, the criminal cause of the infliction, continued as a punishment, and the drawing of it back again a sign of cure; but, on the contrary, the hand which had previously been drawn inwards, owing to disease, can after the completion of the cure be again extended. That, in other instances, about that period, the power of working cures of this kind was in the East ascribed to the favourites of the gods, may be seen from a narrative already adduced, in which, together with the cure of blindness, the restoration of a diseased hand is attributed to Vespasian [13].

But this curative miracle does not appear independently and as an object by itself: the history of it hinges on the fact that the cure was wrought on the Sabbath, and the point of the whole lies in the words by which Jesus vindicates his activity in healing on the Sabbath against the Pharisees. In Luke and Mark this defence consists in the question, *Is it lawful to do good on the sabbath days, or to do evil, to save life or to destroy it?* in Matthew, in a part of this question, together with the aphorism on saving the sheep which might fall into the pit on the sabbath. Luke, who has not this saying on the present occasion, places it (varied by the substitution of ὄνος ἢ βοῦς, *an ass or an ox* for πρόβατον *sheep,* and of φρέαρ, *well* or *pit* for βόθυνος, *ditch,*) in connexion with the cure of an ὑδρωπικὸς *a man who had the dropsy* (xiv. 5.); a narrative which has in general a striking similarity to the one under consideration. Jesus takes food in the house of one of the chief Pha-

[13] Tacit. Hist. iv. 81.

risees, where, as in the other instance in the synagogue, he is watched (here, ἦσαν παρατηρούμενοι, there, παρετήρουν). A dropsical person is present; as, there, a man with a withered hand. In the synagogue, according to Matthew, the Pharisees ask Jesus, εἰ ἔξεστι τοῖς σάββασι θεραπεύειν; *Is it lawful to heal on the sabbath days?* According to Mark and Luke, Jesus asks them whether it be *lawful to save life*, &c.: so, here, he asks them, εἰ ἔξεστι τῷ σαββάτῳ θεραπεύειν; *Is it lawful to heal on the sabbath?* whereupon in both histories the interrogated parties are silent (in that of the withered hand, Mark: οἱ δὲ ἐσιώπων; in that of the dropsical patient, Luke: οἱ δὲ ἡσύχασαν). Lastly, in both histories we have the saying about the animal fallen into a pit, in the one as an epilogue to the cure, in the other (that of Matthew) as a prologue. A natural explanation, which has not been left untried even with this cure of the dropsy[14], seems more than usually a vain labour, where, as in this case, we have before us no particular narrative, resting on its own historical basis, but a mere variation on the theme of the sabbath cures, and the text on the endangered domestic animal, which might come to one (Matthew) in connexion with the cure of a withered hand, to another (Luke) with the cure of a dropsical patient, and to a third in a different connexion still; for there is yet a third story of a miraculous cure with which a similar saying is associated. Luke, namely, narrates (xiii. 10 ff.) the cure of a woman bowed down by demoniacal influence, as having been performed by Jesus on the sabbath; when to the indignant remonstrance of the ruler of the synagogue, Jesus replies by asking, whether every one does not loose his ox or ass from the stall on the sabbath, and lead him away to watering? a question which is undeniably a variation of the one given above. So entirely identical does this history appear with the one last named, that Schleiermacher comes to this conclusion: since in the second there is no reference to the first, and since consequently the repetition is not excused

---

[14] Paulus, exeg. Handb. 2, s. 341 f.

by confession, the two passages Luke xiii. 10, and xiv. 5, cannot have been written one after the other by the same author [15].

Thus we have here, not three different incidents, but only three different frames in which legend has preserved the memorable and thoroughly popular aphorism on the domestic animal, to be rescued or tended on the sabbath. Yet, unless we would deny to Jesus so original and appropriate an argument, there must lie at the foundation a cure of some kind actually performed by him on the sabbath; not, however, a miraculous one. We have seen that Luke unites the saying with the cure of a demoniacal patient: now it might have been uttered by Jesus on the occasion of one of those cures of demoniacs of which, under certain limitations, we have admitted the natural possibility. Or, when Jesus in cases of illness among his followers applied the usual medicaments without regard to the sabbath, he may have found this appeal to the practical sense of men needful for his vindication. Or lastly, if there be some truth in the opinion of rationalistic commentators that Jesus, according to the oriental and more particularly the Essene custom, occupied himself with the cure of the body as well as of the soul, he may, when complying with a summons to the former work on the sabbath, have had occasion for such an apology. But in adopting this last supposition, we must not, with these commentators, seek in the particular supernatural cures which the Gospels narrate, the natural reality; on the contrary, we must admit that this is totally lost to us, and that the supernatural has usurped its place [16]. Further, it cannot have been cures in general with which that saying of Jesus was connected; but any service performed by him or his disciples which might be regarded as a rescuing or preservation of life, and which was accompanied by external labour, might in his position with

---

[15] Ut sup. s. 196.

[16] Winer (bibl. Realw. 1, s. 796) says : We should be contented to refrain from seeking a natural explanation *in individual cases* (of the cures of Jesus), and ever bear in mind that the banishment of the miraculous out of the agency of Jesus can never be effected *so long as the gospels are regarded historically.*

respect to the Pharisaic party, furnish an occasion for such a defence.

Of the two cures on the sabbath narrated in the fourth gospel, one has already been considered with the cures of the blind; the other (v. 1 ff.) might have been numbered among the cures of paralytics, but as the patient is not so designated, it was admissible to reserve it for our present head. In the porches of the pool of Bethesda in Jerusalem, Jesus found a man who, as it subsequently appears, had been lame for thirty-eight years; this sufferer he enables by a word to stand up and carry home his bed, but, as it was the sabbath, he thus draws down on himself the hostility of the Jewish hierarchy. Wool-ston [17] and many later writers have thought to get clear of this history in a singular manner, by the supposition that Jesus here did not cure a real sufferer but merely unmasked a hypo-crite [18]. The sole reason which can with any plausibility be urged in favour of this notion, is that the cured man points out Jesus to his enemies as the one who had commanded him to carry his bed on the sabbath (v. 15; comp. 11 ff.), a circum-stance which is only to be explained on the ground that Jesus had enjoined what was unwelcome. But that notification to the Pharisees might equally be given, either with a friendly in-tention, as in the case of the man born blind (John ix. 11. 25.), or at least with the innocent one of devolving the defence of the alleged violation of the sabbath on a stronger than him-self [19]. The evangelist at least gives it as his opinion that the man was really afflicted, and suffered from a wearisome disease, when he describes him as *having had an infirmity thirty-eight years*, τριάκοντα καὶ ὀκτὼ ἔτη ἔχων ἐν τῇ ἀσθενείᾳ (v. 5): for the forced interpretation once put on this passage by Paulus, refer-ring the thirty-eight years to the man's age, and not to the duration of his disease, he has not even himself ventured to re-

---

[17] Disc. 3.
[18] Paulus, Comm. 4, s. 263 ff. L. J. 1, a. s. 298 ff.
[19] Vid. Lücke and Tholuck, in loc.

produce[20].   On this view of the incident it is also impossible to explain what Jesus says to the cured man on a subsequent meeting (v. 14): *Behold thou art made whole; sin no more lest a worse thing come unto thee.*   Even Paulus is compelled by these words to admit that the man had a real infirmity, though only a trifling one:—in other words he is compelled to admit the inadequacy of the idea on which his explanation of the incident is based, so that here again we retain a miracle, and that not of the smallest.

In relation to the historical credibility of the narrative, it may certainly be held remarkable that so important a sanative institution as Bethesda is described to be by John, is not mentioned either by Josephus or the rabbins, especially if the popular belief connected a miraculous cure with this pool[21] : but this affords nothing decisive.   It is true that in the description of the pool there lies a fabulous popular notion, which appears also to have been received by the writer (for even if v. 4 be spurious, something similar is contained in the words κίνησις τοῦ ὕδατος, v. 3, and ταραχθῇ, v. 7).   But this proves nothing against the truth of the narrative, since even an eye-witness and a disciple of Jesus may have shared a vulgar error.   To make credible, however, such a fact as that a man who had been lame eight-and-thirty years, so that he was unable to walk, and completely bed-ridden, should have been perfectly cured by a word, the supposition of psychological influence will not suffice, for the man had no knowledge whatever of Jesus, v. 13 ; nor will any physical analogy, such as magnetism and the like, serve the purpose: but if such a result really happened, we must exalt that by which it happened above all the limits of the human and the natural.   On the other hand, it ought never to have been thought a difficulty[22] that from among the multitude of the infirm waiting in the porches of the pool, Jesus selected one only as the object of

---

[20] Comp. with Comm. 4, s. 290, his Leben Jesu, 1, a. s. 298.

[21] Bretschneider, Probab. s. 69.

[22] As by Hase, L. J. § 92.

his curative power, since the cure of him whose sufferings had been of the longest duration was not only particularly adapted, but also sufficient, to glorify the miraculous power of the Messiah. Nevertheless, it is this very trait which suggests a suspicion that the narrative has a mythical character. On a great theatre of disease, crowded with all kinds of sufferers, Jesus, the exalted and miraculously gifted physician, appears and selects the one who is afflicted with the most obstinate malady, that by his restoration he may present the most brilliant proof of his miraculous power. We have already remarked that the fourth gospel, instead of extending the curative agency of Jesus over large masses and to a great variety of diseases, as the synoptical gospels do, concentrates it on a few cases which proportionately gain in intensity: thus here, in the narrative of the cure of a man who had been lame thirty-eight years, it has far surpassed all the synoptical accounts of cures performed on persons with diseased limbs, among whom the longest sufferer is described in Luke xiii. 11, only as a woman who had had a spirit of infirmity eighteen years. Without doubt the fourth evangelist had received some intimation (though, as we have gathered from other parts of his history, it was far from precise) of cures of this nature performed by Jesus, especially of that wrought on the paralytic, Matt. ix. 2 ff. parall., for the address to the patient, and the result of the cure are in this narrative in John almost verbally the same as in that case, especially according to Mark's account [23]. There is even a vestige in this history of John, of the circumstance that in the synoptical narrative the cure appears in the light of a forgiveness of sins; for as Jesus in the latter consoles the patient,

---

[23] Mark ii. 9 : (τί ἐστιν εὐκοπώτερον, εἰπεῖν ————) ἔγειραι, καὶ ἆρόν σου τὸν κράββατον καὶ περιπάτει ;

11 : — ἔγειραι, καὶ ἆρον τὸν κράββατόν σου καὶ ὕπαγε εἰς τόν οἶκόν σου.

12 : καὶ ἠγέρθη εὐθέως, καὶ ὥρας τὸν κράββατον ἐξῆλθεν ἐναντίον πάντων.

John v. 8 : ἔγειραι, ἆρον τὸν κράββατον σου, καὶ περιπάτει.

9 : καὶ εὐθέως ἐγένετο ὑγιὴς ὁ ἄνθρωπος, καὶ ἦρε τὸν κράββατον αὑτοῦ καὶ περιεπάτει.

before the cure, with the assurance, *thy sins are forgiven thee*, so in the former, he warns him, after the cure, in the words, *sin no more*, &c. For the rest, this highly embellished history of a miraculous cure was represented as happening on the sabbath, probably because the command to take up the bed which it contained appeared the most suitable occasion for the reproach of violating the sabbath.

§ 100.

RESUSCITATIONS OF THE DEAD.

The evangelists tell us of three instances in which Jesus recalled the dead to life. One of these is common to the three synoptists, one belongs solely to Luke, and one to John.

The instance which is common to the three first evangelists is the resuscitation of a girl, and is in all the three gospels united with the narrative of the woman who had an issue of blood (Matt. ix. 18 f. 23—26 ; Mark v. 22 ff. ; Luke viii. 41 ff.). In the more precise designation of the girl and her father, the synoptical writers vary. Matthew introduces the father generally as ἄρχων εἷς *a certain ruler*, without any name ; the two others as a *ruler of the synagogue named Jairus :* the latter moreover describes the girl as being twelve years old, and Luke states that she was the only child of her father ; particulars of which Matthew is ignorant. A more important difference is, that according to Matthew the ruler in the first instance speaks of his daughter to Jesus as being dead, and intreats him to restore her to life ; whereas according to the two other evangelists, he left her while yet living, though on the point of death, that he might fetch Jesus to avert her actual decease, and first when Jesus was on the way with him, people came out of his house with the information that his daughter had in the mean time expired, so that to trouble Jesus further was in vain. The circumstances of the resuscitation also are differently described, for Matthew knows not that Jesus, as the other evangelists state, took with him only his three most confidential disciples as witnesses. Some theologians, Storr for example, have thought these divergencies so important, that they have supposed two different cases in which, among other similar circumstances, the daughter, in one case of a civil ruler (Matthew), in the other, of a ruler of the synagogue named Jairus (Mark and Luke), was raised from the dead by Jesus [1].

But that, as Storr supposes, and as it is inevitable to suppose on his view, Jesus not only twice resuscitated a girl, but also on both these occasions, healed a woman with an issue immediately before, is a coincidence which does not at all gain in probability by the vague observation of Storr, that it is quite possible for very similar things to happen at different times. If then it must be admitted that the evangelists narrate only one event, the weak attempt to give perfect agreement to their narratives should be forborne. For neither can the expression of Matthew ἄρτι ἐτελεύτησε mean, as Kuinöl maintains [2], *est morti proxima*, nor can that of Mark, ἐσχάτως ἔχει, or of Luke ἀπέθνησκε, imply that death had already taken place : not to mention that according to both, the fact of the death is subsequently announced to the father as something new [3].

Our more modern critics have wisely admitted a divergency between the accounts ; in doing which they have unanimously given the palm of superior accuracy to the intermediate evangelists. Some are lenient towards Matthew, and only attribute to his mode of narration a brevity which might belong even to the representation of an eye-witness [4]; while others regard this want of particularity as an indication that the first gospel had not an apostolic origin [5]. Now that Mark and Luke give the

---

[1] Ueber den Zweck des Evang. und der Briefe Joh. s. 351 ff.

[2] Comm. in Matth. p. 263. Observe his argumentation : *verba* [N.B. *Matthaei*] : ἄρτι ἐτελεύτησεν, *non possunt latine reddi : jam mortua est : nam, auctore* [N.B. *Luca*] *patri adhuc cum Christo colloquenti nuntiabat servus, filiam jam exspirasse ; ergo* [*auctore Matthaeo ?*] *nondum mortua erat, cum pater ad Jesum accederet.*

[3] Compare, on the subject of these vain attempts at reconciliation, Schleiermacher über den Lukas, s. 132, and Fritzsche, in Matth. p. 347 f.

[4] Olshausen, in loc.

[5] Schleiermacher, ut sup. s. 131 ff. ; Schulz, über d. Abendmahl, s. 316 f.

name of the applicant, on which Matthew is silent, and also
that they determine his rank more precisely than the latter,
will just as well bear an unfavourable construction for them, as
the usual favourable one; since the designation of persons by
name, as we have before remarked, is not seldom an addition of
the later legend. For example, the woman with the issue first
receives the name of Veronica in the tradition of John Malala[6];
the Canaanitish woman that of Justa in the Clementine
Homilies[7]; and the two thieves crucified with Jesus, the
names of Gestas and Demas in the gospel of Nicodemus[8].
Luke's μονογενὴς (one only daughter) only serves to make
the scene more touching, and the ἐτῶν δώδεκα twelve years
of age, he, and after him Mark, might have borrowed from
the history of the woman with the issue. The divergency
that, according to Matthew, the maiden is spoken of in the
first instance as dead, according to the two others as only
dying, must have been considered very superficially by those
who have thought it possible to turn it in accordance with our
own rule to the disadvantage of Matthew, on the ground that
his representation serves to aggrandize the miracle. For in
both the other gospels the death of the girl is subsequently announced, and its being supposed in Matthew to have occurred a
few moments earlier is no aggrandizement of the miracle. Nay,
it is the reverse; for the miraculous power of Jesus appears
greater in the former, not indeed objectively, but subjectively,
because it is heightened by contrast and surprise. There, where
Jesus is in the first instance intreated to restore the dead to
life, he does no more than what was desired of him; here, on
the contrary, where supplicated only for the cure of a sick person, he actually brings that person to life again, he does more
than the interested parties seek or understand. There, where
the power of awaking the dead is presupposed by the father to
belong to Jesus, the extraordinary nature of such a power is

[6] Vid. Fabricius, Cod. Apocr. N. T. 2, p. 449 ff.
[7] Homil. ii. 19.
[8] Cap. x.

less marked than here, where the father at first only presupposes the power of healing the sick, and when death has supervened, is diverted from any further hope. In the description of the arrival and the conduct of Jesus in the house where the corpse lay, Matthew's brevity is at least clearer than the diffuse accounts of the two other evangelists. Matthew tells us that Jesus, having reached the house, put forth the minstrels already assembled for the funeral, together with the rest of the crowd, on the ground that there would be no funeral there ; this is perfectly intelligible. But Mark and Luke tell us besides that he excluded his disciples also, with the exception of three, from the scene about to take place, and for this it is difficult to discover a reason. That a greater number of spectators would have been physically or psychologically an impediment to the resuscitation, can only be said on the supposition that the event was a natural one. Admitting the miracle, the reason for the exclusion can only be sought in the want of fitness in the excluded parties, whom however, the sight of such a miracle would surely have been the very means to benefit. But we must not omit to observe that the two later synoptists, in opposition to the concluding statement of Matthew that the fame of this event went abroad in the whole land, represent Jesus as enjoining the strictest silence on the witnesses : so that on the whole it rather appears that Mark and Luke regarded the incident as a mystery, to which only the nearest relatives and the most favoured disciples were admitted. Lastly, the difference on which Schulz insists as favourable to the second and third evangelist, namely, that while Matthew makes Jesus simply take the maiden by the hand, they have preserved to us the words which he at the same time uttered, the former even in the original language ;—can either have no weight at all, or it must fall into the opposite scale. For that Jesus, if he said anything when recalling a girl to life, made use of some such words as ἡ παις ἐγείρου, *maiden, I say unto thee, arise,* the most remote narrator might imagine, and to regard the ταλιθὰ κοῦμι of Mark as an indication that this evangelist drew from a peculiarly original source, is to forget the more

simple supposition that he translated these words from the
Greek of his informant for the sake of presenting the life-giving
word in its original foreign garb, and thus enhancing its mysteriousness, as we have before observed with reference to the
ἐφφαθὰ in the cure of the deaf man. After what we have seen
we shall willingly abstain from finding out whether the individual who originally furnished the narrative in Luke were one
of the three confidential disciples, and whether the one who
originally related it, also put it into writing : a task to which
only the acumen of Schleiermacher is equal [9].

In relation to the facts of the case, the natural interpretation speaks with more than its usual confidence, under the persuasion that it has on its side the assurance of Jesus himself,
that the maiden was not really dead, but merely in a sleep-like
swoon ; and not only rationalists, like Paulus, and semi-
rationalists, like Schleiermacher, but also decided supranaturalists, like Olshausen, believe, on the strength of that
declaration of Jesus, that this was no resuscitation of the dead [10].
The last-named commentator attaches especial importance to
the antithesis in the speech of Jesus, and because the words
οὐκ ἀπέθανε, *is not dead*, are followed by ἀλλὰ καθεύδει, *but
sleepeth*, is of opinion that the former expression cannot be interpreted to mean merely, she is not dead, since I have resolved
to restore her to life ; strange criticism,—for it is precisely
this addition which shows that she was only not dead, in so
far as it was in the power of Jesus to recall her to life. Reference is also made to the declaration of Jesus concerning Lazarus,
John xi. 14, Λάζαρος ἀπέθανε, *Lazarus is dead*, which is directly
the reverse of the passage in question, οὐκ ἀπέθανε τὸ κοράσιον,
the damsel is not dead. But Jesus had before said of Lazarus,

---

[9] Ut sup. s. 129.

[10] Paulus, exeg. Handb. 1, b. s. 526, 31 f. ; Schleiermacher, ut sup. s. 132 ; Olshausen, 1, s. 327. Even Neander does not express himself decidedly against this
interpretation of the words of Jesus ; while with regard to the girl's real condition,
he thinks the supposition of a merely apparent death probable. L. J. Chr. s. 343.
Comp. 338 f.

αὕτη ἡ ἀσθένεια οὐκ ἔστι πρὸς θάνατον, *this sickness is not unto death* (v. 4), and Λάζαρος ὁ φίλος ἡμῶν κεκοίμηται, *our friend Lazarus sleepeth* (v. 11). Thus in the case of Lazarus also, who was really dead, we have just as direct a denial of death, and affirmation of mere sleep, as in the narrative before us. Hence Fritzsche is undoubtedly right when he paraphrases the words of Jesus in our passage as follows : *puellam ne pro mortua habetote, sed dormire existimatote, quippe in vitam mox redituram.* Moreover, Matthew subsequently (xi. 5) makes Jesus say, νεκροὶ ἐγείρονται, *the dead are raised up ;* and as he mentions no other instance of resuscitation by Jesus, he must apparently have had this in his mind [11].

But apart from the false interpretation of the words of Jesus, this view of the subject has many difficulties. That in many diseases conditions may present themselves which have a deceptive resemblance to death, or that in the indifferent state of medical science among the Jews of that age especially, a swoon might easily be mistaken for death, is not to be denied. But how was Jesus to know that there was such a merely apparent death in this particular case? However minutely the father detailed to him the course of the disease, nay, even if Jesus were acquainted beforehand with the particular circumstances of the girl's illness (as the natural explanation supposes) : we must still ask, how could he build so much on this information as, without having seen the girl, and in contradiction to the assurance of the eye-witnesses, decidedly to declare that she was not dead, according to the rationalistic interpretation of his words ? This would have been rashness and folly to boot, unless Jesus had obtained certain knowledge of the true state of the case in a supernatural way [12] : to admit which, however, is to abandon the naturalistic point of view. To return to the explanation of Paulus; between the expressions, ἐκράτησε τῆς χειρὸς αὐτῆς, *he took her by the hand,* and ἠγέρθη τὸ κοράσιον,

---

[11] Comp. de Wette, exeg. Handb. 1, 1, s. 95 ; Weisse, die ev. Geschichte, 1, s. 503.

[12] Comp. Neander. L. J. s. 342.

the maid arose, expressions which are closely enough connected in Matthew, and are still more inseparably linked by the words εὐθέως and παραχρῆμα in the other two gospels, he inserts a course of medical treatment, and Venturini can even specify the different restoratives which were applied [13]. Against such arbitrary suppositions, Olshausen justly maintains that in the opinion of the evangelical narrator the life-giving word of Jesus, (and we might add, the touch of his hand, furnished with divine power,) was the means of restoring the girl to life.

In the case of resuscitation narrated by Luke alone (vii. 11 ff.) the natural explanation has not such a handle as was presented by the declaration of Jesus in the narrative just considered. Nevertheless, the rationalistic commentators take courage, and rest their hopes mainly on the circumstance that Jesus *speaks* to the young man lying in the coffin (v. 14). Now, say they, no one would speak to a dead person, but only to such an one as is ascertained or guessed to be capable of hearing [14]. But this rule would prove that all the dead whom Christ will raise at the last day are only apparently dead, as otherwise they could not hear his voice, which it is expressly said they will do (John v. 28; comp. 1 Thess. iv. 16); it would therefore prove too much. Certainly one who is spok n to must be supposed to hear, and in a certain sense to be living; but in the present instance this holds only in so far as the voice of him who quickens the dead can penetrate even to the ears from which life has departed. We must indeed admit the possibility that with the bad custom which prevailed among the Jews of burying their dead a few hours after their decease, a merely apparent corpse might easily be carried to the grave [15]; but all by which it is attempted to show that this possibility was here a reality, is a tissue of fictions. In order to explain how Jesus, even without any intention to perform a miracle, came to join the funeral procession, and how the

---

[13] Natürliche Geschichte, 2, s. 212.

[14] Paulus, exeg. Handb. 1, b. s. 716, Anm. and 719 f.

[15] Ibid, ut sup. s. 723. Comp. De Wette, exeg. Handb. 1, 2, s. 47.

conjecture could occur to him that the individual about to be buried was not really dead, it is first imagined that the two processions, that of the funeral and that of the companions of Jesus, met precisely under the gate of the city, and as they impeded each other, halted for a while:—directly in opposition to the text, which makes the bearers first stand still when Jesus touches the bier. Affected by the peculiar circumstances of the case, which he had learned during the pause in his progress, Jesus, it is said, approached the mother, and not with any reference to a resurrection which he intended to effect, but merely as a consolatory address, said to her, *Weep not* [16]. But what an empty, presuming comforter would he be, who, when a mother was about to consign her only son to the grave, should forbid her even the relief of tears, without offering to her either real help by recalling the departed one, or ideal, by suggesting grounds for consolation! Now the latter Jesus does not attempt: hence unless we would allow him to appear altogether heartless, he must be supposed to have resolved on the former, and for this he in fact makes every preparation, designedly touching the bier, and causing the bearers to stand still. Here, before the reanimating word of Jesus, the natural explanation inserts the circumstance that Jesus observed some sign of life in the youth, and on this, either immediately or after a previous application of medicaments [17], spoke the words, which helped completely to awake him. But setting aside the fact that those intervening measures are only interpolated into the text, and that the strong words: νεανίσκε, σοὶ λέγω, ἐγέρθητι, *Young man, I say unto thee arise!* resemble rather the authoritative command of a miracle worker than the attempt of a physician to restore animation; how, if Jesus were conscious that the youth was alive when he met him, and was not first recalled to life by himself, could he with a good conscience receive the praise which, according to the narrative, the multitude lavished on him as a great prophet on account of

---

[16] Thus Hase also, L. J. § 87.
[17] Venturini, 2, s. 293.

this deed ? According to Paulus, he was himself uncertain how he ought to regard the result; but if he were not convinced that he ought to ascribe the result to himself, it was his duty to disclaim all praise on account of it; and if he omitted to do this, his conduct places him in an equivocal light, in which he by no means appears in the other evangelical histories, so far as they are fairly interpreted. Thus here also we must acknowledge that the evangelist intends to narrate to us a miraculous resuscitation of the dead, and that according to him, Jesus also regarded his deed as a miracle [18].

In the third history of a resurrection, which is peculiar to John (chap. xi.), the resuscitated individual is neither just dead nor being carried to his grave, but has been already buried several days. Here one would have thought there was little hope of effecting a natural explanation; but the arduousness of the task has only stimulated the ingenuity and industry of the rationalists in developing their conception of this narrative. We shall also see that together with the rigorously consequent mode of interpretation of the rationalists,—which, maintaining the historical integrity of the evangelical narrative throughout, assumes the responsibility of explaining every part naturally, there has appeared another system, which distinguishes certain features of the narrative as additions after the event, and is thus an advance towards the mythical explanation.

The rationalistic expositors set out here from the same premises as in the former narrative, namely, that it is in itself possible for a man who has lain in a tomb four days to come to life again, and that this possibility is strengthened in the present instance by the known custom of the Jews; propositions which we shall not abstractedly controvert. From this they proceed to a supposition which we perhaps ought not to let pass so easily [19], namely, that from the messenger whom the sisters had sent with the news of their brother's illness, Jesus had obtained accurate information of the circumstances of the

---

[18] Comp. Schleiermacher, ut sup. s. 103 f.
[19] Paulus, Comm. 4, s. 535 ff.; L. J. 1, b. s. 55 ff.

disease ; and the answer which he gave to the messenger, *This sickness is not unto death*, (v. 4,) is said to express, merely as an inference which he had drawn from the report of the messenger, his conviction that the disease was not fatal. Such a view of his friend's condition would certainly accord the best with his conduct in remaining two days in Peræa after the reception of the message (v. 6) ; since, according to that supposition, he could not regard his presence in Bethany as a matter of urgent necessity. But how comes it that after the lapse of these two days, he not only resolves to journey thither (v. 8), but also has quite a different opinion of the state of Lazarus, nay, certain knowledge of his death, which he first obscurely (v. 10) and then plainly (v. 14) announces to his disciples ? Here the thread of the natural explanation is lost, and the break is only rendered more conspicuous by the fiction of a second messenger [20], after the lapse of two days, bringing word to Jesus that Lazarus had expired in the interim. For the author of the gospel at least cannot have known of a second messenger, otherwise he must have mentioned him, since the omission to do so gives another aspect to the whole narrative, obliging us to infer that Jesus had obtained information of the death of Lazarus in a supernatural manner. Jesus, when he had resolved to go to Bethany, said to the disciples, *Lazarus sleepeth, but I go that I may awake him out of sleep* (κεκοίμηται—ἐξυπνίσω —v. 11); this the naturalists explain by the supposition that Jesus must in some way have gathered from the statements of the messengers who announced the death of Lazarus, that the latter was only in a state of lethargy. But we can as little here as in a former case impute to Jesus the foolish presumption of giving, before he had even seen the alleged corpse, the positive assurance that he yet lived [21]. From this point of view, it is also a difficulty that Jesus says to his disciples (v. 15) *I am*

---

[20] In the translation of the text in his *Leben Jesu*, 2, b. s. 46, Paulus appears to suppose, besides the message mentioned in the gospel, *three* subsequent messages.

[21] Comp. C. Ch. Flatt, etwas zur Vertheidigung des Wunders der Wiederbelebung des Lazarus, in Süskind's Magazin, 14tes Stück, s. 93 ff.

glad for your sakes that I was not there, to the intent ye may believe (ἵνα πιστεύσητε). Paulus explains these words to imply that Jesus feared lest the death, had it happened in his presence, might have shaken their faith in him ; but, as Gabler [22] has remarked, πιστεύω cannot mean merely the negative : *not to lose faith,* which would rather have been expressed by a phrase such as : ἵνα μὴ ἐκλείπῃ ἡ πίστις ὑμῶν, *that your faith fail not* (see Luke xxii. 32.) ; and moreover we nowhere find that the idea which the disciples formed of Jesus as the Messiah was incompatible with the death of a man, or, more correctly, of a friend, in his presence.

From the arrival of Jesus in Bethany the evangelical narrative is somewhat more favourable to the natural explanation. It is true that Martha's address to Jesus (v. 21 f.), *Lord, if thou hadst been here, my brother had not died, but I know that even now, whatsoever thou wilt ask of God, he will give it thee,* ἀλλὰ καὶ νῦν οἶδα, ὅτι, ὅσα ἂν αἰτήσῃ τὸν θεόν, δώσει σοι ὁ θεός, appears evidently to express the hope that Jesus may be able even to recall the dead one to life.   However, on the assurance of Jesus which follows, *Thy brother shall rise again,* ἀναστήσεται ὁ ἀδελφός σου, she answers despondingly, Yes, at the last day. This is certainly a help to the natural explanation, for it seems retrospectively to give to the above declaration of Martha (v. 22) the general sense, that even now, although he has not preserved the life of her brother, she believes Jesus to be him to whom God grants all that he desires, that is, the favourite of the Deity, the Messiah.   But the expression which Martha there uses is not πιστεύω but οἶδα, and the turn of phrase : I know that this will happen if thou only willest it to be so, is a common but indirect form of petition, and is here the more unmistakeable, because the object of the entreaty is clearly indicated by the foregoing antithesis. Martha evidently means, Thou hast not indeed prevented the death of our brother, but even now it is not too late, for at thy prayer God will restore him to

---

[22] Journal für auserlesene theol. Literatur, 3, 2, s. 261. Anm.

thee and us. Martha's change of mind, from the hope which is but indirectly expressed in her first reply (v. 24) to its extinction in the second, cannot be held very surprising in a woman who here and elsewhere manifests a very hasty disposition, and it is in the present case sufficiently explained by the form of the foregoing assurance of Jesus (v. 23). Martha had expected that Jesus would reply to her indirect prayer by a decided promise of its fulfilment, and when he answers quite generally and with an expression which it was usual to apply to the resurrection at the last day (ἀναστήσεται), she gives a half-impatient, half-desponding reply [23]. But that general declaration of Jesus, as well as the yet more indefinite one (v. 25 f.), *I am the resurrection and the life,* is thought favourable to the rationalistic view : Jesus, it is said, was yet far from the expectation of an extraordinary result, hence he consoles Martha merely with the general hope that he, the Messiah, would procure for those who believed in him a future resurrection and a life of blessedness. As however Jesus had before (v. 11) spoken confidently to his disciples of awaking Lazarus, he must then have altered his opinion in the interim—a change for which no cause is apparent. Further, when (v. 40) Jesus is about to awake Lazarus, he says to Martha, *Said I not unto thee that if thou wouldst believe thou shouldst see the glory of God ?* evidently alluding to v. 23, in which therefore he must have meant to predict the resurrection which he was going to effect. That he does not declare this distinctly, and that he again veils the scarcely uttered promise in relation to the brother (v. 25) in general promises for the believing, is the effect of design, the object of which is to try the faith of Martha, and extend her sphere of thought [24].

When Mary at length comes out of the house with her companions, her weeping moves Jesus himself to tears. To this circumstance the natural interpretation appeals with unusual confidence, asking whether if he were already certain of his

---

[23] Flatt, ut sup. 102 f. ; De Wette, in loc.; Neander, s. 351 f.
[24] Flatt, ut sup. ; Lücke, Tholück and De Wette, in loc.

friend's resurrection, he would not have approached his grave
with the most fervent joy, since he was conscious of being able
to call him again living from the grave in the next moment?   In
this view the words ἐνεβριμήσατο (v. 33) and ἐμβριμώμενος (v. 38)
are understood of a forcible repression of the sorrow caused by
the death of his friend, which subsequently found vent in tears
(ἐδάκρυσεν). But both by its etymology, according to which it signifies *fremere in aliquem* or *in se*, and by the analogy of its use
in the New Testament, where it appears only in the sense of
increpare aliquem (Matt. ix. 30 ; Mark i. 43 ; xiv. 5.), ἐμβριμᾶσθαι is determined to imply an emotion of anger, not of sorrow;
where it is united, not with the dative of another person, but
with τῷ πνεύματι and ἐν ἑαυτῷ, it must be understood of a silent,
suppressed displeasure.   This sense would be very appropriate
in v. 38, where it occurs the second time ; for in the foregoing
observation of the Jews, *Could not this man, who opened the
eyes of the blind, have caused that even this man should not
have died?* there lies an intimation that they were *scandalized,*
the prior conduct of Jesus perplexing them as to his present
demeanour, and vice versâ.   But where the word ἐμβριμᾶσθαι is
first used v. 33, the general weeping seems to have been likely
to excite in Jesus a melancholy, rather than an angry emotion :
yet even here a strong disapproval of the want of faith (ὀλιγο-
πιστία) which was manifested was not impossible.   That Jesus
then himself broke out into tears, only proves that his indignation against the faithless generation around him dissolved into
melancholy, not that melancholy was his emotion from the
beginning.   Lastly, that the Jews (v. 36) in relation to the
tears which Jesus shed, said among themselves, *Behold, how
he loved him!* appears to be rather against than for those who
regard the emotion of Jesus as sorrow for the death of his
friend, and sympathy with the sisters; for, as the character of
the narrative of John in general would rather lead us to expect
an opposition between the real import of the demeanour of
Jesus, and the interpretation put upon it by the spectators, so
in particular *the Jews* in this gospel are always those who either

misunderstand or pervert the words and actions of Jesus. It is true that the mild character of Jesus is urged, as inconsistent with the harshness which displeasure on his part at the very natural weeping of Mary and the rest would imply [25]; but such a mode of thinking is by no means foreign to the Christ of John's gospel. He who gave to the βασιλικὸς, when preferring the inoffensive request that he would come to his house and heal his son, the rebuke, *Except ye see signs and wonders ye will not believe;* he who, when some of his disciples murmured at the hard doctrines of the sixth chapter, assailed them with the cutting questions, *Doth this offend you?* and *Will ye also go away?* (vi. 61, 67.); he who repulsed his own mother, when at the wedding at Cana she complained to him of the want of wine, with the harsh reply, *What have I to do with thee, Woman?* (ii. 4.)—who thus was always the most displeased when men, not comprehending his higher mode of thought or action, showed themselves desponding or importunate,—would here find peculiar reason for this kind of displeasure. If this be the true interpretation of the passage, and if it be not sorrow for the death of Lazarus which Jesus here exhibits, there is an end to the assistance which the natural explanation of the entire event is thought to derive from this particular feature; meanwhile, even on the other interpretation, a momentary emotion produced by sympathy with the mourners is quite reconcileable with the foreknowledge of the resurrection [26]. And how could the words of the Jews v. 37, serve, as rationalistic commentators think, to excite in Jesus the hope that God would now perhaps perform something extraordinary for him? The Jews did not express the hope that he could awake the dead, but only the conjecture that he might perhaps have been able to preserve his friend's life; Martha therefore had previously said more when she declared her belief that even now the Father would grant him what he asked; so that if such hopes were excited in Jesus from without, they must have been

---

[25] Lücke, 2, s. 388.
[26] Flatt, ut sup. s. 104 f.; Lücke, ut sup.

excited earlier, and especially before the weeping of Jesus, to which it is customary to appeal as the proof that they did not yet exist.

Even supranaturalists admit that the expression of Martha when Jesus commanded that the stone should be taken away from the grave, Κύριε, ἤδη ὄζει (v. 39), is no proof at all that decomposition had really commenced, nor consequently that a natural resuscitation was impossible, since it may have been a mere inference from the length of time since the burial [27]. But more weight must be attached to the words with which Jesus, repelling the objections of Martha, persists in having the tomb opened (v. 40): *Said I not unto thee that if thou wouldst believe thou shouldst see the glory of God?* How could he say this unless he was decidedly conscious of his power to re-suscitate Lazarus? According to Paulus, this declaration only implied generally that those who have faith will, in some way or other, experience a glorious manifestation of the divinity. But what glorious manifestation of the divinity was to be seen here, on the opening of the grave of one who had been buried four days, unless it were his restoration to life? and what could be the sense of the words of Jesus, as opposed to the observa-tion of Martha, that her brother was already within the grasp of decay, but that he was empowered to arrest decay? But in order to learn with certainty the meaning of the words τὴν δόξαν τοῦ θεοῦ in our present passage we need only refer to v. 4, where Jesus had said that the sickness of Lazarus was not *unto death*, πρὸς θάνατον, but *for the glory of God*, ὑπὲρ τῆς δόξης τοῦ θεοῦ. Here the first member of the antithesis, *not unto death*, clearly shows that the δόξα τοῦ θεοῦ signifies the glorification of God by the life of Lazarus, that is, since he was now dead, by his resur-rection: a hope which Jesus could not venture to excite in the most critical moment, without having a superior assurance that it would be fulfilled [28]. After the opening of the grave, and before he says to the dead man, *Come forth!* he thanks the

---

[27] Flatt, s. 106; Olshausen, 2, s. 269.
[28] Flatt, s. 97 f.

Father for having heard his prayer. This is adduced, in the rationalistic point of view, as the most satisfactory proof that he did not first recall Lazarus to life by those words, but on looking into the grave found him already alive again. Truly, such an argument was not to be expected from theologians who have some insight into the character of John's gospel. These ought to have remembered how common it is in this gospel, as for example in the expression *glorify thy son*, to represent that which is yet to be effected or which is only just begun, as already performed; and in the present instance it is especially suited to mark the certainty of obtaining fulfilment, that it is spoken of as having already happened. And what invention does it further require to explain, both how Jesus could perceive in Lazarus the evidences of returning life, and how the latter could have come to life again! Between the removal of the stone, says Paulus, and the thanksgiving of Jesus, lies the critical interval when the surprising result was accomplished; then must Jesus, yet some steps removed from the grave, have discerned that Lazarus was living. By what means? and how so quickly and unhesitatingly? and why did he and no one else discern it? He may have discerned it by the movements of Lazarus, it is conjectured. But how easily might he deceive himself with respect to a dead body lying in a dark cavern: how precipitate was he, if without having examined more nearly, he so quickly and decidedly declared his conviction that Lazarus lived! Or, if the movements of the supposed corpse were strong and not to be mistaken, how could they escape the notice of the surrounding spectators? Lastly, how could Jesus in his prayer represent the incident about to take place as a sign of his divine mission, if he was conscious that he had not effected, but only discovered, the resuscitation of Lazarus? As arguments for the natural possibility of a return of life in a man who had been interred four days, the rationalistic explanation adduces our ignorance of the particular circumstances of the supposed death, the rapidity of interment among the Jews, afterwards the coolness of the cave, the strong fragrance of the spices, and lastly, the reanimating draught of warm air which on the rolling away of the stone streamed into the cave. But all these circumstances do not produce more than the lowest degree of possibility, which coincides with the highest degree of improbability: and with this the certainty with which Jesus predicts the result must remain irreconcileable [29].

These decided predictions are indeed the main hindrance to the natural interpretation of this chapter; hence it has been sought to neutralize them, still from the rationalistic position, by the supposition that they did not proceed from Jesus, but may have been added *ex eventu* by the narrator. Paulus himself found the words ἐξυπνίσω αὐτὸν (v. 11) quite too decided, and therefore ventured the conjecture that the narrator, writing with the result in his mind, had omitted a qualifying *perhaps*, which Jesus had inserted [30]. This expedient has been more extensively adopted by Gabler. Not only does he partake the opinion of Paulus as to the above expression, but already in v. 4, he is inclined to lay the words ὑπὲρ τῆς δόξης τοῦ θεοῦ *for the glory of God*, to the account of the evangelist: again v. 15, he conjectures that in the words χαίρω δι' ὑμᾶς, ἵνα πιστεύσητε, ὅτι οὐκ ἤμην ἐκεῖ, *I am glad for your sakes that I was not there, to the intent ye may believe*, there is a slight exaggeration resulting from John's knowledge of the issue; lastly, even in relation to the words of Martha v. 22, ἀλλὰ καὶ νῦν οἶδα κ. τ. λ. he admits the idea of an addition from the pen of the writer [31]. By the adoption of this expedient, the natural interpretation avows its inability by itself to cope with the difficulties in John's narrative. For if, in order to render its application possible, it is necessary

---

[29] Compare on this subject, especially Flatt and Lücke.

[30] Comm. 4, s. 437; in the L. J. 1, b. s. 57, and 2, b. s. 46, this conjecture is no longer employed.

[31] Ut sup. s. 272 ff. Even Neander shows himself not disinclined to such a conjecture as far as regards v. 4, (s. 349). As Gabler believes that these expressions cannot have come from Jesus, but only from John, so Dieffenbach, in Bertholdt's Krit. Journal, 5, s. 7 ff., maintains that they cannot have proceeded from John, and as he holds that the rest of the gospel is the production of that apostle, he pronounces those passages to be interpolations.

to expunge the most significant passages, it is plain that the narrative in its actual state does not admit of a natural explanation. It is true that the passages, the incompatibility of which with the rationalistie mode of explanation is confessed by their excision, are very sparingly chosen; but from the above observations it is clear, that if all the features in this narrative which are really opposed to the natural view of the entire event were ascribed to the evangelist, it would in the end be little short of the whole that must be regarded as his invention. Thus, what *we* have done with the two first narratives of resuscitations, is with the last and most remarkable history of this kind, effected by the various successive attempts at explanation themselves, namely, to reduce the subject to the alternative: that we either receive the event as supernatural, according to the representation of the evangelical narrative; or, if we find it incredible as such, deny that the narrative has an historical character.

In order, in this dilemma, to arrive at a decision with respect to all the three narratives, we must refer to the peculiar character of the kind of miracles which we have now before us. We have hitherto been ascending a ladder of miracles; first, cures of mental disorders, then, of all kinds of bodily maladies, in which, however, the organization of the sufferer was not so injured as to cause the cessation of consciousness and life; and now, the revivification of bodies, from which the life has actually departed. This progression in the marvellous is, at the same time, a gradation in inconceivability. We have indeed been able to represent to ourselves how a mental derangement, in which none of the bodily organs were attacked beyond the nervous system, which is immediately connected with mental action, might have been removed, even in a purely psychical manner, by the mere word, look, and influence of Jesus: but the more deeply the malady appeared to have penetrated into the entire corporeal system, the more inconceivable to us was a cure of this kind. Where in insane persons the brain was disturbed to the extent of raging madness, or where in nervous patients the disorder was so confirmed as to manifest itself in periodical epilepsy; there we could scarcely imagine how permanent benefit could be conferred by that mental influence ; and this was yet more difficult where the disease had no immediate connection with the mind, as in leprosy, blindness, lameness, &c. And yet, up to this point, there was always something present, to which the miraculous power of Jesus could apply itself; there was still a consciousness in the objects, on which to make an impression—a nervous life to be stimulated. Not so with the dead. The corpse from which life and consciousness have flown has lost the last fulcrum for the power of the miracle worker ; it perceives him no longer—receives no impression from him ; for the very capability of receiving impressions must be conferred on him anew. But to confer this, that is, to give life in the proper sense, is a creative act, and to think of this as being exercised by a man, we must confess to be beyond our power.

But even within the limits of our three histories of resurrections, there is an evident climax. Woolston has remarked with justice, that it seems as if each of these narratives were intended to supply what was wanting in the preceding [32]. The daughter of Jairus is restored to life on the same bed on which she had just expired ; the youth of Nain, when already in his coffin, and on his way to interment; lastly, Lazarus, after four days' abode in the tomb. In the first history, a word was the only intimation that the maiden had fallen under the powers of the grave ; in the second, the fact is imprinted on the imagination also, by the picture of the young man being already carried out of the city towards his grave ; but in the third, Lazarus, who had been some time inclosed in the grave, is depicted in the strongest manner as an inhabitant of the nether world : so that, if the reality of the death could be doubted in the first instance, this would become more difficult in the second, and in the third, as good as impossible [33]. With this gradation, there is a corresponding increase in the difficulty of rendering the three events

[32] Disc. 5.
[33] Bretschneider, Probab. s. 61.

conceivable ; if, indeed, when the fact itself is inconceivable, there can exist degrees of inconceivableness between its various modifications. If, however, the resurrection of a dead person in general were possible, it must rather be possible in the case of one just departed, and yet having some remains of vital warmth, than in that of a corpse, cold and being carried to the grave ; and again, in this, rather than in the case of one who had already lain four days in the grave, and in which decay is supposed to have commenced, nay, with respect to which, this supposition, if not confirmed, is at least not denied.

But, setting aside the miraculous part of the histories in question, each succeeding one is both intrinsically more improbable, and externally less attested, than the foregoing. As regards the internal improbability, one element of this, which indeed lies in all, and therefore also in the first, is especially conspicuous in the second. As a motive by which Jesus was induced to raise the young man at Nain, the narrative mentions compassion for the mother (v. 13). Together with this we are to include, according to Olshausen, a reference to the young man himself. For, he observes, man as a conscious being can never be treated as a mere instrument, which would be the case here, if the joy of the mother were regarded as the sole object of Jesus in raising the youth [34]. This remark of Olshausen demands our thanks, not that it removes the difficulty of this and every other resuscitation of the dead, but that it exhibits that difficulty in the clearest light. For the conclusion, that what in itself, or according to enlightened ideas, is not allowable or fitting, cannot be ascribed to Jesus by the evangelists, is totally inadmissible. We should rather (presupposing the purity of the character of Jesus) conclude that when the evangelical narratives ascribe to him what is not allowable, they are incorrect. Now that Jesus, in his resuscitations of the dead, made it a consideration whether the persons to be restored to life might, from the spiritual condition in which they

[34] 1, s. 276 f.

died, derive advantage from the restoration or the contrary, we find no indication ; that, as Olshausen supposes, the corporeal awakening was attended with a spiritual awakening, or that such a result was expected, is nowhere said. These resuscitated individuals, not excepting even Lazarus, recede altogether from our observation after their return to life, and hence Woolston was led to ask why Jesus rescued from the grave precisely these insignificant persons, and not rather John the Baptist, or some other generally useful man ? Is it said, he knew it to be the will of Providence that these men, once dead, should remain so ? But then, it should seem, he must have thought the same of all who had once died, and to Woolston's objection there remains no answer but this : as it was positively known concerning celebrated men, that the breach which their deaths occasioned was never filled up by their restoration to life, legend could not annex the resurrections which she was pleased to narrate to such names, but must choose unknown subjects, in relation to which she was not under the same control.

The above difficulty is common to all the three narratives, and is only rendered more prominent in the second by an accidental expression : but the third narrative is full of difficulties entirely peculiar to itself, since the conduct of Jesus throughout, and, to a considerable extent, that of the other parties, is not easily to be conceived. When Jesus receives the information of the death of Lazarus, and the request of the sisters implied therein, that he would come to Bethany, he remains still two days in the same place, and does not set out toward Judea till after he is certain of the death. Why so ? That it was not because he thought the illness attended with no danger, has been already shown ; on the contrary, he foresaw the death of Lazarus. That indifference was not the cause of the delay, is expressly remarked by the evangelist (v. 5). What then ? Lücke conjectures that Jesus was then occupied with a particularly fruitful ministry in Peræa, which he was not willing to interrupt for the sake of Lazarus, holding it his duty to postpone his less important call as a worker of miracles and a succouring friend, to his higher call as a teacher [35]. But he might here have very well done the one, and not have left the other undone; he might either have left some disciples to carry forward his work in that country, or remaining there himself, have still cured Lazarus, whether through the medium of a disciple, or by the power of his will at a distance. Moreover, our narrator is entirely silent as to such a cause for the delay of Jesus. This view of it, therefore, can be listened to only on the supposition that no other motive for the delay is intimated by the evangelist, and even then as nothing more than a conjecture. Now another motive is clearly indicated, as Olshausen has remarked, in the declaration of Jesus, v. 15, that he is glad he was not present at the death of Lazarus, because, for the object of strengthening the faith of the disciples, the resurrection of his friend would be more effectual than his cure. Thus Jesus had designedly allowed Lazarus to die, that by his miraculous restoration to life, he might procure so much the more faith in himself. Tholuck and Olshausen on the whole put the same construction on this declaration of Jesus; but they confine themselves too completely to the moral point of view, when they speak of Jesus as designing, in his character of teacher, to perfect the spiritual condition of the family at Bethany and of his disciples [36]; since, according to expressions, such as ἵνα δοξασθῇ ὁ υἱὸς τ. θ. (v. 4), his design was rather the messianic one of spreading and confirming faith in himself as the Son of God, though principally, it is true, within that narrow circle. Here Lücke exclaims: by no means! never did the Saviour of the needy, the noblest friend of man, act thus arbitrarily and capriciously [37]; and De Wette also observes, that Jesus in no other instance designedly brings about or increases his miracles [38]. The former, as we have seen, concludes that something external, pre-

---

[35] Comm. 2, s. 376. Also Neander, s. 346.
[36] Tholuck, s. 202; Olshausen, 2, s. 260.
[37] Ut sup.
[38] Andachtsbuch, 1, s. 292 f. Exeg. Handb. 1, 3, s. 134.

occupation elsewhere, detained Jesus; a supposition which is contrary to the text, and which even De Wette finds inadequate, though he points out no other expedient. If then these critics are correct in maintaining that the real Jesus cannot have acted thus; while, on the other hand, they are incorrect in denying that the author of the fourth gospel makes his Jesus act thus: nothing remains but with the author of the Probabilia [39], from this incongruity of the Christ in John's gospel with the Christ alone conceivable as the real one, to conclude that the narrative of the fourth evangelist is unhistorical.

The alleged conduct of the disciples also, v. 12 f., is such as to excite surprise. If Jesus had represented to them, or at least to the three principal among them, the death of the daughter of Jairus as a mere sleep, how could they, when he said of Lazarus, *he sleeps, I will awake him*, κεκοίμηται, ἐξυπνίσω αὐτὸν, think that he referred to a natural sleep? One would not awake a patient out of a healthy sleep; hence it must have immediately occurred to the disciples that here sleep (κοίμησις) was spoken of in the same sense as in the case of the maiden. That, instead of this, the disciples understand the deep expressions of Jesus quite superficially, is entirely in the fourth evangelist's favourite manner, which we have learned to recognise by many examples. If tradition had in any way made known to him, that to speak of death as a sleep was part of the customary phraseology of Jesus, there would immediately spring up in his imagination, so fertile in this kind of antithesis, a misunderstanding corresponding to that figure of speech [40].

The observation of the Jews, v. 37, is scarcely conceivable, presupposing the truth of the synoptical resuscitations of the dead. The Jews appeal to the cure of the man born blind (John ix.), and draw the inference, that he who had restored sight to this individual, must surely have been able to avert the death of Lazarus. How came they to refer to this heterogeneous and

[39] S. 59 f. 79.
[40] Comp. de Wette, exeg. Handb. 1, 3, s. 135.

inadequate example, if there lay before them, in the two resuscitations of the dead, miracles more analogous, and adapted to give hope even in this case of actual death? It is certain that the Galilean resuscitations were prior to this of Lazarus, since Jesus after this period went no more into Galilee; neither could those events remain unknown in the capital [41], especially as we are expressly told that the fame of them *went abroad into all that land, throughout all Judæa, and throughout all the country round about.* To the real Jews therefore these cases must have been well known; and as the fourth evangelist makes his Jews refer to something less to the point, it is probable that he knew nothing of the above events: for that the reference belongs to him, and not to the Jews themselves, is evident from the fact, that he makes them refer to the very cure which he had last narrated.

A formidable difficulty lies also in the prayer which is put into the mouth of Jesus, v. 41 f. After thanking the Father for hearing his prayer, he adds, that for himself he knew well that the Father heard him always, and that he uttered this special thanksgiving only for the sake of the people around him, in order to obtain their belief in his divine mission. Thus he first gives his address a relation to God, and afterwards reduces this relation to a feigned one, intended to exist only in the conceptions of the people. Nor is the sense of the words such as Lücke represents it, namely, that Jesus for his own part would have prayed in silence, but for the benefit of the people uttered his prayer aloud (for in the certainty of fulfilment there lies no motive for silent prayer); they imply that for himself he had no need to thank the Father for a single result, as if surprised, since he was sure beforehand of having his wish granted, so

---

[41] This is what Neander maintains, L. J. Chr. s. 354. He objects that the fourth evangelist must in any case have known of resuscitations of the dead by Jesus, even supposing the narrative in question to be an unhistorical exaggeration. But this objection is refuted by the observation, that, as an inducement to the formation of such a narrative, the general tradition that Jesus had raised the dead would be sufficient, and an acquaintance with particular instances as exemplars was not at all requisite.

that the wish and the thanks were coincident; that is, to speak generally, his relation to the Father did not consist in single acts of prayer, fulfilment, and thanks, but in a continual and permanent interchange of these reciprocal functions, in which no single act of gratitude in and by itself could be distinguished in this manner. If it may be admitted that in relation to the necessities of the people, and out of sympathy with them, such an isolated act could have taken place on the part of Jesus; yet, if there be any truth in this explanation, Jesus must have been entirely borne away by sympathy, must have made the position of the people his own, and thus in that moment have prayed from his own impulse, and on his own behalf [42]. But, here, scarcely has he begun to pray when the reflection arises that he does this from no need of his own; he prays therefore from no lively feeling, but out of cold accommodation, and this must be felt difficult to conceive, nay, even revolting. He who in this manner prays solely for the edification of others, ought in no case to tell them that he prays from their point of view, not from his own; since an audible prayer cannot make any impression on the hearers, unless they suppose the speaker's whole soul to be engaged. How then could Jesus make his prayer ineffective by this addition? If he felt impelled to lay before God a confession of the true state of the case, he might have done this in silence; that he uttered the confession aloud, and that we in consequence read it, could only happen on a calculation of advantage to later Christendom, to the readers of the gospel. While the thanksgiving was, for obvious reasons, needful to awake the faith of the spectators, the more developed faith which the fourth gospel presupposes, might regard it as a difficulty; because it might possibly appear to proceed from a too subordinate, and more particularly, a too little constant relation between the Father and the Son. Consequently the prayer which was necessary for the hearers, must be annulled

---

[42] This argument applies also to De Wette, who, while acknowledging that such an idea would be unsuitable in the *mouth* of Jesus, supposes nevertheless that it was really in his *mind*.

for readers of a later period, or its value restricted to that of a mere accommodation. But this consideration cannot have been present in the mind of Jesus: it could belong only to a Christian who lived later. This has been already felt by one critic, who has hence proposed to throw v. 42 out of the text, as an unauthenticated addition by a later hand [43]. But as this judgment is destitute of any external reason, if the above passage could not have been uttered by Jesus, we must conclude that the evangelist only lent the words to Jesus in order to explain the preceding, v. 41; and to this opinion Lücke has shown himself not altogether disinclined [44]. Assuredly we have here words, which are only lent to Jesus by the evangelist: but if it be so with these words, what is our security that it is so *only* with these? In a gospel in which we have already detected many discourses to be merely lent to the alleged speakers—in a narrative which presents historical improbabilities at all points,—the difficulty contained in a single verse is not a sign that that verse does not belong to the rest, but that the whole taken together does not belong to the class of historical compositions [45].

As regards the gradation in the external testimony to the three narratives, it has already been justly observed by Woolston, that only the resurrection of the daughter of Jairus, in which the miraculous is the least marked, appears in three evangelists; the two others are each related by one evangelist only [46]: and as it is far less easy to understand the omission in the other gospels in relation to the resurrection of Lazarus, than in relation to the raising of the youth at Nain, there is here again a complete climax.

That the last-named event is mentioned by the author of Luke's gospel alone;—especially that Matthew and Mark have it not instead of the resuscitation of the daughter of Jairus, or

---

[43] Dieffenbach, über einige wahrscheinliche Interpolationen im Evangelium Johannis, in Bertholdt's krit. Journal, 5, s. 8 f.

[44] Comm. z. Joh., 1te Aufl., 2, s. 310.

[45] Thus the author of the Probabilia also argues, p. 61.

[46] Disc. 5.

together with that narrative,—is a difficulty in more than one respect [47]. Even viewed generally as a resuscitation of a dead person, one would have thought, as there were few of such miracles according to our gospels, and as they are highly calculated to carry conviction, it could not have been too much trouble to the evangelists to recount it as a second instance; especially as Matthew has thought it worth while, for example, to narrate three cures of blindness, which nevertheless were of far less importance, and of which, therefore, he might have spared two, inserting instead of them either one or the other of the remaining resuscitations of the dead. But admitting that the two first evangelists had some reason, no longer to be discovered, for not giving more than one history of a resurrection, they ought, one must think, to have chosen that of the youth at Nain far rather than that of the daughter of Jairus, because the former, as we have above observed, was a more indubitable and striking resurrection. As nevertheless they give only the latter, Matthew at least can have known nothing of the others; Mark, it is true, probably had it before him in Luke, but he had, as early as iii. 7. or 20. leaped from Luke vi. 12. (17.) to Matt. xii. 15; and only at iv. 35. (21 ff.) returns to Luke viii. 22. (16 ff.) [48]; thus passing over the resurrection of the youth (Luke vii. 11 ff.). But now arises the second question: how can the resurrection of the youth, if it really happened, have remained unknown to the author of the first gospel? Even apart from the supposition that this gospel had an apostolic origin, this question is fraught with no less difficulty than the former. Besides the people, there were present many of his disciples, μαθηταὶ ἱκανοὶ; the place, Nain, according to the account which Josephus gives of its position relative to Mount Tabor, cannot have been far from the ordinary Galilean theatre of the ministry of Jesus [49]; lastly, the fame of the event, as was natural, was widely disseminated (v. 17). Schleiermacher is

[47] Comp. Schleiermacher, über den Lukas, s. 103 ff.
[48] Saunier, über die quellen des Markus, s. 66 ff.
[49] Comp. Winer bibl. Realw. d. A.

of opinion that the authors of the first sketches from the life of Jesus, not being within the apostolic circle, did not generally venture to apply to the much occupied apostles, but rather sought the friends of Jesus of the second order, and in doing so they naturally turned to those places where they might hope for the richest harvests,—to Capernaum and Jerusalem ; events which, like the resuscitation in question, occurred in other places, could not so easily become common property. But first, this conception of the case is too subjective, making the promulgation of the most important deeds of Jesus, dependent on the researches of amateurs and collectors of anecdotes, who went about gleaning, like Papias, at a later period ; secondly, (and these two objections are essentially connected,) there lies at its foundation the erroneous idea that such histories were fixed, like inert bodies once fallen to the ground, in the places to which they belonged, guarded there as lifeless treasures, and only exhibited to those who took the trouble to resort to the spot : instead of which, they were rather like the light-winged inhabitants of the air, flying far away from the place which gave them birth, roaming everywhere, and not seldom losing all association with their original locality. We see the same thing happen daily ; innumerable histories, both true and false, are represented as having occurred at the most widely different places. Such a narrative, once formed, is itself the substance, the alleged locality, the accident : by no means can the locality be the substance, to which the narrative is united as the accident, as it would follow from Schleiermacher's supposition. Since then it cannot well be conceived that an incident of this kind, if it really happened, could remain foreign to the general tradition, and hence unknown to the author of the first gospel : the fact of this author's ignorance of the incident gives rise to a suspicion that it did not really happen.

But this ground of doubt falls with incomparably greater weight, on the narrative of the resurrection of Lazarus in the fourth gospel. If the authors or collectors of the three first gospels knew of this, they could not, for more than one reason, avoid introducing it into their writings. For, first, of all the resuscitations effected by Jesus, nay, of all his miracles, this resurrection of Lazarus, if not the most wonderful, is yet the one in which the marvellous presents itself the most obviously and strikingly, and which therefore, if its historical reality can be established, is a pre-eminently strong proof of the extraordinary endowments of Jesus as a divine messenger [50]; whence the evangelists, although they had related one or two other instances of the kind, could not think it superfluous to add this also. But, secondly, the resurrection of Lazarus had, according to the representation of John, a direct influence in the development of the fate of Jesus; for we learn from xi. 47 ff., that the increased resort to Jesus, and the credit which this event procured him, led to that consultation of the Sanhedrim in which the sanguinary counsel of Caiaphas was given and approved. Thus the event had a double importance—pragmatical as well as dogmatical; consequently, the synoptical writers could not have failed to narrate it, had it been within their knowledge. Nevertheless, theologians have found out all sorts of reasons why those evangelists, even had the fact been known to them, should refrain from its narration. Some have been of opinion that at the time of the composition of the three first gospels, the history was still in every mouth, so that to make a written record of it was superfluous [51]; others, on the contrary, have conjectured that it was thought desirable to guard against its further publication, lest danger should accrue to Lazarus and his family, the former of whom, according to John xii. 10., was persecuted by the Jewish hierarchy on account of the miracle which had been performed in him; a caution for which there was no necessity at the later period at which John wrote his gospel [52]. It is plain that these two reasons nullify each other, and neither of them is in itself worthy of a serious refutation; yet as similar modes of evading a difficulty are still more fre-

[50] Let the reader recollect the well-known expression of Spinoza.

[51] Whitby, Annot. in loc.

[52] Thus Grotius and Herder; Olshausen also adopts this explanation under the form of conjecture, 2, s. 256 f. Anm.

quently resorted to than might be supposed, we ought not to think some animadversion on them altogether thrown away. The proposition, that the resurrection of Lazarus was not recorded by the synoptists because it was generally known in their circle, proves too much; since on this rule, precisely the most important events in the life of Jesus, his baptism, death, and resurrection, must have remained unwritten. Moreover, writings, which, like our gospels, originate in a religious community, do not serve merely to make known the unknown; it is their office also to preserve what is already known. In opposition to the other explanation, it has been remarked by others, that the publication of this history among those who were not natives of Palestine, as was the case with those for whom Mark and Luke wrote, could have done no injury to Lazarus; and even the author of the first gospel, admitting that he wrote in and for Palestine, could hardly have withheld a fact in which the glory of Christ was so peculiarly manifested, merely out of consideration to Lazarus, who, supposing the more improbable case that he was yet living at the time of the composition of the first gospel, ought not, christian as he doubtless was, to refuse to suffer for the name of Christ; and the same observation would apply to his family. The most dangerous time for Lazarus according to John xii. 10, was that immediately after his resurrection, and a narrative which appeared so long after, could scarcely have heightened or renewed this danger; besides, in the neighbourhood of Bethany and Jerusalem whence danger was threatened to Lazarus, the event must have been so well-known and remembered that nothing was to be risked by its publication [53].

It appears then that the resurrection of Lazarus, since it is

---

[53] See these arguments dispersed in Paulus and Lücke on this chapter; in Gabler, ut sup. p. 238 ff; and Hase, L. J. § 119.—A new reason why Matthew in particular is silent on the resurrection of Lazarus, has been excogitated by Heydenreich, (über die Unzulässigkeit der mythischen Auffassung, 2tes Stück, s. 42.). The evangelist, he says, omitted it, because it required to be represented and treated with a tenderness and liveliness of feeling, of which he did not think himself capable. Hence, the modest man chose to avoid the history altogether rather than to deprive it by his manner of narration, of its proper pathos and sublimity.—Idle modesty truly !

not narrated by the synoptists, cannot have been known to them; and the question arises, how was this ignorance possible? Hase gives the mysterious answer, that the reason of this omission lies hid in the common relations under which the synoptists in general were silent concerning all the earlier incidents in Judæa; but this leaves it uncertain, at least so far as the expressions go, whether we ought to decide to the disadvantage of the fourth gospel or of its predecessors. The latest criticism of the gospel of Matthew has cleared up the ambiguity in Hase's answer after its usual manner, determining the nature of those common relations which he vaguely adduces, thus: Every one of the synoptists, by his ignorance of a history which an apostle must have known, betrays himself to be no apostle [54]. But this renunciation of the apostolic origin of the first gospel, does not by any means enable us to explain the ignorance of its author and his compeers of the resurrection of Lazarus. For besides the remarkable character of the event, its occurrence in the very heart of Judæa, the great attention excited by it, and its having been witnessed by the apostles,—all these considerations render it incomprehensible that it should not have entered into the general tradition, and from thence into the synoptical gospels. It is argued that these gospels are founded on Galilean legends, i. e. oral narratives and written notices by the Galilean friends and companions of Jesus; that these were not present at the resurrection of Lazarus, and therefore did not include it in their memoirs; and that the authors of the first gospels, strictly confining themselves to the Galilean sources of information, likewise passed over the event [55]. But there was not such a wall of partition between Galilee and Judæa, that the fame of an event like the resurrection of Lazarus could help sounding over from the one to the other. Even if it did not happen during a feast time, when (John iv. 45.) many Galileans might be eye-

---

[54] Schneckenburger, über den Urspr. s. 10.
[55] Gabler, ut sup. s. 240 f. ; also Neander, s. 357.

witnesses, yet the disciples, who were for the greater part Galileans, were present (v. 16), and must, so soon as they returned
into Galilee after the resurrection of Jesus, have spread abroad
the history throughout this province, or rather, before this, the
Galileans who kept the last passover attended by Jesus, must
have learned the event, the report of which was so rife in the
city. Hence even Lücke finds this explanation of Gabler's un-
satisfactory; and on his own side attempts to solve the enigma
by the observation, that the original evangelical tradition, which
the synoptists followed, did not represent the history of the
passion mainly in a pragmatical light, and therefore gave no heed
to this event as the secret motive of the murderous resolve
against Jesus, and that only John, who was initiated into the
secret history of the Sanhedrim, was in a condition to supply
this explanatory fact [56]. This view of the case would certainly
appear to neutralize one reason why the synoptists must have
noticed the event in question, namely, that drawn from its pragmatical importance; but when it is added, that as a miracle regarded in itself, apart from its more particular circumstances, it
might easily be lost among the rest of those narratives from
which we have in the three first gospels a partly accidental
selection,—we must reply, that the synoptical selection of miracles appears to be an accidental one only when that is at once
assumed which ought first to be proved: namely, that the
miracles in the fourth gospel are historical; and unless the selection be casual to a degree inconsistent with the slightest intelligence in the compilers, such a miracle cannot have been
overlooked [57].

[56] Comm. z. Joh. 2, s. 402.
[57] Comp. De Wette, exeg. Handb. 1, 3, s. 139. In Schleiermacher's Lectures on
the Life of Jesus, (if I may be permitted to refer to a work not yet printed,) the silence in question is explained in the following manner. The synoptical evangelists
in general were ignorant of the relations of Jesus with the family of Bethany, because
perhaps the apostles did not wish an intimate personal connexion of this kind to pass
into the general tradition, from which those evangelists drew; and ignorance of the
relations of Jesus with the family in general, of course included ignorance of this particular fact connected with them. But what motive could the apostles have for such

It has doubtless been these and similar considerations, which have led the latest writers on the controversy concerning the first gospel, to complain of the one-sidedness with which the above question is always answered to the disadvantage of the synoptists, especially Matthew, as if it were forgotten that an answer dangerous to the fourth gospel lies just as near at hand [58]. For our own part, we are not so greatly alarmed by the fulminations of Lücke, as to be deterred from the expression of our opinion on the subject. This theologian, even in his latest editions, reproaches those who, from the silence of the synoptical writers, conclude that this narrative is a fiction and the gospel of John not authentic, with an unparalleled lack of discernment, and a total want of insight into the mutual relations of our gospels (that is, into those relations viewed according to the professional conviction of theologians, which is unshaken even by the often well-directed attacks of the author of the Probabilia). We, nevertheless, distinctly declare that we regard the history of the resurrection of Lazarus, not only as in the highest degree improbable in itself, but also destitute of external evidence ; and this whole chapter, in connexion with those previously examined, as an indication of the unauthenticity of the fourth gospel.

If it is thus proved that all the three evangelical histories of resuscitations are rendered more or less doubtful by negative reasons : all that is now wanting to us is positive proof, that

reserve ? Are we to infer secret, or even, with Venturini, tender ties? Must not such a private relation in the case of Jesus have presented much to edify us ? The intimations which John and Luke afford us on this subject contain in fact much of this description, and from the narrative which the latter gives of the visit of Jesus to Martha and Mary, we see also that the apostles, in furnishing their accounts, were by no means averse to allow something of these relations to appear, so far as they could retain a general interest.   Now in this light, the resurrection of Lazarus, as a pre-eminent miracle, was incomparably more valuable than that visit with its single aphorism " One thing is needful," and involved less of the private relations of Jesus with the family of Bethany ; the supposed effort to keep these secret, could not therefore have hindered the promulgation of the resurrection of Lazarus.

[58] Kern, über den Ursprung des Evang. Matth. Tübing. Zeitschrift, 1834, 2, s. 110.

the tradition of Jesus having raised the dead might easily be formed without historical foundation. According to rabbinical [59], as well as New Testament passages (e. g. John v. 28 f.; vi. 40, 44; 1 Cor. xv.; 1 Thess. iv. 16), the resuscitation of the dead was expected of the Messiah at his coming. Now the παρουσία, the appearance of the Messiah Jesus on earth, was in the view of the early church broken by his death into two parts; the first comprised his preparatory appearance, which began with his human birth, and ended with the resurrection and ascension; the second was to commence with his future advent on the clouds of heaven, in order to open the αἰὼν μέλλων, *the age to come.* As the first appearance of Jesus had wanted the glory and majesty expected in the Messiah, the great demonstrations of messianic power, and in particular the general resurrection of the dead, were assigned to his second, and as yet future appearance on earth.   Nevertheless, as an immediate pledge of what was to be anticipated, even in the first advent some fore-splendours of the second must have been visible in single instances; Jesus must, even in his first advent, by awaking some of the dead, have guaranteed his authority one day to awake all the dead; he must, when questioned as to his messiahship, have been able to adduce among other criteria the fact that the dead were raised up by him (Matt. xi. 5.), and he must have imparted the same power to his disciples (Matt. xi. 8, comp. Acts ix. 40; xx. 10.); but especially as a close prefiguration of the hour *in which all that are in their graves shall hear his voice, and shall come forth* (John v. 28 f.), he must have *cried with a loud voice, Come forth!* to one who *had lain in the grave four days* (John xi. 17, 43).   For the origination of detailed narratives of single resuscitations, there lay, besides, the most appropriate types in the Old Testament. The prophets Elijah and Elisha (1 Kings xvii. 17 ff.; 2 Kings iv. 18 ff.) had awaked the dead, and to these instances Jewish writings appealed as a type of the messianic time [60].   The

---

[59] Bertholdt, Christol. Jud. § 35.

[60] See the passages quoted from Tanchuma, Vol. I. § 14.

object of the resuscitation was with both these prophets a child,
but a boy, while in the narrative common to the synoptists
we have a girl; the two prophets revived him while he
lay on the bed, as Jesus does the daughter of Jairus; both
entered alone into the chamber of death, as Jesus excludes all
save a few confidential friends; only, as it is fitting, the Messiah
needs not the laborious manipulations by which the prophets
attained their object. Elijah in particular raised the son of a
widow, as Jesus did at Nain; he met the widow of Zarephath
at the gate (but before the death of her son) as Jesus met the
widow of Nain, under the gate of the city (after the death of her
son); lastly, it is in both instances told in the same words
how the miracle-worker restored the son to the mother [61]. Even
one already laid in his grave, like Lazarus, was restored to life
by the prophet Elisha; with this difference, however, that the
prophet himself had been long dead, and the contact of his bones
reanimated a corpse which was accidently thrown upon them
(2 Kings xiii. 21). There is yet another point of similarity
between the resuscitations of the dead in the Old Testament and
that of Lazarus; it is that Jesus, while in his former resuscitation he utters the authoritative word without any preliminary,
in that of Lazarus offers a prayer to God, as Elisha, and more
particularly Elijah, are said to have done. While Paulus extends to these narratives in the Old Testament, the natural
explanation which he has applied to those in the New, theologians of more enlarged views have long ago remarked, that the
resurrections in the New Testament are nothing more than
mythi, which had their origin in the tendency of the early
Christian church, to make her Messiah agree with the type of
the prophets, and with the messianic ideal [62].

[61] 1 Kings xvii. 23. LXX : καὶ ἔδωκεν αὐτό τῇ μητρὶ αὐτοῦ, Luke vii. 15 : καὶ
ἔδωκεν αὐτὸν τῇ μητρὶ αὐτοῦ.
[62] Thus the author of the Abhandlung über die verschiedenen Rücksichten, in
welchen der Biograph Jesu arbeiten kann, in Bertholdt's krit. Journ., 5, s. 237 f.
Kaiser, bibl. Theol. 1, s. 202.—A resuscitation strikingly similar to that of the
young man at Nain is narrated by Philostratus, of Apollonius of Tyana. "As according to Luke, it was a young man, the only son of a widow, who was being car-

§ 101.

As in general, at least according to the representations of the three first evangelists, the country around the Galilean sea was the chief theatre of the ministry of Jesus; so a considerable number of his miracles have an immediate reference to the sea. One of this class, the miraculous draught of fishes granted to Peter, has already presented itself for our consideration; besides this, there are the miraculous stilling of the storm which had arisen on the sea while Jesus slept, in the three synoptists; Matthew, Mark, and John; the summary of most of those the walking of Jesus on the sea, likewise during a storm, in incidents which the appendix to the fourth gospel places after the resurrection; and lastly, the anecdote of the coin that was to be angled for by Peter, in Matthew.

The first-named narrative (Matt. viii. 23 ff. parall.) is intended, according to the evangelist's own words, to represent Jesus to us as him whom *the winds and the sea obey* οἱ ἄνεμοι καὶ ἡ θάλασσα ὑπακούουσιν.   Thus, to follow out the gradation in the miraculous which has been hitherto observed, it is here presupposed, not merely that Jesus could act on the human mind and living body in a psychological and magnetic manner; or with a revivifying power on the human organism when it was forsaken by vitality; nay, not merely as in the history of the

---

ried out of the city; so, in Philostratus, it is a young maiden already betrothed, whose bier Apollonius meets.   The command to set down the bier, the mere touch, and a few words, are sufficient here, as there, to bring the dead to life" (Baur, Apollonius v. Tyana und Christus, s. 145).   I should like to know whether Paulus, or any other critic, would be inclined to explain this naturally; if, however, it ought to be regarded as an imitation of the evangelical narrative, (a conclusion which can hardly be avoided,) we must have a preconceived opinion of the character of the books of the New Testament, to evade the consequence, that the resuscitations of the dead which they contain are only less designed imitations of those in the Old Testament; which are themselves to be derived from the belief of antiquity, that a victorious power over death was imparted to the favourites of the gods, (Hercules, Esculapius, &c.,) and more immediately, from the Jewish idea of a prophet.

draught of fishes earlier examined, that he could act immediately with determinative power, on irrational yet animated
existences, but that he could act thus even on inanimate nature. The possibility of finding a point of union between the
alleged supernatural agency of Jesus, and the natural order of
phenomena, here absolutely ceases : here, at the latest, there is
an end to miracles in the wider and now more favoured sense ;
and we come to those which must be taken in the narrowest
sense, or to the miracle proper. The purely supranaturalistic
view is therefore the first to suggest itself. Olshausen has
justly felt, that such a power over external nature is not essentially connected with the destination of Jesus for the human
race and for the salvation of man ; whence he was led to place
the natural phenomenon which is here controlled by Jesus in a
relation to sin, and therefore to the office of Jesus. Storms, he
says, are the spasms and convulsions of nature, and as such the
consequences of sin, the fearful effects of which are seen even on
the physical side of existence[1]. But it is only that limited observation of nature which in noting the particular forgets the
general, that can regard storms, tempests, and similar phenomena, (which in connexion with the whole have their necessary place and beneficial influence,) as evils and departure from
original law : and a theory of the world in which it is seriously
upheld, that before the fall there were no storms and tempests,
as, on the other hand, no beasts of prey and poisonous plants,
partakes—one does not know whether to say, of the fanatical,
or of the childish. But to what purpose, if the above explanation will not hold, could Jesus be gifted with such a power over
nature ? As a means of awakening faith in him, it was inadequate and superfluous : because Jesus found individual adherents without any demonstration of a power of this kind, and
general acceptance even this did not procure him. As little can
it be regarded as a type of the original dominion of man over
external nature, a dominion which he is destined to re-attain ;

[1] Bibl. Comm. 1, s. 287.

for the value of this dominion consists precisely in this, that it is a mediate one, achieved by the progressive reflection and the united efforts of ages, not an immediate and magical dominion, which costs no more than a word. Hence in relation to that part of nature of which we are here speaking, the compass and the steam-vessel are an incomparably truer realization of man's dominion over the ocean, than the allaying of the waves by a mere word. But the subject has another aspect, since the dominion of man over nature is not merely external and practical, but also immanent or theoretical; that is, man even when externally he is subjected to the might of the elements, yet is not internally conquered by them; but, in the conviction that the powers of physical nature can only destroy in him that which belongs to his physical existence, is elevated in the self-certainty of the spirit above the possible destruction of the body. This spiritual power, it is said, was exhibited by Jesus, for he slept tranquilly in the midst of the storm, and when awaked by his trembling disciples, inspired them with courage by his words. But for courage to be shown, real danger must be apprehended: now for Jesus, supposing him to be conscious of an immediate power over nature, danger could in no degree exist: therefore he could not here give any proof of this theoretical power.

In both respects the natural explanation would find only the conceivable and the desirable attributed to Jesus in the evangelical narrative; namely, on the one hand, an intelligent observation of the state of the weather, and on the other, exalted courage in the presence of real peril. When we read that Jesus *commanded the winds* ἐπιτιμᾷν τοῖς ἀνέμοις, we are to understand simply that he made some remark on the storm, or some exclamations at its violence: and his calming of the sea we are to regard only as a prognostication, founded on the observation of certain signs, that the storm would soon subside. His address to the disciples is said to have proceeded, like the celebrated saying of Cæsar, from the confidence that a man who was to leave an impress on the world's history, could not so lightly be cut short in his career by an accident. That those who were in the ship regarded the subsidence of the storm as the effect of the words of Jesus, proves nothing, for Jesus nowhere confirms their inference[2]. But neither does he disapprove it, although he must have observed the impression which, in consequence of that inference, the result had made on the people;[3] he must therefore, as Venturini actually supposes, have designedly refrained from shaking their high opinion of his miraculous power, in order to attach them to him the more firmly. But, setting this altogether aside, was it likely that the natural presages of the storm should have been better understood by Jesus, who had never been occupied on the sea, than by Peter, James, and John, who had been at home on it from their youth upwards[4]?

It remains then that, taking the incident as it is narrated by the evangelists, we must regard it as a miracle: but to raise this from an exegetical result to a real fact, is, according to the above remarks, extremely difficult: whence there arises a suspicion against the historical character of the narrative. Viewed more nearly however, and taking Matthew's account as the basis, there is nothing to object to the narrative until the middle of v. 26. It might really have happened that Jesus in one of his frequent passages across the Galilean sea, was sleeping when a storm arose; that the disciples awaked him with alarm, while he, calm and self-possessed, said to them, *Why are ye fearful, O ye of little faith?* What follows—the commanding of the waves, which Mark with his well-known fondness for such authoritative words, reproduces as if he were giving the exact words of Jesus in a Greek translation ($\sigma\iota\acute{\omega}\pi\alpha, \pi\epsilon\phi\acute{\iota}\mu\omega\sigma o$!)—might have been added in the propagation of the anecdote from one to another. There was an inducement to attribute to Jesus such a command over the winds and the sea, not only in the

[2] Thus Paulus, exeg. Handb., 1, b. s. 468 ff.; Venturini, 2, s. 166 ff.; Kaiser, bibl. Theol. 1, s. 197. Hase, also, § 74, thinks this view probable.

[3] Neander, L. J. Chr., s. 363, who for the rest here offers but a weak defence against the natural explanation.

[4] Hase, ut sup.

c c 2

opinion entertained of his person, but also in certain features of the Old Testament history. Here, in poetical descriptions of the passage of the Israelites through the Red Sea, Jehovah is designated as he who *rebuked the Red Sea,* ἐπετίμησε τῆ ἐρυθρᾶ θαλάσσῃ, (Psa. cvi. 9 ; LXX. comp. Nahum i. 4,) so that it retreated. Now, as the instrument in this partition of the Red Sea was Moses, it was natural to ascribe to his great successor, the Messiah, a similar function ; accordingly we actually find from rabbinical passages, that a drying up of the sea was expected to be wrought by God in the messianic times, doubtless through the agency of the Messiah, as formerly through that of Moses [5]. That instead of drying up the sea Jesus is said only to produce a calm, may be explained, on the supposition that the storm and the composure exhibited by Jesus on the occasion were historical, as a consequence of the mythical hav ing combined itself with this historical element ; for, as according to this, Jesus and his disciples were on board a ship, a drying up of the sea would have been out of place.

Still it is altogether without any sure precedent, that a mythical addition should be engrafted on the stem of a real incident, so as to leave the latter totally unmodified. And there is one feature, even in the part hitherto assumed to be historical, which, more narrowly examined, might just as probably have been invented by the legend as have really happened. That Jesus, before the storm breaks out, is sleeping, and even when it arises, does not immediately awake, is not his voluntary deed, but chance [6] ; it is this very chance, however, which alone gives the scene its full significance, for Jesus sleeping in

---

[5] Vid. Vol. 1, § 14, note 9.

[6] Neander alters the fact, when he describes Jesus as falling asleep in the midst of the fury of the storm and the waves, and thus manifesting a tranquillity of soul which no terror of nature could disturb (s. 362.).   Luke says expressly, *as they sailed he fell asleep: and there came down a storm,* &c., πλεόντων δὲ αὐτῶν ἀφύπνωσε· καὶ κατέβη λαῖλαψ κ. τ. λ., and according to the representation of the other evangelists also, the sleeping of Jesus appears to have preceded the breaking out of the storm, since otherwise the timorous disciples would not have awaked him—they would rather not have allowed him to go to sleep.

the storm is by the contrast which he presents, a not less emblematical image than Ulysses sleeping when, after so many storms, he was about to land on his island home. Now that Jesus really slept at the time that a storm broke out, may indeed have happened by chance in one case out of ten; but in the nine cases also, when this did not happen, and Jesus only showed himself calm and courageous during the storm, I am inclined to think that the legend would so far have understood her interest, that, as she had represented the contrast of the tranquillity of Jesus with the raging of the elements to the intellect, by means of the words of Jesus, so she would depict it for the imagination, by means of the image of Jesus sleeping in the ship (or as Mark has it [7], on a pillow in the hinder part of the ship). If then that which may possibly have happened in a single case, must certainly have been invented by the legend in nine cases; the expositor must in reason prepare himself for the undeniable possibility, that we have before us one of the nine cases, instead of that single case [8]. If then it be granted that nothing further remains as an historical foundation for our narrative, than that Jesus exhorted his disciples to show the firm courage of faith in opposition to the raging waves of the sea, it is certainly possible that he may once have done this in a storm at sea; but just as he said: if ye have faith as a grain of mustard seed, ye may say to this mountain, Be thou removed and cast into the sea (Matt. xxi. 21.), or to this tree, Be thou plucked up by the root, and be thou planted in the sea (Luke xvii. 6.), and both shall be done (καὶ ὑπήκουσεν ἂν ὑμῖν, Luke): so he might, not merely on the sea, but in any situation, make use of the figure, that to him who has faith, winds and waves shall be obedient at a word (ὅτι καὶ τοῖς ἀνέμοις ἐπιτάσσει καὶ τῷ ὕδατι, καὶ ὑπακούουσιν αὐτῷ, Luke). If we now take into account what even Olshausen remarks, and Schneckenburger

[7] Comp. Saunier, über die Quellen des Markus, s. 82.

[8] This may serve as an answer to Tholuck's accusation, Glaubwürdigkeit, s. 110.

has shown [9], that the contest of the kingdom of God with the world was in the early times of Christianity commonly compared to a voyage through a stormy ocean; we see at once, how easily legend might come to frame such a narrative as the above, on the suggestions afforded by the parallel between the Messiah and Moses, the expressions of Jesus, and the conception of him as the pilot who steers the little vessel of the kingdom of God through the tumultuous waves of the world. Setting this aside, however, and viewing the matter only generally, in relation to the idea of a miracle-worker, we find a similar power over storms and tempests, ascribed, for example, to Pythagoras [10].

We have a more complicated anecdote connected with the sea, wanting in Luke, but contained in John vi. 16 ff., as well as in Matt. xiv. 22 ff., and Mark vi. 45 ff., where a storm overtakes the disciples when sailing by night, and Jesus appears to their rescue, walking towards them on the sea. Here, again, the storm subsides in a marvellous manner on the entrance of Jesus into the ship; but the peculiar difficulty of the narrative lies in this, that the body of Jesus appears so entirely exempt from a law which governs all other human bodies without exception, namely, the law of gravitation, that he not only does not sink under the water, but does not even dip into it; on the contrary, he walks erect on the waves as on firm land. If we are to represent this to ourselves, we must in some way or other, conceive the body of Jesus as an etherial phantom, according to the opinion of the Docetæ; a conception which, the Fathers of the Church condemned as irreligious, and which we must reject as extravagant. Olshausen indeed says, that in a superior corporeality, impregnated with the powers of a higher

---

[9] Ueber den Ursprung, u. s. f. s. 68 f.

[10] According to Jamblich. vita Pyth. 135, ed. Kiessling, there were narrated of Pythagoras, ἀνέμων βιαίων χαλαζῶν τε χύσεως παραυτίκα κατευνήσεις καὶ κυμάτων ποταμίων τε καὶ θαλασσίων ἀπευδιασμοὶ πρὸς εὐμαρῆ τῶν ἑταίρων διάβασιν, *instantaneous tranquillizings of violent winds and hailstorms, and soothings of the waves of rivers and seas, to afford easy transit to his companions.* Comp. Porphyr. v. p. 29 same ed.

world, such an appearance need not create surprise[11] : but these
are words to which we can attach no definite idea.   If the
spiritual activity of Jesus which refined and perfected his corporeal nature, instead of being conceived as that which more
and more completely emancipated his body from the psychical
laws of passion and sensuality, is understood as if by its means
the body was exempted from the physical law of gravity:—this
is a materialism of which, as in a former case, it is difficult to
decide whether it be more fantastical or childish.   If Jesus
did not sink in the water, he must have been a spectre, and the
disciples in our narrative would not have been wrong in taking
him for one.   We must also recollect that on his baptism in
the river Jordan, Jesus did not exhibit this property, but was
submerged like an ordinary man.   Now had he at that time
also the power of sustaining himself on the surface of the
water, and only refrained from using it ? and did he thus increase or reduce his specific gravity by an act of his will ? or
are we to suppose, as Olshausen would perhaps say, that at the
time of his baptism he had not attained so far in the process of
subtilizing his body, as to be freely borne up by the water, and
that he only reached this point at a later period ?   These are
questions which Olshausen justly calls absurd : nevertheless
they serve to open a glimpse into the abyss of absurdities in
which we are involved by the supranaturalistic interpretation,
and particularly by that which this theologian gives of the
narrative before us.

To avoid these, the natural explanation has tried many expedients.   The boldest is that of Paulus, who maintains that
the text does not state that Jesus walked on the water ; and
that the miracle in this passage is nothing but a philological
mistake, since περιπατεῖν ἐπὶ τῆς θαλάσσης is analogous to the
expression στρατοπεδεύειν ἐπὶ τῆς θαλάσσης, Exod. xiv. 2, and signifies to walk, as the other to encamp, over the sea, that is, on

[11] Ut sup. s. 491.

the elevated sea-shore [12]. According to the meaning of the words taken separately, this explanation is possible : its real applicability in this particular instance, however, must be determined by the context. Now this represents the disciples as having rowed twenty-five or thirty furlongs (John), or as being in the midst of the sea (Matthew and Mark), and then it is said that Jesus came towards the ship, and so near that he could speak to them, περιπατῶν ἐπὶ τῆς θαλάσσης. How could he do this if he remained on the shore ? To obviate this objection, Paulus conjectures that the disciples in that stormy night probably only skirted the shore ; but the words ἐν μέσῳ τῆς θαλάσσης, in the midst of the sea, though not, we grant, to be construed with mathematical strictness, yet, even taken according to the popular mode of speaking, are too decidedly opposed to such a supposition, for it to be worth our further consideration. But this mode of interpretation encounters a fatal blow in the passage where Matthew says of Peter, that having come down out of the ship he walked on the water, καταβὰς ἀπὸ τοῦ πλοίου περιεπάτησεν ἐπὶ τὰ ὕδατα (v. 29) ; for as it is said shortly after that Peter began to sink (καταποντίζεσθαι), walking merely on the shore cannot have been intended here ; and if not here, neither can it have been intended in the former instance relating to Jesus, the expressions being substantially the same [13].

But if Peter, in his attempt to walk upon the waters, περιπατεῖν ἐπὶ τὰ ὕδατα, began to sink, may we not still suppose that both he and Jesus merely swam in the sea, or waded through its shallows? Both these suppositions have actually been advanced [14]. But the act of wading must have been expressed by περιπατεῖν διὰ τῆς θαλάσσης, and had that of swim-

[12] Paulus, Memorabilien, 6, Stück, No. V. ; exeg. Handb. 2, s. 238 ff.

[13] Against the extremely arbitrary expedient which Paulus has here adopted, see Storr, Opusc. acad. 3, p. 288.

[14] The former by Bolten, Bericht des Matthäus, in loc ; the latter in Henke's neuem Magazin, 6, 2, s. 327 ff.

ming been intended, one or other of the parallel passages would
certainly have substituted the precise expression for the ambiguous one : besides, it must be alike impossible either to
swim from twenty-five to thirty furlongs in a storm, or to wade
to about the middle of the sea, which certainly was beyond the
shallows; a swimmer could not easily be taken for a spectre ; and lastly, the prayer of Peter for special permission
to imitate Jesus, and his failure in it from want of faith, point
to something supernatural [15].

The reasoning on which the natural mode of interpretation
rests here as elsewhere, has been enunciated by Paulus in connexion with this passage in a form which reveals its fundamental error in a particularly happy manner.   The question, he
says, in such cases is always this : which is more probable, that
the evangelical writer should use an expression not perfectly
exact, or that there should be a departure from the course of nature ?   It is evident that the dilemma is falsely stated, and
should rather be put thus : Is it more probable that the author
should express himself inaccurately, (rather, in direct contradiction to the supposed sense,) or that he should mean to narrate a departure from the course of nature ?   For only what he
means to narrate is the immediate point of inquiry ; what really
happened is, even according to the distinction of the judgment
of a writer from the fact that he states, on which Paulus ever-
lastingly insists, an altogether different question.   Because according to our views a departure from the course of nature cannot have taken place, it by no means follows, that a writer
belonging to the primitive age of Christianity could not have
credited and narrated such a case [16] ; and therefore to abolish
the miraculous, we must not explain it away from the narrative,
but rather inquire whether the narrative itself, either in whole
or in part, must not be excluded from the domain of history.
In relation to this inquiry, first of all, each of our three ac-

---

[15] Comp. Paulus and Fritzsche, in loc.
[16] See the excellent passage in Fritzsche, Comm. in Matth. p. 505.

counts has peculiar features which in an historical light are
suspicious.

The most striking of these features is found in Mark v.
48, where he says of Jesus that he came walking on the sea towards
the disciples, *and would have passed by them*, καὶ ἤθελε παρελθεῖν
αὐτούς, but that he was constrained by their anxious cries to
take notice of them. With justice Fritzsche interprets Mark's
meaning to be, that it was the intention of Jesus, supported by
divine power, to walk across the whole sea as on firm land.
But with equal justice Paulus asks, Could anything have been
more useless and extravagant than to perform so singular a
miracle without any eye to witness it? We must not however
on this account, with the latter theologian, interpret the words
of Mark as implying a natural event, namely, that Jesus, being
on the land, was going to pass by the disciples who were sailing
in a ship not far from the shore, for the miraculous interpretation
of the passage is perfectly accordant with the spirit of our evangelist. Not contented with the representation of his informant,
that Jesus, on this one occasion, adopted this extraordinary
mode of progress with special reference to his disciples, he
aims by the above addition to convey the idea of walking on
the water being so natural and customary with Jesus, that without any regard to the disciples, whenever a sheet of water lay
in his road, he walked across it as unconcernedly, as if it had
been dry land. But such a mode of procedure, if habitual with
Jesus, would presuppose most decidedly a subtilization of his
body such as Olshausen supposes; it would therefore presuppose what is inconceivable. Hence this particular of Mark's
presents itself as one of the most striking among those, by
which the second evangelist now and then approaches to the
exaggerations of the apocryphal gospels [17].

In Matthew, the miracle is in a different manner, not so

---

[17] Mark's inclination to exaggerate shows itself also in his concluding sentence, v.
51, (comp. vii. 37) : *and they were sore amazed in themselves beyond measure and
wondered ;* which will scarcely be understood to import, as Paulus supposes (2, s.
266), a disapproval of the excessive astonishment.

much heightened as complicated; for there, not only Jesus, but Peter also makes an experiment in walking on the sea, not indeed altogether successful. This trait is rendered suspicious by its intrinsic character, as well as by the silence of the two other narrators. Immediately on the word of Jesus, and in virtue of the faith which he has in the beginning, Peter actually succeeds in walking on the water for some time, and only when he is assailed by fear and doubt does he begin to sink. What are we to think of this? Admitting that Jesus, by means of his etherialized body, could walk on the water, how could he command Peter, who was not gifted with such a body, to do the same? or if by a mere word he could give the body of Peter a dispensation from the law of gravitation, can he have been a man? and if a God, would he thus lightly cause a suspension of natural laws at the caprice of a man? or lastly, are we to suppose that faith has the power instantaneously to lessen the specific gravity of the body of a believer? Faith is certainly said to have such a power in the figurative discourse of Jesus just referred to, according to which, the believer is able to remove mountains and trees into the sea,—and why not also himself to walk on the sea? The moral that as soon as faith falters, power ceases, could not be so aptly presented by either of the two former figures as by the latter, in the following form: as long as a man has faith he is able to walk unharmed on the unstable sea, but no sooner does he give way to doubt than he sinks, unless Christ extend to him a helping hand. The fundamental thought, then, of Matthew's episodical narrative is, that Peter was too confident in the firmness of his faith, that by its sudden failure he incurred great danger, but was rescued by Jesus; a thought which is actually expressed in Luke xxii. 31 f. where Jesus says to Simon: *Satan hath desired to have you that he may sift you as wheat; but I have prayed for thee that thy faith fail not.* These words of Jesus have reference to Peter's coming denial: this was the occasion when his faith, on the strength of which he had just before offered to go with Jesus to prison and to death, would have wavered, had not the Lord by

his intercession, procured him new strength.   If we add to this
the above-mentioned habit of the early Christians to represent the
persecuting world under the image of a turbulent sea, we cannot fail, with one of the latest critics, to perceive in the description of Peter courageously volunteering to walk on the sea,
soon, however, sinking from faintheartedness, but borne up by
Jesus, an allegorical and mythical representation of that trial
of faith which this disciple who imagined himself so strong,
met so weakly, and which higher assistance alone enabled him
to surmount [18].

But the account of the fourth gospel also is not wanting in
peculiar features, which betray an unhistorical character.   It
has ever been a cross to harmonists, that while according to
Matthew and Mark, the ship was only in the middle of the sea
when Jesus reached it : according to John, it immediately after
arrived at the opposite shore; that while, according to the
former, Jesus actually entered into the ship, and the storm
thereupon subsided : according to John, on the contrary, the
disciples did indeed wish to take him into the ship, but their
actually doing so was rendered superfluous by their immediate
arrival at the place of disembarkation.   It is true that here also
abundant methods of reconciliation have been found.   First,
the word ἤθελον, *they wished*, added to λαβεῖν, *to receive*, is said
to be a mere redundancy of expression ; then, to signify simply
the joyfulness of the reception, as if it had been said. ἐθέλοντες
ἔλαβον ; then, to describe the first impression which the recognition of Jesus made on the disciples, his reception into the
ship, which really followed, not being mentioned [19].   But the
sole reason for such an interpretation lies in the unauthorized
comparison with the synoptical accounts : in the narrative of
John, taken separately, there is no ground for it, nay, it is excluded.   For the succeeding sentence : εὐθέως τὸ πλοῖον ἐγένετο
ἐπὶ τῆς γῆς, εἰς ἣν ὑπῆγον, *immediately the ship was at the land*

[18] Schneckenburger, über den Ursprung u. s. f. s. 68 f. ; Weisse, die evang. Geschichte, 1, s. 521.

[19] Vid. Lücke and Tholuck.

whither they went, though it is united, not by δὲ but by καὶ, can nevertheless only be taken antithetically, in the sense that the reception of Jesus into the ship, notwithstanding the readiness of the disciples, did not really take place, because they were already at the shore. In consideration of this difference, Chrysostom held that there were two occasions on which Jesus walked on the sea. He says that on the second occasion, which John narrates, Jesus did not enter into the ship, *in order that the miracle might be greater* ἵνα τὸ θαῦμα μεῖζον ἐργάσηται [20]. This view we may transfer to the evangelist, and say: if Mark has aggrandized the miracle, by implying that Jesus intended to walk past the disciples across the entire sea; so John goes yet farther, for he makes him actually accomplish this design, and without being taken into the ship, arrive at the opposite shore [21]. Not only, however, does the fourth evangelist seek to aggrandize the miracle before us, but also to establish and authenticate it more securely. According to the synoptists, the sole witnesses were the disciples, who saw Jesus come towards them, walking on the sea: John adds to these few immediate witnesses, a multitude of mediate ones, namely, the people who were assembled when Jesus performed the miracle of the loaves and fishes. These, when on the following morning they no longer find Jesus on the same spot, make the calculation, that Jesus cannot have crossed the sea by ship, for he did not get into the same boat with the disciples, and no other boat was there (v. 22); while, that he did not go by land, is involved in the circumstance that the people when they have forthwith crossed the sea, find him on the opposite shore (v. 25), whither he could hardly have arrived by land in the short interval. Thus in the narrative of the fourth gospel, as all natural means of passage are cut off from Jesus, there re-

---

[20] Homil. in Joann. 43.

[21] In De Wette's objection, that the opinion of an exaggeration of the miracle in John, is discountenanced by the addition that they were immediately at the land (ex. Handb. 1, 3, s. 79,) there appears to me only a misunderstanding : but his assertion that in John the manner in which Jesus goes over the sea is not represented as a miracle, (s. 78,) is to me thoroughly incomprehensible.

mains for him only a supernatural one, and this consequence
is in fact inferred by the multitude in the astonished question
which they put to Jesus, when they find him on the opposite
shore: *Rabbi, when camest thou hither?* As this chain of
evidence for the miraculous passage of Jesus depends on the
rapid transportation of the multitude, the evangelist hastens to
procure *other boats* ἄλλα πλοιάρια for their service (v. 23).
Now the multitude who take ship (v. 22, 26 ff.) are described as
the same whom Jesus had miraculously fed, and these amounted
(according to v. 10) to about 5000.   If only a fifth, nay, a
tenth of these passed over, there needed for this, as the author
of the Probabilia has justly observed, a whole fleet of ships,
especially if they were fishing boats; but even if we suppose
them vessels of freight, these would not all have been bound
for Capernaum, or have changed their destination for the sake
of accommodating the crowd.   This passage of the multitude,
therefore, appears only to have been invented[22], on the one
hand, to confirm by their evidence the walking of Jesus on the
sea; on the other, as we shall presently see, to gain an opportunity for making Jesus, who according to the tradition had
gone over to the opposite shore immediately after the multiplication of the loaves, speak yet further with the multitude on
the subject of this miracle.

After pruning away these offshoots of the miraculous which
are peculiar to the respective narratives, the main stem is still
left, namely, the miracle of Jesus walking on the sea for a considerable distance, with all its attendant improbabilities as above
exposed.   But the solution of these accessory particulars, as it
led us to discover the causes of their unhistorical origin, has
facilitated the discovery of such causes for the main narrative,
and has thereby rendered possible the solution of this also.   We
have seen, by an example already adduced, that it was usual
with the Hebrews and early Christians, to represent the power
of God over nature, a power which the human spirit when

---

[22] Bretschneider, Probab p. 81.

united to him was supposed to share, under the image of supremacy over the raging waves of the sea.   In the narrative of the Exodus this supremacy is manifested by the sea being driven out of its place at a sign, so that a dry path is opened to the people of God in its bed; in the New Testament narrative previously considered, the sea is not removed out of its place, but only so far laid to rest that Jesus and his disciples can cross it in safety in their ship : in the anecdote before us, the sea still remains in its place as in the second, but there is this point of similarity to the first, that the passage is made on foot, not by ship, yet as a necessary consequence of the other particular, on the surface of the sea, not in its bed. Still more immediate inducements to develop in such a manner the conception of the power of the miracle-worker over the waves, may be found both in the Old Testament, and in the opinions prevalent in the time of Jesus.   Among the miracles of Elisha, it is not only told that he divided the Jordan by a stroke of his mantle, so that he could go through it dry shod (2 Kings ii. 14.), but also that he caused a piece of iron which had fallen into the water to swim (2 Kings vi. 6.) ; an ascendancy over the law of gravitation which it would be imagined the miracle-worker might be able to evince in relation to his own body also, and thus to exhibit himself, as it is said of Jehovah Job ix. 8, LXX., περιπατῶν ὡς ἐπ' ἐδάφους ἐπὶ θαλάσσης, *walking upon the sea as upon a pavement.*   In the time of Jesus much was told of miracle-workers who could walk on the water. Apart from conceptions exclusively Grecian [23], the Greco-oriental legend feigned that the hyperborean Abaris possessed an arrow, by means of which he could bear himself up in the air, and thus traverse rivers, seas, and abysses [24], and popular superstition attributed to many wonder-workers the power of walking on water [25].   Hence the possibility that with all these elements and inducements existing, a similar legend should be formed

[23] See the passages in Wetstein, p. 417 f.
[24] Jamblich, vita Pythagoræ, 136 ; comp. Porphyr. 29.
[25] Lucian. Philopseudes, 13.

concerning Jesus, appears incomparably stronger, than that a real event of this kind should have occurred :—and with this conclusion we may dismiss the subject.

The *manifestation* φανέρωσις of Jesus *at the sea of Tiberias* ἐπὶ τῆς θαλάσσης τῆς Τιβεριάδος narrated John xxi. has so striking a resemblance to the sea anecdotes hitherto considered, that although the fourth gospel places it in the period after the resurrection, we are induced, as in an earlier instance we brought part of it under notice in connexion with the narrative of Peter's draught of fishes, so here to institute a comparison between its other features, and the narrative of Jesus walking on the sea. In both cases, Jesus is perceived by the disciples in the twilight of early morning ; only in the latter instance he does not, as in the former, walk on the sea, but stands on the shore, and the disciples are in consternation, not because of a storm, but because of the fruitlessness of their fishing.   In both instances they are afraid of him ; in the one, they take him for a spectre, in the other, not one of them ventures to ask him who he is, *knowing that it is the Lord.*   But especially the scene with Peter, peculiar to the first gospel, has its corresponding one in the present passage.   As, there, when Jesus walking on the sea makes himself known to his disciples, Peter entreats permission to go to him on the water : so here, as soon as Jesus is recognized standing on the shore, Peter throws himself into the water that he may reach him the shortest way by swimming. Thus, that which in the earlier narrative was the miraculous act of walking on the sea, becomes in the one before us, in relation to Jesus, the simple act of standing on the shore, in relation to Peter, the natural act of swimming ; so that the latter history sounds almost like a rationalistic paraphrase of the former: and there have not been wanting those who have maintained that at least the anecdote about Peter in the first gospel, is a traditional transformation of the incident in John xxi. 7. into a miracle [26].   Modern criticism is restrained from

---

[26] Schneckenburger, über den Urspr. s. 68.

extending this conjecture to the anecdote of Jesus walking on the sea, by the fact that the supposed apostolic fourth gospel itself has this feature in the earlier narrative (vi. 16 ff.). But from our point of view it appears quite possible, that the history in question either came to the author of this gospel in the one form, and to the author of the appendix in the other ; or that it came to the one author of both in a double form, and was inserted by him in separate parts of his narrative.   Meanwhile, if the two histories are to be compared, we ought not at once to assume that the one, John xxi., is the original, the other, Matt. xiv. parall., the secondary ; we must first ask which of the two bears intrinsic marks of one or the other character. Now certainly if we adhere to the rule that the more miraculous narrative is the later, that in John xxi. appears, in relation to the manner in which Jesus approaches the disciples, and in which Peter reaches Jesus, to be the original.   But this rule is connected in the closest manner with another ; namely, that the more simple narrative is the earlier, the more complex one the later, as the conglomerate is a later formation than the homo geneous stone ; and according to this rule, the conclusion is reversed, and the narrative in John xxi. is the more traditional, for in it the particulars mentioned above are interwoven with the miraculous draught of fishes, while in the earlier narrative they form in themselves an independent whole.   It is indeed true, that a greater whole may be broken up into smaller parts ; but such fragments have not at all the appearance of the separate narratives of the draught of fishes and the walking on the sea, since these, on the contrary, leave the impression of being each a finished whole.   From this interweaving with the miracle of the draught of fishes,—to which we must add the circumstance that the entire circle of events turns upon the risen Jesus, who is already in himself a miracle,—it is apparent how, contrary to the general rule, the oft-named particulars could lose their miraculous character, since by their combination with other miracles they were reduced to mere accessories, to a sort of natural scaffolding.   If then the narrative in John xxi. is entirely secondary, its historical value has already been estimated with that of the narratives which furnished its materials.

If, before we proceed further, we take a retrospect of the series of sea-anecdotes hitherto examined, we find, it is true, that the two extreme anecdotes are altogether dissimilar, the one relating mainly to fishing, the other to a storm; nevertheless, on a proper arrangement, each of them appears to be connected with the preceding by a common feature. The narrative of the call of the fishers of men (Matt. iv. 18 ff. par.) opens the series; that of Peter's draught of fishes (Luke v. 1 ff.) has in common with this the saying about the fishers of men, but the fact of the draught of fishes is peculiar to it; this fact reappears in John xxi., where the circumstances of Jesus standing on the shore in the morning twilight, and the swimming of Peter towards him, are added; these two circumstances are in Matt. xiv. 22 ff. parall. metamorphosed into the act of walking on the sea on the part of Jesus and of Peter, and at the same time a storm, and its cessation on the entrance of Jesus into the ship, are introduced; lastly, in Matt. viii. 23 ff. parall. we have an anecdote single in its kind, namely, that of the stilling of the storm by Jesus.

We come to a history for which a place is less readily found in the foregoing series, in Matt. xvii. 24 ff. It is true that here again there is a direction of Jesus to Peter to go and fish, to which, although it is not expressly stated, we must suppose that the issue corresponded: but first, it is only one fish which is to be caught, and with an angle; and secondly, the main point is, that in its mouth is to be found a piece of gold to serve for the payment of the temple tribute for Jesus and Peter. from the latter of whom this tax had been demanded. This narrative as it is here presented has peculiar difficulties, which Paulus well exhibits, and which Olshausen does not deny. Fritzsche justly remarks, that there are two miraculous particulars presupposed: first, that the fish had a coin in its mouth; secondly, that Jesus had a foreknowledge of this. On the one hand, we must regard the former of these particulars as extravagant, and consequently the latter also ; and on the other, the whole miracle appears to have been unnecessary. Certainly, that metals and other valuables have been found in the bodies of fish is elsewhere narrated [27], and is not incredible ; but that a fish should have a piece of money in its mouth, and keep it there while it snapped at the bait—this even Dr. Schnappinger [28] found inconceivable. Moreover, the motive of Jesus for performing such a miracle could not be want of money, for even if at that time there was no store in the common fund, still Jesus was in Capernaum, where he had many friends, and where consequently he could have obtained the needful money in a natural way. To exclude this possibility, we must with Olshausen confound borrowing with begging, and regard it as inconsistent with the *decorum divinum* which must have been observed by Jesus. Nor after so many proofs of his miraculous power, could Jesus think this additional miracle necessary to strengthen Peter's belief in his messiahship.

Hence we need not wonder that rationalistic commentators have attempted to free themselves at any cost from a miracle which even Olshausen pronounces to be the most difficult in the evangelical history, and we have only to see how they proceed in this undertaking. The pith of the natural explanation of the fact lies in the interpretation of the word εὑρήσεις, *thou shalt find*, in the command of Jesus, not of an immediate discovery of a stater in the fish, but of a mediate acquisition of this sum by selling what was caught [29]. It must be admitted that the above word may bear this signification also ; but if we are to give it this sense instead of the usual one, we must in the particular instance have a clear intimation to this effect in the context. Thus, if it were said in the present passage : Take the first fine fish, carry it to the market, *κἀκεῖ εὑρήσεις στατῆρα, and there thou shalt find a stater*, this explanation would be

---

[27] See the examples in Wetstein, in loc.
[28] Die h. Schrift des n. Bundes, 1, s. 314, 2te Aufl.
[29] Paulus, ex. Handb. 2, 502 ff. Comp. Hase, L. J. § 111.

in place; as however instead of this, the word εὑρήσεις is preceded by ἀνοίξας τὸ στόμα αὐτοῦ, *when thou hast opened his mouth*,—as, therefore, no place of sale, but a place inside the fish, is mentioned, as that on the opening of which the coin is to be obtained,—we can only understand an immediate discovery of the piece of money in this part of the fish [30]. Besides, to what purpose would the opening of the fish's mouth be mentioned, unless the desideratum were to be found there? Paulus sees in this only the injunction to release the fish from the hook without delay, in order to keep it alive, and thus to render it more saleable. The order to open the mouth of the fish might indeed, if it stood alone, be supposed to have the extraction of the hook as its object and consequence; but as it is followed by εὑρήσεις στατῆρα, *thou shalt find a stater*, it is plain that this is the immediate end of opening the mouth. The perception that, so long as the opening of the fish's mouth is spoken of in this passage, it will be inferred that the coin was to be found there, has induced the rationalistic commentators to try whether they could not refer the word στόμα, *mouth*, to another subject than the fish, and no other remained than the fisher, Peter. But as στόμα appeared to be connected with the fish by the word αὐτοῦ, which immediately followed it, Dr. Paulus, moderating or exaggerating the suggestion of a friend, who proposed to read ἀνθευρήσεις, instead of—αὐτοῦ, εὑρήσεις— allowed αὐτοῦ to remain, but took it adverbially, and translated the passage thus: thou hast then only to open thy mouth to offer the fish for sale, and thou wilt on the spot (αὐτοῦ) receive a stater as its price. But, it would still be asked, how could a single fish fetch so high a price in Capernaum, where fish were so abundant? Hence Paulus understands the words, τὸν ἀναβάντα πρῶτον ἰχθὺν ἆρον, *take up the fish that first cometh up*, collectively thus: continue time after time to take the fish that first comes to thee, until thou hast caught as many as will be worth a stater.

---

[30] Comp. Storr, in Flatt's Magazin, 2, s. 68 ff

If the series of strained interpretations which are necessary to a natural explanation of this narrative throw us back on that which allows it to contain a miracle; and if this miracle appear to us, according to our former decision, both extravagant and useless, nothing remains but to presume that here also there is a legendary element. This view has been combined with the admission, that a real but natural fact was probably at the foundation of the legend: namely, that Jesus once ordered Peter to fish until he had caught enough to procure the amount of the temple tribute; whence the legend arose that the fish had the tribute money in its mouth [31]. But, in our opinion, a more likely source of this anecdote is to be found in the much-used theme of a catching of fish by Peter, on the one side, and on the other, the well-known stories of precious things having been found in the bodies of fish. Peter, as we learn from Matt. iv., Luke v., John xxi., was the fisher in the evangelical legend to whom Jesus in various forms, first symbolically, and then literally, granted the rich draught of fishes. The value of the capture appears here in the shape of a piece of money, which, as similar things are elsewhere said to have been found in the belly of fishes, is by an exaggeration of the marvel said to be found in the mouth of the fish. That it is the stater, required for the temple tribute, might be occasioned by a real declaration of Jesus concerning his relation to that tax; or conversely, the stater which was accidentally named in the legend of the fish angled for by Peter, might bring to recollection the temple tribute, which amounted to that sum for two persons, and the declaration of Jesus relative to this subject.

With this tale conclude the sea anecdotes.

§ 102.

THE MIRACULOUS MULTIPLICATION OF THE LOAVES AND FISHES.

As, in the histories last considered, Jesus determined and mitigated the motions of irrational and even of inanimate ex-

---

[31] Kaiser, bibl. Theol. 1, s. 200. Comp. Hase, ut sup.

istences; so, in the narratives which we are about to examine, he exhibits the power of multiplying not only natural objects, but also productions of nature which had been wrought upon by art.

That Jesus miraculously multiplied prepared articles of food, feeding a great multitude of men with a few loaves and fishes, is narrated to us with singular unanimity by all the evangelists (Matt. xiv. 13 ff.; Mark vi. 30 ff.; Luke ix. 10 ff.; John vi. 1 ff.). And if we believe the two first, Jesus did not do this merely once; for in Matt. xv. 32 ff.; Mark viii. 1 ff. we read of a second multiplication of loaves and fishes, the circumstances of which are substantially the same as those of the former. It happens somewhat later; the place is rather differently described, and the length of time during which the multitude stayed with Jesus is differently stated; moreover, and this is a point of greater importance, the proportion between the stock of food and the number of men is different, for, on the first occasion, five thousand men are satisfied with five loaves and two fishes, and, on the second, four thousand with seven loaves and a few fishes; on the first twelve baskets are filled with the fragments, on the second only seven. Notwithstanding this, not only is the substance of the two histories exactly the same—the satisfying of a multitude of people with disproportionately small means of nourishment; but also the description of the scene in the one, entirely corresponds in its principal features to that in the other. In both instances, the locality is a solitary region in the vicinity of the Galilean sea; Jesus is led to perform the miracle because the people have lingered too long with him; he manifests a wish to feed the people from his own stores, which the disciples regard as impossible; the stock of food at his disposal consists of loaves and fishes; Jesus makes the people sit down, and, after giving thanks, distributes the provisions to them through the medium of the disciples; they are completely satisfied, and yet a disproportionately great quantity of fragments is afterwards collected in baskets; lastly, in the one case as in the other, Jesus after thus feeding the multitude, crosses the sea.

This repetition of the same event creates many difficulties. The chief of these is suggested by the question: Is it conceivable that the disciples, after they had themselves witnessed how Jesus was able to feed a great multitude with a small quantity of provision, should nevertheless on a second occasion of the same kind, have totally forgotten the first, and have asked, *Whence should we have so much bread in the wilderness as to feed so great a multitude?* To render such an obliviousness on the part of the disciples probable, we are reminded that they had, in just as incomprehensible a manner, forgotten the declarations of Jesus concerning his approaching sufferings and death, when these events occurred [1]; but it is equally a pending question, whether after such plain predictions from Jesus, his death could in fact have been so unexpected to the disciples. It has been supposed that a longer interval had elapsed between the two miracles, and that during this there had occurred a number of similar cases, in which Jesus did not think fit to afford miraculous assistance [2]: but, on the one hand, these are pure fictions; on the other, it would remain just as inconceivable as ever, that the striking similarity of the circumstances preceding the second feeding of the multitude to those preceding the first, should not have reminded even one of the disciples of that former event. Paulus therefore is right in maintaining, that had Jesus once already fed the multitude by a miracle, the disciples, on the second occasion, when he expressed his determination not to send the people away fasting, would confidently have called upon him for a repetition of the former miracle.

---

[1] Olshausen, 1, s. 512. This theologian, in the note on the same page, observes, that according to the words, *We have taken no bread,* Matt. xvi. 7, the disciples, even after the second feeding, were not alive to the fact, that there was no necessity for providing themselves with food for the body in the neighbourhood of the Son of man. But this instance is not to the point, for the circumstances are here altogether different. That from the miraculous feeding of the people when they were accidentally belated in the wilderness, the disciples did not draw the same convenient conclusion with the biblical commentator, can only redound to their honour.

[2] Ibid.

In any case then, if Jesus on two separate occasions fed a multitude with disproportionately small provision, we must suppose, as some critics have done, that many features in the narrative of the one incident were transferred to the other, and thus the two, originally unlike, became in the course of oral tradition more and more similar; the incredulous question of the disciples especially having been uttered only on the first occasion, and not on the second[3]. It may seem to speak in favour of such an assimilation, that the fourth evangelist, though in his numerical statement he is in accordance with the first narrative of Matthew and Mark, yet has, in common with the second, the circumstances that the scene opens with an address of Jesus and not of the disciples, and that the people come to Jesus on a mountain. But if the fundamental features be allowed to remain,—the wilderness, the feeding of the people, the collection of the fragments,—it is still, even without that question of the disciples, sufficiently improbable that the scene should have been repeated in so entirely similar a manner. If, on the contrary, these general features be renounced in relation to one of the histories, it is no longer apparent, how the veracity of the evangelical narratives as to the *manner* in which the second multiplication of loaves and fishes took place can be questioned on all points, and yet their statement as to the *fact* of its occurrence be maintained as trustworthy, especially as this statement is confined to Matthew and his imitator Mark.

Hence later critics have, with more[4] or less[5] decision, expressed the opinion, that here one and the same fact has been doubled, through a mistake of the first evangelist, who was followed by the second. They suppose that several narratives of the miraculous feeding of the multitude were current which pre-

---

[3] Gratz, Comm. z. Matth. 2, s. 90 f. ; Sieffert, über den Ursprung, s. 97.

[4] Thiesz, Krit. Commentar. 1, s. 168 ff. ; Schulz. über das Abendmahl, s. 311. Comp. Fritzsche, in Matth. p. 523.

[5] Schleiermacher, über den Lukas, s. 145 ; Sieffert, ut sup. s. 95 ff. ; Hase, § 97. Neander is undecided, L. J. Chr., s. 372 ff. Anm.

sented divergencies from each other, especially in relation to
numbers, and that the author of the first gospel, to whom every
additional history of a miracle was a welcome prize, and who
was therefore little qualified for the critical reduction of two
different narratives of this kind into one, introduced both into
his collection. This fully explains how on the second occasion
the disciples could again express themselves so incredulously ;
namely, because in the tradition whence the author of the first
gospel obtained the second history of a miraculous multiplication of loaves and fishes, it was the first and only one, and the
evangelist did not obliterate this feature because, apparently,
he incorporated the two narratives into his writing just as he
read or heard them. Among other proofs that this was the
case, may be mentioned the constancy with which he and Mark,
who copied him, not only in the account of the events, but
also in the subsequent allusion to them (Matt. xvi. 9 f. ; Mark
viii. 19 f.), call the baskets in the first feeding, κόφινοι, in the
second σπυρίδες. It is indeed correctly maintained, that the
apostle Matthew could not possibly take one event for two, and
narrate a new history which never happened [7] : but this proposition does not involve the reality of the second miraculous
feeding of the multitude, unless the apostolic origin of the first
gospel be at once presupposed, whereas this yet remains to be
proved. Paulus further objects, that the duplication of the history in question could be of no advantage whatever to the design of the evangelist ; and Olshausen, developing this idea
more fully, observes that the legend would not have left the
second narrative as simple and bare as the first. But this argument, that a narrative cannot be fictitious, because if it were so
it would have been more elaborately adorned, may very properly be at once dismissed, since its limits being altogether un-
defined, it might be repeated under all circumstances, and in
the end would prove fable itself not sufficiently fabulous. But,
in this case particularly, it is totally baseless, because it pre-

[6] Comp. Saunier, ut sup. s. 105.
[7] Paulus, ex. Handb. 2, s. 315 ; Olshausen, ut sup.

supposes the narrative of the first feeding of the multitude to be historically accurate; now, if we have already in this a legendary production, the other edition of it, namely, the second history of a miraculous feeding, needs not to be distinguished by special traditionary features. But not only is the second narrative not embellished as regards the miraculous, when compared with the first; it even diminishes the miracle, for, while increasing the quantity of provision, it reduces the number of those whom it satisfied : and this retrogression in the marvellous is thought the surest proof that the second feeding of the multitude really occurred ; for, it is said, he who chose to invent an additional miracle of this kind, would have made it surpass the first, and instead of five thousand men would have given, not four, but ten thousand [8]. This argument, also, rests on the unfounded assumption that the first narrative is of course the historical one; though Olshausen himself has the idea that the second might with probability be regarded as the historical basis, and the first as the legendary copy, and then the fictitious would have the required relation to the true—that of exaggeration.   But when in opposition to this, he observes, how improbable it is that an unscrupulous narrator would place the authentic fact, being the less imposing, last, and eclipse it beforehand by the false one,—that such a writer would rather seek to outdo the truth, and therefore place his fiction last, as the more brilliant,—he again shows that he does not comprehend the mythical view of the biblical narratives, in the degree necessary for forming a judgment on the subject.   For there is no question here of an unscrupulous narrator, who would designedly surpass the true history of the miraculous multiplication of the loaves and fishes, and least of all is Matthew pronounced to be such a narrator : on the contrary, it is held that with perfect honesty, one account gave five thousand, another four, and that, with equal honesty, the first evangelist copied from both ; and for the very reason that he went to work innocently

---

[8] Olshausen, s. 513.

and undesignedly, it was of no importance to him which of the two histories stood first and which last, the more important or the less striking one; but he allowed himself to be determined on this point by accidental circumstances, such as that he found the one connected with incidents which appeared to him the earlier, the other with such as he supposed to be the later. A similar instance of duplication occurs in the Pentateuch in relation to the histories of the feeding of the Israelites with quails, and of the production of water out of the rock, the former of which is narrated both in Exod. xvi. and Numb. xi., the latter in Exod. xvii. and again in Numb. xx., in each instance with an alteration in time, place, and other circumstances [9]. Meanwhile, all this yields us only the negative result that the double narratives of the first gospels cannot have been founded on two separate events. To determine which of the two is historical, or whether either of them deserves that epithet, must be the object of a special inquiry.

To evade the pre-eminently magical appearance which this miracle presents, Olshausen gives it a relation to the moral state of the participants, and supposes that the miraculous feeding of the multitude was effected through the intermediation of their spiritual hunger. But this is ambiguous language, which, on the first attempt to determine its meaning, vanishes into nothing. For in cures, for example, the intermediation here appealed to consists in the opening of the patient's mind to the influence of Jesus by faith, so that when faith is wanting, the requisite fulcrum for the miraculous power of Jesus is also wanting: here therefore the intermediation is real. Now if the same kind of intermediation took place in the case before us, so that on those among the multitude who were unbelieving the satisfying power of Jesus had no influence, then must the satisfaction of hunger here, (as, in the above cases, the cure,) be regarded as something effected by Jesus directly in the body of the hungry persons, without any antecedent augmentation of the

---

[9] See the proof in De Wette, Kritik der mos. Gesch. s. 220 ff., 314 ff.

external means of nourishment. But such a conception of the matter, as Paulus justly remarks, and as even Olshausen intimates, is precluded by the statement of the evangelists, that real food was distributed among the multitude; that each enjoyed as much as he wanted; and that at the end the residue was greater than the original store. It is thus plainly implied that there was an external and objective increase of the provisions, as a preliminary to the feeding of the multitude. Now, this cannot be conceived as effected by means of the faith of the people in a real manner, in the sense that that faith co-operated in producing the multiplication of the loaves. The intermediation which Olshausen here supposes, can therefore have been only a teleological one, that is, we are to understand by it, that Jesus undertook to multiply the loaves and fishes for the sake of producing a certain moral condition in the multitude. But an intermediation of this kind affords me not the slightest help in forming a conception of the event; for the question is not *why*, but *how* it happened. Thus all which Olshausen believes himself to have done towards rendering this miracle more intelligible, rests on the ambiguity of the expression, *intermediation ;* and the inconceivableness of an immediate influence of the will of Jesus on irrational nature, remains chargeable upon this history as upon those last examined.

But there is another difficulty which is peculiar to the narrative before us. We have here not merely, as hitherto, a modification or a direction of natural objects, but a multiplication of them, and that to an enormous extent. Nothing, it is true, is more familiar to our observation than the growth and multiplication of natural objects, as presented to us in the parable of the sower, and the grain of mustard seed, for example. But, first, these phenomena do not take place without the co-operation of other natural agents, as earth, water, air, so that here, also, according to the well known principle of physics, there is not properly speaking an augmentation of the substance, but only a change in the accidents; secondly, these processes of growth and multiplication are carried forward so as to pass through their various stages in corresponding intervals of time. Here, on the contrary, in the multiplication of the loaves and fishes by Jesus, neither the one rule nor the other is observed: the bread in the hand of Jesus is no longer, like the stalk on which the corn grew, in communication with the maternal earth, nor is the multiplication gradual, but sudden.

But herein, it is said, consists the miracle, which in relation to the last point especially, may be called the acceleration of a natural process. That which comes to pass in the space of three quarters of a year, from seed-time to harvest, was here effected in the minutes which were required for the distribution of the food; for natural developments are capable of acceleration, and to how great an extent we cannot determine [10]. It would, indeed, have been an acceleration of a natural process, if in the hand of Jesus a grain of corn had borne fruit a hundred-fold, and brought it to maturity, and if he had shaken the multiplied grain out of his hands as they were filled again and again, that the people might grind, knead, and bake it, or eat it raw from the husk in the wilderness where they were;—or if he had taken a living fish, suddenly called forth the eggs from its body, and converted them into full-grown fish, which then the disciples or the people might have boiled or roasted, this, we should say, would have been an acceleration of a natural process. But it is not corn that he takes into his hand, but bread; and the fish also, as they are distributed in pieces, must have been prepared in some way, perhaps, as in Luke xxiv. 42, comp. John xxi. 9, broiled or salted. Here then, on both sides, the production of nature is no longer simple and living, but dead and modified by art: so that to introduce a natural process of the above kind, Jesus must, in the first place, by his miraculous power have metamorphosed the bread into corn again, the roasted fish into raw and living ones; then instantaneously have effected the described multiplication: and lastly, have restored the whole from the natural to the artificial state. Thus

---

[10] Thus Olshausen, in loc. after Pfenninger. Comp. Hase, § 97.

the miracle would be composed, 1st, of a revivification, which would exceed in miraculousness all other instances in the gospels; 2ndly, of an extremely accelerated natural process; and 3rdly, of an artificial process, effected invisibly, and likewise extremely accelerated, since all the tedious proceedings of the miller and baker on the one hand, and of the cook on the other, must have been accomplished in a moment by the word of Jesus. How then can Olshausen deceive himself and the believing reader, by the agreeably sounding expression, *accelerated natural process*, when this nevertheless can designate only a third part of the fact of which we are speaking [11] ?

But how are we to represent such a miracle to ourselves, and in what stage of the event must it be placed? In relation to the latter point, three opinions are possible, corresponding to the number of the groups that act in our narrative; for the multiplication may have taken place either in the hands of Jesus, or in those of the disciples who dispensed the food, or in those of the people who received it. The last idea appears, on the one hand, puerile even to extravagance, if we are to imagine Jesus and the apostles distributing, with great carefulness, that there might be enough for all, little crumbs which in the hands of the recipients swelled into considerable pieces: on the other hand, it would have been scarcely a possible task, to get a particle, however small, for every individual in a multitude of five thousand men, out of five loaves, which according to Hebrew custom, and particularly as they were carried by a boy, cannot have been very large; and still less out of two fishes. Of the two other opinions I think, with Olshausen, the one most suitable is that which supposes that the food was augmented under the creative hands of Jesus, and that he time after time dispensed new quantities to the disciples. We may

---

[11] This lamentable observation of mine, according to Olshausen, has its source in something worse than intellectual incapacity, namely, in my total disbelief in a living God; otherwise assuredly it would not have appeared so great a difficulty to me that the Divine causality should have superseded human operations (s. 479, der 3ten Aufl.).

then endeavour to represent the matter to ourselves in two ways: first we may suppose that as fast as one loaf or fish was gone, a new one came out of the hands of Jesus, or secondly, that the single loaves and fishes grew, so that as one piece was broken off, its loss was repaired, until on a calculation the turn came for the next loaf or fish. The first conception appears to be opposed to the text, which as it speaks of fragments ἐκ τῶν πέντε ἄρτων, *of the five loaves* (John vi. 13.), can hardly be held to presuppose an increase of this number; thus there remains only the second, by the poetical description of which Lavater has done but a poor service to the orthodox view [12]. For this miracle belongs to the class which can only appear in any degree credible so long as they can be retained in the obscurity of an indefinite conception [13]: no sooner does the light shine on them, so that they can be examined in all their parts, than they dissolve like the unsubstantial creations of the mist. Loaves, which in the hands of the distributors expand like wetted sponges,—broiled fish, in which the severed parts are replaced instantaneously, as in the living crab gradually,— plainly belong to quite another domain than that of reality.

What gratitude then do we not owe to the rationalistic interpretation, if it be true that it can free us, in the easiest manner, from the burden of so unheard-of a miracle? If we are to believe Dr. Paulus [14], the evangelists had no idea that they were narrating anything miraculous, and the miracle was first conveyed into their accounts by expositors. What they narrate is, according to him, only thus much: that Jesus caused his small store of provisions to be distributed, and that in consequence of this the entire multitude obtained enough to eat. Here, in any case, we want a middle term, which would distinctly inform us, how it was possible that, although Jesus had so little food to offer, the whole multitude obtained enough to eat. A very

[12] Jesus Messias, 2, Bd. No. 14, 15 and 20.
[13] For this reason Neander (s. 377) passes over the miracle with a few entirely general remarks.
[14] Exeg. Handb. 2, s. 205 ff.

natural middle term however is to be gathered, according to
Paulus, out of the historical combination of the circumstances.
As, on a comparison with John vi. 4, the multitude appear to
have consisted for the greater part of a caravan on its way to.
the feast, they cannot have been quite destitute of provisions,
and probably a few indigent persons only had exhausted their
stores. In order then to induce the better provided to share
their food with those who were in want, Jesus arranged that
they should have a meal, and himself set the example of
imparting what he and his disciples could spare from their own
little store ; this example was imitated, and thus the distribution
of bread by Jesus having led to a general distribution, the
whole multitude were satisfied. It is true that this natural
middle term must be first mentally interpolated into the text ;
as, however, the supernatural middle term which is generally
received is just as little stated expressly, and both alike
depend upon inference, the reader can hardly do otherwise than
decide for the natural one. Such is the reasoning of Dr.
Paulus : but the alleged identity in the relation of the two
middle terms to the text does not in fact exist. For while the
natural explanation requires us to suppose a new distributing
subject, (the better provided among the multitude,) and a new
distributed object, (their provisions,) together with the act of
distributing these provisions : the supranatural explanation
contents itself with the subject actually present in the text,
(Jesus and his disciples,) with the single object there given,
(their little store,) and the described distribution of this ; and
only requires us to supply from our imagination the means by
which this store could be made sufficient to satisfy the hunger
of the multitude, namely its miraculous augmentation under the
hands of Jesus (or of his disciples). How can it be yet maintained that neither of the two middle terms is any more suggested
by the text than the other ? That the miraculous multiplication
of the loaves and fishes is not expressly mentioned, is explained
by the consideration that the event itself is one of which no clear
conception can be formed, and therefore it is best conveyed by

the result alone. But how will the natural theologian account for nothing being said of the distribution, called forth by the example of Jesus, on the part of those among the multitude who had provisions? It is altogether arbitrary to insert that distribution between the sentences, *He gave them to the disciples, and the disciples to the multitude* (Matt. xiv. 19), and, *they did all eat and were filled* (v. 20); while the words, καὶ τοὺς δύο ἰχθύας ἐμέρισε πᾶσι, *and the two fishes divided he among them all*, (Mark vi. 41,) plainly indicate that only the two fishes—and consequently only the five loaves—were the object of distribution for all [15]. But the natural explanation falls into especial embarrassment when it comes to the baskets which, after all were satisfied, Jesus caused to be filled with the fragments that remained. The fourth evangelist says : συνήγαγον οὖν, καὶ ἐγέμισαν δώδεκα κοφίνους κλασμάτων ἐκ τῶν πέντε ἄρτων τῶν κριθίνων, ἃ ἐπερίσσευσε τοῖς βεβρωκόσιν, *therefore they gathered them together, and filled twelve baskets with the fragments of the five barley loaves, which remained over and above unto them that had eaten* (vi. 13). This seems clearly enough to imply that out of those identical five loaves, after five thousand men had been satisfied by them, there still remained fragments enough to fill twelve baskets,—more, that is, than the amount of the original store. Here, therefore, the natural expositor is put to the most extravagant contrivances in order to evade the miracle. It is true, when the synoptists simply say that the remnants of the meal were collected, and twelve baskets filled with them, it might be thought from the point of view of the natural explanation, that Jesus out of regard to the gift of God, caused the fragments which the crowd had left from their own provisions to be collected by his disciples. But as, on the one hand, the fact that the people allowed the remains of the repast to lie, and did not appropriate them, seems to indicate that they treated the nourishment presented to them as the property of another ; so, on the other

---

[15] Olshausen, in loc.

hand, Jesus, when, without any preliminary, he directs his disciples to gather them up, appears to regard them as his own property. Hence Paulus understands the words ἦραν κ. τ. λ. of the synoptists, not of a collection first made after the meal, of that which remained when the people had been satisfied, but of the overplus of the little store belonging to Jesus and the disciples, which the latter, after reserving what was necessary for Jesus and themselves, carried round as an introduction and inducement to the general repast. But how, when the words ἔφαγον καὶ ἐχορτάσθησαν πάντες, *they did all eat and were filled,* are immediately followed by καὶ ἦραν, *and they took up,* can the latter member of the verse refer to the time prior to the meal? Must it not then have necessarily been said at least ἦραν γὰρ, *for they took up?* Farther, how, after it had just been said that the people did eat and were filled, can τὸ περισσεῦσαν, *that which remained,* especially succeeded as it is in Luke by αὐτοῖς, *to them,* mean anything else than what the people had left? Lastly, how is it possible that out of five loaves and two fishes, after Jesus and his disciples had reserved enough for themselves, or even without this, there could in a natural manner be twelve baskets *filled* for distribution among the people? But still more strangely does the natural explanation deal with the narrative of John. Jesus here adds, as a reason for gathering up the fragments, ἵνα μή τι ἀπόληται, *that nothing be lost;* hence it appears impossible to divest the succeeding statement that they filled twelve baskets with the remains of the five loaves, of its relation to the time after the meal; and in this case, it would be impossible to get clear of a miraculous multiplication of the loaves. Paulus therefore, although the words συνήγαγον οὖν καὶ ἐγέμισαν δώδεκα κοφίνους κ. τ. λ., *therefore they gathered them together and filled twelve baskets,* &c., form a strictly coherent whole, chooses rather to detach συνήγαγον οὖν, and, by a still more forced construction than that which he employed with the synoptical text, makes the narrative pass all at once, without the slightest notice, into the pluperfect, and thus leap back to the time before the meal.

Here, then, the natural explanation once more fails to fulfil its task: the text retains its miracle, and if we have reason to think this incredible, we must inquire whether the narrative of the text deserve credence. The agreement of all the four evangelists is generally adduced in proof of its distinguished credibility: but this agreement is by no means so perfect. There are minor differences, first between Matthew and Luke; then between these two and Mark, who in this instance again embellishes; and lastly, between the synoptists collectively and John, in the following points: according to the synoptists, the scene of the event is a *desert place*, according to John, a *mountain;* according to the former, the scene opens with an address from the disciples, according to John, with a question from Jesus (two particulars in which, as we have already remarked, the narrative of John approaches that of the second feeding in Matthew and Mark); lastly, the words which the three first evangelists put into the mouth of the disciples indefinitely, the fourth in his individualizing manner ascribes to Philip and Andrew, and the same evangelist also designates the bearer of the loaves and fishes as a *boy* ($\pi\alpha\iota\delta\acute{\alpha}\rho\iota\omicron\nu$). These divergencies however may be passed over as less essential, that we may give our attention only to one, which has a deeper hold. While, namely, according to the synoptical accounts, Jesus had been long teaching the people and healing their sick, and was only led to feed them by the approach of evening, and the remark of the disciples that the people needed refreshment: in John, the first thought of Jesus, when he lifts up his eyes and sees the people gathering round him, is that which he expresses in his question to Philip: *Whence shall we buy bread that these may eat?* or rather, as he asked this merely to *prove* Philip, well knowing himself *what he would do,* he at once forms the resolution of feeding the multitude in a miraculous manner. But how could the design of feeding the people arise in Jesus immediately on their approach? They did not come to him for this, but for the sake of his teaching and his curative power. He must therefore have conceived this design entirely

E E 2

of his own accord, with a view to establish his miraculous power by so signal a demonstration. But did he ever thus work a miracle without any necessity, and even without any inducement,—quite arbitrarily, and merely for the sake of working a miracle? I am unable to describe strongly enough how impossible it is that eating should here have been the first thought of Jesus, how impossible that he could thus obtrude his miraculous repast on the people. Thus in relation to this point, the synoptical narrative, in which there is a reason for the miracle, must have the preference to that of John, who, hastening towards the miracle, overlooks the requisite motive for it, and makes Jesus create instead of awaiting the occasion for its performance. An eye-witness could not narrate thus [16]; and if, therefore, the account of that gospel to which the greatest authority is now awarded, must be rejected as unhistorical; so, with respect to the other narratives, the difficulties of the fact itself are sufficient to cast a doubt on their historical credibility, especially if in addition to these negative grounds we can discover positive reasons which render it probable that our narrative had an unhistorical origin.

Such reasons are actually found both within the evangelical history itself, and beyond it in the Old Testament history, and the Jewish popular belief. In relation to the former source, it is worthy of remark, that in the synoptical gospels as well as in John, there are more or less immediately appended to the feeding of the multitude by Jesus with literal bread, figurative discourses of Jesus on bread and leaven: namely, in the latter, the declarations concerning the bread of heaven, and the bread of life which Jesus gives (John vi. 27 ff.); in the former, those concerning the false leaven of the Pharisees and Sadducees, that is, their false doctrine and hypocrisy [17] (Matt. xvi. 5 ff.;

---

[16] Against Neander's attempt at reconciliation, compare De Wette, exeg. Handb. 1, 3, s. 77.

[17] This indication has been recently followed up by Weisse. He finds the key to the history of the miraculous multiplication of the loaves, in the question addressed by Jesus to the disciples when they misunderstand his admonition against the leaven

Mark viii. 14 ff. ; comp. Luke xii. 1.) ; and on both sides, the figurative discourse of Jesus is erroneously understood of literal bread. It would not then be a very strained conjecture, that as in the passages quoted we find the disciples and the people generally, understanding literally what Jesus meant figuratively; so the same mistake was made in the earliest Christian tradition. If, in figurative discourses, Jesus had sometimes represented himself as him who was able to give the true bread of life to the wandering and hungering people, perhaps also placing in opposition to this, the leaven of the Pharisees : the legend, agreeably to its realistic tendency, may have converted this into the fact of a miraculous feeding of the hungry multitude in the wilderness by Jesus. The fourth evangelist makes the discourse on the bread of heaven arise out of the miracle of the loaves ; but the relation might very well have been the reverse, and the history owe its origin to the discourse, especially as the question which introduces John's narrative, *Whence shall we buy bread that these may eat?* may be more easily conceived as being uttered by Jesus on the first sight of the people, if he alluded to feeding them with the word of God (comp. John iv. 32 ff.), to appeasing their spiritual hunger (Matt. v. 6), in order to exercise ($\pi\epsilon\iota\rho\acute{\alpha}\zeta\omega\iota$) the higher understanding of his disciples, than if he really thought of the satisfaction of their bodily hunger, and only wished to try whether his disciples

of the Pharisees and Sadducees. He asks them whether they did not remember, how many baskets they had been able to fill from the five and again from the seven loaves, and then adds, *How is it that ye do not understand that I spake it not to you concerning bread,* &c., (Matt. xvi. 11.).   Now, says Weisse, the parallel which Jesus here institutes between his discourse on the leaven, and the history of the feeding of the multitude, shows that the latter also is only to be interpreted parabolically (s. 511 ff.). But the form of the question of Jesus : $\tau\acute{o}\sigma o\upsilon\varsigma$ $\kappa o\phi\acute{\iota}\nu o\upsilon\varsigma$ ($\sigma\pi\upsilon\rho\acute{\iota}\delta\alpha\varsigma$) $\grave{\epsilon}\lambda\acute{\alpha}\beta\epsilon\tau\epsilon$; *how many baskets ye took up,* presupposes a real event; we can form no conception, as we have already remarked in relation to the history of the temptation, of a parable in which Jesus and his disciples would have played a principal part ; moreover, the inference which Jesus would convey is, according to the text, not that because the present narrative was figurative, so also must be the interpretation of the subsequent discourse, but that after the earlier proof how superfluous was any solicitude about physical bread where Jesus was at hand, it was absurd to understand his present discourse as relating to such.

would in this case confide in his miraculous power. The synoptical narrative is less suggestive of such a view; for the figurative discourse on the leaven could not by itself originate the history of the miracle. Thus the gospel of John stands alone with reference to the above mode of derivation, and it is more agreeable to the character of this gospel to conjecture that it has applied the narrative of a miracle presented by tradition to the production of figurative discourses in the Alexandrian taste, than to suppose that it has preserved to us the original discourses out of which the legend spun that miraculous narrative.

If then we can discover, beyond the limits of the New Testament, very powerful causes for the origination of our narrative, we must renounce the attempt to construct it out of materials presented by the gospels themselves. And here the fourth evangelist, by putting into the mouth of the people a reference to the manna, that bread of heaven which Moses gave to the fathers in the wilderness (v. 31), reminds us of one of the most celebrated passages in the early history of the Israelites (Exod. xvi.), which was perfectly adapted to engender the expectation that its antitype would occur in the messianic times; and we in fact learn from rabbinical writings, that among those functions of the first Goël which were to be revived in the second, a chief place was given to the impartation of bread from heaven [18]. If the Mosaic manna presents itself as that which was most likely to be held a type of the bread miraculously augmented by Jesus; the fish which Jesus also multiplied miraculously, may remind us that Moses gave the people, not only a substitute for bread in the manna, but also animal food in the quails (Exod. xvi. 8; xii. 13; Numb. xi. 4 ff.). On comparing these Mosaic narratives with our evangelical ones, there appears a striking resemblance even in details. The locality in both cases is the wilderness; the inducement to the miracle here as there, is fear lest the people should suffer from

[18] Vid. Vol. I. § 14.

want in the wilderness, or perish from hunger; in the Old Testament history, this fear is expressed by the people in loud murmurs, in that of the New Testament, it results from the shortsightedness of the disciples, and the benevolence of Jesus. The direction of the latter to his disciples that they should give the people food, a direction which implies that he had already formed the design of feeding them miraculously, may be parallelled with the command which Jehovah gave to Moses to feed the people with manna (Exod. xvi. 4.), and with quails (Exod. xvi. 12; Numb. xi. 18—20.). But there is another point of similarity which speaks yet more directly to our present purpose. As, in the evangelical narrative, the disciples think it an impossibility that provision for so great a mass of people should be procured in the wilderness, so, in the Old Testament history, Moses replies doubtingly to the promise of Jehovah to satisfy the people with flesh (Numb. xi. 21 f.). To Moses, as to the disciples, the multitude appears too great for the possibility of providing sufficient food for them; as the latter ask, whence they should have so much bread in the wilderness, so Moses asks ironically whether they should slay the flocks and the herds (which they had not). And as the disciples object, that not even the most impoverishing expenditure on their part would thoroughly meet the demand, so Moses, clothing the idea in another form, had declared, that to satisfy the people as Jehovah promised, an impossibility must happen (the fish of the sea be gathered together for them); objections which Jehovah there, as here Jesus, does not regard, but issues the command that the people should prepare for the reception of the miraculous food.

But though these two cases of a miraculous supply of nourishment are thus analogous, there is this essential distinction, that in the Old Testament, in relation both to the manna and the quails, it is a miraculous procuring of food not previously existing which is spoken of, while in the New Testament it is a miraculous augmentation of provision already present, but inadequate; so that the chasm between the Mosaic narrative and the evangelical one is too great for the latter to have been derived immediately from the former. If we search for an intermediate step, a very natural one between Moses and the Messiah is afforded by the prophets. We read of Elijah, that through him and for his sake, the little store of meal and oil which he found in the possession of the widow of Zarephath was miraculously replenished, or rather was made to suffice throughout the duration of a famine (1 Kings xvii. 8—16). This species of miracle is developed still farther, and with a greater resemblance to the evangelical narrative, in the history of Elisha (2 Kings iv. 42 ff.). As Jesus fed five thousand men in the wilderness with five loaves and two fishes, so this prophet, during a famine, fed a hundred men with twenty loaves, (which like those distributed by Jesus in John, are called barley loaves,) together with some ground corn, (כַּרְמֶל, LXX : παλάθας) ; a disproportion between the quantity of provisions and the number of men, which his servant, like the disciples in the other instance, indicates in the question : *What! should I set this before a hundred men?* Elisha, like Jesus, is not diverted from his purpose, but commands the servant to give what he has to the people ; and as in the New Testament narrative great stress is laid on the collection of the remaining fragments, so in the Old Testament it is specially noticed at the close of this story, that notwithstanding so many had eaten of the store, there was still an overplus [19]. The only important difference here is, that on the side of the evangelical narrative, the number of the loaves is smaller, and that of the people greater ; but who does not know that in general the legend does not easily imitate, without at the same time surpassing, and who does not see that in this particular instance it was entirely suited to the position of the Messiah, that his miraculous power, compared with that

---

[19] 2 Kings iv. 43, LXX : τί δῶ τοῦτ; ἐνώπιον ἑκατὸν ἀνδρῶν ;

Ibid. v. 44 : καὶ ἔφαγον, καὶ κατέλιπον κατὰ τὸ ῥῆμα Κυρίου.

John vi. 9 : ἀλλὰ ταῦτα τί ἐστιν εἰς τοσούτους ;

Matth. xiv. 20 : καὶ ἔφαγον πάντες, καὶ ἐχορτάσθησαν, καὶ ἦραν τὸ περισσεῦον τῶν κλασμάτων, κ. τ. λ.

of Elisha, should be placed, as it regards the need of natural means, in the relation of five to twenty, but as it regards the supernatural performance, in that of five thousand to one hundred ? Paulus indeed, in order to preclude the inference, that as the two narratives in the Old Testament are to be understood mythically, so also is the strikingly similar evangelical narrative, extends to the former the attempt at a natural explanation which he has pursued with the latter, making the widow's cruse of oil to be replenished by the aid of the scholars of the prophets, and the twenty loaves suffice for one hundred men by means of a praiseworthy moderation [20]; a mode of explanation which is less practicable here than with the New Testament narrative, in proportion as, by reason of the greater remoteness of these anecdotes, they present fewer critical, (and, by reason of their merely mediate relation to Christianity, fewer dogmatical,) motives for maintaining their historical veracity.

Nothing more is wanting to complete the mythical derivation of this history of the miraculous feeding of the multitude, except the proof, that the later Jews also believed of particularly holy men, that by their means a small amount of provision was made sufficient, and of this proof the disinterested industry of Dr. Paulus as a collector, has put us in possession. He adduces a rabbinical statement that in the time of a specially holy man, the small quantity of show-bread more than sufficed for the supply of the priests [21]. To be consequent, this commentator should try to explain this story also naturally,—by the moderation of the priests, for instance: but it is not in the canon, hence he can unhesitatingly regard it as a fable, and he only so far admits its striking similarity to the evangelical narrative as to observe, that in consequence of the Jewish belief in such augmentations of food, attested by that rabbinical state-

---

[20] Exeg. Handb. 2, s. 237 f.
[21] Joma f. 39, 1: *Tempore Simeonis justi benedictio erat super duos pane: pentecostales et super decem panes προθέσεως, ut singuli sacerdotes, qui pro rata parte acciperent quantitatem olivæ, ad satietatem comederent, imo ut adhuc reliquiæ superessent.*

ment, the New Testament narrative may in early times have been understood by judaizing Christians in the same (miraculous) sense. But our examination has shown that the evangelical narrative was designedly composed so as to convey this sense, and if this sense was an element of the popular Jewish legend, then is the evangelical narrative without doubt a product of that legend [22].

§ 103.

JESUS TURNS WATER INTO WINE.

Next to the history of the multiplication of the loaves and fishes, may be ranged the narrative in the fourth gospel (ii. 1 ff.), of Jesus at a wedding in Cana of Galilee turning water into wine. According to Olshausen, both miracles fall under the same category, since in both a substratum is present, the substance of which is modified [1]. But he overlooks the logical distinction, that in the miracle of the loaves and fishes, the modification is one of quantity merely, an augmentation of what was already existing, without any change of its quality (bread becomes *more* bread, but remains *bread*); whereas at the wedding in Cana the substratum is modified in quality—out of a certain substance there is made not merely more of the same kind, but something else (out of water, wine); in other words, a real transubstantiation takes place. It is true there are changes in quality which are natural results, and the instantaneous effectuation of which by Jesus would be even more easy to conceive, than an equally rapid augmentation of quantity; for example, if he had suddenly changed must into wine, or wine into vinegar, this would only have been to conduct in an accelerated manner the same vegetable substratum, the vinous juice, through various conditions natural to it. The miracle would be already heightened if Jesus had imparted to the juice of another fruit, the apple for instance, the quality of

---

[22] Comp. De Wette, ex Handb. 1, 1, s. 133 f.
[1] Bibl. Comm. 2, s. 74.

that of the grape, although even in this his agency would have
been within the limits of the same kingdom of nature. But
here, where water is turned into wine, there is a transition from
one kingdom of nature to another, from the elementary to the
vegetable ; a miracle which as far exceeds that of the multiplication of the loaves, as if Jesus had hearkened to the counsel of
the tempter, and turned stones into bread [2].

To this miracle as to the former, Olshausen, after Augustine [3],
applies his definition of an accelerated natural process, by which
we are to understand that we have here simply the occurrence,
in an accelerated manner, of that which is presented yearly in
the vine in a slow process of development. This mode of viewing the matter would have some foundation, if the substratum
on which Jesus operated had been the same out of which wine
is wont to be naturally produced ; if he had taken a vine in his
hand, and suddenly caused it to bloom, and to bear ripe grapes,
this might have been called an accelerated natural process.
Even then indeed we should still have no wine, and if Jesus
were to produce this also from the vine which he took into his
hand, he must add an operation which would be an invisible
substitute for the wine-press, that is, an accelerated artificial
process ; so that on this supposition the category of the
accelerated natural process would already be insufficient. In
fact, however, we have no vine as a substratum for this production of wine, but water, and in this case we could only
speak with propriety of an accelerated natural process, if by any
means, however gradual, wine were ever produced out of water.
Here it is urged, that certainly out of water, out of the moisture
produced in the earth by rain and the like, the vine draws its
sap, which in due order it applies to the production of the

---

[2] Neander is of opinion that an analogy may be found for this miracle yet more
easily than for that of the loaves—in the mineral springs, the water of which is rendered so potent by natural agencies, that it produces effects which far exceed those
of ordinary water, and in part resemble those of wine ! (s. 369.)

[3] In Joann. tract. 8 : *Ipse vinum fecit in nuptiis, qui omni anno hoc facit in
vitibus.*

grape, and of the wine therein contained; so that thus yearly, by means of a natural process, wine does actually come out of water [4]. But apart from the fact that water is only one of the elementary materials which are required for the fructification of the vine, and that to this end, soil, air, and light, must concur; it could not be said either of one, or of all these elementary materials together, that they produce the grape or the wine, nor, consequently, that Jesus, when he produced wine out of water, did the same thing, only more quickly, which is repeated every year as a gradual process: on the contrary, here again there is a confusion of essentially distinct logical categories. For we may place the relation of the product to the producing agent, which is here treated of, under the category of power and manifestation, or of cause and effect: never can it be said that water is the power or the cause, which produces grapes and wine, for the power which gives existence to them is strictly the vegetable individuality of the vine-plant, to which water, with the rest of the elementary agencies, is related only as the solicitation to the power, as the stimulus to the cause. That is, without the co-operation of water, air, &c., grapes certainly cannot be produced, any more than without the vine-plant; but the distinction is, that in the vine the grape, in itself or in its germ, is already present, and water, air, &c., only assist in its development; whereas in these elementary substances, the grape is present neither *actu* nor *potentiâ;* they can in no way produce the fruit out of themselves, but only out of something else—the vine. To turn water into wine is not then to make a cause act more rapidly than it would act in a natural way, but it is to make the effect appear without a cause, out of a mere accessory circumstance; or, to refer more particularly to organic nature, it is to call forth the organic product without the producing organism, out of the simple inorganic materials, or rather out of one of these materials only. This is about the

---

[4] Thus Augustine, ut sup. approved by Olshausen: *sicut enim, quod miserunt ministri in hydrias, in vinum conversum est opere Domini, sic et quod nubes fundunt, in vinum convertitur ejusdem opere Domini.*

same thing as to make bread out of earth without the intervention of the corn plant, flesh out of bread without a previous
assimilation of it by an animal body, or in the same immediate
manner, blood out of wine. If the supranaturalist is not here
contented with appealing to the incomprehensibleness of an omni-
potent word of Jesus, but also endeavours, with Olshausen, to
bring the process which must have been contained in the
miracle in question nearer to his conception, by regarding it in
the light of a natural process; he must not, in order to render
the matter more probable, suppress a part of the necessary
stages in that process, but exhibit them all. They would then
present the following series: 1st, to the water, as one only of
the elementary agents, Jesus must have added the power of the
other elements above named; 2ndly, (and this is the chief
point,) he must have procured, in an equally invisible manner,
the organic individuality of the vine; 3rdly, he must have accelerated, to the degree of instantaneousness, the natural process resulting from the reciprocal action of these objects upon
one another, the blooming and fructification of the vine, together with the ripening of the grape; 4thly, he must have
caused the artificial process of pressing, and so forth, to occur
invisibly and suddenly; and lastly, he must again have accelerated the further natural process of fermentation, so as to render
it momentary. Thus, here again, the designation of the
miracle as an accelerated natural process, would apply to two
stages only out of five, the other three being such as cannot
possibly be brought under this point of view, though the two
first, especially the second, are of greater importance even than
belonged to the stages which were neglected in the application
of this view to the history of the miraculous feeding: so that
the definition of an accelerated natural process is as inadequate
here as there[5]. As, however, this is the only, or the extreme

[5] Even Lücke, 1, s. 405, thinks the analogy with the above natural process deficient and unintelligible, and does not know how to console himself better than by
the consideration, that a similar inconvenience exists in relation to the miracle of the
loaves.

category, under which we can bring such operations nearer to
our conception and comprehension; it follows that if this category be shown to be inapplicable, the event itself is inconceivable.

Not only, however, has the miracle before us been impeached
in relation to possibility, but also in relation to utility and fitness.   It has been urged both in ancient[6] and modern[7] times,
that it was unworthy of Jesus that he should not only remain
in the society of drunkards, but even further their intemperance
by an exercise of his miraculous power.   But this objection
should be discarded as an exaggeration, since, as expositors
justly observe, from the words *after men have well drunk* ὅταν
μεθυσθῶσι (v. 10), which *the ruler of the feast* ἀρχιτρίκλινος
uses with reference to the usual course of things at such feasts,
nothing can with certainty be deduced with respect to the occasion in question.   We must however still regard as valid an
objection, which is not only pointed out by Paulus and the
author of the Probabilia[8], but admitted even by Lücke and
Olshausen to be at the first glance a pressing difficulty:
namely, that by this miracle Jesus did not, as was usual with
him, relieve any want, any real need, but only furnished an
additional incitement to pleasure; showed himself not so much
helpful as courteous; rather, so to speak, performed a miracle
of luxury, than of true beneficence.   If it be here said that it
was a sufficient object for the miracle to confirm the faith of the
disciples[9], which according to v. 11 was its actual effect; it
must be remembered that, as a general rule, not only had the
miracles of Jesus, considered with regard to their form, i. e. as
extraordinary results, something desirable as their consequence,
for instance, the faith of the spectators; but also, considered
with regard to their matter, i. e. as consisting of cures, multi-
plications of loaves, and the like, were directed to some really

[6] Chrysost. hom. in Joann. 21.
[7] Woolston, Disc. 4.
[8] P. 42.
[9] Tholuck, in loc.

beneficent end. In the present miracle this characteristic is wanting, and hence Paulus is not wrong when he points out the contradiction which would lie in the conduct of Jesus, if towards the tempter he rejected every challenge to such miracles as, without being materially beneficent, or called for by any pressing necessity, could only formally produce faith and astonishment, and yet in this instance performed a miracle of that very nature [10].

The supranaturalist was therefore driven to maintain that it was not faith in general which Jesus here intended to produce, but a conviction entirely special, and only to be wrought by this particular miracle. Proceeding on this supposition, nothing was more natural than to be reminded by the opposition of water and wine on which the miracle turns, of the opposition between him who baptized with water (Matt. iii. 11), who at the same time came neither eating nor drinking (Luke i. 15; Matt. xi. 18.), and him who, as he baptized with the Holy Ghost and with fire, so he did not deny himself the ardent, animating fruit of the vine, and was hence reproached with being a *wine-bibber* οἰνοπότης (Matt. xi. 19); especially as the fourth gospel, in which the narrative of the wedding at Cana is contained, manifests in a peculiar degree the tendency to lead over the contemplation from the Baptist to Jesus. On these grounds Herder [11], and after him some others [12], have held the opinion, that Jesus by the above miraculous act intended to symbolize to his disciples, several of whom had been disciples of the Baptist, the relation of his spirit and office to those of John, and by this proof of his superior power, to put an end to the offence which they might take at his more liberal mode of life. But here the reflection obtrudes itself, that Jesus does not avail himself of this symbolical miracle, to enlighten his disciples by explanatory discourses concerning his relation to the Baptist;

[10] Comm. 4, s. 151 f.

[11] Von Gottes Sohn u. s. f. nach Johannes Evangelium, s. 131 f.

[12] C. Ch. Flatt, über die Verwandlung des Wassers in Wein, in Süskind's Magazin, 14. Stück, s. 86 f.; Olshausen, ut sup. s. 75 f.; comp. Neander, L. J. Chr., s. 372.

an omission which even the friends of this interpretation pronounce to be surprising [13].   How needful such an exposition
was, if the miracle were not to fail of its special object, is evident from the fact, that the narrator himself, according to v. 11,
understood it not at all in this light, as a symbolization of a
particular maxim of Jesus, but quite generally, as a *manifestation* φανέρωσις of his glory [14].   Thus if that special lesson were
the object of Jesus in performing the miracle before us, then
the author of the fourth gospel, that is, according to the supposition of the above theologians, his most apprehensive pupil,
misunderstood him, and Jesus delayed in an injudicious manner to prevent this misunderstanding ; or if both these conclusions are rejected, there still subsists the difficulty, that
Jesus, contrary to the prevailing tendency of his conduct,
sought to attain the general object of proving his miraculous
power, by an act for which apparently he might have substituted
a more useful one.

Again, the disproportionate quantity of wine with which
Jesus supplies the guests, must excite astonishment.   Six vessels, each containing from two to three μετρητὰς, supposing the
Attic μετρητὴς, corresponding to the Hebrew *bath*, to be equivalent to 1½ Roman *amphoræ*, or twenty-one Wirtemburg measures *, would yield 252—378 measures [15].   What a quantity
for a company who had already drunk freely !   What enormous vessels !   exclaims Dr. Paulus, and leaves no effort
untried to reduce the statement of measures in the text.
With a total disregard of the rules of the language, he gives to
the preposition ἀνὰ a collective meaning, instead of its proper
distributive one, so as to make the six *water pots* (ὑδρίαι) contain, not each, but altogether, from two to three μετρητὰς ; and

[13] Olshausen, ut sup.

[14] Lücke also thinks this symbolical interpretation too far-fetched, and too little
supported by the tone of the narrative, s. 406.   Comp. De Wette, ex. Handb. 1, 3,
s. 37.

* [A Wirtemburg wine Maas, or measure, is equal to about 3⅓ pints English, or
more exactly 3.32.—Tr.]

[15] Wurm, de ponderum, mensurarum etc. rationibus, ap. Rom. et Graec, p. 123,
126.   Comp. Lücke, in loc.

even Olshausen consoles himself, after Semler, with the fact, that it is nowhere remarked that the water in all the vessels was turned into wine. But these are subterfuges; they to whom the supply of so extravagant and dangerous a quantity of wine on the part of Jesus is incredible, must conclude that the narrative is unhistorical.

Peculiar difficulty is occasioned by the relation in which this narrative places Jesus to his mother, and his mother to him. According to the express statement of the evangelist, the turning of water into wine was the *beginning* of the miracles of Jesus, ἀρχὴ τῶν σημείων; and yet his mother reckons so confidently on his performing a miracle here, that she believes it only necessary to point out to him the deficiency of wine, in order to induce him to afford supernatural aid; and even when she receives a discouraging answer, she is so far from losing hope, that she enjoins the servants to be obedient to the directions of her son (v. 3, 5). How is this expectation of a miracle on the part of the mother of Jesus to be explained? Are we to refer the declaration of John, that the metamorphosis of the water was the first miracle of Jesus, merely to the period of his public life, and to presuppose as real events, for his previous years, the apocryphal miracles of the Gospel of the Infancy? Or, believing that Chrysostom was right in regarding this as too uncritical [16], are we rather to conjecture that Mary, in consequence of her conviction that Jesus was the Messiah, a conviction wrought in her by the signs that attended his birth, expected miracles from him, and as perhaps on some earlier occasions, so now on this, when the perplexity was great, desired from him a proof of his power [17]? Were only that early conviction of the relatives of Jesus that he was the Messiah somewhat more probable, and especially the extraordinary events of the childhood, by which it is supposed to have been produced, better accredited! Moreover, even pre-

[16] Homil. in Joann. in loc.
[17] Tholuck, in loc.

supposing the belief of Mary in the miraculous power of her son, it is still not at all clear how, notwithstanding his discouraging answer, she could yet confidently expect that he would just on this occasion perform his first miracle, and feel assured that she positively knew that he would act precisely so as to require the assistance of the servants [18]. This decided knowledge on the part of Mary, even respecting the manner of the miracle about to be wrought, appears to indicate an antecedent disclosure of Jesus to her, and hence Olshausen supposes that Jesus had given his mother an intimation concerning the miracle on which he had resolved. But when could this disclosure have been made? Already as they were going to the feast? Then Jesus must have foreseen that there would be a want of wine, in which case Mary could not have apprised him of it as of an unexpected embarrassment. Or did Jesus make the disclosure after her appeal, and consequently in connexion with the words: *What have I to do with thee, woman*, &c.? But with this answer, it is impossible to conceive so opposite a declaration to have been united; it would therefore be necessary, on Olshausen's view, to imagine that Jesus uttered the negative words aloud, the affirmative in an under tone, merely for Mary: a supposition which would give the scene the appearance of a comedy. Thus it is on no supposition to be understood how Mary could expect a miracle at all, still less precisely such an one. The first difficulty might indeed be plausibly evaded, by maintaining that Mary did not here apply to Jesus in expectation of a miracle, but simply that she might obtain her son's advice in the case, as she was wont to do in all difficult circumstances [19]: his reply however shows that he regarded the words of his mother as a summons to perform a miracle, and moreover the direction which Mary gave to the servants remains on this supposition totally unexplained.

---

[18] This argument is valid against Neander also, who appeals to the faith of Mary chiefly as a result of the solemn inauguration at the baptism, (s. 370.)

[19] Hess, Gesch. Jesu, 1, s. 135.   Comp. also Calvin, in loc.

The answer of Jesus to the intimation of his mother (v. 4) has been just as often blamed with exaggeration [20] as justified on insufficient grounds. However truly it may be urged that the Hebrew phrase, וָלָךְ מַה־לִּי, to which the Greek τί ἐμοὶ καὶ σοὶ corresponds, appears elsewhere as an expression of gentle blame, e. g. 2 Sam. xvi. 10 [21]; or that with the entrance of Jesus on his special office his relation to his mother as regarded his actions was dissolved [22] : it nevertheless remains undeniable, that it was fitting for Jesus to be modestly apprised of opportunities for the exercise of his miraculous power, and if one who pointed out to him a case of disease and added an intreaty for help, did not deserve reprehension, as little and even less did Mary, when she brought to his knowledge a want which had arisen, with a merely implied intreaty for assistance. The case would have been different had Jesus considered the occasion not adapted, or even unworthy to have a miracle connected with it; he might then have repelled with severity the implied summons, as an incitement to a false use of miraculous power (instanced in the history of the temptation); as, on the contrary, he immediately after showed by his actions that he held the occasion worthy of a miracle, it is absolutely incomprehensible how he could blame his mother for her information, which perhaps only came to him a few moments too soon [23].

Here again it has been attempted to escape from the numerous difficulties of the supranatural view, by a natural interpretation of the history. The commentators who advance this explanation set out from the fact, that it was the custom among the Jews to make presents of oil or wine at marriage feasts. Now Jesus, it is said, having brought with him five new disciples as uninvited guests, might foresee a deficiency of wine, and wished out of pleasantry to present his gift in an unexpected and mysterious manner. The δόξα (glory) which he manifested by

[20] E. g. by Woolston, ut sup.
[21] Flatt, ut sup. s. 90 ; Tholuck, in loc.
[22] Olshausen, in loc.
[23] Comp. also the Probabilia, p. 41 f.

this proceeding, is said to be merely his humanity, which in the proper place did not disdain to pass a jest; the πίστις, (*faith*) which he thereby excited in his disciples, was a joyful adherence to a man who exhibited none of the oppressive severity which had been anticipated in the Messiah. Mary was aware of her son's project, and warned him when it appeared to her time to put it in execution; but he reminded her playfully not to spoil his jest by over-haste. His causing water to be drawn, seems to have belonged to the playful deception which he intended; that all at once wine was found in the vessels instead of water, and that this was regarded as a miraculous metamorphosis, might easily happen at a late hour of the night, when there had already been considerable drinking; lastly, that Jesus did not enlighten the wedding party as to the true state of the case, was the natural consequence of his wish not himself to dissipate the delusion which he had playfully caused[24]. For the rest, how the plan was effected, by what arrangements on the part of Jesus the wine was conveyed in the place of the water, this, Paulus thinks, is not now to be ascertained; it is enough for us to know that all happened naturally. As however, according to the opinion of this expositor, the evangelist was aware in a general manner, that the whole occurrence was natural, why has he given us no intimation to that effect? Did he wish to prepare for the reader the same surprise that Jesus had prepared for the spectators? still he must afterwards have solved the enigma, if he did not intend the delusion to be permanent. Above all, he ought not to have used the misleading expression, that Jesus by this act *manifested forth his glory* (τὴν δόξαν αὐτοῦ, v. 11), which, in the phraseology of this gospel, can only mean his superior dignity; he ought not to have called the incident a *sign* (σημεῖον), by which something supernatural is implied; lastly, he ought not, by the expression, *the water that was made wine* (τὸ ὕδωρ οἶνον γεγενημένον, v. 9), and still less by the subsequent designa-

[24] Paulus, Comm. 4, s. 150 ff.; L. J. 1, a. s. 169 ff.; Natürliche Gesch. 2, s. 61 ff.

tion of Cana as the place *where he made the water wine* (ὅπου ἐποίησεν ὕδωρ οἶνον), to have occasioned the impression, that he approved the miraculous conception of the event [25]. The author of the Natural History sought to elude these difficulties by the admission, that the narrator himself, John, regarded the event as a miracle, and meant to describe it as such. Not to mention, however, the unworthy manner in which he explains this error on the part of the evangelist [26], it is not easy to conceive of Jesus that he should have kept his disciples in the same delusion as the rest of the guests, and not have given to them at least an explanation concerning the real course of the event. It would therefore be necessary to suppose that the narrator of this event was not one of the disciples of Jesus : a supposition which goes beyond the sphere of this system of interpretation. But even admitting that the narrator himself, whoever he may have been, was included in the same deception with those who regarded the affair as a miracle, in which case his mode of representation and the expressions which he uses would be accounted for ; still the procedure of Jesus, and his mode of acting, are all the more inconceivable, if no real miracle were on foot. Why did he with refined assiduity arrange the presentation of the wine, so that it might appear to be a miraculous gift ? Why, in particular, did he cause the vessels in which he intended forthwith to present the wine, to be filled beforehand with water, the necessary removal of which could only be a hindrance to the secret execution of his plan ? unless indeed it be supposed, with Woolston, that he merely imparted to the water the taste of wine, by pouring into it some liquor. Thus there is a double difficulty; on the one hand, that of imagining how the wine could be introduced into the vessels already filled with water ; on the other, that of freeing Jesus from the suspicion of having wished to create the appearance of a miraculous transmutation of the water. It may have been the perception of these difficulties which induced the author of

[25] Compare on this point, Flatt, ut sup. s. 77 ff. and Lücke, in loc.
[26] He makes the word μεθύσκεσθαι, v. 10, refer to John also.

the Natural History entirely to sever the connexion between the water which was poured in, and the wine which subsequently appeared, by the supposition that Jesus had caused the water to be fetched, because there was a deficiency of this also, and Jesus wished to recommend the beneficial practice of washing before and after meals, but that he afterwards caused the wine to be brought out of an adjoining room where he had placed it :—a conception of the matter which requires us either to suppose the intoxication of all the guests, and especially of the narrator, as so considerable, that they mistook the wine brought out of the adjoining room, for wine drawn out of the water vessels; or else that the deceptive arrangements of Jesus were contrived with very great art, which is inconsistent with the straightforwardness of character elsewhere ascribed to him.

In this dilemma between the supranatural and the natural interpretations, of which, in this case again, the one is as insufficient as the other, we should be reduced, with one of the most recent commentators on the fourth gospel, to wait "until it pleased God, by further developments of judicious Christian reflection, to evolve a solution of the enigma to the general satisfaction;"[27] did we not discern an outlet in the fact, that the history in question is found in John's gospel alone. Single in its kind as this miracle is, if it were also the first performed by Jesus, it must, even if all the twelve were not then with Jesus, have yet been known to them all; and even if among the rest of the evangelists there were no apostle, still it must have passed into the general Christian tradition, and from thence into the synoptical memoirs: consequently, as John alone has it, the supposition that it arose in a region of tradition unknown to the synoptists, seems easier than the alternative, that it so early disappeared out of that from which they drew; the only question is, whether we are in a condition to show how such a legend could arise without historical grounds. Kaiser points for this purpose to the extravagant spirit of the oriental legend,

[27] Lücke, s. 407.

which has ever been so fertile in metamorphoses: but this
source is so wide and indefinite, that Kaiser finds it necessary
also to suppose a real jest on the part of Jesus [28], and thus
remains uneasily suspended between the mythical and the natural explanations, a position which cannot be escaped from,
until there can be produced points of mythical connexion and
origin more definite and exact. Now in the present case we
need halt neither at the character of eastern legend in general,
nor at metamorphoses in general, since transmutations of this
particular element of water are to be found within the narrower
circle of the ancient Hebrew history. Besides some narratives
of Moses procuring for the Israelites water out of the flinty rock
in the wilderness (Exod. xvii. 1 ff.; Numb. xx. 1 ff.)—a bestowal of water which, after being repeated in a modified manner in the history of Samson, (Judges xv. 18 f.) was made a
feature in the messianic expectations [29];—the first transmutation of water ascribed to Moses, is the turning of all the water
in Egypt into blood, which is enumerated among the so-called
plagues (Exod. vii. 17 ff.). Together with this *mutatio in
deterius*, there is in the history of Moses a *mutatio in melius*,
also effected in water, for he made bitter water sweet, under the
direction of Jehovah (Exod. xiv. 23 ff. [30]); as at a later era,
Elisha also is said to have made unhealthy water good and
innoxious (2 Kings ii. 19 ff. [31]). As, according to the rabbinical passage quoted, the *bestowal* of water, so also, according
to this narrative in John, the *transmutation* of water appears to
have been transferred from Moses and the prophets to the
Messiah, with such modifications, however, as lay in the nature
of the case. If namely, on the one hand, a change of water

[28] Bibl. Theol. 1, s. 200.

[29] In the passages cited Vol. I. § 14, out of Midrasch Koheleth, it is said among
other things : *Goël primus—ascendere fecit puteum : sic quoque Goël postremus ascendere faciet aquas, etc.*

[30] A natural explanation of this miracle is given by Josephus in a manner worthy
of notice, Antiq. iii. 1, 2.

[31] We may also remind the reader of the transmutation of water into oil, which
Eusebius (H. E. vi. 9.) narrates of a Christian bishop.

for the worse, like that Mosaic transmutation into blood—if a miracle of this retributive kind might not seem well suited to the mild spirit of the Messiah as recognised in Jesus: so on the other hand, such a change for the better as, like the removal of bitterness or noxiousness, did not go beyond the *species* of water, and did not, like the change into blood, alter the substance of the water itself, might appear insufficient for the Messiah; if then the two conditions be united, a change of water for the better, which should at the same time be a specific alteration of its substance, must almost of necessity be a change into wine. Now this is narrated by John, in a manner not indeed in accordance with reality, but which must be held all the more in accordance with the spirit of his gospel. For the harshness of Jesus towards his mother is, historically considered, incredible; but it is entirely in the spirit of the fourth gospel, to place in relief the exaltation of Jesus as the divine Logos by such demeanour towards suppliants (as in John iv. 48.), and even towards his mother [32]. Equally in the spirit of this gospel is it also, to exhibit the firm faith which Mary maintains notwithstanding the negative answer of Jesus, by making her give the direction to the servants above considered, as if she had a preconception even of the manner in which Jesus would perform his miracle, a preconception which is historically impossible [33].

[32] Compare the Probabilia, ut sup.

[33] De Wette thinks the analogies adduced from the Old Testament too remote; according to him, the metamorphosis of wine into water by Bacchus, instanced by Wetstein, would be nearer to the subject, and not far from the region of Greek thought, out of which the gospel of John arose. The most analogous mythical derivation of the narrative would be to regard this supply of wine as the counterpart to the supply of bread, and both as corresponding to the bread and wine in the last supper. But, he continues, the mythical view is opposed, 1, by the not yet overthrown authenticity of the fourth gospel; 2, by the fact that the narrative bears less of a legendary than a subjective impress, by the obscurity that rests upon it, and its want of one presiding idea, together with the abundance of practical ideas worthy of Jesus which it embodies. By these observations De Wette seems to intimate his approval of a natural explanation, built on the self-deception of John; an explanation which is encumbered with the difficulties above noticed.

§ 104.

The anecdote of the fig-tree which Jesus caused to wither by his word, because when he was hungry he found no fruit on it, is peculiar to the two first gospels (Matt. xxi. 18 ff.; Mark xi. 12 ff.), but is narrated by them with divergencies which must affect our view of the fact. One of these divergencies of Mark from Matthew, appears so favourable to the natural explanation, that, chiefly in consideration of it, a tendency towards the natural view of the miracles of Jesus has been of late ascribed to this evangelist; and for the sake of this one favourable divergency, he has been defended in relation to the other rather inconvenient one, which is found in the narrative before us.

If we were restricted to the manner in which the first evangelist states the consequence of the curse of Jesus: *and immediately the fig-tree withered away καὶ ἐξηράνθη παραχρῆμα ἡ συκῆ*, it would be difficult here to carry out a natural explanation; for even the forced interpretation of Paulus, which makes the word παραχρῆμα (*immediately*) only exclude farther human accession to the fact, and not a longer space of time, rests only on an unwarranted transference of Mark's particulars into the narrative of Matthew. In Mark, Jesus curses the fig-tree on the morning after his entrance into Jerusalem, and not till the following morning the disciples remark, in passing, that the tree is withered. Through this interim, which Mark leaves open between the declaration of Jesus and the withering of the tree, the natural explanation of the whole narrative insinuates itself, taking its stand on the possibility, that in this interval the tree might have withered from natural causes. Accordingly, Jesus is supposed to have remarked in the tree, besides the lack of fruit, a condition from which he prognosticated that it would soon wither away, and to have uttered this prediction in the

words : No one will ever again gather fruit from thee. The
heat of the day having realized the prediction of Jesus with
unexpected rapidity, and the disciples remarking this the next
morning, they then first connected this result with the words of
Jesus on the previous morning, and began to regard them as a
curse : an interpretation which, indeed, Jesus does not confirm,
but impresses on the disciples, that if they have only some self-
reliance, they will be able, not only to predict such physiolo-
gically evident results, but also to know and effect things far
more difficult[1]. But even admitting Mark's statement to be
the correct one, the natural explanation still remains impossible.
For the words of Jesus in Mark (v. 14) : μηκέτι ἐκ σοῦ εἰς τὸν
αἰῶνα μηδεὶς καρπὸν φάγοι, *No man eat fruit of thee hereafter
for ever*, if they had been meant to imply a mere conjecture as
to what would probably happen, must necessarily have had a
potential signification given to them by the addition of ἂν ; and
in the expression of Matthew : μηκέτι ἐκ σοῦ καρπὸς γένηται,
Let no fruit grow on thee henceforward for ever, the command is not to be mistaken, although Paulus would only find
in this also the expression of a possibility. Moreover the circumstance that Jesus addresses the tree itself, as also the
solemn εἰς τὸν αἰῶνα, *for ever*, which he adds, speaks against
the idea of a mere prediction, and in favour of a curse ; Paulus
perceives this fully, and hence with unwarrantable violence he
interprets the words λέγει αὐτῇ *he saith to it*, as if they introduced a saying merely in reference to the tree, while he depre-
ciates the expression εἰς τὸν αἰῶνα, by the translation : *in time
to come*. But even if we grant that the evangelists, owing to
their erroneous conception of the incident, may have somewhat
altered the words of Jesus, and that he in reality only prognosticated the withering of the tree ; still, when the prediction was
fulfilled, Jesus did nevertheless ascribe the result to his own
supernatural influence. For in speaking of what he has done
in relation to the fig-tree, he uses the verb ποιεῖν (v. 21 Matt.);

[1] Paulus, exeg. Handb. 3, a. s. 157 ff.

which cannot, except by a forced interpretation, be referred to a
mere prediction. But more than this, he compares what he has
done in relation to the fig-tree, with the removal of mountains;
and hence, as this, according to every possible interpretation, is
an act of causation, so the other must be regarded as an influence on the tree. In any case, when Peter spoke of the fig-tree
as having been cursed by Jesus (v. 21 Mark), either the latter
must have contradicted the construction thus put on his words,
or his silence must have implied his acquiescence. If then
Jesus in the issue ascribes the withering of the tree to his influence, he either by his address to it designed to produce an
effect, or he ambitiously misused the accidental result for the
sake of deluding his disciples; a dilemma, in which the words
of Jesus, as they are given by the evangelists, decidedly direct
us to the former alternative.

Thus we are inexorably thrown back from the naturalistic
attempt at an explanation, to the conception of the supranaturalists, pre-eminently difficult as this is in the history
before us.   We pass over what might be said against the
physical possibility of such an influence as is there presupposed; not, indeed, because, with Hase, we could comprehend
it through the medium of natural magic [2], but because another
difficulty beforehand excludes the inquiry, and does not allow
us to come to the consideration of the physical possibility.
This decisive difficulty relates to the moral possibility of such
an act on the part of Jesus.   The miracle he here performs is
of a punitive character.   Another example of the kind is not
found in the canonical accounts of the life of Jesus; the apocryphal gospels alone, as has been above remarked, are full of
such miracles.   In one of the synoptical gospels there is, on
the contrary, a passage often quoted already (Luke ix. 55 f.),
in which it is declared, as the profound conviction of Jesus,
that the employment of miraculous power in order to execute
punishment or to take vengeance, is contrary to the spirit of

[2] L. J. § 128.

his vocation; and the same sentiment is attributed to Jesus by the evangelist, when he applies to him the words of Isaiah: *He shall not break a bruised reed,* &c. (Matt. xii. 20.). Agreeably to this principle, and to his prevalent mode of action, Jesus must rather have given new life to a withered tree, than have made a green one wither; and in order to comprehend his conduct on this occasion, we must be able to show reasons which he might possibly have had, for departing in this instance from the above principle, which has no mark of unauthenticity. The occasion on which he enunciated that principle was when, on the refusal of a Samaritan village to exercise hospitality towards Jesus and his disciples, the sons of Zebedee asked him whether they should not rain down fire on the village, after the example of Elijah. Jesus replied by reminding them of the nature of the spirit to which they belonged, a spirit with which so destructive an act was incompatible. In our present case Jesus had not to deal with men who had treated him with injustice, but with a tree which he happened not to find in the desired state. Now, there is here no special reason for departing from the above rule; on the contrary, the chief reason which in the first case might possibly have moved Jesus to determine on a judicial miracle, is not present in the second. The moral end of punishment, namely, to bring the punished person to a conviction and acknowledgment of his error, can have no existence in relation to a tree; and even punishment in the light of retribution, is out of the question when we are treating of natural objects destitute of volition [3]. For one to be irritated against an inanimate object, which does not happen to be found just in the desired state, is with reason pronounced to be a proof of an uncultivated mind; to carry such indignation to the destruction of the object is regarded as barbarous, and unworthy of a reasonable being; and hence Woolston is not wrong in maintaining, that in any other person than Jesus,

---

[3] Augustin. de verbis Domini in ev. sec. Joann. sermo 44 : *Quid arbor fecerat, fructum non afferendo ? quæ culpa arboris infœcunditas ?*

such an act would be severely blamed [4]. It is true that when a natural object is intrinsically and habitually defective, it may very well happen, that it may be removed out of the way, in order to put a better in its place ; a measure, however, for which, in every case, only the owner has the adequate motive and authority (comp. Luke xiii. 7.). But that this tree, because just at that time it presented no fruit, would not have borne any in succeeding years, was by no means self-evident :— nay, the contrary is implied in the narrative, since the form in which the curse of Jesus is expressed, that fruit shall never more grow on the tree, presupposes, that without this curse the tree might yet have been fruitful.

Thus the evil condition of the tree was not habitual but temporary ; still further, if we follow Mark, it was not even objective, or existing intrinsically in the tree, but purely subjective, that is, a result of the accidental relation of the tree to the momentary wish and want of Jesus. For according to an addition which forms the second feature peculiar to Mark in this narrative, it was not then the time of figs (v. 13) ; it was not therefore a defect, but, on the contrary, quite in due order, that this tree, as well as others, had no figs on it, and Jesus (in whom it is already enough to excite surprise that he expected to find figs on the tree so out of season) might at least have reflected, when he found none, on the groundlessness of his expectation, and have forborne so wholly unjust an act as the cursing of the tree. Even some of the fathers stumbled at this addition of Mark's, and felt that it rendered the conduct of Jesus enigmatical [5] ; and to descend to later times, Woolston's ridicule is

---

[4] Disc. 4.

[5] Orig. Comm. in Matth. Tom. xvi. 29 : Ὁ δὲ Μάρκος ἀναγράψας τὰ κατὰ τὸν τόπον, ἀπεμφαῖνόν τι ὡς πρὸς τὸ ῥητὸν προσέθηκε, ποιήσας, ὅτι—οὐ γὰρ ἦν καιρὸς σύκων. —Εἴποι γὰρ ἄν τις· εἰ μὴ ὁ καιρὸς σύκων ἦν, πῶς ἦλθεν ὁ Ἰ. ὡς εὑρήσων τι ἐν αὐτῇ, καὶ πῶς δικαίως εἶπεν αὐτῇ· μηκέτι εἰς τὸν αἰῶνα ἐκ σοῦ μηδεὶς καρπὸν φάγῃ ; comp. Augustin ut sup. *Mark, in relating this event, adds something which seems not to tally well with his statement, when he observes that it was not the season for figs. It might be urged : if it was not the season for figs, why should Jesus go and look for fruit on the tree, and how could he, with justice, say to it, Let no man eat fruit of thee for ever ?*

not unfounded, when he says that if a Kentish countryman were to seek for fruit in his garden in spring, and were to cut down the trees which had none, he would be a common laughing-stock. Expositors have attempted to free themselves from the difficulty which this addition introduces, by a motley series of conjectures and interpretations. On the one hand, the wish that the perplexing words did not stand in the text, has been turned into the hypothesis that they may probably be a subsequent gloss [6]. On the other hand, as, if an addition of this kind must stand there, the contrary statement, namely, that it was then the time of figs, were rather to be desired, in order to render intelligible the expectation of Jesus, and his displeasure when he found it deceived; it has been attempted in various ways to remove the negative out of the proposition. One expedient is altogether violent, οὖ being read instead of οὐ, a point inserted after ἦν, and a second ἦν supplied after σύκων, so that the translation runs thus : *ubi enim tum versabatur* (Jesus), *tempus ficuum erat* [7] ; another expedient, the transformation of the sentence into an interrogatory one, *nonne enim*, etc., is absurd [8]. A third expedient is to understand the words καιρὸς σύκων as implying the time of the fig-gathering, and thus to take Mark's addition as a statement that the figs were not yet gathered, i. e. were still on the trees [9], in support of which interpretation, appeal is made to the phrase καιρὸς τῶν καρπῶν (Matt. xxi. 34.). But this expression strictly refers only to the *antecedent* of the harvest, the existence of the fruits in the fields or on the trees; when it stands in an affirmative proposition, it can only be understood as referring to the *consequent*, namely, the possible gathering of the fruit, in so far as it also includes the *antecedent*, the existence of the fruits in the field : hence ἔστι καιρὸς καρπῶν can only mean thus much : the (ripe) fruits stand in

[6] Toupii emendd. in Suidam, 1, p. 330 f.

[7] Heinsius and others, ap. Fritzsche, in loc.

[8] Maji Obs. ib.

[9] Dahme, in Henke's n. Magazin, 2. Bd. 2. Heft, s. 252. Kuinöl, in Marc, p. 150 f.

the fields, and are therefore ready to be gathered. In like manner, when the above expression stands in a negative proposition, the *antecedent*, the existence of the fruits in the field, on the trees, &c., is primarily denied, that of the *consequent* only secondarily and by implication; thus οὐκ ἔστι καιρὸς σύκων, means: the figs are not on the trees, and therefore not ready to be gathered; by no means the reverse: they are not yet gathered, and therefore are still on the trees. But this unexampled figure of speech, by which, while according to the words, the *antecedent* is denied, according to the sense only the *consequent* is denied, and the *antecedent* affirmed, is not all which the above explanation entails upon us; it also requires the admission of another figure which is sometimes called synchisis, sometimes hyperbaton. For, as a statement that the figs were then still on the trees, the addition in question does not show the reason why Jesus found none on that tree, but why he expected the contrary; it ought therefore, say the advocates of this explanation, to stand, not after *he found nothing but leaves*, but after *he came, if haply he might find any thing thereon;* a transposition, however, which only proves that this whole explanation runs counter to the text. Convinced, on the one hand, that the addition of Mark denies the prevalence of circumstances favourable to the existence of figs on that tree, but, on the other hand, still labouring to justify the expectation of Jesus, other expositors have sought to give to that negation, instead of the general sense, that it was not the right season of the year for figs, a fact of which Jesus must unavoidably have been aware, the particular sense, that special circumstances only, not necessarily known to Jesus, hindered the fruitfulness of the tree. It would have been a hindrance altogether special, if the soil in which the tree was rooted had been an unfruitful one; hence, according to some, the words καιρὸς σύκων actually signify *a soil favourable to figs* [10]. Others with more regard to the verbal meaning of καιρὸς, adhere it is true to the inter-

---

[10] Vid. Kuinöl, in loc.

pretation of it as *favourable time*, but instead of understanding the statement of Mark universally, as referring to a regular, annual season, in which figs were not to be obtained, they maintain it to mean that that particular year was from some incidental causes unfavourable to figs [11]. But the immediate signification of καιρὸς is the right, in opposition to the wrong season, not a favourable season as opposed to an unfavourable one. Now, when any one, even in an unproductive year, seeks for fruits at the time in which they are wont to be ripe, it cannot be said that it is the wrong season for fruit; on the contrary, the idea of a bad year might be at once conveyed by the statement, that *when the time for fruit came,* ὅτε ἦλθεν ὁ καιρὸς τῶν καρπῶν, there was none to be found. In any case, if the whole course of the year were unfavourable to figs, a fruit so abundant in Palestine, Jesus must almost as necessarily have known this, as that it was the wrong season; so that the enigma remains, how Jesus could be so indignant that the tree was in a condition which, owing to circumstances known to him, was inevitable.

But let us only remember who it is, to whom we owe that addition. It is Mark, who, in his efforts after the explanatory and the picturesque, so frequently draws on his own imagination; and in doing this, as it has been long ago perceived, and as we also have had sufficient opportunities of observing on our way, he does not always go to work in the most considerate manner. Thus, here, he is arrested by the first striking particular that presents itself, namely, that the tree was without fruit, and hastens to furnish the explanation, that it was not the time for figs, not observing that while he accounts physically for the barrenness of the tree, he makes the conduct of Jesus morally inexplicable. Again, the above-mentioned divergency from Matthew in relation to the time within which the tree withered, far from evincing more authentic information [12], or a tendency to

---

[11] Paulus, exeg. Handb., 3, a. s. 175; Olshausen, b. Comm. 1, s. 782.

[12] As Sieffert thinks, ueber den Urspr. s. 113 ff. Compare my reviews, in the Charakteristiken and Kritiken, s. 272.

the natural explanation of the marvellous on the part of Mark, is only another product of the same dramatising effort as that which gave birth to the above addition. The idea of a tree suddenly withering at a word, is difficult for the imagination perfectly to fashion ; whereas it cannot be called a bad dramatic contrivance, to lay the process of withering behind the scenes, and to make the result be first noticed by the subsequent passers by. For the rest, in the assertion that it was then, (a few days before Easter,) no time for figs, Mark is so far right, as it regards the conditions of climate in Palestine, that at so early a time of the year the new figs of the season were not yet ripe, for the early fig or boccore is not ripe until the middle or towards the end of June ; while the proper fig, the kermus, ripens only in the month of August. On the other hand, there might about Easter still be met with here and there, hanging on the tree, the third fruit of the fig tree, the late kermus, which had remained from the previous autumn, and through the winter [13] : as we read in Josephus that a part of Palestine (the shores of the Galilean sea, more fruitful, certainly, than the country around Jerusalem, where the history in question occurred,) *pro-duces figs uninterruptedly during ten months of the year*, σῦκον δέκα μησὶν ἀδιαλείπτως χορηγεῖ [14].

But even when we have thus set aside this perplexing addition of Mark's, that the tree was not really defective, but only appeared so to Jesus in consequence of an erroneous expectation : there still subsists, even according to Matthew, the incongruity that Jesus appears to have destroyed a natural object on account of a deficiency which might possibly be merely temporary. He cannot have been prompted to this by economical considerations, since he was not the owner of the tree ; still less can he have been actuated by moral views, in relation to an inanimate object of nature ; hence the expedient has been adopted of substituting the disciples as the proper object on which Jesus here intended to act, and of regarding the tree and what Jesus does

[13] Vid. Paulus, ut sup. s. 168 f. ; Winer, b. Realw. d. A. Feigenbaum.
[14] Bell. Jud. III. x. 8.

to it, as a mere means to his ultimate design. This is the symbolical interpretation, by which first the fathers of the church and of late the majority of orthodox theologians among the moderns, have thought to free Jesus from the charge of an unsuitable action. According to them, anger towards the tree which presented nothing to appease his hunger, was not the feeling of Jesus, in performing this action; his object, not simply the extermination of the unfruitful plant: on the contrary, he judiciously availed himself of the occasion of finding a barren tree, in order to impress a truth on his disciples more vividly and indelibly than by words. This truth may either be conceived under a special form, namely, that the Jewish nation which persisted in rendering no pleasing fruit to God and to the Messiah, would be destroyed; or under the general form, that every one who was as destitute of good works as this tree was of fruit, had to look forward to a similar condemnation [15]. Other commentators however with reason maintain, that if Jesus had had such an end in view in the action, he must in some way have explained himself on the subject; for if an elucidation was necessary when he delivered a parable, it was the more indispensable when he performed a symbolical action, in proportion as this, without such an indication of an object lying beyond itself, was more likely to be mistaken for an object in itself [16]; it is true that, here as well as elsewhere, it might be supposed, that Jesus probably enlarged on what he had done, for the instruction of his disciples, but that the narrators, content with the miracle, have omitted the illustrative discourse. If however Jesus gave an interpretation of his act in the alleged symbolical sense, the evangelists have not merely been silent concerning this discourse, but have inserted a false one in its place; for they represent Jesus, after his procedure with respect to the tree, not as being silent, but as giving, in answer to an expression of astonishment on the part of his disciples, an explanation which

---

[15] Ullman, über die Unsündlichkeit Jesu, in his Studien, 1, s. 50; Sieffert, ut sup. s. 115 ff.; Olshausen, 1, s. 783 f.; Neander, L. J. Chr. s. 378.

[16] Paulus, ut sup. s. 170; Hase, L. J. § 128; also Sieffert, ut sup.

is not the above symbolical one, but a different, nay, an opposite one.   For when Jesus says to them that they need not wonder at the withering of the fig-tree, since with only a little faith they will be able to effect yet greater things, he lays the chief stress on his agency in the matter, not on the condition and the fate of the tree as a symbol: therefore, if his design turned upon the latter, he would have spoken to his disciples so as to contravene that design; or rather, if he so spoke, that cannot have been his design.   For the same reason, falls also Sieffert's totally unsupported hypothesis, that Jesus, not indeed after, but before that act, when on the way to the fig-tree, had held a conversation with his disciples on the actual condition and future lot of the Jewish nation, and that to this conversation the symbolical cursing of the tree was a mere key-stone, which explained itself: for all comprehension of the act in question which that introduction might have facilitated, must, especially in that age when there was so strong a bias towards the miraculous, have been again obliterated by the subsequent declaration of Jesus, which regarded only the miraculous side of the fact.   Hence Ullmann has judged rightly in preferring to the symbolical interpretation, although he considers it admissible, another which had previously been advanced [17]: namely, that Jesus by this miracle intended to give his followers a new proof of his perfect power, in order to strengthen their confidence in him under the approaching perils.   Or rather, as a special reference to coming trial is nowhere exhibited, and as the words of Jesus contain nothing which he had not already said at an earlier period (Matt. xvii. 20; Luke xvii. 6), Fritzsche is more correct in expressing the view of the evangelists quite generally, thus: Jesus used his displeasure at the unfruitfulness of the tree, as an occasion for performing a miracle, the object of which was merely the general one of all his miracles, namely, to attest his Messiahship [18].   Hence Euthymius speaks entirely in the spirit of the narrators, as

[17] Heydenreich, in the Thecl. Nachrichten, 1814, Mai., s. 121 ff.
[18] Comm. in Matth. p. 637.

described by Fritzsche[19], when he forbids all investigation into the special end of the action, and exhorts the reader only to look at it in general as a miracle[20]. But it by no means follows from hence that we too should refrain from all reflection on the subject, and believingly receive the miracle without further question; on the contrary, we cannot avoid observing, that the particular miracle which we have now before us, does not admit of being explained as a real act of Jesus, either upon the general ground of performing miracles, or from any peculiar object or motive whatever. Far from this, it is in every respect opposed both to his theory and his prevailing practice, and on this account, even apart from the question of its physical possibility, must be pronounced more decidedly than any other, to be such a miracle as Jesus cannot really have performed.

It is incumbent on us, however, to adduce positive proof of the existence of such causes as, even without historical foundation, might give rise to a narrative of this kind. Now in our usual source, the Old Testament, we do, indeed, find many figurative discourses and narratives about trees, and fig-trees in particular; but none which has so specific an affinity to our narrative, that we could say the latter is an imitation of it. But we need not search long in the New Testament, before we find, first in the mouth of the Baptist (Matt. iii. 10.), then in that of Jesus (vii. 19.), the apothegm of the tree, which, because it bears no good fruit, is cut down and cast into the fire; and farther on (Luke xiii. 6 ff.) this theme is dilated into the fictitious history of a man who for three years in vain seeks for fruit on a fig-tree in his vineyard, and on this account determines to cut it down, but that the gardener intercedes for

[19] Comm. in Marc. p. 481 : *Male—vv. dd. in eo hæserunt, quod Jesus sine ratione innocentem ficum aridam reddidisse videretur, mirisque argutiis usi sunt, ut aliquod hujus rei consilium fuisse ostenderent. Nimirum apostoli, evangelistæ et omnes primi temporis Christiani, qua erant ingeniorum simplicitate, quid quantumque Jesus portentose fecisse diceretur, curarunt tantummodo, non quod Jesu in edendo miraculo consilium fuerit, subtiliter et argute quæsiverunt.*

[20] Μὴ ἀκριβολογοῦ διατί τετιμώρηται τὸ φυτὸν, ἀναίτιον ὄν· ἀλλὰ μόν ν ὅρα τὸ θαῦμα, καὶ θαυμάζε τὸν θαυματουργόν.

another year's respite. It was already an idea of some Fathers of the church, that the cursing of the fig-tree was only the parable of the barren fig-tree carried out into action [21]. It is true that they held this opinion in the sense of the explanation before cited, namely, that Jesus himself, as he had previously exhibited the actual condition and the approaching catastrophe of the Jewish people in a figurative discourse, intended on the occasion in question to represent them by a symbolical action; which, as we have seen, is inconceivable. Nevertheless, we cannot help conjecturing, that we have before us one and the same theme under three different modifications: first, in the most concentrated form, as an apothegm; then expanded into a parable; and lastly realized as a history. But we do not suppose that what Jesus twice described in words, he at length represented by an action; in our opinion, it was tradition which converted what it met with as an apothegm and a parable, into a real incident. That in the real history the end of the tree is somewhat different from that threatened in the apothegm and parable, namely, withering instead of being cut down, need not amount to a difficulty. For had the parable once become a real history, with Jesus for its subject, and consequently its whole didactic and symbolical significance passed into the external act, then must this, if it were to have any weight and interest, take the form of a miracle, and the natural destruction of the tree by means of the axe, must be transformed into an immediate withering on the word of Jesus. It is true that there seems to be the very same objection to this conception of the narrative which allows its inmost kernel to be symbolical, as to the one above considered; namely, that it is contravened by the words of Jesus which are appended to the narrative. But on our view of the gospel histories we are warranted to say, that with the transformation of the parable into a history, its original sense also was lost, and as the miracle began to be regarded as constituting the pith of the matter, that discourse

[21] Ambrosius, Comm. in Luc, in loc. Neander adopts this opinion, ut sup.

on miraculous power and faith, was erroneously annexed to it. Even the particular circumstance that led to the selection of the saying about the removal of the mountain for association with the narrative of the fig-tree, may be shown with probability. The power of faith, which is here represented by an effectual command to a mountain: *Be thou removed and be thou cast into the sea,* is elsewhere (Luke xvii. 6.) symbolized by an equally effectual command to a species of fig-tree (συκ-άμινος): *Be thou plucked up by the root, and be thou planted in the sea.* Hence the cursing of the fig-tree, so soon as its withering was conceived to be an effect of the miraculous power of Jesus, brought to mind the tree or the mountain which was to be transported by the miraculous power of faith, and this saying became appended to that fact. Thus, in this instance, praise is due to the third gospel for having preserved to us the parable of the barren συκῆ, and the apothegm of the συκάμινος to be transplanted by faith, distinct and pure, each in its original form and significance; while the two other synoptists have transformed the parable into a history, and have misapplied the apothegm (in a somewhat altered form) to a false explanation of that pretended history [22].

[22] Conceptions of the narrative in the main accordant with that here given, may be found in De Wette, exeg. Handb., 1, 1, s. 176 f.; 1, 2, s. 174 f., and Weisse, die evang. Gesch. 1, s. 576 f.

END OF VOL. II.

G. Woodfall and Son, Printers, Angel Court, Skinner Street, London.

Made in the USA
Middletown, DE
27 February 2023

25774715R00279